# THIS DATE IN
# PHILADELPHIA
# phillies
# HISTORY

# THIS DATE IN
# PHILADELPHIA
# phillies
# HISTORY

A day by day listing of events in the
history of the Philadelphia National League
Baseball Team

## Allen Lewis
### and
## Larry Shenk

**SB**
**A SCARBOROUGH BOOK**
STEIN AND DAY/*Publishers*/New York

First published in 1979
Copyright © 1979 by Allen Lewis and Larry Shenk
All rights reserved
Designed by Palisade Printing Co. and Art Ballant
Printed in the United States of America
Stein and Day/*Publishers*/Scarborough House
Briarcliff Manor, N.Y. 10510

Library of Congress Cataloging in Publication Data
Lewis, Allen
        This date in Philadelphia Phillies history.

        1. Philadelphia. Baseball club (National League) —
History, I. Shenk, Larry, joint author. II. Title.
GV875. P45L48        796.375'64'0974811        78-24075
ISBN O-8128-6019-5

# ACKNOWLEDGEMENTS

We would like to express our gratitude to the following for their enormous contributions to this book.

To "The Sporting News" for allowing us to use material from their publications: *Official Baseball Guide, Official Baseball Register, Official World Series Records, The Sporting News Official Baseball Record Book, Official Baseball Dope Book,* and *Daguerreotypes.*

To Joseph L. Reichler, Special Assistant to the Baseball Commissioner and Editor of *The Baseball Encyclopedia,* Macmillan Publishing Company, Inc., New York.

To Bill Giles, Executive Vice President of the Philadelphia Phillies, our sincere thanks for all his courtesies and encouragements.

To Chris Wheeler, Assistant Public Relations Director of the Philadelphia Phillies, for his interest in our project and the time he generously gave to it.

To Larre Hoke, James Smith, Jr., Joseph Smagala, Jr., and Skip Clayton for their endless hours of research and assistance.

To Karen Boghosian and Art Ballant, our editors at Stein and Day, for their encouragement.

To Muriel Fritsche, for her aid in typing our statistical material.

# CONTENTS

# THIS DATE IN PHILADELPHIA PHILLIES HISTORY

Baseball was a popular game in Philadelphia long before there were any organized leagues. In 1866, the Philadelphia Athletics won their first national championship; by 1869, the city boasted three outstanding teams, and in 1871 both the Athletics and Quakers were Philadelphia teams in baseball's first professional league, the National Association.

The Quakers are generally regarded as the forerunner of the Phillies, but it was the Athletics who were awarded the Philadelphia franchise when the National League was organized on February 2, 1876.

But the Athletics, along with the New York Mutuals, refused to make the season's last Western trip in 1876, and both were expelled. It wasn't until 1883 that the city again had a National League franchise, the Phillies, who have been members ever since.

In 1901, the Philadelphia Athletics joined the newly-formed American League and for more than thirty years were one of the most successful teams in baseball. But the Phillies became the more popular and successful team after World War II, and the Athletics moved to Kansas City after the 1954 season.

The Phillies have won pennants only in 1915 and 1950 but captured Eastern Division crowns for three straight years, starting in 1976, and have been one of baseball's attendance leaders since moving to Veterans Stadium from Connie Mack Stadium after the 1970 season.

What follows is a mini-history of the Phillies, in chronological order, followed by a number of listings and tables about the team and its players.

In the chronological listings, a B after a player's name indicates he was born on this date. Then come the year or years in which he played or managed the Phillies, his primary position or positions, and the total number of games he played for the Phillies. Games managed are found in a separate listing. In the case of those who both played ánd managed, only the games appeared in as a player are shown. Where games appear in the chronological listing, a (P) indicates the game was played in Philadelphia, and an (A) that the game was played away from Philadelphia.

At the end of the chronological listing, information is shown about Phillies players for whom complete birth dates are unavailable.

While the 1876 Philadelphia National League team was known as the Athletics, not the Phillies, players on that team and important events during that season are included in order to make this a more complete history of National League baseball in Philadelphia.

# JANUARY 1

1856 — Tim Keefe — B 1891-93 P G-72

1874 — Ned Garvin — B 1896 P G-2

1884 — Tom Downey — B 1912 3B G-54

1888 — Benny Meyer — B 1925 2B G-1

1904 — Ethan Allen — B 1934-36 OF G-331

1924 — Earl Torgeson — B 1953-55 1B G-293

## January 2

1858 — Jack Neagle — B 1883 OF-P G-18

1871 — Phil Saylor — B 1891 P G-1

1905 — Pinky Whitney — B 1928-33,36-39 3B G-1,157

1919 — Bill Harman — B 1941 C-P G-15

1926 — Stan Hollmig — B 1949-51 OF G-94

1951 — Jim Essian — B 1973-75 C G-21

## January 3

1874 — Roy Brashear — B 1903 2B G-20

1899 — Buzz Arlett — B 1931 OF G-121

1906 — Gus Suhr — B 1939-40 1B G-70

1941 — John Sullivan — B 1968 C G-12

## January 4

1906 — Blondy Ryan — B 1935 SS G-39

1947 — Ken Reynolds — B 1970-72 P G-88

## January 5

1885 — Art Fletcher — B 1920, 22-26 SS-MGR G-212

1912 — Red Dooin signs two-year contract to manage Phillies.

1928 — Bob Oldis — B 1962-63 C G-85

1948 — Bill Laxton — B 1970 P G-2

## January 6

1870 — Joe Sullivan — B 1894-96 SS-OF G-217

1890 — Vern Duncan — B 1913 OF G-8

1897 — By Speece — B 1930 P G-11

1933 — Lee Walls — B 1960-61 IF-OF G-156  1936 — Ruben Amaro — B 1960-65 SS G-668

1933 — Lee Walls — B 1960-61 IF-OF G-156

1936 — Ruben Amaro — B 1960-65 SS G-668

## January 7

1875 — Kitty Bransfield — B 1905-11 1B G-814

1900 — Carl Lord — B 1923 3B G-17

1904 — Al Todd — B 1932-35 C G-304

1922 — Alvin Dark — B 1960 3B G-55

1931 — Ray Semproch — B 1958-59 P G-76

1933 — Infielder Barney Friberg sold to Boston Red Sox.

1947 — Scott Reid — B 1969-70 OF G-38

## January 8

1891 — Bud Weiser — B 1915-16 OF P-41

1922 — Ralph LaPointe — B 1947 SS G-56

1934 — Gene Freese — B 1959 3B G-132

1948 — Jesus Hernaiz — B 1974 P G-27

## January 9

1887 — Harry Hoch — B 1908 P G-3

1916 — Charley Stanceu — B 1946 P G-14

1919 — Charlie Sproull — B 1945 P G-34

1927 — In three-way trade, Phillies sent outfielder George Harper to New York Giants and catcher Butch Henline to Brooklyn Dodgers, and received second baseman Fresco Thompson and pitcher Jack Scott from Giants.

1944 — Dick Thoenen — B 1967 P G-1

4

## January 10

1835 — Harry Wright — B 1884-93 MGR

1856 — Doc Bushong — B 1876 C G-5

1882 — Johnny Bates — B 1909-10 OF G-211

1910 — Johnny Peacock — B 1944-45 C G-116

1966 — Outfielder Wes Covington traded to Chicago Cubs for outfielder Doug Clemens.

## January 11

1868 — Bill Magee B 1899, 1902 P G-17

1876 — Elmer Flick — B 1898-1901 OF G-537

1900 — Lefty Taber — B 1926-27 P G-9

1910 — Schoolboy Rowe — B 1943, 46-49 P G-209

1911 — Roy Hughes — B 1939-40, 46 IF-P G-155

1960 — Outfielder Richie Ashburn traded to Chicago Cubs for infielders Alvin Dark and Jim Woods and pitcher John Buzhardt.

## January 12

1862 — John Crowley — B 1884 C G-48

1876 — George Browne — B 1901-02, 12 OF G-84

1889 — Doc Imlay — B 1913 P G-9

1895 — Jack Knight — B 1925-26 P G-80

1900 — George Knothe — B 1932 2B G-6

## January 13

1916 — Bama Rowell — B 1948 IF-OF G-77

1950 — Mike Buskey — B 1977 SS G-6

1954 — Pitcher Andy Hansen, infielder Jack Lohrke, and cash traded to Pittsburgh Pirates for pitcher Murry Dickson.

1959 — John Quinn, Milwaukee Braves general manager, hired as Phillies vice-president and general manager, succeeding Roy Hamey, who resigns to return to New York Yankees.

1975 — Pitcher Joe Hoerner signed as free agent.

## January 14

1867 — Bill Kling — B 1891 P G-13

1871 — Art Madison — B 1895 IF G-11

1894 — Art Decatur — B 1925-27 P G-56

1903 — Russ Scarritt — B 1932 OF G-11

1923 — Ken Johnson — B 1950-51 P G-57

1943 — Ron Clark — B 1975 PH G-1


## January 15

1896 — Mike Cantwell — B 1919-20 P G-10

1913 — William H. Locke acquires Phillies and is named president of club.

1937 — Bob Sadowski — B 1961 3B G-16

1973 — Catcher John Bateman released.


## January 16

1891 — Erskine Mayer — B 1912-18 P G-206

1907 — Buck Jordan — B 1938 3B-1B G-87

1934 — Jim Owens — B 1955-56, 58-62 P G-120

1944 — Gene Stone — B 1969 1B G-18


## January 17

1899 — Tripp Sigman — B 1929-30 OF G-62

1915 — Mayo Smith — B 1955-58 MGR

1920 — Jocko Thompson — B 1948-51 P G-43

1944 — Denny Doyle — B 1970-73 2B G-446


## January 18

1884 — Ralph Caldwell — B 1904-05 P G-13

1911 — Pinky May — B 1939-43 3B G-665

1946 — Billy Grabarkewitz — B 1973-74 IF G-59

## January 19

1903 — Fred Lucas — B 1935 OF G-20

1913 — Hugh Poland — B 1947 C G-4

1914 — Benny Culp — B 1942-44 C G-15

## January 20

1904 — Denny Sothern — B 1926, 28-30 OF G-231

1907 — Bob Adams — B 1931-32 P G-5

1910 — Pitcher Harry Coveleskie traded to Cincinnati Reds for pitcher Ad Brennan.

1969 — Catcher Clay Dalrymple traded to Baltimore Orioles for outfielder Ron Stone.

## January 21

1899 — Lew Fonseca — B 1925 2B-1B G-126

1914 — Blix Donnelly — B 1946-50 P G-113

1919 — Third baseman Milt Stock, catcher Pickles Dillhoefer, and pitcher Frank Davis traded to St. Louis Cardinals for infielders Doug Baird and Stuffy Stewart, pitcher Eugene Packard, and cash.

1946 — Johnny Oates — B 1975-76 C G-135

## January 22

1876 — Warren McLaughlin — B 1900, 03 P G-4

1877 — Ed Murphy — B 1898 P G-7

1904 — John Milligan — B 1928-31 P G-33

1908 — Prince Oana — B 1934 OF G-6

1921 — Pitcher Eppa Rixey traded to Cincinnati Reds for pitcher Jimmy Ring and outfielder Greasy Neale.

1925 — Bobby Young — B 1958 2B G-32

1940 — Pitcher Ray Harrell sold to Pittsburgh Pirates.

1943 — First baseman Nick Etten traded to New York Yankees for catcher Tom Padden, pitcher Al Gerheauser, and cash.

1946 — Third baseman Jim Tabor purchased from Boston Red Sox.

7

## January 23

1873 — Red Donahue — B 1898-1901 P G-137

1907 — Bobby Burke — B 1937 P G-2

1930 — Frank Sullivan — B 1961-62 P G-68

## January 24

1898 — Cliff Heathcote — B 1932 1B G-30

1901 — Flint Rhem — B 1932-33 P G-54

1902 — Mickey Finn — B 1933 2B G-51

## January 25

1933 — Mel Roach — B 1962 IF G-65

1934 — Ted Kazanski — B 1953-58 IF G-417

## January 26

1874 — Kaiser Wilhelm — B 1921-22 P-MGR G-4

1884 — Tubby Spencer — B 1911 C G-11

1886 — Hick Cady — B 1919 C G-34

1909 — Israel Durham named president of Phillies.

1920 — Dick Mauney — B 1945-47 P G-62

1935 — Bob Uecker — B 1966-67 C G-96

## January 27

1871 — Berk Inks — B 1896 P G-3

## January 28

1874 — Al Burris — B 1894 P G-1

1898 — Jim Bishop — B 1923-24 P G-22

1934 — Bill White — B 1966-68 1B G-396

## January 29

1880 — Bill Burns — B 1911 P G-21

1883 — Marty Martel — B 1909 C G-24

## January 30

1925 — Bill Glynn — B 1949 1B G-8

1943 — Dave Johnson — B 1977-78 IF G-122

## January 31

1914 — Mel Mazzera — B 1940 OF-1B G-69

1974 — Catcher Mike Ryan traded to Pittsburgh Pirates for shortstop Jackie Hernandez.

# FEBRUARY 1

1867 —Pete Wood — B 1889 P G-3

1917 —Elmer Burkart   B 1936-39 P G-16

1934 — Bob Conley — B 1958 P G-2

## February 2

1875 — Charlie Ziegler — B 1900 3B G-3

1952 — Warren Brusstar — B 1977-78 P G-104

## February 3

1896 — Chicken Hawks — B 1925 1B G-105

1901 — Ernie Maun — B 1926 P G-14

1949 — Bake McBride — B 1977-78 OF G-208

1951 — Mike Wallace — B 1973-74 P G-28

1977 — Infielder Dave Johnson signed as free agent.

## February 4

1890 — Possum Whitted — B 1915-19 OF G-523

1896 — Andy Woehr — B 1923-24 3B G-63

## February 5

1928 — Don Hoak — B 1963-64 3B G-121

1946 — Pitcher Al Jurisich and outfielder Johnny Wyrostek purchased from St. Louis Cardinals.

## February 6

1892 — Goldie Rapp — B 1921-23 3B G-218

1927 — Smoky Burgess — B 1952-55 C G-327

## February 7

1876 — Pat Moran — B 1910-18 C-MGR G-117

1905 — Cy Moore — B 1933-34 P G-71

1924 — Paul Owens — B 1972 MGR

1927 — Joe Lonnett — B 1956-59 C G-143

1948 — Outfielder Johnny Wyrostek traded to Cincinnati Reds for infielder Eddie Miller.


## February 8

1914 — Bert Haas — B 1948-49 3B-1B G-97

1920 — Buddy Blattner — B 1949 IF G-64

1923 — Outfielder DeWitt Lebourveau sold to Cincinnati Reds.

1942 — Costen Shockley — B 1964 1B G-11

1972 — Infielder-outfielder-catcher Bobby Pfeil traded to Milwaukee Brewers for third baseman Chico Vaughns.


## February 9

1867 — Sumner Bowman — B 1890 P G-1

1916 — Freddy Schmidt — B 1947 P G-29

1917 — Moon Mullen — B 1944 2B G-118

1945 — Jim Nash — B 1972 P G-9

1946 — Pitcher Whit Wyatt released.


## February 10

1882 — Ches Crist — B 1906 C G-6

1894 — Cotton Tierney — B 1923 2B G-121

1917 — Roy Bruner — B 1939-41 P G-19

1938 — Pitcher Bill Hallahan signed after release by Cincinnati Reds.

1945 — First baseman Jimmie Foxx signed as free agent.

1955 — Outfielder Peanuts Lowrey signed as free agent.

1897 — Red Miller — B 1923 P G-1

1923 — Pitcher George Smith traded to Brooklyn Dodgers for pitcher Clarence Mitchell.

1934 — Pitcher Flint Rhem sold to St. Louis Cardinals.

1944 — Ollie Brown — B 1974-77 OF G-272

## February 12

1864 — Jim Fogarty — B 1884-89 OF-IF G-660

1893 — George Stutz — B 1926 SS G-6

1902 — Kiddo Davis — B 1932, 34 OF G-237

1912 — Dutch Dietz — B 1943 P G-21

1919 — Monk Dubiel — B 1948 P G-38

## February 13

1907 — Wayne LaMaster — B 1937-38 P G-69

## February 14

1858 — Arthur Irwin — B 1886-89, 94-95 SS-MGR G-345

1867 — Morgan Murphy — B 1898, 1900 C G-36

1908 — Oscar Judd — B 1945-48 P G-121

1945 — Bob Terlecki — B 1972 P G-9

1949 — Larry Fritz — B 1975 PH G-1

## February 15

1895 — Jimmy Ring — B 1921-25, 28 P G-220

1905 — Hal Lee — B 1931-33 OF G-239

## February 16

1865 — Ben Sanders — B 1888-89 P-OF G-101

1866 — Billy Hamilton — B 1890-95 OF G-729

1866 — John Scheible — B 1894 P G-1

1897 — Alex Ferguson — B 1927-29 P G-71

1912 — Ray Harrell — B 1939 P G-22

## February 16 (continued)

1936 — Don Landrum — B 1957 OF G-2

1952 — Barry Foote — B 1977-78 C G-56

1953 — Pitcher Russ Meyer traded to Boston Braves for first baseman Earl Torgeson.

## February 17

1931 — Roger Craig — B 1966 P G-14

## February 18

1897 — Huck Betts — B 1920-25 P G-161

1927 — Herm Wehmeier — B 1954-56 P G-62

1929 — Cal Neeman — B 1960-61 C G-78

## February 19

1914 — Stan Sperry — B 1936 2B G-20

1915 — Isidore Leon — B 1945 P G-14

## February 20

1917 — John Bolling — B 1939 1B G-69

## February 21

1876 — John Titus — B 1903-12 OF G-1218

1907 — Snipe Hansen — B 1930, 32-35 P G-146

1937 — Ted Savage — B 1962 OF G-127

## February 22

1874 — Barney McFadden — B 1902 P G-1

1891 — Clarence Mitchell — B 1923-28 P G-236

1907 — Marty Hopkins — B 1934 3B G-10

1909 — Art Bramhall — B 1935 SS-3B G-2

1920 — Karl Drews — B 1951-54 P G-93

1929 — Ryne Duren — B 1963-64, 65 P G-42

1934 — Sparky Anderson — B 1959 2B G-152

1948 — Mike Rogodzinski — B 1973-75 OF G-99

## February 22 (continued)

1966 — First baseman Dick Stuart traded to New York Mets for catcher Jim Schaffer and infielders Bobby Klaus and Wayne Graham.

## February 23

1874 — Bill Lauder — B 1898-99 3B G-248

1877 — Rudy Hulswitt — B 1902-04 SS G-379

1918 — Jim Carlin — B 1941 OF G-16

1932 — Jim Bolger — B 1959 OF G-35

## February 24

1869 — Con Lucid — B 1895-96 P G-15

1873 — Joe Dolan — B 1899-1901 IF G-145

1887 — Bill Hilly — B 1914 OF G-8

1907 — Earl Grace — B 1936-37 C G-166

1919 — Del Wilber — B 1951-52 C G-86

## February 25

1897 — Bob Vines — B 1925 P G-3

1908 — Al Hollingsworth — B 1938-39 P G-39

1924 — Lucky Lohrke — B 1952-53 IF G-37

1940 — Danny Cater — B 1964 OF-IF G-60

1972 — Pitcher Rick Wise traded to St. Louis Cardinals for pitcher Steve Carlton.

## February 26

1863 — Ed Sixsmith — B 1884 C G-1

1887 — Grover Alexander — B 1911-17, 30 P G-345

1907 — Cy Malis — B 1934 P G-1

1930 — Ron Negray — B 1955-56 P G-58

## February 27

1886 — Walter Moser — B 1906 P G-6

1904 — Chick Fullis — B 1933-34 OF G-179

13

1917 — Rube Melton — B 1941-42 P G-67

1920 — Connie Ryan — B 1952-53 2B G-244

## February 28

1881 — Moose McCormick — B 1908 OF G-11

1899 — Lil Stoner — B 1931 P G-7

1909 — Lefty Bertrand — B 1936 P G-1

## February 29

1896 — Ralph Miller — B 1920-21 IF G-154

# MARCH 1

1915 — Nick Strincevich — B 1948 P G-6

1917 — Ike Pearson — B 1939-42, 46 P G-143

1921 — Howie Fox — B 1952 P G-13

## March 2

1912 — Bennie Warren — B 1939-42 C G-335

1917 — Jim Konstanty — B 1948-54 P G-314

1932 — Chico Fernandez — B 1957-59 SS G-342

## March 3

1903 — Walt Lerian — B 1928-29 C G-201

1918 — Bill Hoffman — B 1939 P G-3

1925 — George Eyrich — B 1943 P G-9

1934 — Bobby Locke — B 1962-64 P G-22

## March 4

1862 — Tom Gunning — B 1887 C G-28

1863 — Al McCauley — B 1890 1B G-116

1870 — Bill Whitrock — B 1896 P G-2

1890 — Johnny Enzmann — B 1920 P G-17

1897 — Lefty O'Doul — B 1929-30 OF G-294

1915 — Art Rebel — B 1938 OF G-7

1924 — John Brittin — B 1950-51 P G-6

1933 — John Easton — B 1955, 59 PH G-4

### March 5

1860 — Sam Thompson — B 1889-98 OF G-1034

1911 — Earl Browne — B 1937-38 OF-1B G-126

1916 — Harry Shuman — B 1944 P G-18

1917 — Al Monchak — B 1940 IF G-19

1921 — Elmer Valo — B 1956, 61 OF G-148

1936 — Jacke Davis — B 1962 OF G-48

### March 6

1863 — John Coleman — B 1883-84 P-OF G-133

1938 — First baseman Dolf Camilli traded to Brooklyn Dodgers for outfielder Ed Morgan and $50,000.

1939 — Cookie Rojas — B 1963-69 2B-OF G-880

### March 7

1933 — Ed Bouchee — B 1956-60 1B G-410

1962 — Catcher Sammy White signed as free agent.

### March 8

1895 — Jack Bentley — B 1926 1B G-75

1941 — Phillies pitcher Hugh Mulcahy becomes first major league player drafted into Armed Forces in World War II.

1942 — Richie Allen — B 1963-69, 75-76 3B-1B-OF G-1070

1942 — Outfielder Lloyd Waner and infielder Al Glossop traded to Brooklyn Dodgers for first baseman Babe Dahlgren.

### March 9

1869 — John McPherson — B 1904 P G-15

1872 — Tom Delahanty — B 1894 2B G-1

## March 10

1921 — Johnny Blatnik — B 1948-50 OF G-131

1942 — Tom Hilgendorf — B 1975 P G-53

1944 — John Briggs — B 1964-71 OF G-695

1948 — Wayne Twitchell — B 1971-77 P G-188

## March 11

1893 — Ralph Capron — B 1913 OF G-2

1903 — Art Ruble — B 1934 OF G-19

1913 — Del Young — B 1937-40 SS-2B G-309

1933 — Jack Spring — B 1955 P G-2

1975 — Outfielder Nelson Garcia traded to Cleveland Indians for pitcher Tom Hilgendorf.

## March 12

1869 — Bill Hulen — B 1896 IF-OF G-88

1885 — Charlie Johnson — B 1908 OF G-4

1939 — Johnny Callison — B 1960-69 OF G-1432

1945 — Horacio Pina — B 1978 P G-2

## March 13

1918 — Eddie Pellagrini — B 1951 2B G-86

1928 — Bob Greenwood — B 1954-55 P G-13

## March 14

1963 — Pitcher Ryne Duren purchased from Los Angeles Angels.

## March 15

1871 — Bill Bernhard — B 1899-1900 P G-53

1890 — Fred Mollenkamp — B 1914 1B G-3

1944 — Dave Watkins — B 1969 C G-69

## March 16

1859 — Jerry Denny — B 1891 3B G-19

1906 — Lloyd Waner — B 1942 OF G-100

1912 — Bud Bates — B 1939 OF G-15

1954 — First baseman Eddie Waitkus sold to Baltimore Orioles.

## March 17

1871 — Chick Fraser — B 1899-1900, 02-04 P G-174

1874 — Bill Duggleby — B 1898, 1901-02, 03-07 P G-230

1885 — Paddy Mayes — B 1911 OF G-5

1975 — Pitcher Cy Acosta purchased from Chicago White Sox.

## March 18

1874 — Nixey Callahan — B 1894 P G-9

1893 — Russ Wrightstone — B 1920-28 IF-OF G-879

1918 — Dick Mulligan — B 1946 P G-19

1924 — Garvin Hamner — B 1945 IF G-32

## March 19

1887 — Billy Maharg — B 1916 OF G-1

1927 — Richie Ashburn — B 1948-59 OF G-1794

1932 — Outfielder Fred Leach sold to Boston Braves.

1955 — Pitcher Dave Cole purchased from Chicago Cubs.

## March 20

1875 — Willie Greene — B 1902 3B G-19

1907 — Vern Kennedy — B 1944-45 P G-27

1941 — Pat Corrales — B 1964-65 C G-65

## March 21

1952 — Pitcher Ken Johnson sold to Detroit Tigers.

## March 22

1856 — Bill McClellan — B 1883-84 SS G-191

1866 — Jack Boyle — B 1893-98 1B-C G-484

1892 — Lew Wendell — B 1924-26 C G-40

1927 — Paul Stuffel — B 1950, 52-53 P G-7

1933 — Al Schroll — B 1959 P G-3

1936 — Gene Oliver — B 1967 C G-85

1953 — Danny Boitano — B 1978 P G-1

1967 — Dick Ellsworth — B 1967 P G-32

1973 — Pitcher Jim Nash released.

## March 23

1880 — Peaches Graham — B 1912 C G-24

1881 — Gavvy Cravath — B 1912-20 OF-MGR G-1103

1895 — Frank Parkinson — B 1921-24 IF G-378

1902 — Johnny Moore — B 1934-37 OF G-489

1918 — Lou Lucier — B 1944-45 P G-14

1928 — Jim Lemon — B 1963 OF G-31

1932 — Jack Meyer — B 1955-61 P G-202

1978 — Second baseman Fred Andrews and cash traded to New York Mets for infielder Bud Harrelson.

## March 24

1874 — Roy Thomas — B 1899-1908, 10-11 OF G-1286

1997 — Gus Dugas — B 1933 1B G-37

1943 — Catcher-infielder Bobby Bragan traded to Brooklyn Dodgers for pitcher Jack Kraus and cash.

1962 — Pitcher Cal McLish acquired from Chicago White Sox as replacement for third baseman Andy Carey, who refused to report following his trade to Phillies.

## March 25

1884 — Jimmy Lavender — B 1917 P G-29

1886 — Jimmy Walsh — B 1910-13 OF-IF G-259

1900 — Russ Miller — B 1927-28 P G-38

1909 — Dutch Leonard — B 1947-48 P G-66

## March 25 (continued)

1946 — Catcher Rollie Hemsley purchased from New York Yankees.

1963 — Pitcher Johnny Klippstein purchased from Cincinnati Reds.

## March 26

1888 — Brad Hogg — B 1918-19 P G-64

1939 — Al Neiger — B 1960 P G-6

1940 — Outfielder Chuck Klein signed as free agent after release by Pittsburgh Pirates.

## March 27

1856 — Jim Tyng — B 1888 P G-1

1903 — Marty Walker — B 1928 — P G-1

1906 — Fred Tauby — B 1937 OF G-11

1911 — Walter Stephenson — B 1937 C G-10

1915 — Newt Kimball — B 1943 P G-34

1932 — Wes Covington — B 1961-65 OF G-522

1946 — Mike Jackson — B 1970 P G-5

1947 — Pitcher Andy Karl traded to Boston Braves for catcher Don Padgett.

1951 — Dick Ruthven — B 1973-75, 78 P G-107

## March 28

1907 — Walt Masters — B 1937 P G-1

1911 — Clarence Pickrel — B 1933 P G-9

1936 — Jim Coker — B 1958, 60-62 C G-99

1945 — Pitcher Whit Wyatt purchased from Brooklyn Dodgers.

1954 — Infielder Dick Young and cash traded to Brooklyn Dodgers for infielder Bobby Morgan.

## March 29

1855 — Bill Harbridge — B 1883 OF-IF-C G-73

1873 — Duff Cooley — B 1896-99 OF-1B G-440

1912 — Gibby Brack — B 1938-39 OF G-163

19

## March 30

1842 — Al Wright — B 1876 MGR

1867 — Bill Hallman — B 1888-89, 92-97, 1901-03 IF-OF-C G-1060

1897 — Eddie Sicking — B 1919 SS-2B G-61

1925 — Infielder Lew Fonseca purchased from Cincinnati Reds.

1926 — Dick Koecher — B 1946-48 P G-7

## March 31

1862 — Art Benedict — B 1883 2B G-3

1891 — Johnny Couch — B 1923-25 P G-83

1905 — Sam Dailey — B 1929 P G-20

1938 — John Herrnstein — B 1962-66 OF-1B G-213

1945 — Pitcher Al Gerheauser traded to Pittsburgh Pirates for Vince DiMaggio.

1959 — Catcher Stan Lopata and infielders Johnny O'Brien and Ted Kazanski traded to Milwaukee Braves for pitcher Gene Conley, shortstop Joe Koppe, and infielder-outfielder Harry Hanebrink.

1977 — Pitcher Ron Schueler sold to Minnesota Twins.

## APRIL 1

1893 — Claude Cooper — B 1916-17 OF G-80

1935 — Tom Qualters — B 1953, 57-58 P G-8

1948 — Willie Montanez — B 1970-75 1B-OF G-633

1963 — Infielder Billy Klaus signed as free agent.

1976 — Outfielder-first baseman Bobby Tolan signed after being released by San Diego Padres.

## April 2

1869 — Hughie Jennings — B 1901-02 1B-SS-2B G-160

1894 — Harry O'Donnell — B 1927 C G-16

## April 3

1860 — Tom Lynch — B 1884-85 OF G-26

1921 — Dick Conger — B 1943 P G-13

1950 — Infielder Eddie Miller sold to St. Louis Cardinals.

1961 — Infielder Ted Lepcio sold to Chicago White Sox.

1969 — First baseman Bill White traded to St. Louis Cardinals for infielder Jerry Buchek and infielder-catcher Jim Hutto.

## April 4

1918 — Infielder Bert Niehoff traded to St. Louis Cardinals with cash for pitcher Mule Watson.

1927 — Don Hasenmayer — B 1945-46 IF G-11

1937 — Al Kenders — B 1961 C G-10

1942 — Eddie Watt — B 1974 P G-42

## April 5

1859 — Ed Andrews — B 1884-89 OF G-557

1936 — Jimmie Schaffer — B 1966-67 C G-20

1957 — Outfielder Elmer Valo. shortstop Mel Geho, first baseman Tim Harkness, pitchers Ben Flowers and Ron Negray and $75,000 traded to Brooklyn Dodgers for shortstop Chico Fernandez.

1975 — Outfielder Bill Robinson traded to Pittsburgh Pirates for pitcher Wayne Simpson.

## April 6

1914 — Dee Moore — B 1943, 46 C-IF G-48

1937 — Wayne Graham — B 1963 OF G-10

## April 7

1933 — Bobby Del Greco — B 1960-61, 65 OF G-149

1948 — Infielder Ralph LaPointe and $20,000 traded to St. Louis Cardinals for first baseman Dick Sisler.

1969 — Shortstop Bobby Wine sent to Montreal Expos as replacement for pitcher Larry Jackson, who was selected in expansion draft but retired.

1975 — Pitcher Eddie Watt released.

21

## April 8

1897 — Dick Attreau — B 1926-27 1B G-61

1898 — Lerton Pinto — B 1922, 24 P G-12

1899 — Ted Kleinhans — B 1934 P G-5

1914 — Andy Karl — B 1943-46 P G-159

1915 — Kirby Higbe — B 1939-40 P G-75

1934 — Dick Farrell — B 1956-61, 67-69 P G-359

1949 — Mac Scarce — B 1972-74 P G-141

1969 — Rookie shortstop Don Money hits two home runs, bats in five runs but Phillies lose season opener, 7-6, in eleven innings at Chicago.

1970 — First baseman Willie Montanez acquired from St. Louis Cardinals to replace outfielder Curt Flood, who refused to report after being traded October 7, 1969.

1976 — Pitcher Wayne Simpson sold to California Angels.


## April 9

1879 — Jack Townsend — B 1901 P G-19

Doc White — B 1901-02 P-OF G-92

1905 — Earl Caldwell — B 1928 P G-5

1908 — Claude Passeau — B 1936-39 P G-153

1913 — In first National League game ever played in Brooklyn's Ebbets Field, Phillies won, 1-0, as Tom Seaton beat Nap Rucker.


## April 10

1879 — Tom Barry — B 1904 P G-1

1895 — Bob McGraw — B 1928-29 P G-80

1909 — Jim Spotts — B 1930 C G-3

1963 — Phillies score eight runs in seventh inning to beat Cincinnati, 8-7 (P).

1967 — First baseman Tito Francona purchased from St. Louis Cardinals.

1971 — Phillies beat Montreal, 4-1, in first game ever played in Veterans Stadium before 55,352, then the largest crowd in Pennsylvania baseball history.

## April 11

1886 — Al Nixon — B 1926-28 OF G-172

1907 — Frank Corridon pitches one-hitter as Phillies win season opener at New York, 3-0.

1916 — Joe Antolick — B 1944 C G-4

1921 — Jim Hearn — B 1957-59 P G-81

1965 — Pitcher Dallas Green sold to Washington Senators.

1966 — Pitcher Roger Craig signed as free agent after release by Cincinnati Reds.


## April 12

1926 — Lou Possehl — B 1946-48, 51-52 P G-16

1940 — Woodie Fryman — B 1968-72 P G-157

1944 — Terry Harmon — B 1967, 69-77 IF G-547

1965 — Phillies win season opener, 2-0, in first National League game ever played in Houston's Astrodome as Chris Short pitches four-hitter and Dick Allen hits two-run home run.


## April 13

1864 — Billy Murray — B 1907-09 MGR

1866 — Herman Long — B 1904 2B G-1

1875 — Kid Elberfeld — B 1898 3B G-14

1910 — Infielder Kid Gleason released.

1944 — First baseman Tony Lupien purchased from Boston Red Sox.

1965 — Pitcher Ryne Duren signed as free agent after release by Cincinnati Reds.

1966 — Pitcher Steve Ridzik purchased from Washington Senators.


## April 14

1931 — Chuck Klein becomes third member of Phillies to hit two home runs in season opener, but New York wins, 9-5 (P).

1960 — Eddie Sawyer resigns as manager of Phillies after opening day 9-4 loss on April 12 in Cincinnati. Minneapolis Manager Gene Mauch named new manager of Phillies.

## April 15

1871 —  Bill Grey — B 1890-91 OF-IF-C G-57

1877 —  Ed Abbaticchio — B 1897-98 3B-2B G-28

1926 —  Cy Williams hits grand-slam home run in 8-4 win over Boston (P).

1930 —  Les Sweetland pitches three-hitter, doubles and scores only run in 1-0 opening day victory at Brooklyn.

1946 —  Ted Sizemore — B 1977-78 2B G-260

## April 16

1867 —  Piggy Ward — B 1883, 89 IF-OF G-8

1937 —  Pitcher Joe Bowman traded to Pittsburgh Pirates for first baseman Earle Browne.

1943 —  Jim Lonborg — B 1973-78 P G-184

1951 —  Pitcher Blix Donnelly sold to Boston Braves.

1953 —  Phillies second baseman Connie Ryan gets six consecutive hits (four singles, two doubles) in six at bats in 14-12 loss at Pittsburgh. Phillies score nine runs, Pirates six in fifth inning to tie modern National League record.

1959 —  Dave Philley gets major league record ninth hit in row as pinch-hitter (eight in 1958) as Phillies lose at Milwaukee, 7-3.

1972 —  Rookie Burt Hooton pitches 4-0, no-hit victory against Phillies at Chicago.

1978 —  Bob Forsch pitches 5-0, no-hit victory against Phillies at St. Louis.

## April 17

1863 —  Charlie Ferguson — B 1884-87 P-OF-IF G-257

1904 —  Elmer Miller — B 1929 P-OF G-31

1907 —  Eddie Delker — B 1932-33 2B G-55

Bobby Stevens — B 1931 SS G-12

1911 —  Charlie Sheerin — B 1936 IF G-39

1914 —  Lefty Smoll — B 1940 P G-33

1917 —  Stan Andrews — B 1945 C G-13

1923 —  Solly Hemus — B 1956-58 2B-3B G-253

## April 17 (continued)

Phillies and Brooklyn tie in fourteen innings, 5-5, in longest National League opener (A).

1940 — Roberto Pena — B 1968 SS G-138

1964 — Phillies hit three home runs (pitcher Art Mahaffey, Dick Allen and Roy Sievers) and Chicago hits two in fifth inning to tie major league record for one inning as Phillies win, 10-8 (A).

1969 — Montreal's Bill Stoneman pitches 7-0, no-hit victory against Phillies (P).

1976 — Mike Schmidt ties major league record by hitting four consecutive home runs, and bats in eight runs as Phillies win, 18-16, in ten innings after trailing, 12-1 and 13-2, tying National League record for comeback (A).

## April 18

1877 — Tully Sparks — B 1897, 1903-10 P G-224

1892 — Jack Scott — B 1927 P G-83

1908 — Ed Boland — B 1934-35 OF G-38

1929 — Lefty O'Doul hits two home runs but Phillies lose season opener to New York, 11-9 (P).

1948 — Ron Schueler — B 1974-76 P G-125

1954 — Error by pitcher Curt Simmons in sixth inning allows Pittsburgh's Curt Roberts to score, ending streak of thirty-two straight scoreless innings by Phillies pitchers in 7-1 Phillies victory (P) (2nd game).

## April 19

1887 — Jack Martin — B 1914 IF G-83

1900 — Phillies won at Boston in ten innings, 19-17, in highest scoring season opener in National League history. Boston scored nine runs in ninth inning to tie.

1904 — Phillies and New York play 15-inning, 1-1 tie (P).

1909 — Bucky Walters — B 1934-38 P-3B G-267

1920 — John O'Neil — B 1946 SS G-46

1935 — Dolf Camilli hits two home runs and bats in seven runs, and Lou Chiozza scored five runs in 18-7 win over New York (P).

1938 — Emmett Mueller of Phillies and Brooklyn's Ernie Koy each hit a home run in first major league time at bat in first inning of 12-5 Brooklyn victory in season opener (P).

1976 — Catcher Tim Blackwell purchased from Boston Red Sox.

## April 20

1869 — Tommy Dowd — B 1897 OF G-91

1891 — Dave Bancroft — B 1915-20 SS G-681

1921 — Bill Peterman — B 1942 C G-1

1946 — Tommy Hutton — B 1972-77 1B-OF G-662

1949 — Willie Jones hit four doubles in row to tie major league record in 6-5 loss at Boston.

## April 21

1898 — Pitcher Bill Duggleby hits grand-slam home run in first major league at bat in second inning, a feat which has never been duplicated by any player, in game against New York (P).

1901 — Lefty Weinert — B 1919-24 P G-100

1935 — Mack Burk — B 1956, 58 C G-16

1955 — Brooklyn beats Phillies, 14-4, sets modern major league record with tenth win in row at start of season (A).

1964 — Pitcher Ed Roebuck purchased from Washington Senators.

1966 — Pitcher Ferguson Jenkins, outfielder Adolfo Phillips, and outfielder-first baseman John Herrnstein traded to Chicago Cubs for pitchers Bob Buhl and Larry Jackson.

## April 22

1876 — Boston wins at Philadelphia, 6-5, in first National League game ever played.

1902 — Ray Benge — B 1928-32, 36 P G-217

1908 — Fabian Kowalik — B 1936 P G-42

1909 — Tom Lanning — B 1938 P G-3

1910 — Earl Moore and Bert Humphries combine to pitch 3-0, one-hit victory over Boston (P).

1971 — Outfielder John Briggs traded to Milwaukee Brewers for pitcher Ray Peters and catcher-outfielder-infielder Pete Koegel.

## April 23

1886 — Harry Coveleski — B 1907-09 P G-34

1907 — Dolf Camilli — B 1934-37 1B G-540

1917 — Tony Lupien — B 1944-45 1B G-169

1926 — Chuck Harmon — B 1957 OF-IF G-57

1950 — Phillies win, 6-5, at Boston in first major league day game ever completed under lights (second game).

1961 — Phillies win doubleheader shutout over Chicago, winning 1-0 behind Frank Sullivan and 6-0 behind Art Mahaffey. Mahaffey sets club record for strikeouts with seventeen (P).

1966 — Infielder-outfielder Harvey Kuenn purchased from Chicago Cubs.

## April 24

1873 — Bob Ewing — B 1910-11 P G-38

1894 — Infielder Lave Cross hits for cycle in 22-5 victory over Brooklyn.

1895 — Dixie Parker — B 1923 C G-4

1913 — Herb Harris — B 1936 P G-4

1926 — Frank Lucchesi — B 1970-72 MGR

1933 — Shortstop Dick Bartell becomes first major league player to get four consecutive doubles in nine-inning game in 7-1 victory over Boston (P).

1943 — Joe Verbanic — B 1966 P G-17

## April 25

1873 — Frank Figgemeier — B 1894 P G-1

1972 — Steve Carlton pitches 3-0, one-hit victory (Chris Speier single in first inning) at San Francisco and ties club record for left-handed pitchers with fourteen strikeouts.

## April 26

1900 — Hack Wilson — B 1934 OF G-7

1918 — Tex Kraus — B 1943, 45 P G-85

1920 — Ron Northey — B 1942-44, 46-47, 57 OF G-600

1921 — Gene Lambert — B 1941-42 P G-3

1927 — Granny Hamner — B 1944-59 IF-P G-1501

1957 — In first major league start, Don Cardwell pitches 5-0, four-hit victory over New York (P).

1965 — Phillies win at Los Angeles, 4-3, and end Sandy Koufax's nine-game winning streak against them, dating back to 1961.

1972 — Phillies ground into five double plays in first six innings in ten-inning, 8-6 loss at San Francisco.

1975 — Mike Schmidt hits two home runs in 10-9 victory over Cincinnati to tie major league record for home runs in April with eleven (P).

## April 27

1865 — Bill Vinton — B 1884-85 P G-30

1889 — John Dodge — B 1912-13 3B G-33

1914 — Larry Crawford B 1937 P G-6

1950 — Outfielder Johnny Blatnik traded to St. Louis Cardinals for pitcher Ken Johnson.

1965 — Phillies tie their club record with six home runs but lose at San Francisco, 14-13.

## April 28

1890 — Frank Scanlan — B 1909 P G-6

1921 — Infielder Ralph Miller hits grand-slam home run in first inning and pitcher Lee Meadows hits one in eighth inning against Boston (P).

1922 — Outfielder Lee King bats in seven runs in game at Brooklyn.

1934 — Jackie Brandt — B 1966-67 OF G-98

1935 — Pete Ramos — B 1967 P G-6

1962 — Pitcher Don Ferrarese traded to St. Louis Cardinals for pitcher Bobby Locke and cash.

## April 29

1928 — Freddy Rodriguez — B 1959 P G-1

1929 — Steve Ridzik — B 1950, 52-55, 66 P G-107

1934 — Phillies lose to Brooklyn, 8-7, in their first legal Sunday game at home.

1946 — Pitcher Si Johnson released and signed by Boston Braves.

1954 — Robin Roberts pitched 4-0, one-hit victory (Del Crandall double in third inning) at Milwaukee.

## April 30

1851 — Dave Eggler — B 1876 OF G-39

1887 — Phillies beat New York, 19-10, in first game played at Broad and Huntingdon Streets park, later known as Baker Bowl.

1897 — Walt Walsh — B 1920 PR G-2

1902 — Bill Dietrick — B 1927-28 OF-SS G-57

1919 — Phillies and Brooklyn set major league record by scoring three runs apiece in nineteenth inning of twenty-inning, 9-9 tie (P).

1936 — Infielder Mickey Haslin traded to Boston Braves for third baseman Pinky Whitney.

1943 — First baseman-outfielder Jimmy Wasdell purchased from Pittsburgh Pirates.

1955 — Catcher Smoky Burgess, pitcher Steve Ridzik and outfielder Stan Palys traded to Cincinnati Reds for outfielders Jim Greengrass and Glen Gorbous and catcher Andy Seminick.

Infielder Roy Smalley purchased from Milwaukee Braves.

1962 — Phillies beat Warren Spahn, 6-4, after losing 11 games in row to the Milwaukee left-hander (P).

# MAY 1

1883 — In Philadelphia's first National League game since 1876, Phillies lose to Providence and pitcher Old Hoss Radbourn, 4-3 (P).

1885 — George McQuillan — B 1907-10, 15-16 P G-149

1903 — Fritz Knothe — B 1933 IF G-41

1906 — John Lush pitches 6-0, no-hit victory at Brooklyn.

1930 — Stan Palys — B 1953-55 OF G-19

1946 — Outfielder Vince DiMaggio traded to New York Giants for catcher Clyde Kluttz, who was then traded to St. Louis Cardinals for second baseman Emil Verban.

1958 — Pitcher Tom Qualters sold to Chicago White Sox.

1972 — Dick Selma pitches 2-1 victory at Los Angeles for fifth straight complete game by Phillies staff.

## May 2

1886 — Larry Cheney — B 1919 P G-9

1895 — Rebuilt grandstand at Philadelphia Park, which had burned down August 6, 1894, is opened to the public. The cantilever construction is called "probably the finest in the world."

1899 — Skinny O'Neal — B 1925, 27 P G-13

1915 — Ken Richardson — B 1946 2B G-6

1954 — Bobby Moreland — B 1978 C G-1

1957 — Robin Roberts ties then club record by striking out thirteen Chicago Cubs in 4-2 victory in which Phillies infield had no assists to tie major league record (P).

1970 — Both Phillies catchers, Tim McCarver and Mike Ryan, suffer broken bones in their hands in sixth inning of 3-1 loss at San Francisco.

1973 — First baseman Deron Johnson traded to Oakland Athletics for third baseman-outfielder Jack Bastable.

## May 3

1891 — Eppa Rixey — B 1912-17, 19-20 P G-254

1899 — Ed Delahanty becomes first member of Phillies to hit four doubles in one game and ties major league record.

1916 — Ken Silvestri — B 1949-51 C G-19

1926 — Stan Jok — B 1954 3B G-3

1947 — Outfielder Ron Northey and $50,000 traded to St. Louis Cardinals for outfielder Harry Walker and pitcher Fred Schmidt.

1974 — Pitcher Mike Wallace traded to New York Yankees for pitcher Ken Wright.

## May 4

1854 — Flip Lafferty — B 1876 P G-1

1891 — Frank Bruggy — B 1921 C G-86

1919 — Phillies win, 4-3, in first legal Sunday game in New York.

1929 — Chicago beats Phillies 16-0, scoring most runs against Phillies in shutout game in post-1900 era (P).

1952 — Fred Andrews — B 1976-77 2B G-16

1961 — Pitcher Dick Farrell and shortstop Joe Koppe traded to Los Angeles Dodgers for third baseman Charlie Smith and outfielder Don Demeter.

1963 — Outfielder Jim Lemon purchased from Minnesota Twins.

1973 — Phillies beat Atlanta in twenty innings, 5-4, in longest game in Veterans Stadium history, matching longest home game in club history.

1975 — First baseman Willie Montanez traded to San Francisco Giants for outfielder Garry Maddox.

## May 5

1863 — Paul Cook — B 1884 C G-3

1867 — Tom Vickery — B 1890, 93 P G-61

1883 — Chief Bender — B 1916-17 P G-48

1935 — Jose Pagan — B 1973 IF G-46

1938 — Pitcher Hal Kelleher gives up modern National League record twelve runs in eighth inning of 21-2 loss at Chicago. Losing pitcher Wayne LaMaster left game with 3-1 count on leadoff batter Stan Hack in first inning.

1947 — Catcher Rollie Hemsley released.

Larry Hisle — B 1968-71 OF G-314

1965 — Jim Bunning hits home run off Warren Spahn to win, 1-0, at New York, giving him a career record against Mets of six starts, six complete game victories, three shutouts and only four runs scored against him in fifty-four innings.

1969 — Outfielder Don Lock traded to Boston Red Sox for outfielder Bill Schlesinger.

## May 6

1941 — Pitcher Vito Tamulis traded to Brooklyn Dodgers for pitcher Lee Grissom.

1966 — In 8-7 victory, Phillies score five runs in eleventh inning to win after Pittsburgh scored four, the nine runs setting a modern National League record for an eleventh inning.

## May 7

1880 — Mickey Doolan — B 1905-13 SS G-1301

1896 — Tom Zachary — B 1936 P G-8

1909 — Ed Heusser — B 1938, 48 P G-34

1922 — Jesse Barnes pitches 6-0, no-hit victory against Phillies at New York.

1925 — Home game with New York is postponed, the Phillies eighth postponement in a row.

1975 — Catcher Jim Essian and outfielder Barry Bonnell traded to Atlanta Braves for first baseman Dick Allen and catcher Johnny Oates.

## May 8

1858 — Dan Brouthers — B 1896 1B G-57

1893 — Ed Hemingway — B 1918 IF G-33

1899 — Fritz Henrich — B 1924 OF G-36

1934 — Pitcher Ted Kleinhans and outfielder Wes Schulmerich traded to Cincinnati Reds for pitcher Syl Johnson and outfielder Johnny Moore.

1945 — Outfielder Buster Adams traded to St. Louis Cardinals for infielders John Antonelli and Glen Crawford.

1962 — Infielder Bobby Consolo sold to Los Angeles Angels.

1967 — Pitcher Dick Farrell purchased from Houston Astros.

1973 — Pitcher Dick Selma released.

## May 9

1892 — Mickey Devine — B 1918 C G-4

1902 — George Durning — B 1925 OF G-5

1937 — Second baseman Alex Kampouris hits three home runs and bats in eight runs, and catcher Ernie Lombardi gets six hits in six at bats for Cincinnati in 21-10 victory at Philadelphia.

1947 — Pitcher Ken Heintzelman purchased from Pittsburgh Pirates.

1950 — Infielder Jimmy Bloodworth purchased from Cincinnati Reds.

1973 — Catcher Johnny Bench hits three home runs and bats in seven runs for Cincinnati in 9-7 victory at Philadelphia.

## May 10

1872 — Klondike Douglas — B 1898-1904 1B-C G-541

1895 — Phillies play their 182nd straight game without being shut out.

1906 — Gene Connell — B 1931 C G-6

1931 — Bob Bowman — B 1955-59 OF G-256

1947 — First baseman Howie Schultz purchased from Brooklyn Dodgers.

1954 — Third baseman-outfielder Stan Jok sold to Chicago White Sox.

1957 — Outfielder Glen Gorbous traded to St. Louis Cardinals for outfielder Chuck Harmon.

1966 — Pitcher Terry Fox purchased from Detroit Tigers.

## May 11

1867 — Lave Cross — B 1892-97 IF-C-OF G-674

1879 — Jesse Purnell — B 1904 3B G-7

1900 — Phillies score 20 runs against Cincinnati.

1910 — Lou Chiozza — B 1934-36 IF-OF G-402

1923 — Second baseman Johnny Rawlings purchased from New York Giants.

Phillies hit six home runs, including three by Cy Williams, and St. Louis hits four to set two-team National League record in Phillies 20-14 victory (P). St. Louis has forty-one total bases and Phillies thirty-eight for major league record total of seventy-nine.

1928 — Catcher Jimmie Wilson traded to St. Louis Cardinals for catcher Spud Davis and outfielder Homer Peel.

1936 — Mel Ott bats in eight runs for New York in 13-12 victory at Philadelphia.

1947 — Largest Philadelphia major league baseball crowd at the time, 40,720, watch Phillies beat Brooklyn, 7-3 and 5-4.

1949 — Jerry Martin — B 1974-78 OF G-444

1950 — Dane Iorg — B 1977 1B G-12

1956 — Pitchers Murry Dickson and Herm Wehmeier and infielder Bobby Morgan traded to St. Louis Cardinals for pitchers Ben Flowers and Harvey Haddix.

1958 — Centerfielder Richie Ashburn plays in 473rd straight game but pulls muscle in first inning of 10-4, first-game loss, and sits out second game.

1962 — Don Demeter bats in six runs, including four on second career grand-slam home run, in 12-2 win at Chicago.

## May 12

1899 — Tod Dennehy — B 1923 OF G-9

1905 — Charlie Butler — B 1933 P G-1

1916 — Hank Borowy — B 1949-50 P G-31

1925 — Pitcher Jimmy Ring hits grand-slam home run off Pittsburgh's Vic Aldridge (P).

1952 — Catcher Del Wilber sold to Boston Red Sox.

1959 — Pitcher Seth Morehead traded to Chicago Cubs for pitcher Taylor Phillips.

## May 12 (continued)

1960 — Outfielder-first baseman Dave Philley sold to San Francisco Giants.

Pitcher Curt Simmons released, and later signed with St. Louis Cardinals.

## May 13

1884 — Alex Main — B 1918 P G-9

Bert Niehoff — B 1915-17 2B G-408

1902 — Cincinnati gets twenty-eight hits in victory over Phillies.

1954 — Robin Roberts pitches 8-1, one-hit victory against Cincinnati, retiring twenty-seven batters in order after Bobby Adams leads off game with home run (P).

1956 — Phillies end ten-game losing streak after 11-9 defeat at Pittsburgh in first game of doubleheader.

1957 — Infielder Bobby Morgan sold to Chicago Cubs.

1958 — Robin Roberts sets club record with 191st career victory, beating Milwaukee, 5-2 (P).

1960 — First baseman Ed Bouchee and pitcher Don Cardwell traded to Chicago Cubs for second baseman Tony Taylor and catcher Cal Neeman.

Phillies lose at Cincinnati, 1-0, after losing 1-0 games the previous two days in San Francisco.

1961 — Phillies beat St. Louis, 3-1, behind Art Mahaffey to end ten-game losing streak (P).

1964 — Pitcher Ryne Duren sold to Cincinnati Reds.

## May 14

1904 — Chicago hits two bases-loaded triples against Phillies.

1913 — Howie Gorman — B 1937-38 OF G-14

1915 — Jim Shilling — B 1939 IF G-11

1927 — Section of stands collapses during seventh inning of 12-4 victory over St. Louis (P). Game is called and Phillies played last twelve games of May home stand at Shibe Park, starting May 16.

1947 — First baseman Frank McCormick released, signed by Boston Braves.

1956 — Infielder Bobby Morgan traded to St. Louis Cardinals for infielder Solly Hemus.

1963 — Phillies win their first game in Dodger Stadium, 5-1, after losing all nine there in 1962, and end Don Drysdale's streak of thirteen wins in row against them, dating back to 1958.

## May 15

1895 — Jimmy Smith — B 1921-22 IF G-105

1911 — Phillies get fourty-three total bases in game against Cincinnati (P).

1914 — Jimmy Wasdell — B 1943-46 OF-1B G-434

1922 — St. Louis scores in every inning except the fifth in 19-7 victory over Phillies (A).

1923 — Dale Matthewson — B 1943-44 P G-29

1935 — Pittsburgh beats Phillies, 20-5 (P).

1936 — Outfielder George Watkins released and signed by Brooklyn Dodgers.

1955 — Robin Roberts wins, 9-1, in second game of doubleheader at Milwaukee to snap Phillies thirteen-game losing streak.

1960 — In 14-3 victory in first game of doubleheader at Cincinnati, Reds pitcher Raul Sanchez hits third Phillies batter in inning, pitcher Gene Conley, setting off a brawl between the two teams.

## May 16

1886 — Clarence Lehr — B 1911 OF-IF G-23

1902 — Outfielder Elmer Flick sold to Cleveland Indians.

1917 — George Jumonville — B 1940-41 IF G-17

1920 — Dave Philley — B 1958-60 OF-1B G-204

1953 — Curt Simmons pitches 3-0, one-hit victory (Bill Bruton leadoff single in first inning) at Milwaukee, retiring last twenty-seven Braves in order.

1959 — Infielder Granny Hamner traded to Cleveland Indians for pitcher Humberto Robinson.

1967 — Pitcher Bob Buhl released.

1972 — Greg Luzinski hits 500-foot home run off Liberty Bell in center field stands at Veterans Stadium in fourth inning for Phillies only run in 8-1 loss to Chicago.

## May 17

1894 — Hal Carlson — B 1924-27 P G-127

1894 — Frank Woodward — B 1918-19 P G-19

1907 — Ed Baecht — B 1926-28 P G-38

1908 — Leo Norris — B 1936-37 IF G-270

1934 — In his first game in Philadelphia since being traded by Phillies to Chicago, Chuck Klein hits two home runs to help Cubs win, 10-3.

1963 — Don Nottebart pitches 4-1, no-hit victory against Phillies at Houston. Phillies score unearned run in fifth inning on Don Hoak's sacrifice fly.

1975 — Gene Garber ties major league record for relief pitchers by beating Atlanta, 9-8, for his third victory in three consecutive games (P).

## May 18

1898 — Harvey MacDonald — B 1928 OF G-13

1921 — John Fick — B 1944 P G-4

1922 — Sam File — B 1940 SS G-7

1929 — Jack Sanford — B 1956-58 P G-74

Brooklyn beats Phillies, 20-16, as Babe Herman and Johnny Frederick each get five hits for Dodgers (P).

1964 — Third baseman Don Hoak released.

Jim Bunning pitches 4-0, one-hit victory (Jim Wynn single in fifth inning) against Houston (A).

## May 19

1874 — Pop Williams — B 1903 P G-2

1886 — Red Nelson — B 1912-13 P G-6

1919 — Earl Naylor — B 1942-43 OF-P G-109

1929 — Curt Simmons — B 1947-50, 52-60 P G-357

1970 — Chris Short pitches 2-0 victory at Pittsburgh to snap Phillies ten-game losing streak.

## May 20

1914 — Stan Benjamin — B 1939-42 OF G-228

1927 — Cy Williams hits grand-slam home run in 15-2 win over Cincinnati (P) (second game).

1930 — Brooklyn scores in eight of nine innings in 16-9 victory over Phillies (P).

## May 20 (continued)

1940 — Phillies score seven runs in ninth inning to beat Pittsburgh, 8-7 (P).

1943 — Phillies take doubleheader shutout from Chicago, winning behind Charley Fuchs, 3-0, and Al Gerheauser, 2-0 (P).

1951 — Phillies win at Pittsburgh, 17-0 and 12-4, as Richie Ashburn gets four hits in each game.

1958 — Shortstop Roy Smalley released.

1964 — Phillies win at San Francisco, 7-2, ending Juan Marichal's twelve-game winning streak. John Callison gets four singles and home run in five at bats.

## May 21

1883 — Eddie Grant — B 1907-10 3B-SS G-526

1918 — Neb Stewart — B 1940 OF G-10

1936 — Outfielder Ethan Alen and pitcher Curt Davis traded to Chicago Cubs for outfielder Chuck Klein, pitcher Fabian Kowalik, and $50,000.

1961 — Phillies score nine runs in third inning but lose to Pittsburgh, 13-11 (P).

1967 — Phillies beat Cincinnati in eighteen innings, 2-1 (P).

## May 22

1890 — George Mangus — B 1912 OF G-10

1913 — Bill Lohrman — B 1934 P G-4

1923 — Pitcher Lee Meadows and second baseman Johnny Rawlings traded to Pittsburgh Pirates for pitcher Whitey Glazner and second baseman Cotton Tierney.

1927 — Brooklyn beats Phillies, 20-4 (A).

1937 — Phillies win at Cincinnati, 19-9.

1956 — Outfielder Elmer Valo signed after release by Kansas City A's.

1959 — Pitcher Jim Hearn released.

## May 23

1874 — Nap Shea — B 1902 C G-3

1878 — Dave Shean — B 1908-09 2B-SS G-50

1909 — Chile Gomez — B 1935-36 2B-SS G-175

37

1952 — Pitcher Bubba Church traded to Cincinnati Reds for outfielder Johnny Wyrostek and pitcher Kent Peterson.

1955 — Pitcher Bob Kuzava purchased from Baltimore Orioles.

## May 24

1876 — Fred Jacklitsch — B 1900-02, 07-10 C-IF G-231

1891 — Joe Oeschger — B 1914-19, 24 P G-149

1903 — Jack Berly — B 1932-33 P G-34

1935 — Phillies lose first night game in major league history, 2-1, at Cincinnati.

1953 — Brooklyn scores twelve runs with none out in eight inning of 16-2 victory at Philadelphia.

1963 — Infielder Billy Klaus released.

## May 25

1876 — Phillies and Louisville tie in fourteen innings, 2-2, first tie in National League history.

1889 — Jimmie Keenan — B 1920-21 P G-16

1904 — Buz Phillips — B 1930 P G-14

1917 — Bert Hodge — B 1942 3B G-8

## May 26

1891 — Gene Paulette — B 1919-20 IF G-210

1904 — Frank Ragland — B 1933 P G-11

1933 — Chuck Klein hits for cycle in 5-4, fourteen-inning loss at St. Louis.

1962 — Sandy Koufax strikes out sixteen Phillies for second time in less than three years in 6-3 victory at Los Angeles.

1966 — Phillies lose in fourteen innings to Juan Marichal at San Francisco in longest 1-0 defeat in club history.

## May 27

1873 — Jack Taylor — B 1892-97 P G-207

1908 — Euel Moore — B 1934-35, 36 P G-55

1912 — Terry Moore — B 1954 MGR

1913 — Hal Spindel — B 1945-46 C G-37

## May 27 (continued)

1919 — Pitcher Joe Oeschger traded to New York Giants for pitcher George Smith and infielder Ed Sicking.

1922 — Phillies end twelve-game losing streak and Brooklyn's eight-game winning streak with 3-2 victory (P) (second game).

1923 — Cy Williams hits fifteenth home run of month off Giants Rosy Ryan in New York to set record for homers in May. It was his eighteenth home run of season, setting National League record for home runs by end of May.

1972 — Phillies end ten-game losing streak with 2-1, twelve-inning victory at Pittsburgh.

## May 28

1867 — Pearce Chiles — B 1899-1900 OF-IF G-130

1899 — Bob Rice — B 1926 3B G-19

1920 — Art Lopatka — B 1946 P G-4

1923 — Bob Kuzava — B 1955 P G-17

1928 — Pitcher Clarence Mitchell released and signed by St. Louis Cardinals.

1934 — Bobby Gene Smith — B 1960-61 OF G-177

1973 — Andy Messersmith strikes out first six Phillies in 5-1 victory at Los Angeles.

## May 29

1875 — Dave Fultz — B 1889-99 OF-IF G-78

1899 — Ace Elliott — B 1929-32 P G-120

1915 — Vance Dinges — B 1945-46 1B-OF G-159

1918 — Bill Burich — B 1942, 46 SS-3B G-27

1939 — Pitcher Claude Passeau traded to Chicago Cubs for outfielder Joe Marty, pitchers Ray Harrell and Kirby Higbe, and $50,000.

1965 — Dick Allen hits measured 529-foot home run completely over Connie Mack Stadium's left center field roof off Larry Jackson in first inning of 4-2 win over Chicago.

1978 — Garry Maddox steals four bases to help Phillies beat Pittsburgh, 4-3, in fourteen innings (P).

## May 30

1897 — Wally Kimmick — B 1925-26 IF G-90

1908 — Hugh Willingham — B 1931-33 IF G-28

1935 — Babe Ruth goes hitless in his final game as Boston beats Phillies, 11-6 (P) (first game).

1965 — Pitcher Lew Burdette purchased from Chicago Cubs.

## May 31

1884 — Bill Foxen — B 1908-10 P G-56

1892 — George Smith — B 1919-22 P G-155

1945 — Pitcher Oscar Judd purchased from Boston Red Sox.

1959 — Gene Freese hits his fifth home run of season as pinch-hitter, one short of major league record, but Phillies lose at Milwaukee, 2-1 (second game).

1975 — Houston scores twelve runs in eighth inning of 15-3 win at Philadelphia.

# JUNE 1

1883 — John Castle — B 1910 OF G-3

1889 — Duke Sedgwick — B 1921 P G-16

1900 — Dutch Schesler — B 1931 P G-17

1919 — Phillies win in eighteen innings, 10-9, at Brooklyn.

1923 — Three New York players get five or more hits and Giants score in all nine innings in 22-5 victory at Philadelphia.

1927 — Pitcher Wayland Dean sold to Chicago Cubs.

1939 — Phillies play first home night game in their history and lose to Pittsburgh, 5-2.

1943 — Outfielders Danny Litwhiler and Earl Naylor traded to St. Louis Cardinals for outfielders Buster Adams, Dain Clay, and Coaker Triplett.

1965 — Left-hander Bob Veale sets Pittsburgh club record by striking out sixteen Phillies as Pirates win, 4-0, for their twelfth straight win (A).

1968 — Phillies beat Cincinnati, 12-0, behind Woodie Fryman in most one-sided game in Philadelphia since 1963.

1969 — Dick Allen hits home run in fifth straight game as Phillies lose to Los Angeles, 12-4 (P).

1921 — Outfielder Greasy Neale sold to Cincinnati Reds.

## June 2 (continued)

1928 — Two Phillies pinch-hitters and one St. Louis pinch-hitter hit home runs in 13-12 Cardinal victory (P).

1931 — Larry Jackson — B 1966-68 P G-115

1946 — Roger Freed — B 1971-72 OF G-191

1949 — Phillies hit six home runs, five in ten-run eighth inning, in 12-3 victory over Cincinnati (P). Andy Seminick hits three home runs, two in eighth inning.

1962 — Dennis Bennett pitches 7-0, four-hit victory as Phillies end thirteen-game Los Angeles winning streak (P).

## June 3

1863 — Woodie Wagenhurst — B 1888 3B G-2

1916 — Maxie Wilson — B 1940 P G-3

1928 — Dick Young — B 1951-52 2B G-20

1930 — Grover Alexander's major league career ends as Phillies release him.

1941 — Tommy Hughes pitches 7-0, one-hit victory (Lou Novikoff single) against Chicago (P).

1972 — Paul Owens promoted from farm system director to general manager of Phillies, succeeding John Quinn, who held post for 14½ years.

1978 — Dave Johnson becomes first pinch-hitter in major league history to hit two grand-slam home runs in one season. This one came with none out in ninth inning and gave Phillies 5-1 victory over Los Angeles (P). First came April 30 with score tied in fifth inning of 11-4 victory over San Diego (P).

## June 4

1902 — George Watkins — B 1936-36 OF G-169

1908 — Orville Jorgens — B 1935-37 P G-144

1913 — Joe Holden — B 1934-36 C G-17

1932 — Pitcher Flint Rhem and infielder Eddie Delker purchased from St. Louis Cardinals.

1938 — Art Mahaffey — B 1960-65 P G-173

1939 — Phil Linz — B 1966-67 IF G-63

1953 — Pitcher Curt Simmons cuts off end of his left big toe in his power lawn mower and does not start a game for Phillies for a month.

## June 4 (continued)

1964 — Sandy Koufax pitches 3-0, no-hit, victory for Los Angeles against Phillies (P).

## June 5

1878 — Fred Mitchell — B 1903-04 P G-54

1915 — Grover Alexander pitches 5-0, one-hit, victory at St. Louis.

1948 — Richie Ashburn tied modern National League rookie record by hitting safely in twenty-third straight game in 6-5 victory at Chicago (second game). Ashburn hit .439 (43 for 98) during streak.

1959 — Third baseman Willie Jones traded to Cleveland Indians for outfielder Jim Bolger.

1967 — Pitcher Pedro Ramos released.

## June 6

1897 — Ray Pierce — B 1925-26 P G-62

1902 — Fresco Thompson — B 1927-30 2B G-575

1915 — Ray Stoviak — B 1938 OF G-10

1928 — Cy Williams hits second home run in succession as pinch-hitter in 5-3 victory over Chicago (P). Previous home run as pinch-hitter was hit on June 2 in 13-12 loss to St. Louis (P).

1930 — Denny Sothern hits four doubles to tie major league record and scores five runs as Phillies beat Cincinnati, 14-5 (P).

1937 — Umpire Ziggy Sears forfeits game to St. Louis with two out in fifth inning and Phillies behind, 8-2 (P) (second game).

1943 — Outfielder Dain Clay traded to Cincinnati Reds for shortstop Charlie Brewster.

1944 — Bud Harrelson — B 1978 IF G-71

1948 — Phillies pitcher Charlie Bicknell gives up four home runs and eighteen total bases in sixth inning as Phillies lose, 11-1, at St. Louis (second game).

1965 — John Callison hits three home runs in 10-9 victory at Chicago (second game).

## June 7

1888 — George Chalmers — B 1910-16 P G-121

1927 — Pitcher Hal Carlson traded to Chicago Cubs for pitcher Tony Kaufmann and shortstop Jimmy Cooney.

## June 7 (continued)

1939 — Outfielder Chuck Klein released and signed by Pittsburgh Pirates.

1947 — Don Money — B 1968-72 3B-SS G-524

1957 — Rookie Jack Sanford ties Phillies club record by striking out thirteen in 1-0 victory over Chicago (P).

1966 — Jim Bunning strikes out career-equalling high of fourteen, beats Cincinnati, 5-1, for eighth victory in row, matching his career high set in 1964 (P).

1967 — Catcher Bob Uecker traded to Atlanta Braves for catcher-first baseman Gene Oliver.

## June 8

1907 — Lew Moren pitches one-hit vicotry for Phillies against St. Louis.

1913 — Art Mahan — B 1940 1B G-146

1919 — Charley Schanz — B 1944-47 P G-141

1920 — Shortstop Dave Bancroft traded to New York Giants for shortstop Art Fletcher, pitcher Bill Hubbell, and $100,000.

1925 — Del Ennis — B 1946-56 OF G-1630

1934 — Bill Smith — B 1962 P G-24

1942 — Larry Colton — B 1968 P G-1

1951 — Outfielder Dick Whitman and cash traded to Brooklyn Dodgers for outfielder-infielder Tommy Brown.

1965 — Pitcher Ryne Duren released, signed by Washington Senators.

1968 — Pinch-hitter Howie Bedell's sacrifice fly in Phillies fifth inning ends Don Drysdale's major league record streak of 58 2/3 scoreless innings as Los Angeles wins, 5-3 (A).

## June 9

1893 — Irish Meusel — B 1918-21 OF G-486

1893 — Mack Wheat — B 1920-21 C G-88

1902 — Lee Dunham — B 1926 1B G-5

1911 — Frank McCormick — B 1946-47 1B G-150

1926 — Roy Smalley — B 1955-58 SS G-186

1939 — Doug Clemens — B 1966-68 OF G-177

## June 9 (continued)

1949 — Phillies beat Pittsburgh in eighteen innings, 4-3, as both teams have sixty-eight at bats, sixteen hits, twenty-one assists, and three errors, and winners fail to draw a walk (P).

1959 — Outfielder Solly Drake purchased from Los Angeles Dodgers.

1963 — Home runs by Don Demeter, pinch-hitter Jim Lemon, and Johnny Callison in five-run ninth inning enable Phillies to tie, and they beat Cincinnati in tenth, 8-7 (P) (first game).

## June 10

1920 — Johnny Podgajny — B 1940-43 P G-96

1921 — Al Verdel — B 1944 P G-1

1926 — Phillies Russ Wrightstone hits for cycle in 13-11 victory over Pittsburgh (P).

1928 — Ken Lehman — B 1961 P G-42

## June 11

1866 — Pop Schriver — B 1888-90 C G-152

1887 — Bill Culp — B 1910 P G-4

1929 — Frank Thomas — B 1964-65 1B G-74

1934 — First baseman Don Hurst traded to Chicago Cubs for first baseman Dolf Camilli.

1944 — Catcher Johnny Peacock purchased from Boston Red Sox.

1948 — Dave Cash — B 1974-76 2B G-484

1952 — Chicago outfielder Hank Sauer hits three solo home runs off Curt Simmons as Phillies lose, 3-2, at Chicago.

1977 — Phillies outfielder Greg Luzinski hits grand-slam home run, three-run double to bat in seven runs as Phillies win, 13-10, at Atlanta.

## June 12

1879 — Red Dooin — B 1902-14 C-MGR G-1218

1884 — Otto Knabe — B 1907-13 2B G-946

1886 — Lou Schettler — B 1910 P G-27

1918 — Bitsy Mott — B 1945 IF G-90

44

## June 12 (continued)

1922 — St. Louis gets National League record ten hits in row, scores seven runs in sixth inning to beat Phillies, 14-8 (P). One of the ten hits was an apparent home run by George Torporcer, but he passed preceeding runner and was credited with single.

1941 — Del Bates — B 1970 C G-22

1943 — Sam Parrilla — B 1970 OF G-11

1950 — Pitcher Hank Borowy sold to Pittsburgh Pirates.

1954 — Pitcher Herm Wehmeier purchased from Cincinnati Reds.

Jim Wilson pitches 2-0, no-hit victory against Phillies at Milwaukee.

1967 — First baseman Tito Francona sold to Atlanta Braves.

1971 — Infielder Tony Taylor traded to Detroit Tigers for pitchers Carl Cavanaugh and Mike Fremuth.

## June 13

1894 — Henry Baldwin — B 1927 SS-3B G-6

1918 — Phillies and St. Louis tie in nineteen innings, 8-8 (P).

1938 — Pitcher Bucky Walters traded to Cincinnati Reds for catcher Spud Davis, pitcher Al Hollingsworth, and $55,000.

1958 — Catcher Joe Lonnett traded to Milwaukee Braves for catcher Carl Sawatski.

## June 14

1861 — Charlie Buffinton — B 1887-89 P-OF G-159

1876 — Phillies George Hall becomes first major league player to hit for the cycle.

1887 — Walt Tragesser — B 1919-20 C G-97

1891 — Frank Withrow — B 1920, 22 C G-58

1914 — George Myatt — B 1968, 69 MGR

1934 — Third baseman Bucky Walters purchased from Boston Red Sox.

1947 — Pitcher Ken Raffensberger and catcher Hugh Poland traded to Cincinnati Reds for catcher Al Kaleman.

1959 — Catcher Jim Hegan sold to San Francisco Giants.

1965 — Catcher Gus Triandos sold to Houston Astros.

1972 — Catcher Tim McCarver traded to Montreal Expos for catcher John Bateman.

1978 — Outfielders Jay Johnstone and Bobby Brown traded to New York Yankees for pitcher Rawly Eastwick.

## June 15

1887 — New York wins, 29-1, scoring cost most runs ever against Phillies.

1894 — Phillies beat Cincinnati, 21-8.

1912 — Babe Dahlgren — B 1943 IF G-136

1925 — Infielder Barney Friberg purchased from Chicago Cubs.

1927 — Ben Flowers — B 1956 P G-32

1934 — Outfielder Chick Fullis traded to St. Louis Cardinals for outfielder Kiddo Davis.

1940 — Outfielder Morrie Arnovich traded to Cincinnati Reds for outfielder Johnny Rizzo.

1941 — Phillies score eight runs in sixth inning to end streak of twenty-eight straight scoreless innings in 8-4 victory at Chicago (second game).

1945 — Catcher Johnny Peacock traded to Brooklyn Dodgers for pitcher-outfielder Ben Chapman.

1949 — Eddie Waitkus shot by deranged nineteen-year old Ruth Ann Steinhagen in her Chicago hotel room, sidelining Phillies first baseman for the rest of the season.

1952 — Infielder-outfielder Tommy Brown sold to Chicago Cubs.

1954 — Pitcher Karl Drews sold to Cincinnati Reds.

1955 — First baseman Earl Torgeson sold to Detroit Tigers.

1960 — Outfielders Harry Anderson and Wally Post and first baseman Fred Hopke traded to Cincinnati Reds for outfielder Tony Gonzalez and infielder-outfielder Lee Walls.

1962 — Phillies score ten runs in third inning, their biggest inning in thirteen years, in 13-8 victory over Cincinnati (P).

1968 — Gene Mauch fired as manager of Phillies after 8½ years, and is replaced by Bob Skinner, manager of the club's San Diego farm team.

1972 — Pitcher Joe Hoerner and first baseman Andre Thornton traded to Atlanta Braves for pitchers Jim Nash and Gary Neibauer.

1977 — Pitcher Wayne Twitchell and catcher Tim Blackwell traded to Montreal Expos for catcher Barry Foote and pitcher Dan Warthen.

Pitcher Tom Underwood, outfielder Rick Bosetti, and first baseman Dane Iorg traded to St. Louis Cardinals for outfielder Bake McBride and pitcher Steve Waterbury.

1978 — Pitcher Gene Garber traded to Atlanta Braves for pitcher Dick Ruthven.

## June 16

1847 — Libe Washburn — B 1903 P-OF G-8

1853 — Lon Knight — B 1876 P-IF-OF G-55

1886 — Jack Rowan — B 1911 P G-12

1894 — Ed Delahanty gets six hits in six times at bat.

1926 — Bob Miller — B 1949-58 P G-261

1929 — Ray Benge strikes out thirteen to tie Phillies club record in 7-2 victory at Chicago.

1934 — Pancho Herrera — B 1958, 60-61 IF G-300

## June 17

1876 — George Hall becomes first player to score five runs and first to hit two home runs in a nine-inning National League game.

1884 — Charley Ferguson pitches 7-2 victory to end Boston streak of twenty-one straight wins over Phillies (fourteen in 1883).

1897 — Bill Hubbell — B 1920-25 P G-156

1903 — Ben Shields — B 1931 P G-4

1910 — Joe Bowman — B 1935-36 P G-93

1914 — Phillies outfielder Sherry Magee ties major league record with four doubles in game against St. Louis (P).

1930 — Chuck Klein hits in twenty-sixth straight game to set Phillies modern record, compiling .482 batting average (53 for 110) from May 18 through June 17. Klein again hits in twenty-six straight games from July 12 through August 3 (first game), compiling .434 average (49 for 113).

1933 — Third baseman Pinky Whitney and outfielder Hal Lee traded to Boston Braves for outfielder Wes Schulmerich, infielder Fritz Knothe, and cash.

1943 — Luis Peraza — B 1969 P G-8

1957 — Outfielder Frankie Baumholtz released.

1961 — Outfielder Elmer Valo signed as free agent.

## June 18

1862 — Charlie Ganzel B 1885-86 C G-35

1898 — George Stallings fired as manager of Phillies after year and one-half in job.

1933 — Taylor Phillips — B 1959-60 P G-42

1941 — Paul Brown — B 1961-63, 68 P G-36

1948 — Pitcher Robin Roberts makes major league debut and loses to Pittsburgh, 2-0 (P).

## June 19

1905 — Togie Pittinger's eight-game winning streak ends as Phillies lose at Chicago, 3-2.

1929 — Don Ferrarese — B 1961-62 P G-48

1931 — Hank Mason — B 1958, 60 P G-4

1955 — Phillies win in fifteen innings, 1-0, at Chicago, matching Phillies longest 1-0 victory (first game).

## June 20

1883 — Boston wins, 29-4, scoring most runs ever against Phillies.

1903 — Wayland Dean — B 1926-27 P G-66

1967 — Larry Jackson pitches 4-0, one-hit victory (Tommy Davis double in second inning) against New York (P). It was Jackson's eighteenth win over Mets without defeat. Streak ended with 8-3 loss on August 14.

## June 21

1891 — Bert Adams — B 1915-19 C G-240

1900 — Brooklyn scores seven runs in eleventh inning for 20-13 lead. When Phillies stalled in last of eleventh, hoping the game would be called by darkness, Umpire Hank O'Day forfeited the game to the visitors.

1904 — Phillies win in thirteen innings, 1-0, at Brooklyn for the only major league victory in the career of pitcher John McPherson.

1952 — Dave Downs — B 1972 P G-4

1964 — Jim Bunning pitches first complete perfect game in National League in eighty-four years, winning at New York, 6-0, in first game of doubleheader. Second baseman Tony Taylor's diving stop of Jesse Gonder's line smash in the fifth inning was closest thing to a hit. Taylor knocked the ball down and threw to first while on his knees to retire the Met catcher by a stride. The game ended with Bunning striking out pinch-hitter Johnny Stephenson for the right-hander's tenth strikeout.

48

Phillies won second game, 8-2, for rookie Rick Wise's first victory and set National League record by holding Mets to three hits in doubleheader.

1974 — Pitcher Pete Richert purchased from St. Louis Cardinals.

## June 22

1884 — Charlie Roy — B 1906 P G-8

1890 — Mike Fitzgerald — B 1918 OF G-66

1944 — Phillies win, 1-0, on Ron Northey's home run in fifteenth inning at Boston, matching longest 1-0 victory in club history.

1951 — Mike Anderson — B 1971-75 OF G-409

1959 — Sandy Koufax strikes out sixteen Phillies in 6-2 victory at Los Angeles, a figure no rival pitcher has exceeded against Phillies.

1967 — Shortstop Dick Groat sold to San Francisco Giants.

## June 23

1875 — Jerry Nops — B 1896 P G-1

1902 — Leon Pettit — B 1937 P G-3

1907 — Dusty Cooke — B 1948 MGR

1915 — John Humphries — B 1946 P G-10

1922 — Deacon Donahue — B 1943-44 P G-8

1929 — Pitcher Phil Collins hits grand-slam home run off Kent Greenfield but Phillies lose, 7-5, at Boston (second game).

1930 — Chicago beats Phillies, 21-8 (A).

1960 — Infielder Alvin Dark traded to Milwaukee Braves for third baseman Joe Morgan.

1961 — Phillies overcome 9-0 and 11-2 leads with four runs in eighth inning and six runs in ninth to win, 12-11, at Pittsburgh.

1964 — Ray Culp pitches 9-0, one-hit victory (Len Gabrielson single in sixth inning) against Chicago (P) (second game).

1968 — Dick Allen hits sixth homer in last seven games but Phillies lose at Houston, 7-4.

1971 — Rick Wise pitches 4-0, no-hit victory at Cincinnati and becomes first pitcher in major league history to hit two home runs in no-hitter. Only

## June 23 (continued)

a walk to Dave Concepcion with one out in sixth inning deprived Wise of a perfect game. Rookie third baseman John Vukovich made the best defensive play, diving to make a backhand stop of Tommy Helms smash to open the third inning.

1973 — Ken Brett sets major league record for pitchers by hitting a home run in his fourth straight game while pitching Phillies to 7-2 victory at Montreal. Other three home runs were hit on June 9 in his 4-1 win over San Diego, on June 13 in his 16-3 win over Los Angeles, and on June 18 in his 9-6 win over New York, all at Veterans Stadium.

1978 — Phillies beat Chicago twice by 6-1 scores at Veterans Stadium to take over National League's Eastern Division lead, which they held for rest of season.

## June 24

1855 — Charlie Reilly — B 1892-95 3B G-283

1864 — Jack Clements — B 1884-97 C G-997

1865 — Billy Nash — B 1896-98 3B-MGR G-189

1892 — George Harper — B 1924-26 OF G-297

1907 — Rollie Hemsley — B 1946-47 C G-51

1914 — Hal Kelleher — B 1935-38 P G-53

1915 — Buster Adams — B 1943-45, 47 OF G-345

1917 — Al Gerheauser — B 1943-44 P G-70

1969 — Phillies Manager Bob Skinner suspends slugger Dick Allen for failing to show up for twilight-night doubleheader at New York. Suspension lasts until July 20.

1974 — Outfielder Ollie Brown purchased from Houston.

## June 25

1902 — June Green — B 1928-29 P G-32

1928 — New York third baseman Fred Lindstrom ties major league record with nine hits in 12-4, 8-2 doubleheader sweep by Giants at Philadelphia.

1930 — Humberto Robinson — B 1959-60 P G-64

1935 — Don Demeter — B 1961-63 OF-3B G-413

1953 — With 13-2 victory at Chicago, Phillies beat Cubs for eleventh time in row this season. Streak ends when Cubs win, 5-3, on July 19 (P).

## June 26

1910 — Jim Henry — B 1939 — P G-9

50

1915 — Grover Alexander pitches 4-0, one-hit victory against Brooklyn (P).

1943 — Bill Robinson — B 1972-74 OF G-306

1955 — Manny Seoane — B 1977 P G-2

1957 — Pitcher Warren Hacker purchased from Cincinnati Reds.

## June 27

1876 — Dave Force becomes first National League player to get six hits in nine-inning game.

1926 — Al Porto — B 1948 P G-3

1952 — Eddie Sawyer is fired as manager of Phillies and is succeeded by Steve O'Neill on June 28.

1963 — Phillies outfielder, John Callison hits for cycle in 13-4 victory at Pittsburgh. In same game, Phillies center fielder Tony Gonzalez fumbles single in seventh inning, ending major league record streak for outfielder of 205 consecutive errorless games.

## June 28

1887 — Phillies shut out Indianapolis, 24-0, the highest score in shutout victory in history of club.

1892 — Phillies tie their club record with their sixteenth straight victory, beating Boston, 8-1 (P). Boston ended streak with 9-1 win June 29.

1909 — Phillies president Israel Durham dies suddenly in Atlantic City. Durham had been named president on February 26 after he and two partners had acquired the club's stock from Alfred Reach and John Rogers.

1921 — Infielder Jimmy Smith purchased from Cincinnati Reds.

1923 — Phillies go into last of ninth inning trailing Brooklyn, 7-0, but rally for eight runs to win, 8-7.

1937 — Cal Emery — B 1963 1B G-16

1940 — Gary Wagner — B 1965-69 P G-118

1960 — Pancho Herrera hits home run in seventh inning of 2-0 victory over Los Angeles (P) to run ninth longest hitting streak in Phillies history to twenty games. Streak ends next night with three hitless at bats against Dodgers (first game).

1961 — Phillies and San Francisco play fifteen-inning, 7-7 tie in what was then the longest night game by time in major league history, lasting five hours, eleven minutes.

1963 — Outfielder Jim Lemon sold to Chicago White Sox.

## June 28 (continued)

1974 — Pitcher George Culver released.

## June 29

1873 — Jack Sutthoff — B 1904-05 P G-32

1876 — Patsy Flaherty — B 1910 OF-P G-2

1877 — She Donahue — B 1904 IF G-58

1912 — Grover Alexander ties Phillies club record by striking out thirteen Brooklyn batters in eleven-inning, 3-2 victory (P).

1916 — Phillies pitcher Eppa Rixey hurls one-hit victory at New York.

1925 — Nippy Jones — B 1952 1B G-8

1926 — Bobby Morgan — B 1954-56, 57 IF G-281

1945 — Ben Chapman named player-manager of Phillies, succeeding Fred Fitzsimmons.

1961 — Willie Mays hit three home runs, including one in tenth inning, to give San Francisco 8-7 victory at Philadelphia (first game).

1964 — Pitcher Johnny Klippstein sold to Minnesota Twins.

## June 30

1913 — Manny Salvo — B 1943 P G-1

New York scores ten runs in tenth inning to beat Phillies, 11-1.

1914 — Dino Chiozza — B 1935 SS G-2

1921 — Jack Albright — B 1947 SS G-41

Second baseman Johnny Rawlings and outfielder Casey Stengel traded to New York Giants for infielder Joe Rapp and outfielders Lee King and Curt Walker.

1932 — Chuck Klein hits twenty-third and twenty-fourth runs in 9-3 victory over Brooklyn (P), the most home runs ever hit at that time by the end of June by a National League player.

1935 — Syl Johnson wins, 15-5, at Boston for his eighth straight victory.

1938 — New York beats Phillies, 14-1, in final major league game at Baker Bowl.

1967 — Cookie Rojas pitches scoreless ninth inning in 12-3 loss to San Francisco (second game). Rojas has now filled all nine positions since joining Phillies in 1963, and played eight positions this season.

52

# JULY 1

1857 — Roger Connor — B 1892 1B G-155

1925 — New York's Hack Wilson hits two home runs in third inning at Philadelphia (second game).

1931 — Chuck Klein hits for cycle, bats in five runs in 11-6 victory over Chicago (P).

1951 — Russ Meyer and Jim Konstanty combine to pitch one-hitter (Peewee Reese two-run triple in third), but Phillies lose at Brooklyn, 2-0.

1952 — Kerry Dineen — B 1978 OF G-5

1975 — Catcher Tim McCarver signed after release by Boston Red Sox.

## July 2

1869 — Walter Plock — B 1891 OF G-2

1897 — Chet Nichols — B 1930-32 P G-39

1900 — Joe Bennett — B 1923 3B G-1

1914 — Bob Allen — B 1937 P G-3

1915 — Hal Wanger — B 1948-49 C G-4

1961 — Outfielder Bobby Del Greco traded to Kansas City A's for outfielder Wes Covington.

1962 — Pitcher Johnny Podres ties major league record by striking out eight Phillies in succession in 5-1 victory at Los Angeles.

1969 — Phillies win, 14-4, at Pittsburgh for their ninth straight victory, all on the road in the longest road winning streak in club history. Streak ends on July 4 when Montreal beats Phillies, 8-5 (P) (first game).

## July 3

1883 — Cliff Curtis — B 1911-12 P G-18

1896 — Curt Walker — B 1921-24 OF G-333

1897 — Heinie Sand — B 1923-28 SS G-848

1922 — Howie Schultz — B 1947-48 1B G-120

1928 — Alex Ferguson pitches 15-0, seven-hit victory at Boston for first shutout of season by Phillies pitcher.

1930 — Jim Westlake — B 1955 PH G-1

1931 — Ed Roebuck — B 1964-66 P G-110

1940 — Cesar Tovar — B 1973 IF-OF G-97

1965 — During batting practice before 10-8 loss to Cincinnati (P), Phillies infielders Dick Allen and Frank Thomas fight. Thomas placed on waivers after game in which he hit game-tying home run as pinch-hitter in eighth inning.

## July 4

1860 — Charlie Bastian — B 1885-88, 91 IF G-348

1890 — Milt Reed — B 1913-14 IF G-57

1904 — Ed Cotter — B 1926 3B-SS G-17

1908 — Hooks Wiltse pitches 1-0, no-hit, ten-inning victory against Phillies at New York (A.M. game). Pitcher George McQuillan, who lost the game on an error with none out in the tenth, was hit by a pitch with two out in the ninth to spoil Wiltse's bid for a perfect game.

1921 — First baseman Ed Nonetchy purchased from Brooklyn Dodgers.

1931 — Bobby Malkmus — B 1960-62 IF G-208

1938 — Phillies lose to Boston, 10-5, in first game of doubleheader in their first game at Shibe Park since moving permanently out of Baker Bowl. Phillies won second game, 10-2.

1954 — Dan Larson — B 1978 P G-1

1967 — Catcher Clay Dalrymple ties National League record by drawing six walks as Phillies sweep doubleheader from Houston, 9-0 and 4-3 in eleven innings (P).

## July 5

1841 — Wes Fisler — B 1876 OF-IF G-59

1857 — Jack Farrell — B 1886 2B G-17

1886 — Beals Becker — B 1913-15 OF G-338

1904 — Phillies win in ten innings to end New York's eighteen-game winning streak (P).

1915 — Grover Alexander pitches 2-0, one-hit victory against New York (P).

## July 6

1891 — Steve O'Neill — B 1952-54 MGR

1893 — John Boyle gets six hits for Phillies in eleven-inning game.

1899 — Lenny Mets — B 1923-25 SS G-30

## July 6 (continued)

1908 — Cy Blanton — B 1940-42 P G-47

1918 — Hal Marnie — B 1940-42 IF G-96

1929 — St. Louis scores ten runs in first inning and ten runs in fifth inning, beats Phillies, 28-6, with most runs in modern National League history (P) (second game). Outfielders Taylor Douthit and Chick Hafey get five hits apiece, and Hafey and first baseman Jim Bottomley hit grand-slam home runs for Cardinals.

1930 — Angelo LiPetri — B 1956, 58 P G-10

1939 — John Boozer — B 1962-64, 66-69 P G-172

1943 — Pitcher Dick Barrett purchased from Chicago Cubs.

1951 — Richie Ashburn hits safely in twentieth straight game in 6-2 loss to Brooklyn (P).

## July 7

1910 — Ernie Sulik — B 1936 OF G-122

1919 — Phillies tie major league record by stealing eight bases in ninth inning against New York (P) (first game).

1924 — Ed Sanicki — B 1949, 51 OF G-20

1926 — Mel Clark — B 1951-55 OF G-210

1928 — Sammy White — B 1962 C G-41

1964 — John Callison hits three-run home run in ninth inning to give National League 7-4 victory in thirty-fifth Major League All-Star Game at New York's Shea Stadium.

## July 8

1895 — Ray Crumpler — B 1925 P G-3

1898 — Red Donahue pitches 5-0, no-hit victory against Boston (P). He allowed just one batter to pass first. Herman Long, who reached base on an error to start the game, stole second and was stranded. Only three other batters reached base.

1919 — Charlie Gilbert — B 1946-47 OF G-171

1924 — Phillies set major league record by playing twenty-five inning doubleheader without committing an error (A). Cincinnati won sixteenth-inning first game, 2-1.

1930 — Glen Gorbous — B 1955-57 OF G-109

1933 — Chick Fullis hits safely in twenty-second straight game but Phillies lose, 3-0, at Pittsburgh (second game).

55

1939 — Ed Keegan — B 1959, 62 P G-8

1940 — Darrell Brandon — B 1971-73 P G-130

1941 — Gary Kroll — B 1964 P G-2

1943 — George Culver — B 1973-74 P G-28

Pitcher Andy Karl purchased from Boston Red Sox.

Pinch-hitter Pinky May singles with two out in fourteenth inning to drive in only run and Dick Barrett goes route to beat Cincinnati, 1-0 (P).

1946 — Pitcher Blix Donnelly purchased from St. Louis Cardinals.

1952 — National League beats American League, 3-2, in twentieth Major League All-Star Game before 32,785 at Shibe Park. Phillies pitcher Curt Simmons and A's pitcher Bobby Shantz star on mound in game halted by rain after five innings.

## July 9

1889 — Jack Boyle — B 1912 3B-SS G-15

1906 — Johnny Vergez — B 1935-36 3B G-163

1925 — First baseman Walter Holke sold to Cincinnati Reds.

1929 — Wally Post — B 1958-60 OF G-276

1939 — Kirby Higbe pitches 3-1, six-hit victory at Boston to end eleven-game Phillies losing streak.

1953 — Robin Roberts is relieved by winner Bob Miller in two-run eighth inning in Phillies 6-5 victory over Brooklyn (P), ending his streak of consecutive complete games at twenty-eight. Streak began August 28, 1952, covered his last eight starts in 1952, and went through his first twenty starts in 1953, including 2-0 victory at Pittsburgh on July 5 for number twenty-eight.

1955 — Pitcher Saul Rogovin signed as free agent after release by Baltimore Orioles.

1959 — Third baseman Gene Freese hits his third grand-slam home run of season in 11-0 victory over St. Louis (P) (first game).

1961 — Catcher Darrell Johnson signed as free agent.

1967 — Dick Allen becomes first player to hit home run over center field fence between stands and flagpole at Connie Mack Stadium since fence was raised in 1934 to thirty-two feet. Blow came off Nelson Briles in eighth inning of 4-3 victory over St. Louis.

## July 10

1867 — Bob Allen — B 1890-94 SS G-567

1882 — Dutch Rudolph — B 1903 PH G-1

1906 — Ad Liska — B 1932-33 P G-55

1921 — Pitcher Cecil Causey traded to New York Giants for pitcher Jesse Winters and infielder John Monroe.

1936 — Chuck Klein becomes fourth major league player to hit four home runs in a game in ten-inning, 9-6 Phillies victory at Pittsburgh.

1965 — First baseman Frank Thomas sold to Houston Astros.

1972 — General Manager Paul Owens takes on added duty of field manager of Phillies, succeeding Frank Lucchesi for remainder of season.

1974 — Infielder Billy Grabarkewitz sold to Chicago Cubs.

## July 11

1873 — Jimmy Slagle — B 1900-01 OF G-189

1893 — Milt Stock — B 1915-18 3B G-474

1910 — First baseman Kitty Bransfield bats in eight runs as Phillies get twenty hits in 18-0 victory over Pittsburgh (P).

1911 — Vito Tamulis — B 1941 P G-6

1931 — New York gets twenty-eight hits in 23-8 victory at Philadelphia (first game).

1954 — Phillies third baseman Jim Command's first major league hit is a grand-slam home run off Carl Erskine in eighth inning of 8-7 loss at Brooklyn (first game).

1967 — Infielder Phil Linz traded to New York Mets for infielder Chuck Hiller.

1971 — First baseman Deron Johnson hits three home runs in game (extending streak to four home runs in succession) in 11-5 victory over Montreal (P).

## July 12

1889 — Harry Pearce — B 1917-19 IF G-135

1894 — Lee Meadows — B 1919-23 P G-131

1900 — Noodles Hahn pitches 4-0, no-hit, victory against Phillies at Cincinnati.

1905 — George Darrow — B 1934 P G-17

## July 12 (continued)

1917 — Infielder Johnny Evers purchased from Boston Braves.

1919 — Johnny Wyrostek — B 1946-47, 52-54 OF G-588

1931 — Paul Penson — B 1954 P G-5

1936 — Joe Bowman, with relief help from Claude Passeau with none out in ninth inning, pitches 4-0, one-hit victory (Kiki Cuyler triple) at Cincinnati.

## July 13

1874 — Wiley Piatt — B 1898-1900 P G-103

1887 — Gene Packard — B 1919 P G-27

1896 — Ed Delahanty hits four home runs and single in five times at bat and drives in six runs against Adonis Terry, but Phillies lose at Chicago, 9-8.

1900 — Third baseman Harry Wolverton collects five hits, including three triples, in 23-8 victory over Pittsburgh.

1927 — Ruben Gomez — B 1959-60, 67 P G-53

1943 — American League beats National League, 5-3, in eleventh Major League All-Star Game before 31,938 at Shibe Park in first All-Star Game ever played at night.

1968 — Phillies win, 3-2, in sixteen innings at Pittsburgh to sweep four-game series from Pirates. Phillies win three more road games for longest road winning streak in more than a quarter of century.

1976 — National League beats American League, 7-1, in fourty-seventh Major League All-Star Game before what was then a Pennsylvania record baseball crowd of 63,974 at Veterans Stadium.

## July 14

1879 — Fred Burchell — B 1903 P G-6

1893 — John Peters — B 1921-22 C G-110

1900 — Chick Fraser pitches 1-0, one-hit victory over Boston (P).

1913 — Gene Schott — B 1939 P G-8

1919 — Pitchers Elmer Jacobs and Frank Woodward and third baseman Doug Baird traded to St. Louis Cardinals for pitcher Lee Meadows and first baseman Gene Paulette.

1934 — Phillies score eleven runs in second inning in 18-0 victory over Cincinnati (P) (first game).

1945 — Pitcher Bill Lee sold to Boston Braves.

1961 — Jack Baldschun relieves in eighth straight Phillies game, one short of then major league record, and is credited with 7-5, ten-inning victory at Los Angeles.

1962 — Pitcher Frank Sullivan is released, signed by Minnesota Twins.

## July 15

1900 — John Jackson — B 1933 P G-10

1908 — Jake Powell — B 1945 OF G-48

1909 — Pitchers Buster Brown and Lew Richie and infielder Dave Shean traded to Boston Braves for outfielder Johnny Bates and infielder Charlie Starr.

1915 — John Antonelli — B 1945 3B G-125

Lefty Scott — B 1945 P G-8

1926 — Jesse Levan — B 1947 OF G-2

1946 — Ron Diorio — B 1973-74 P G-25

1954 — Steve O'Neill fired as manager of the Phillies and former St. Louis Cardinal outfielder Terry Moore named his successor.

1957 — Phillies beat St. Louis, 6-2, to take over first place in the National League for the first time after May since 1950 (P).

1972 — Phillies score eleven runs in seventh inning in 11-4 victory at San Francisco, their biggest inning in thirty-eight years.

## July 16

1893 — Doc Prothro — B 1939-41 MGR

1907 — Reggie Grabowski — B 1932-34 P G-51

1937 — Si Johnson and St. Louis beat Bucky Walters and Phillies, 10-3, in first game, and Johnson beats Walters, 18-10, as both relieve in tenth-inning second game (P).

1948 — Ben Chapman fired as manager of Phillies and is succeeded by interim manager Dusty Cooke.

1964 — First baseman Roy Sievers sold to Washington Senators.

Phillies win, 7-5, at Pittsburgh, take National League lead. They hold it until September 27 when Milwaukee wins, 14-8, at Philadelphia to hand Phillies seventh straight defeat in ten-game losing streak that cost them the pennant.

## July 17

1895 — Chicago scores twelve runs in fourth inning against Phillies (P).

1914 — Charlie Frye — B 1940 P G-18

1918 — Chicago wins, 2-1, in twenty-one innings in longest game in history of the Phillies (A). Lefty Tyler beats Mule Watson as both pitchers go the route, and the two teams set major league record for longest errorless game.

1938 — Deron Johnson — B 1969-73 1B-3B-OF G-563

1939 — In his first series in Philadelphia since leaving the Phillies and signing with Pittsburgh, Chuck Klein hits two home runs in 7-4 Pirate victory.

1948 — Granny Hamner bats in seven runs with two doubles and a single in 11-10 Phillies victory at St. Louis.

1963 — Phillies overcome 7-0 and 9-2 deficits to beat Houston, 10-9, in ten innings (P).

1965 — Johnny Callison hits third career grand-slam home run as Phillies get twenty-two hits to win at Cincinnati, 14-7.


## July 18

1844 — George Zettlein — B 1876 P G-32

1881 — Ad Brennan — B 1910-13 P G-93

1897 — Pat Murray — B 1919 P G-8

1954 — Infielder Floyd Baker purchased from Boston Red Sox.

Phillies are leading, 8-1, in fifth inning at St. Louis (second game) when game is forfeited because of stalling by Cardinals.

1964 — Cincinnati beats Phillies, 14-4, as Reds Pete Rose hits first grand-slam home run of his major league career in fifth inning (A).


## July 19

1890 — Rube Marshall — B 1912-14 P G-43

1891 — Earl Hamilton — B 1924 P G-3

1949 — Phillies left-hander Ken Heintzelman beats Chicago, 1-0, for his third 1-0 victory of season (P).

1960 — Pinch-hitter Clay Dalrymple's single to center with two out in eighth inning is only hit off San Francisco's Juan Marichal, who beats Phillies, 2-0, in his major league debut (A).

## July 19 (continued)

1963 — Roy Sievers hits 300th career home run with one man on base and one out in ninth inning to beat New York, 2-1, and hand Roger Craig his thirteenth straight defeat.

## July 20

1879 — Red Kleinow — B 1911 C G-4

1912 — Emmett Mueller — B 1938-41 IF-OF G-441

1933 — Babe Herman hits three home runs and a single, bats in eight runs in 10-1 victory over Phillies at Chicago.

1955 — Curt Simmons beats Cincinnati, 4-2, for fifth straight complete game victory by Phillies pitching staff in three days (P).

1970 — Bill Singer pitches 5-0, no-hit victory against Phillies at Los Angeles.

## July 21

1881 — Wally Clement — B 1908-09 OF G-19

1881 — Johnny Evers — B 1917 2B G-56

1918 — Mitch Chetkovich — B 1945 P G-4

1923 — Phillies score twelve runs in sixth inning to match their all-time high for one inning in 17-4 victory over Chicago (P) (first game).

1935 — Phillies win doubleheader shutout at Cincinnati behind Curt Davis, 4-0, in first game and behind Joe Bowman, 2-0, in second game.

1942 — John Bateman — B 1972 C G-82

1955 — Gus Bell hits three solo home runs for Cincinnati but Phillies win, 5-3 (P).

1960 — Robin Roberts pitches 3-0, one-hit victory (Felipe Alou single in fifth inning) at San Francisco for third one-hitter of his major league career.

1964 — Pitcher Cal McLish released by Phillies.

## July 22

1899 — Ginger Beaumont gets six infield hits in six times at bat and scores six runs against Phillies at Pittsburgh.

1927 — Outfielder Freddy Leach hits grand-slam home run to beat Chicago, 6-5 (P).

1930 — Pitcher Phil Collins, who finished major league career with only three home runs, hits home runs in fourth and fifth innings of 11-5 victory over Pittsburgh (P).

1936 — Outfielder Johnny Moore hits three consecutive home runs, bats in six runs in 16-4 victory over Pittsburgh (P).

1955 — Longest Phillies winning streak since 1892 reaches eleven games with 6-3 victory over St. Louis in opener of doubleheader, but streak ends in 8-1 defeat in second game (P). All eleven games were played at home.

1958 — Mayo Smith fired as manager of Phillies, and Eddie Sawyer is named to succeed him, his second term as manager of Phillies.

1964 — Phillies first baseman Danny Cater suffers broken left arm in 4-1 victory at Milwaukee.

1965 — Catcher Ed Bailey bats in eight runs with four hits, including his seventh career grand-slam home run, to help Chicago beat Phillies, 10-6 (A).

1966 — Pitcher Gaylord Perry strikes out fifteen Phillies to set club record in 4-1 victory at San Francisco.

## July 23

1897 — Hod Ford — B 1924 2B G-145

1900 — Jimmie Wilson — B 1923-28, 34-38 C-MGR G-838

1901 — Ed Holley — B 1932-34 P G-80

1912 — Al Glossop — B 1942 2B G-121

1930 — Phillies set modern club record with fourty-eight total bases in 16-15, thirteen-inning loss to Pittsburgh (P) (second game).

1955 — Del Ennis hits three home runs, bats in all seven runs in 7-2 victory over St. Louis (P).

1966 — Pitchers Roger Craig and Ed Roebuck released.

1978 — Phillies pitcher Steve Carlton becomes seventy-eighth pitcher to win 200th major league game in 13-2 victory over Houston (P).

## July 24

1864 — Tommy McCarthy — B 1886-87 OF-IF G-26

1893 — Joe Schultz — B 1924-25 OF G-112

1922 — Duane Pillette — B 1956 P G-20

## July 25

1907 — Bill Andrus — B 1937 3B G-3

1910 — LeGrant Scott — B 1939 OF G-76

## July 25 (continued)

1913 — Pittsburgh's Max Carey scores five runs without getting a hit against Phillies (A).

1921 — Outfielder Irish Meusel traded to New York giants for catcher Butch Henline, outfielder Curt Walker, pitcher Jesse Winters, and $30,000.

1950 — Phillies win doubleheader shutout over Chicago, winning first game behind Bubba Church, 7-0, and second game behind Robin Roberts, 1-0; take over National League lead and hold it for remainder of season.

## July 26

1890 — Phillies win, 5-2, at Cleveland for their sixteenth straight victory, tying their all-time club record. Streak ended July 28 with 12-4 loss at Chicago.

1892 — Phillies beat Cincinnati, 26-6.

1917 — Jimmy Bloodworth — B 1950-51 2B G-75

1925 — Jack Mayo — B 1948-53 OF G-139

1930 — Hack Wilson hits three home runs, bats in five runs in Chicago's 16-2 victory at Philadelphia.

1936 — Frank Demaree hits two home runs and three singles, bats in seven runs in Chicago's 18-5 victory at Philadelphia.

1948 — Eddie Sawyer, who had been managing club's Toronto farm team, named manager of Phillies, succeeding interim manager Dusty Cooke.

1960 — Phillies end streak of thirty-eight straight scoreless innings with run in sixth inning of 4-3 victory at Chicago. Streak began with last six innings on July 21 at San Francisco, and continues with 2-0, 2-0 and 9-0 losses at Los Angeles July 22-24.

## July 27

1849 — Davy Force — B 1876 SS G-60

1882 — Huck Wallace — B 1912 P G-4

1883 — Harry Kane — B 1905-06 P G-8

1928 — Charlie Bicknell — B 1948-49 P G-30

1931 — Pitcher Sheriff Blake purchased from Chicago Cubs.

1936 — Don Lock — B 1967-69 OF G-215

1950 — Del Ennis gets a double and a home run, bats in seven runs in seventh and eighth innings to tie National League record in 13-3 victory over Chicago (P).

## July 27 (continued)

1958 — Catcher John Turk and cash traded to Detroit Tigers for catcher Jim Hegan.

1966 — Sandy Koufax strikes out sixteen Phillies in eleven innings of twelve-inning, 2-1 victory at Los Angeles. Jim Bunning strikes out twelve Dodgers in eleven innings.

## July 28

1867 — Bill Day — B 1889-90 P G-8

1868 — Duke Esper — B 1890-92 P G-67

1874 — Newt Fisher — B 1898 C G-9

1901 — Freddie Fitzsimmons — B 1943-45 MGR

1930 — Ted Lepcio — B 1960 IF G-69

1939 — Pitcher Max Butcher traded to Pittsburgh Pirates for first baseman Gus Suhr.

1943 — Brooklyn pitcher Freddie Fitzsimmons named manager of Phillies, succeeding Bucky Harris.

1951 — Russ Meyer pitches Phillies fourth shutout in row, winning, 1-0, at Chicago. Streak of scoreless innings by Phillies staff ends at forty-one on July 29 at Chicago. Robin Roberts pitched 2-0 shutout at St. Louis on July 25; Ken Johnson pitched 7-0 shutout at St. Louis on July 26; and Bubba Church pitched 2-0 shutout at Chicago on July 27.

## July 29

1878 — Earl Moore — B 1908-13 P G-172

1902 — Luther Roy — B 1929 P G-21

1961 — Orlando Cepeda's first major league grand-slam home run in first inning gives San Francisco 4-3 victory and starts Phillies on modern major league record twenty-three game losing streak (P).

1965 — Phillies and Pittsburgh break modern major league record with two-team total of twenty-six strikeouts. Despite sixteen strikeouts, Phillies win, 5-0, behind Ray Culp's two-hitter (A).

1968 — George Culver pitches 6-1, no-hit victory for Cincinnati against Phillies (P) (second game). Phillies score unearned run in second inning.

## July 30

1890 — Casey Stengel — B 1920-21 OF G-153

1912 — Johnny Rizzo — B 1940-41 OF G-202

1929 — Pinky Whitney hits for cycle in 13-5 victory at Pittsburgh.

1930 — Gus Triandos — B 1964-65 C G-103

1937 — Phillies first baseman Dolf Camilli ties major league record by playing nine-inning game without a putout in 1-0 victory at Cincinnati.

1953 — Phillies score nine runs in sixth inning of 17-8 victory at Cincinnati.

1957 — Ron Northey signs as free agent with Phillies in afternoon, then ties major league record that night with ninth career home run as pinch-hitter with one man on base in eighth inning to help Phillies win at Cincinnati, 8-5.

## July 31

1883 — Red Munson — B 1905 C G-9

1892 — Erv Kantlehner — B 1916 P G-3

1913 — Lee Handley — B 1947 IF G-101

1921 — Phillies third baseman Goldie Rapp's major league rookie record twenty-three game hitting streak ends in Chicago.

1935 — Terry Fox — B 1966 P G-38

1937 — Fred Van Dusen — B 1955 PH G-1

1947 — Pete Koegel — B 1971-72 C-IF-OF G-53

John Vukovich — B 1970-71, 76-77 3B-SS G-83

# AUGUST 1

1921 — Ray Hamrick — B 1943-44 IF G-118

1932 — Pinky Whitney hits two doubles in seven-run fourth inning of 18-5 victory over Pittsburgh (P).

1951 — Pete Mackanin — B 1978 IF G-5

1972 — New York beats Phillies in eighteenth-inning, first game, 3-2. In second game, Phillies win, 4-1, but Mets end pitcher Steve Carlton's streak of thirty straight scoreless innings with run in fourth inning (A).

## August 2

1882 — Red Ames — B 1919 P G-3

1919 — In game at Chicago, Phillies first baseman Fred Luderus plays in his 479th consecutive game, breaking the major league record held by Eddie Collins of the Chicago White Sox. The Luderus streak began on

## August 2 (continued)

June 2, 1916, and ended after 533 games in the 1920 season opener. It ranks as the second longest in the history of the Phillies.

1923 — Pitcher Johnny Couch purchased from Cincinnati Reds.

1929 — Phillies first baseman Don Hurst sets National League record by hitting a home run in his sixth consecutive game in 2-0 victory at Pittsburgh. During streak that started July 28, Hurst got no other hits in the six games.

1935 — Dolf Camilli, who led all National League first basemen in fielding percentage two seasons later, sets major league record for first basemen by committing three errors in first inning as Phillies lose to Brooklyn, 8-3 (P).

1962 — Phillies pitcher Art Mahaffey gives up two home runs to Frank Thomas and two home runs to Marv Throneberry, but his own grand-slam home run in third inning helps him win, 9-4, at New York.

## August 3

1869 — George Wheeler — B 1896-99 P G-50

1874 — Ed McFarland — B 1897-1901 C G-423

1902 — Doug Taitt — B 1931-32 OF G-42

1917 — Milo Candini — B 1950-51 P G-33

1920 — Jim Hegan — B 1958-59 C G-50

1943 — Catcher Mickey Livingston traded to Chicago Cubs for pitcher Bill Lee.

1948 — Second baseman Emil Verban sold to Chicago Cubs.

1969 — Cincinnati scores ten runs in fifth inning, gets twenty-five hits in 19-17 victory over Phillies (P). The thirty-six total runs are the most by two teams in any Phillies game since Brooklyn won, 20-16, on May 18, 1929 (P) (first game).

## August 4

1883 — Lew Moren — B 1907-10 P G-138

1894 — Jim Grant — B 1923 P G-2

1896 — Cliff Lee — B 1921-24 OF-1B G-338

1902 — Bill Hallahan — B 1938 P G-21

1910 — Tuck Stainback —B 1938— OF G-30

1934 — Dallas Green — B 1960-64, 67 P G-189

## August 4 (continued)

New York's Mel Ott ties modern major league record by scoring six runs in 21-4 victory at Philadelphia (second game). New York scores eleven runs in ninth inning as Phillies pitcher Reggie Grabowski gives up modern National League record eleven hits in the inning.

1936 — Pitcher Ray Benge purchased from Boston Braves.

1974 — Phillies first baseman Willie Montanez hits safely in twenty-fourth straight game in 6-1 victory at St. Louis. The streak, which came within two games of the Phillies club record ended in second game of this doubleheader.

## August 5

1890 — Hal Irelan — B 1914 2B G-67

1927 — Phillies outfielder Cy Williams hits for cycle in four at bats in 9-7 victory at Pittsburgh.

1951 — Phillies pitcher Bubba Church hurls 5-1, one-hit victory (Ralph Kiner home run in seventh inning) at Pittsburgh (first game).

1953 — Rick Bosetti — B 1976 OF G-13

1975 — Phillies set major league record by getting eight hits in row at start of their first inning (four singles, two doubles, two home runs) in 13-5 victory over Chicago (P).

## August 6

1872 — Sam Mertes — B 1896 OF-IF G-37

1884 — Sherry Magee — B 1904-14 OF G-1520

1894 — On open date during series with Baltimore at home, Phillies stands burn down. Park reopens on August 18 with stands temporarily rebuilt.

1903 — Hal Wiltse — B 1931 P G-1

During game with Brooklyn at Philadelphia, fans crowd to edge of balcony to watch a fire on 15th Street and left field bleachers collapse, killing 12 and injuring 232 others.

1912 — Bud Hafey — B 1939 OF G-18

1914 — Tommy Reis — B 1938 P G-4

1941 — Ray Culp B 1963-66 P G-131

1974 — Phillies tie National League record by making only one assist in 8-3 victory over Chicago (P). This is sixth time Phillies have had only one assist in a game and no other team has done it more than twice.

1978 — Infielder Dave Johnson traded to Chicago Cubs for pitcher Larry Anderson.

## August 7

1951 — Phillies beat Boston, 1-0, in fifteen innings as Ken Heintezelman defeats Warren Spahn (P) (second game).

1964 — Pitcher Gary Kroll, outfielder Wayne Graham, and cash traded to New York Mets for outfielder-first baseman Frank Thomas.

1969 — Bob Skinner quits as manager of Phillies after little more than 13½ months, claiming front office failed to back him in his disciplining of first baseman Dick Allen. Coach George Myatt finishes season as manager.

## August 8

1870 — Dan Leahy — B 1896 SS G-2

1891 — Chick Keating — B 1926 IF G-4

1903 — Clise Dudley — B 1931-32 P G-67

1915 — Phillies outfielder Gavvy Cravath hits four doubles to tie major league record and bats in club record eight runs in 14-7 victory at Cincinnati.

1917 — Ken Raffensberger — B 1943-47 P G-93

1922 — Pittsburgh sets major league record with total of forty-six hits in 19-8 and 7-3 doubleheader sweep of Phillies (A).

1938 — Pitcher Wayne LaMaster traded to Brooklyn Dodgers for pitcher Max Butcher.

1967 — In their longest winning streak in almost four years, Phillies win their eighth game in a row, beating San Francisco, 5-4, in ten innings (P).

1968 — Phillies Rick Wise pitches 1-0, one-hit victory (Bart Shirley singles in third inning) at Los angeles.

## August 9

1867 — John Grim — B 1888 OF-2B G-2

1887 — Charlie Buffinton pitches second straight, one-hit victory for Phillies. John Cahill singled for lone Indianapolis hit on August 6 and Fred Pfeffer homered for Chicago's only hit on August 9.

1890 — Leo Callahan — B 1919 OF G-81

1896 — Phillies score ten runs in first inning at Louisville.

1904 — Augie Walsh — B 1927-28 P G-40

1911 — Justin Stein — B 1938 IF G-11

1921 — Wild Bill Donovan is fired as manager of Phillies and former major league pitcher Kaiser Wilhelm is named to succeed him.

## August 9 (continued)

1931 — Chuck Essegian — B 1958 OF G-39

1956 — Kevin Saucier — B 1978 P G-1

1960 — Third baseman Joe Morgan sold to Cleveland Indians.

1964 — In 6-0 victory over New York, Phillies pitcher Jim Bunning extends his streak of perfect no-hit innings against Mets to fifteen before Joe Christopher beats out a bunt with two out in fifth inning (P).

1965 — Former Phillies star Robin Roberts shuts out his old team, 8-0, with a four-hitter at Houston in his first National League start since September 10, 1961.

## August 10

1859 — Sid Farrar — B 1883-89 1B G-816

1892 — Elmer Jacobs — B 1914, 18-19 P G-49

1930 — Phillies win, 18-0, at Cincinnati, matching their highest score in a shutout victory in the post-1900 era.

1973 — Pitcher George Culver purchased from Los Angeles Dodgers.

## August 11

1893 — Red Causey — B 1920-21 P G-52

1917 — Frank Hoerst — B 1940-42, 46-47 P G-98

1926 — Cincinnati beats Phillies, 21-3 (P).

1943 — Leroy Reams — B 1969 PH G-1

1946 — Phillies win doubleheader from Brooklyn, 7-6 and 6-4, to end major league record streak of eighteen straight Dodger victories in Philadelphia, dating back to May 5, 1945.

1956 — Stan Lopata's two-run homerun for Phillies in second inning ends pitcher Don Newcombe's streak of consecutive scoreless innings at 39 2/3, but Brooklyn beats Phillies, 5-2 (A).

1970 — Phillies pitcher Jim Bunning wins, 6-5, at Houston to become the second pitcher in history to win at least 100 games in each major league.

## Ausust 12

1867 — Tom Dowse — B 1892 C G-16

1905 — Don Hurst — B 1928-34 1B G-854

1928 — Bob Buhl — B 1966-67 P G-35

1950 — Phillies and New York engage in brawl after Phillies catcher Andy Seminick and Giants infielder tangle at second base in Phillies eleven-inning, 5-4 victory (P).

1951 — New York Giants beat Phillies, 3-2 and 2-1, at Polo Grounds to start miracle comeback that saw them win thirty-nine of fourty-seven games and the National League pennant after playoff with Brooklyn.

1977 — Phillies hit six home runs in 10-3 victory at Chicago.

## August 13

1869 — John Sharrott — B 1893 OF-P G-50

1908 — George Susce — B 1929 C G-17

1910 — Lou Finney — B 1947 PH G-4

1917 — Phillies steal five bases in one inning against Boston.

1939 — New York hits four home runs in fourth inning and seven in the game for 11-2 victory over Phillies (A) (first game). Phillies pitcher Bill Kersieck gives up six of the home runs, including the four in the fourth.

1948 — Erskine Thomason — B 1974 P G-1

Phillies score ten runs in first inning of 12-7 victory over New York (P).

## August 14

1868 — Cupid Childs — B 1888 2B G-2

1901 — Les Sweetland — B 1927-30 P G-154

1942 — Phillies end their streak of thirty straight scoreless innings by scoring once in second inning of 5-2 loss at New York.

1956 — Pitchers Harvey Haddix and Curt Simmons each wins his seventh straight game as Phillies beat Pittsburgh, 3-0 and 11-2 (P).

1961 — Catcher Darrell Johnson sold to Cincinnati Reds.

Phillies lose seventeenth straight game, 9-2, as eleventh straight complete game is pitched against them — this one by Dick Ellsworth at Chicago.

1966 — Lefthander Denny Lemaster strikes out fourteen Phillies in 7-1 victory at Atlanta.

1973 — Infielder Bill Grabarkewitz acquired from California Angels for player to be named later. Deal completed December 6.

## August 15

1875 — Bob Becker — B 1897-98 P G-6

1934 — Seth Morehead — B 1957-59 P G-64

1936 — John Buzhardt — B 1960-61 P G-73

1944 — Mike Compton — B 1970 C G-47

1946 — Joe Lis — B 1970-72 OF-1B G-134

1948 — Phillies pitcher Ken Heintzelman hurls 8-1, one-hit victory (Whitey Lockman triples in seventh inning) against New York (P) (first game).

1964 — Pitcher Bobby Shantz purchased from Chicago Cubs.

## August 16

1866 — Ed Mayer — B 1890-91 3B G-185

1908 — Phillies pitcher George McQuillan hurls 1-0, one-hit victory at Chicago.

1925 — Willie Jones — B 1947-59 3B G-1250

1941 — Larry Loughlin — B 1967 P G-3

1952 — Phillies lose, 15-0, at Brooklyn in game ended by rain with one out in top of seventh inning.

1968 — Dick Allen walks in all five times at bat in 7-5 loss at Los Angeles.

1969 — Rick Wise pitches Phillies fourth shutout victory in row, beating Houston, 7-0 (P). Streak of consecutive scoreless innings ends at thirty-nine in first inning August 17 when Houston's Sandy Valdespino steals home.

1973 — Infielder Jose Pagan released.

1977 — Phillies win, 7-5, at Montreal for their thirteenth straight victory, setting their modern club record in their longest streak since 1892. Montreal ended streak the next night with 13-0 victory.

## August 17

1866 — George Harper — B 1894 P G-12

1874 — Bill Keister — B 1903 OF G-100

1892 — Johnny Rawlings — B 1920-21 2B G-158

1894 — Phillies get their most runs, hits (thirty-six) and total bases (forty-nine)              their history in 29-4 victory over Louisville (P). Outfielder Sam Thompson hits three singles, a double, triple and home run in seven at bats, and Phillies hit arecord twenty-eight singles.

71

## August 17 (continued)

1897 — Ed Lennon — B 1928 P G-5

1906 — Johnny Watwood — B 1939 1B G-2

1941 — Joe Marty gets five hits and bats in five runs in 18-2 victory over New York (P) (second game).

1972 — In longest winning streak by Phillies pitcher in history, Steve Carlton beats Cincinnati, 9-4, for his fifteenth straight victory (P). Streak, which began with 3-1 win over Houston on June 7, ends in eleven-inning, 2-1 loss to Atlanta on August 21.

## August 18

1899 — Barney Friberg — B 1925-32 IF G-795

1915 — Gavvy Cravath bats in eight runs in game against Pittsburgh (P).

1931 — Phillies outfielder Chuck Klein extends hitting streak to twenty-two games in 14-5 loss to Pittsburgh (P).

1934 — Billy Consolo — B 1962 3B G-13

1936 — Claude Passeau pitches 7-0, three-hit victory at Boston to end Phillies fourteen-game losing streak, the second longest in the club's history.

1947 — Lowell Palmer — B 1969-71 P G-67

1960 — Lew Burdette pitches 1-0, no-hit victory against Phillies at Milwaukee.

## August 19

1872 — Davey Dunkle — B 1897-98 G-19

1892 — Rags Faircloth — B 1919 P G-2

1903 — Phillies suffer all-time record ninth consecutive postponement (August 10-19).

1915 — Bill Nagel — B 1941 IF-OF G-17

1925 — Phillies beat Cincinnati, 5-4, and end streak of twenty straight victories against them by pitcher Pete Donohue (P).

1933 — Chuck Klein hits three home runs and bats in six runs in 12-2 and 3-0 doubleheader sweep of Cincinnati (P).

1952 — Tim Blackwell — B 1976-77 C G-5

Robin Roberts wins his ninth straight game in longest winning streak of his career as Phillies win, 10-5, at Pittsburgh. Streak ended in 3-0 defeat at Chicago on August 24 in his next start.

1954 — Phillies pitcher Murry Dickson loses tenth game in row, 5-0, at New York. Streak ends on August 22 with 6-0 victory at Brooklyn.

## August 19 (continued)

1963 — Pitcher Dennis Bennett shuts out New York, 1-0 (P), as Phillies extend their longest winning streak since 1955 to eight games. Streak ended the next night when Grover Powell pitched 4-0 shutout for Mets in his first major league start and the only victory of his major league career.

1968 — Phillies first baseman Dick Allen strikes out four times in a game for the seventh time this season to set a major league record as Phillies lose to Bob Gibson and St. Louis, 2-0 (P).

1974 — Cincinnati second baseman Joe Morgan bats in seven runs as Phillies lose, 15-2, at Cincinnati.

## August 20

1906 — Lee Riley — B 1944 OF G-4

1910 — Bill Crouch — B 1941 P G-20

1913 — Infielder-outfielder Cozy Dolan traded to Pittsburgh Pirates for pitcher Howie Camnitz and third baseman Bobby Byrne.

1958 — Phillies third baseman Willie Jones hits single, two-run double and a pair of three-run home runs and bats in eight runs in 12-2 victory at St. Louis.

1961 — Phillies set modern major league record by losing twenty-third straight game (including then modern National League record seventeen in row on road) in first game of doubleheader, 5-2, at Milwaukee. Streak ends when pitcher John Buzhardt beats Braves, 7-4, in second game and snaps ten-game Milwaukee winning streak.

## August 21

1865 — Cannonball Titcomb — B 1886 P G-5

1883 — Providence beats Phillies, 28-0, in highest shutout score in major league history (A).

1910 — Wes Schulmerich — B 1933-34 OF G-112

1916 — Murry Dickson — B 1954-56 P G-79

1917 — Chief Bender pitches one-hit victory for Phillies against Chicago.

1923 — Hilly Flitcraft — B 1942 P G-3

1935 — Chicago scores twelve runs in sixth inning of 19-5 victory over Phillies (P) (second game).

1948 — Craig Robinson — B 1972-73 SS G-51

1949 — Umpires forfeit second game of doubleheader to New York when fans at Shibe Park throw debris on field after second-base umpire George Barr rules that Phillies center fielder Richie Ashburn trapped liner off bat of New York's Joe Lafata with one out in ninth inning and Giants leading, 4-2 (P).

1951 — John Stearns — B 1974 C G-1

## August 22

1881 — Howie Camnitz — B 1913 P G-9

1919 — Ed Freed — B 1942 OF G-13

1943 — Cincinnati beats Phillies, 20-6 (P) (second game).

1954 — Pitcher Jim Konstanty, first relief pitcher ever to win Most Valuable Player Award (1950), sold to New York Yankees.

1961 — Phillies pitcher Art Mahaffey hurls 6-0, one-hit victory (Ron Santo single in first inning) against Chicago (P) to end personal ten-game losing streak.

## August 23

1883 — Lew Richie — B 1906-09 P G-94

1883 — Phillies charged with twenty-seven errors in game with Providence (walks, wild pitches, and passed balls all were charged as errors prior to 1888).

1894 — Roy Leslie — B 1922 1B G-141

1919 — Ed Murphy — B 1942 1B G-13

1941 — John Morris — B 1966 P G-13

1967 — Third baseman Dick Allen suffers serious cuts on right hand when headlight of old automobile he was pushing breaks. He is sidelined for remainder of season.

## August 24

1864 — Lew Hardie — B 1884 C G-3

1875 — Jerry Donovan — B 1906 C G-61

1894 — Jimmy Cooney — B 1927 SS G-76

1896 — Bevo LeBourveau — B 1919-22 OF G-268

1898 — John Monroe — B 1921 IF G-41

1905 — Chicago beats Phillies, 2-1, in twenty innings in Phillies longest game at home.

1922 — Outfielder Cy Williams becomes first Phillies player to hit for the cycle in twenty-eight years in game at Pittsburgh.

1940 — Rick Joseph — B 1967-70 IF-OF G-253

1947 — Cincinnati scores nine runs in tenth inning to win, 12-3, at Philadelphia (first game).

1958 — Phillies outfielder Rip Repulski hits second consecutive home run as pinch-hitter in 13-8 victory at Chicago. First was hit August 22 at St. Louis in 9-1 loss.

1964 — Outfielder Wes Covington bats in six runs with two home runs and a double but Phillies lose, 12-9, at Milwaukee.

## August 25

1869 — John McFetridge — B 1890, 1903 P G-15

1893 — Bob Gandy — B 1916 OF G-1

1911 — Fred Frink — B 1934 OF G-2

1918 — Paul Busby — B 1941, 43 OF G-36

1921 — Al Jurisich — B 1946-47 P G-47

1922 — In highest scoring game in major league history, Phillies lose, 26-23, at Chicago. Phillies get twenty-six hits to twenty-five for Chicago, which scores ten runs in second inning and fourteen in fourth inning. Nine Cubs and seven Phils score two or more runs.

1928 — Darrell Johnson — B 1961 C G-21

1937 — Choo Choo Coleman — B 1961 C G-34

1953 — Infielder Connie Ryan sold to Chicago White Sox.

1972 — Pitcher Ken Reynolds ties Phillies club record by losing twelfth straight game in 6-1 defeat at Cincinnati. Streak ended with 11-1 victory at Atlanta on September 1.

## August 26

1941 — Fred Wenz — B 1970 P G-22

Outfielder Dom Dallessandro hits two singles, a double, and home run, and bats in seven runs in 11-3 Chicago victory over Phillies (P) (second game).

1951 — Niles Jordan pitches 2-0 shutout victory against Cincinnati in first major league start (P) (second game).

75

## August 27

1879 — Paul Sentelle — B 1906-07 IF G-66

1900 — Phil Collins — B 1929-35 P G-278

1903 — Phillies pitchers issue seventeen bases on balls in game with Brooklyn (P).

1915 — Emil Verban — B 1946-48 2B G-348

1918 — Peanuts Lowrey — B 1955 OF-IF G-54

1921 — Nick Picciuto — B 1945 3B G-36

1923 — Don Grate — B 1945-46 P G-8

1951 — Phillies catcher Del Wilber hits three solo home runs in his only times at bat and Ken Johnson pitches 3-0 victory against Cincinnati in second game after Jocko Thompson beats Reds, 2-0, in first game (P).

1965 — Los Angeles pitcher Don Drysdale ends personal nine-game losing streak to Phillies with 9-8 victory (P). It was Drysdale's first victory over Phillies since June 1, 1962, when he beat them for the thirteenth straight time.

## August 28

1881 — Dode Paskert — B 1911-17 OF G-953

1936 — Tony Gonzalez — B 1960-68 OF G-1157

1938 — Billy Cowan — B 1967 OF G-34

1948 — Phillies hit six home runs in 11-7 victory at Pittsburgh (second game).

1970 — Phillies shortstop Larry Bowa steals home for second time this season in 5-2 victory over Atlanta (P).

1971 — Pitcher Rick Wise hits solo home run in fifth inning and grand-slam home run in seventh inning of 7-3 victory over San Francisco (P) (second game). It was Wise's second two-home run game of season, tying major league record for pitchers.

## August 29

1885 — Phillies pitcher Charlie Ferguson hurls 1-0, no-hit victory over Providence (P).

1889 — Frank Nicholson — B 1912 P G-2

1898 — Hap Collard — B 1930 P G-31

1903 — Jack Warner — B 1933 IF G-107

1930 — Dave Cole — B 1955 P G-7

## August 30

1878 — Charlie Starr — B 1909 2B G-3

1883 — Bill Brinker — B 1912 OF-3B G-9

1889 — Tom Seaton — B 1912-13 P G-96

1893 — Ralph Head — B 1923 G-35

1913 — With Phillies leading, 8-6, in top of ninth inning, Philadelphia fans in one section of bleachers try to distract New York batters by waving handkerchiefs, newspapers, and straw hats, and Umpire William Brennan forfeits game to Giants. National League President Thomas Lynch overrules Brennan three days later and declares Phillies the winners, but Giants appeal and National League Board of Directors orders game to be completed in New York on October 2. Phillies finally win the game, 8-6, then split the doubleheader which followed.

1916 — Johnny Lindell — B 1953-54 P G-18

1931 — Phillies pitcher Phil Collins hurls 3-0, one-hit victory (Shanty Hogan single) at New York.

1944 — Tug McGraw — B 1975-78 P G-214

1952 — Infielder Tommy Glaviano purchased from St. Louis Cardinals.

## August 31

1869 — Monte Cross — B 1898-1901 S G-573

1881 — Buster Brown — B 1907-09 P G-32

1894 — Phillies outfielder Billy Hamilton ties major league record by stealing seven bases in eight innings against Washington (P). He steals second base five times and third base twice.

1900 — Phillies draw six bases on balls in succession from pitcher Brickyard Kennedy in second inning at Brooklyn.

1905 — Frank Pearce — B 1933-35 P G-32

1916 — Danny Litwhiler — B 1940-43 OF G-374

1953 — Bill Nahorodny — 1976 C G-3

Pitcher Johnny Lindell purchased from Pittsburgh Pirates.

## SEPTEMBER 1

1900 — Hub Pruett — B 1927-28 P G-44

1912 — Ham Schulte — B 1940 2B G-120

1913 — Joe Marty — B 1939-41 OF G-351

## September 1 (continued)

1945 — Phillies outfielder Vince DiMaggio ties National League record by hitting his fourth grand slam home run of the season in 8-3 victory at Boston. Blow came off pitcher Elmer Singleton.

1949 — Garry Maddox — B 1975-78 OF G-539

1964 — In 4-3 Phillies victory over Houston, outfielders John Callison and Wes Covington and first baseman Frank Thomas hit solo home runs in last of seventh inning (P).

1967 — Pitcher Woodie Fryman strikes out fifteen Phillies batters in 3-0 victory at Pittsburgh.

## September 2

1884 — Joe Ward — B 1906, 09-10 IF G-157

1908 — Phillies beat Brooklyn, 2-1, in seventeen innings and winning pitcher Frank Corridon goes the route without walking a batter (P).

1940 — Phillies outfielder Danny Litwhiler bats in six runs with single, double, and home run in 11-2 victory over New York (P).

1966 — Phillies pitcher Jim Bunning hurls 6-0 victory, making his career record against Mets in New York eight complete-game victories in eight starts, with five shutouts and only four runs scored against him.

1975 — Pitcher John Montague purchased from Montreal Expos.

## September 3

1854 — Harry Decker — B 1889-90 2B-C G-16

1871 — Bill Goeckel — B 1899 1B G-37

1873 — Mike Kahoe — B 1905 C G-16

1885 — Ed Konetchy — B 1921 1B G-72

1917 — Phillies pitcher Grover Alexander hurls 5-0 and 9-3 complete-game victories in doubleheader at Brooklyn, and ties major league record by issuing only one walk.

1925 — New York beats Phillies, 24-10 (P).

1951 — Alan Bannister — B 1974-75 OF G-50

1961 — Phillies beat Cincinnati, 3-2 (P) after losing their first seventeen games with Reds this season.

1972 — Steve Carlton wins, 8-0, at Atlanta for his eighth 1972 shutout, the most for a Phillies pitcher since Grover Alexander had eight in 1917.

1977 — Phillies beat Cincinnati, 9-3, for their sixteenth straight victory at home, a club record.

## September 4

1917 — Phillies play fourteen-inning scoreless tie at Brooklyn as Joe Oeschger and Jeff Pfeffer both pitch complete game with the latter holding the Phillies to three hits.

1919 — Eddie Waitkus — B 1949-53, 55 1B G-613

1962 — Phillies lose at Houston, 4-1, after winning first seventeen games of season from Colt 45s.

1966 — Chris Short wins at New York, 5-0, for the fifth straight complete game victory by the Phillies pitching staff.

## September 5

1872 — Al Orth — B 1895-1901 P-OF G-230

1875 — Nap Lajoie — B 1896-1900 2B G-492

1893 — Don Rader — B 1921 SS G-9

1900 — Merv Shea — B 1944 C G-7

1913 — Phillies tie a major league record by scoring the only run in a doubleheader. Phillies win opener, 1-0, and play ten-inning scoreless tie in second game at Boston.

1919 — Pitcher Red Ames purchased from St. Louis Cardinals.

1965 — Phillies first baseman Dick Stuart hits ninth career grand-slam home run in first inning and two-run home run in seventh inning, but Phillies lose at Cincinnati, 10-9.

## September 6

1903 — Tommy Thevenow — B 1929-30 SS G-246

1912 — Vince DiMaggio — B 1945-46 OF G-133

New York's Jeff Tesreau pitches 3-0, no-hit, victory against Phillies (P) (first game).

1930 — Phillies lose at Brooklyn, 22-8.

1950 — First-place Phillies suffer their third consecutive shutout defeat as Brooklyn wins, 2-0, but end streak of scoreless innings at thirty-two in first inning of 3-2 defeat in second game (P).

1952 — Robin Roberts gives up six runs in first eight innings to trail, 6-2, but goes the route to beat Boston, 7-6, on leadoff home run by Del Ennis in seventeenth inning (P) (first game).

1964 — San Francisco's Juan Marichal strikes out thirteen Phillies, including seven in a row, in 4-3 victory (P).

1969 — Pitcher Gary Wagner traded to Boston Red Sox for pitcher Mike Jackson.

## September 7

1862 — Ed Daily — B 1885-87 P-OF G-155

1884 — Henry Matteson — B 1914 P G-15

1903 — Curt Davis — B 1934-36 P G-108

1928 — Ray Benge gives up eleven hits, three walks in 4-0 shutout victory over Boston (P) (first game).

1944 — Barry Lersch — B 1969-73 P G-176

1947 — Dave Wallace — B 1973-74 P G-7

1959 — Wally Post's sixth-inning home run in 6-4 victory at Cincinnati gives Phillies outfielder twenty home runs for the year and at least one in every National League park this season.

1972 — Phillies Steve Carlton pitches 2-1 victory over St. Louis (P), strikes out 9 for 272, breaking one-season club record of 268, set by Jim Bunning in 1965. Carlton's twenty-third victory also breaks club record for left-handers, set in 1916 by Eppa Rixey. Carlton finished this season with 310 strikeouts and twenty-seven victories.

## September 8

1872 — Deke White — B 1895 P G-3

1883 — New York scores thirteen runs in third inning in victory over Phillies.

1886 — Al Demaree — B 1915-16 P G-71

1896 — Johnny Schulte — B 1928 C G-65

1915 — Len Gabrielson — B 1939 1B G-5

1949 — Russ Meyer pitches 3-1, one-hit victory (Connie Ryan doubles in first inning) at Boston.

1954 — With a 3-2 count, Phillies outfielder Richie Ashburn fouls off fourteen straight pitches by Cincinnati's Corky Valentine before walking as Phillies lose, 9-3 (P).

1962 — Phillies pitcher Chris Short, who finished his career with a .126 batting average, hits double and three singles in four times at bat against Warren Spahn as Phillies win, 4-2, at Milwaukee.

1964 — First baseman Frank Thomas fractures his right thumb sliding back to second base on fourth-inning double play as Los Angeles beats Phillies, 3-2 (P). The loss of Thomas was a major factor in the failure of the Phillies to win the pennant this season.

## September 8 (continued)

1977 — Catcher Bill Nahorodny sold to Chicago White Sox.

## September 9

1886 — Dots Miller — B 1920-21 IF G-182

1911 — First baseman Kitty Bransfield sold to Chicago Cubs.

1913 — Hugh Mulcahy — B 1935-40, 45-46 P G-221

1914 — Boston's George Davis pitches 7-0, no-hit victory against Phillies (A).

1926 — Six Brooklyn pinch-hitters hit safely in nine-inning game at Philadelphia.

1931 — Earl Averill — B 1963 C G-47

1942 — Ron Stone — B 1969-72 OF G-362

1945 — Jimmie Foxx hits 7th home run of season and 534th and last of his career in Phillies 14-3 victory at Pittsburgh (second game). Foxx also homered in 4-3 loss in 1st game.

1964 — First baseman Vic Power obtained from Los Angeles Angels for pitcher Marcelino Lopez and cash.

## September 10

1872 — Joe Berry — B 1902 C G-1

1905 — Irv Jeffries — B 1934 2B-3B G-56

1910 — Eddie Sawyer — B 1948-52, 58-60 MGR

1931 — Harry Anderson — B 1957-60 OF G-438

1942 — Phillies beat Pittsburgh in eleven innings, 2-1, to end their thirteen-game losing streak (P).

1963 — Chris Short pitches four-hitter as Phillies beat Houston, 16-0, in their most one-sided shutout game since 1951 (P).

1965 — Phillies pitcher Ferguson Jenkins makes major league debut, beats St. Louis, 5-4, in 12 innings with 4 1/3 innings of relief in Phillies 10,000th game to decision since 1900.

## September 11

1884 — John Quinn — B 1911 C G-1

1893 — Ray Grimes — B 1926 1B G-32

1924 — Lou Grasmick — B 1948 P G-2

1947 — Larry Cox — B 1973-75 C G-42

81

## September 12

1885 — Fred Luderus — B 1910-20 1B G-1311

1908 — Jim McLeod — B 1933 3B G-67

1910 — Pitcher Earl Moore sets Phillies club record by striking out thirteen batters in 3-0 victory at Brooklyn.

1920 — Andy Seminick — B 1943-51, 55-57 C G-985

1924 — Bubba Church — B 1950-52 P G-80

1925 — Stan Lopata — B 1948-58 C-1B G-821

1940 — Rich Barry — B 1969 OF G-20

1948 — John Montague — B 1975 P G-3

1951 — Second baseman Mike Goliat sold to St. Louis Browns.

1961 — Phillies outfielder Don Demeter hits single and three home runs, scores five runs and bats in seven runs in 19-10 victory at Los Angeles.

1972 — Phillies third baseman Don Money makes his first error after setting National League record with 163 straight errorless chances in 4-3 victory over New York (P).

## September 13

1883 — Cleveland's Hugh Dailey pitches 1-0, no-hit victory against Phillies (P).

1886 — Ed McDonough — B 1909-10 C G-6

1894 — Mickey O'Brien — B 1923 C G-15

1925 — Dazzy Vance pitches 10-1, no-hit victory against Phillies at Brooklyn (first game). In Phillies second inning, left fielder Jimmy Johnston dropped Chicken Hawks easy fly for a two-base error, then threw wildly to second. Braney Friberg's sacrifice fly brought in Hawks with the unearned run.

1926 — Pitcher Jack Bentley sold to New York Giants.

1930 — Lefty O'Doul hits his second home run in a row as a pinch-hitter in 7-5 Phillies victory over Chicago (P). First came four days earlier in 8-6 victory over Cincinnati (P).

1945 — Rick Wise — B 1964, 66-71 P G-223

1948 — Catcher Hal Wagner purchased from Detroit Tigers.

1963 — Chris Short sets Phillies club record for left-handed pitcher by striking out fourteen in 3-2 victory over Los Angeles (P) (first game).

1964 — Phillies pitcher Jim Bunning beats San Francisco in ten innings, 4-1, for his eighth straight victory (A).

1968 — Phillies pitcher Chris Short beats Chicago, 3-1, for his eighth straight victory (P) (first game).

1974 — Phillies set National League record by using twenty-seven players in a game during seventeen-inning, 7-3 victory over St. Louis (P). St. Louis uses twenty-four players to tie two-club major league record of fifty-one.

## September 14

1869 — Kid Nichols — B 1905-06 P G-21

1882 — Tom Madden — B 1911 C G-28

1920 — Phillies beat Cincinnati, 21-10 (P).

1949 — Phillies outfielder Ed Sanicki hits three-run home run in his first major league at bat in 12-4 victory at Pittsburgh.

1962 — Phillies outfielder Johnny Callison hits game-winning, ninth-inning home run for second game in row in 2-1 victory over St. Louis (P). The night before, his home run beat Milwaukee, 2-1.

## September 15

1870 — Frank O'Connor — B 1893 P G-3

1890 — Mike Prendergast — B 1918-19 P G-38

1900 — Bud Clancy — B 1934 1B G-20

Harry McCurdy — B 1930-3 C G-281

1922 — Phillies catcher Butch Henline hits three home runs in 10-9 victory over St. Louis (P). His third home run tied the score in ninth inning and Clif Lee then hit game-winning home run.

1928 — St. Louis sets National League record by leaving eighteen men on base in 8-6 victory over Phillies (P) (second game).

1937 — Charley Smith — B 1961 3B G-112

1940 — Frank Linzy — B 1974 P G-22

1950 — In their longest game ever at Shibe Park, Phillies beat Cincinnati, 8-7, in nineteen innings. Ed Waitkus and Del Ennis each get five hits for winners.

1967 — Phillies outfielder Tony Gonzalez doubles and singles in four at bats to give him thirty hits in his last fifty-five times at bat, but Phillies lose to Los Angeles, 1-0. Phillies also lose second game, 1-0, in their first doubleheader shutout since August 2, 1955.

## September 16

1926 — Roger McKee — B 1943-44 P G-5

In 23-3 victory over Phillies, thirteen St. Louis players get at least one hit (P) (first game).

1930 — Ron Mrozinski — B 1954-55 P G-37

Phillies score five runs in ninth inning to tie the score and five more in the tenth inning after Pittsburgh had scored four to win 15-14 (P).

1940 — Phillies rookie outfielder Danny Litwhiler singles in both games of 3-2 and 7-1 losses to St. Louis to extend his hitting streak through twenty-one straight games (P).

1942 — Catcher Johnny Peacock traded to Brooklyn Dodgers for pitcher-outfielder Ben Chapman.

1960 — Warren Spahn pitches 4-0, no-hit victory against Phillies at Milwaukee, striking out fifteen. Loser John Buzhardt suffers his eleventh straight defeat.

1964 — Pitching with only two days rest, Phillies Jim Bunning loses at Houston, 6-5, ending his eight-game winning streak.

1967 — Pinch-hitter Rick Joseph hits grand-slam home run in eleventh inning to give Phillies 8-4 victory over Los Angeles (P).

## September 17

1850 — Ezra Sutton — B 1876 IF G-54

1876 — Otto Krueger — B 1905 IF-OF G-46

1882 — Wildfire Schulte — B 1971 OF G-64

1893 — Whitey Glazner — B 1923-24 P G-63

1899 — Sheriff Blake — B 1931 P G-14

1909 — Ernie Koy — B 1942 OF G-91

1938 — Bobby Wine — B 1960, 62-68 SS G-731

1939 — Jim Woods — B 1960-61 3B G-34

## September 18

1903 — Phillies pitcher Chick Fraser hurls 10-0 no-hit victory at Chicago (second game). This was the only major league game ever pitched by his mound opponent, Peaches Graham.

1925 — Harvey Haddix — B 1956-57 P G-87

## September 18 (continued)

1928 — Phillies lose, 4-2, as St. Louis beats them for the twentieth time in twenty-two games this season, the Phillies worst record against any team (P). One of the two victories came on July 30 in sixteen innings, 8-7 (P).

1947 — Billy Champion — B 1969-72 P G-99

1948 — Ken Brett — B 1973 P G-37

1963 — Phillies win, 5-1, behind Chris Short in final major league game ever played in New York's famed Polo Grounds.

## September 19

1872 — Henry Lampe B 1895 P G-7

1890 — Stuffy McInnis — B 1927 1B-MGR G-1

1909 — Cap Clarke — B 1938 C G-52

Herschel Martin — B 1937-40 OF G-405

1913 — Nick Etten — B 1941-42, 47 1B G-304

1937 — Chris Short — B 1959-72 P G-459

1959 — Phillies outfielder Richie Ashburn singles off the bag at first base in seventh inning of 9-3 loss to Milwaukee (P) for club record 2,212th hit. Ashburn finished his final season with Phillies with 2,217 hits.

## September 20

1893 — Doc Wallace — B 1919 SS G-2

1916 — Phillies pitcher Al Demaree hurls 7-0 and 3-2 complete game victories over Pittsburgh (P).

1967 — St. Louis pitcher Steve Carlton strikes out sixteen Phillies batters in eight innings, but loses, 3-1 (P).

## September 21

1858 — Dick Buckley — B 1894-95 C G-81

1910 — Max Butcher — B 1938-39 P G-31

1911 — Phillies pitcher Grover Alexander hurls his fourth straight shutout, winning at Chicago. Previously he pitched shutouts on September 7 at Boston, on September 13 against Brooklyn (P), and September 17 at Cincinnati.

## September 21 (continued)

1915 — Ed Walczak — B 1945 IF G-20

1942 — Bill Wilson — B 1969-73 P G-179

1964 — Infielder Chico Ruiz steals home with two out and Frank Robinson at bat in sixth inning to give Cincinnati 1-0 victory and start Phillies on ten-game losing streak that costs them the pennant (P).

## September 22

1869 — Dummy Stephenson — B 1892 OF G-8

1875 — Doc Marshall — B 1904 C G-8

1879 — Bert Conn — B 1898, 1900-01 P-2B G-12

1888 — Patsy McGaffigan — B 1917-18 IF G-73

1908 — Jim Holloway — B 1929 P G-3

1958 — In a fourteen-inning, 3-2 victory over Pittsburgh, Phillies pitchers set major league record with twenty-one strikeouts (P). By striking out the first six batters he faced, Jack Meyer sets major league record for relief pitcher.

1965 — Phillies pitcher Jim Bunning strikes out nine batters in 11-5 victory at Chicago (first game) to break club record for one season of 241, set by Grover Alexander in 1915. Bunning finishes season with 268 strikeouts.

1967 — Pitcher Dallas Green released.

## September 23

1895 — John Mokan — B 1922-27 OF G-532

1913 — Pete Sivess — B 1936-38 P G-62

1916 — Phillies pitcher Grover Alexander pitches 7-3 and 4-0 complete game victories over Cincinnati (P), issuing only one base on balls to tie a major league record. It was Alexander's sixteenth shutout of the season and his fifth against Cincinnati, tying two more major league records.

1924 — Phillies lose to St. Louis, 8-7 (P), and the season's thirty-fourth one-run defeat broke what was then the major league record.

1939 — Brooklyn third baseman Cookie Lavagetto gets six hits in six at bats and Dodgers get twenty-seven hits in 22-4 victory at Philadelphia (first game).

1942 — Jim Morrison — B 1977-78 2B-3B G-58

1943 — Marcelino Lopez — B 1963 P G-5

1956 — Catcher Stan Lopata hits two home runs in 6-2 victory at New York to set Phillies club record for right-handed batter of thirty-two in one season.

1960 — With 6-1 victory at Cincinnati, pitcher John Buzhardt ends his personal eleven-game losing streak, one shy of Phillies club record.

## September 24

1859 — Cyclone Miller — B 1884 P G-1

1911 — St. Louis scores in sixth inning for the first run off Phillies rookie pitcher Grover Alexander after fourty-one consecutive scoreless innings (A).

## September 25

1911 — Bill Atwood — B 1936-40 C G-342

1946 — Phillies first baseman Frank McCormick makes first error of season after setting major league record of 131 straight errorless games in 11-9 victory at Brooklyn.

1956 — Brooklyn pitcher Sal Maglie hurls 5-0, no-hit victory against Phillies (A).

1960 — Phillies win, 7-1, at Cincinnati to end streak of sixteen consecutive Sunday defeats.

## September 26

1880 — Bert Humphries — B 1910-11 P G-16

1912 — Phillies score total of eighteen runs while shutting out Brooklyn in both ends of doubleheader for club record (A).

1923 — Bobby Shantz — B 1964 P G-14

1954 — In eleven-inning, 3-2 loss to New York in final game of the season (P), outfielder Richie Ashburn plays in his 730th consecutive game to set Phillies record. Streak began on June 7, 1950, and ended in the 1955 season opener because an injury late in the exhibition season prevented his appearance.

1969 — Frank Lucchesi, who spent nineteen years managing in minor leagues, including fourteen in Phillies farm system, signs two-year contract as Phillies manager.

1976 — Phillies clinch their first National League Eastern Division title with 4-1 victory at Montreal (first game). Jim Lonborg pitches four-hitter and Greg Luzinski hits three-run home run in sixth inning.

## September 27

1891 — Doug Baird — B 1919 3B G-66

1895 — Mike Loan — B 1912 C G-1

1907 — Whit Wyatt — B 1945 P G-10

1928 — Thornton Kipper — B 1953-55 P G-55

1930 — Dick Hall — B 1967-68 P G-80

1940 — Pitcher Hugh Mulcahy ends Phillies club record-equaling twelve-game losing streak with 6-0 victory at New York.

1944 — Gary Sutherland — B 1966-68 IF-OF G-173

1949 — Mike Schmidt — B 1972-78 3B G-924

1964 — Despite three home runs by outfielder Johnny Callison, Phillies lose to Milwaukee, 14-8 (P), for seventh loss in row, fall to second place for first time since July 15.

1967 — Phillies pitcher Jim Bunning ties National League record by losing his fifth 1-0 game of the season, bowing in eleven innings at Houston.

1975 — Phillies pitcher Steve Carlton hurls 8-1, one-hit victory (Felix Millan double in sixth inning) against New York (P).

1977 — Phillies clinch their second straight National League Eastern Division title with 15-9 victory at Chicago as winning pitcher Larry Christenson hits grand-slam home run in seventh inning.

## September 28

1876 — Shad Barry — B 1901-04 OF G-378

1885 — Wilbur Good — B 1916 OF G-75

1906 — Dick Barrett — B 1943-45 P G-96

1919 — Phillies lose at New York, 6-1 in fifty-one minutes, the fastest game in major league history (first game).

1941 — Phillies lose at Brooklyn, 5-1, in the final game of the season, and that 111th defeat still stands as a Phillies club record for losses.

1942 — Grant Jackson — B 1965-70 P G-180

1952 — Phillies pitcher Robin Roberts wins at New York, 7-4, on final day of the season for his twenty-eighth victory and his thirtieth complete game, the most by any Phillies pitcher since Grover Alexander won thirty games and completed thirty-five in 1917.

1958 — In a race that went down to this final game, Phillies outfielder Richie Ashburn wins his second National League batting title with three hits in four at bats in 6-4, ten-inning victory at Pittsburgh. In same game, the Phillies Dave Philley sets a one-season, major league record by getting his eighth consecutive hit as a pinch-hitter.

## September 29

1886 — Gus Weyhing — B 1892-95 P G-149

1901 — Stan Benton — B 1922 2B G-6

Tony Rensa — B 1930-31 C G-73

1907 — Phillies pitcher George McQuillan pitches two-hit victory against Cincinnati and sets major league record with thirty-two consecutive scoreless innings at start of career.

1912 — Glen Stewart — B 1943-44 IF G-228

1915 — Phillies pitcher Grover Alexander hurls 5-0, one-hit victory (Sherry Magee single in fourth inning) at Boston to clinch Phillies first National League pennant. Gavvy Cravath's three-run home run in the first inning was the big blow in Alexander's thirty-first victory, his twelfth shutout and his major league record fourth one-hitter of the season. Alexander walked leadoff batter Herbie Moran and two outs later right fielder Cravath muffed Magee's fly ball for Phillies lone error. Only other base-runner for Boston was Magee, who singled with one out in fourth inning.

1918 — Eddie Feinberg — B 1938-39 IF-OF G-16

1935 — Howie Bedell — B 1968 PH G-9

1941 — Jeff James — B 1968-69 P G-35

1958 — Second baseman Solly Hemus traded to St. Louis Cardinals for infielder Gene Freese.

1968 — Phillies outfielder Dick Allen hits three home runs, including his third career grand slam, bats in seven runs in 10-3 victory at New York.

## September 30

1874 — Cy Vorhees — B 1902 P G-10

1910 — Jennings Poindexter — B 1939 P G-11

1926 — Robin Roberts — B 1948-1961 P G-541

1929 — Marv Blaylock — B 1955-57 1B G-286

1938 — Jimmie Wilson resigns as manager of Phillies after five years in the job.

1951 — Catcher Andy Seminick becomes first Phillies player to draw five walks in a game in fourteen-inning, 9-8 loss to Brooklyn (P).

1952 — Infielder Tommy Glaviano purchased from St. Louis Cardinals.

1956 — Phillies pitcher Robin Roberts gives up one home run to pitcher Al Worthington and two home runs to first baseman Bill White in 8-3 loss to New York (P) (first game), and the season home run total of forty-six off Roberts sets major league record.

1977 — Greg Luzinski, Richie Hebner, and Garry Maddox hit consecutive home runs in second inning of 9-4 victory against Montreal (P).

1978 — Winning pitcher Randy Lerch hits two home runs and outfielder Greg Luzinski hits three-run home run as Phillies rally to win, 10-8, at Pittsburgh and clinch their third straight National League Eastern Division title in next to last game of season. Phillies victory ended twenty-four game home winning streak of the Pirates.

# OCTOBER 1

1869 — Frank Motz — B 1890 1B G-1

1919 — Barney Mussill — B 1944 P G-16

1935 — Chuck Hiller — B 1967 2B G-31

1950 — Phillies win, 4-1, in ten innings on final day of season at Brooklyn on Dick Sisler's three-run home run off Don Newcombe to clinch their second National League pennant. Robin Roberts goes the route to become Phillies first twenty-game winner since 1917. Center fielder Richie Ashburn prevented a Dodger victory and a playoff with Brooklyn by throwing out Cal Abrams at the plate with the score tied in the ninth inning.

1970 — Phillies beat Montreal, 2-1, in ten innings in final major league game ever played in Connie Mack Stadium, which opened in 1909 as Shibe Park.

## October 2

1865 — Dan Casey B 1886-89 P G-142

1897 — Phillies score twelve runs in second inning at New York.

1907 — Phillies third baseman Eddie Grant gets seven hits in seven at bats in doubleheader at New York against Rube Marquard and Christy Mathewson. The latter lost to the Phillies for the sixth time this season.

1958 — Pitcher Ken Lehman purchased from Baltimore Orioles.

## October 2 (continued)

1964 — Phillies execute third triple play of season to tie major league record in 4-3 victory at Cincinnati. Others were on May 17 at Houston and August 15 at New York.

1965 — Phillies pitcher Jim Bunning wins, 6-0, at New York (first game) for his seventh shutout of season, most by a Phillies pitcher since Grover Alexander hurled eight in 1917.

In eighteen-inning scoreless tie, the longest 0-0 night game in major league history, Phillies pitcher Chris Short strikes out eighteen batters in the fifteen innings he pitches at New York (second game).

1966 — Pitcher Chris Short beats Los Angeles, 4-3 (P) (first game), to become Phillies first lefthanded twenty-game winner since Eppa Rixey in 1916.

## October 3

1895 — Bert Lewis — B 1924 P G-12

1915 — Charlie Letchas — B 1939, 44, 46 2B-3B-SS G-134

1931 — Bob Skinner — B 1968-69 MGR

1955 — Outfielder Peanuts Lowrey released.

1972 — Phillies hit six home runs in 11-1 victory at Chicago as pitcher Steve Carlton wins his twenty-seventh game, most by a Phillies pitcher since 1952.

## October 4

1871 — Charlie Jordan — B 1896 P G-2

1927 — Rip Repulski — B 1957-58 OF G-219

1938 — James (Doc) Prothro, veteran minor league manager, named to manage the Phillies, succeeding interim manager Hans Lobert.

1948 — Outfielder Harry Walker traded to Chicago Cubs for outfielder Bill Nicholson.

1950 — New York beats Phillies, 1-0, in World Series opener as Vic Raschi defeats relief ace Jim Konstanty, who was making his first start for the Phillies after 133 regular-season relief appearances since 1948. Bobby Brown doubled and came around on two long flies for the only run of the game in the fourth inning at Shibe Park.

1977 — Phillies win, 7-5, at Los Angeles in first game of National League Championship Series. Phillies had 5-1 lead until Ron Cey's grand-slam home run off Steve Carlton tied the score in the seventh inning. Singles by Bake McBride, Larry Bowa, and Mike Schmidt highlight winning two-run, ninth-inning rally.

## October 4 (continued)

1978 — Los Angeles beats Phillies, 9-5, in National League Championship Series opener at Veterans Stadium. Dodger first baseman Steve Garvey bats in four runs with two home runs and triple.

## October 5

1871 — Jack Fifield — B 1897-99 P G-62

1906 — Si Johnson — B 1940-43, 46 P G-137

1939 — Dennis Bennett — B 1962-64 P G-95

1950 — Joe DiMaggio, hitless in his four previous times at bat, hits leadoff home run in tenth inning off Robin Roberts to give New York 2-1 victory over the Phillies in second World Series game (P). Allie Reynolds pitched a seven-hitter to win.

1977 — Los Angeles beats Phillies, 7-1, at Dodger Stadium to even National League Championship Series at one game apiece. Dusty Baker's grand-slam home run off Jim Lonborg snapped 1-1 tie in fourth inning.

1978 — Lefthander Tommy John pitches four-hitter as Los Angeles takes 2-0 lead in National League Championship Series with 4-0 victory over Phillies (P). Dodger second baseman bats in three runs off Dick Ruthven with home run, single, and triple.

## October 6

1866 — Eddie Burke — B 1890 OF G-100

1872 — Jack Dunn — B 1900-01 P G-12

1884 — Barney Slaughter — B 1910 P G-8

1908 — Tom Padden B 1943 C G-17

1909 — Walt Bashore — B 1936 OF G-10

1910 — Boston beats Phillies, 20-7 (A).

1923 — In fourth inning of 4-1 loss in five-inning game at Boston, Phillies first baseman Walter Holke lines out to shortstop Ernie Padgett, who steps on second base to double Cotton Tierney and then tags Cliff Lee for an unassisted triple play, the first in modern National League history. Doubleheader loss dropped Phillies into last place.

1950 — New York defeats Phillies, 3-2, at Yankee Stadium in third game of World Series. Jerry Coleman single off losing relief pitcher Russ Meyer with two out in ninth inning to score Gene Woodling with the winning run. Yankees had tied the score with an unearned run in the eighth inning on shortstop Granny Hamner's fumble of ground ball with two out.

## October 6 (continued)

1978 — Phillies beat Los Angeles, 9-4, at Dodger Stadium in third game of National League Championship Series. Left-hander Steve Carlton pitches complete game and bats in four runs with a three-run home run and single off loser Don Sutton.

## October 7

1898 — Phillies pitcher Wiley Piatt hurls 3-0, one-hit victory against Washington (P).

1904 — Chuck Klein — B 1928-33, 36,39, 39-44 OF G-1405

1918 — Frankie Baumholtz — B 1956-57 OF G-78

1919 — Tommy Hughes — B 1941-42, 46-47 P G-140

1943 — Jose Cardenal — B 1978 1B-OF G-87

1940 — Morrie Steevens — B 1964 P G-10

1950 — New York completes four-game sweep over Phillies in World Series with 5-2 victory (A). Yankee rookie left-hander Whitey Ford has shutout with two out in ninth inning when left fielder Gene Woodling drops Andy Seminick's fly ball. After Mike Goliat singles, Allie Reynolds relieves Ford and strikes out pinch-hitter Stan Lopata to end the Series.

1966 — Pitcher Ray Herbert and infielder-outfielder Harvey Kuenn released.

1969 — First baseman Dick Allen, infielder-outfielder Cookie Rojas, and pitcher Jerry Johnson traded to St. Louis Cardinals for catcher Tim McCarver, outfielders Curt Flood and Buron Browne, and pitcher Joe Hoerner.

1977 — Los Angeles scores three runs after two were out in ninth inning to beat Phillies, 6-5, at Veterans Stadium and take 2-1 lead in National League Championship Series. Key Dodger hits off relief pitcher Gene Garber were Manny Mota's double off the glove of left fielder Greg Luzinski, a game-tying single off the glove of third baseman Mike Schmidt, and Bill Russell's run-scoring single to center.

1978 — Los Angeles beats Phillies, 4-3, in ten innings (A) in fourth National League Championship Series game to win second pennant in row. A two-out walk, center-fielder Garry Maddox's muff of Dusty Baker's sinking line drive, and Bill Russell's single to center off losing relief pitcher Tug McGraw produce winning run.

## October 8

1857 — John Bergh — B 1876 — OF-C G-1

1885 — Johnny Lush — B 1904-07 P-OF-1B G-205

1887 — Phillies end season with 6-3 victory at New York for their sixteenth straight victory, a winning streak which has been equalled twice but never surpassed in the club's history.

## October 8 (continued)

1915 — Phillies beat Boston, 3-1, at Baker Bowl in opener of World Series behind Grover Alexander, who outpitched Ernie Shore. Gavvy Cravath's infield grounder drove in the run that snapped 1-1 tie in eighth-inning, 2-run rally in which not one ball was hit out of the infield. The Phillies scored in the fourth inning, Possum Whitted's infield hit driving in a run, and the Red Sox tied with a run in the eighth inning on a walk, an infield out, and a single by Duffy Lewis, who starred with a .444 batting average and five runs batted in for the Series.

1917 — Danny Murtaugh — B 1941-43, 46 2B G-348

1934 — Mickey Harrington — B 1963 PR G-1

1956 — Catcher Andy Seminick released and signed as coach.

1977 — Los Angeles beats Phillies, 4-1, in fourth National League Championship Series game to win pennant in game played in steady rain at Veterans Stadium before 64,924 fans, the largest baseball crowd in the history of Pennsylvania. Dodger left-hander Tommy John outpitches Steve Carlton, and Dusty Baker's two-run home run in second inning is decisive blow.

## October 9

1865 — Al Maul — B 1887, 1900 P-OF G-21

1884 — Phillies outfielder Jack Manning hits three home runs in a game (A), the first time any Phillies batter has ever hit as many as three in one game.

1886 — Charley Ferguson pitches 5-1 and 6-1 complete-game victories, with the second game being called after six innings.

1915 — Boston beats Phillies, 2-1, in second game of World Series (P), attended by Woodrow Wilson, the first President to attend a World Series game. George Foster outpitched Erskine Mayer and singled home Larry Gardner with the winning run in the ninth inning.

1954 — Randy Lerch — B 1975-78 P G-70

1976 — Cincinnati beats Phillies, 6-3, in National League Championship Series opener at Veterans Stadium. Don Gullett beats Steve Carlton as Reds snap 1-1 tie with two runs in sixth inning.

## October 10

1868 — Dave Anderson — B 1889-90 P G-8

1868 — Ad Gumbert — B 1896 P G-11

1877 — Pep Deininger — B 1908-09 OF G-56

1887 — Paul Fittery — B 1917 P G-19

94

## October 10 (continued)

Bill Killefer — B 1911-17 C G-636

1888 — Toots Shultz — B 1911-12 P G-28

1902 — Homer Peel — B 1929 OF G-53

1905 — Wally Berger — B 1940 OF G-20

1916 — Floyd Baker — B 1954-55 3B G-28

1922 — Saul Rogovin — B 1955-57 P G-39

1976 — Cincinnati wins second game of National League Championship Series from Phillies, 6-2 (P). Phillies pitcher Jim Lonborg has 2-0 lead and a no-hitter after five innings, but Reds score four times in sixth inning to win.

## October 11

1878 — Frank Roth — B 1903-04 C G-149

1882 — Buck Washer — B 1905 P G-1

1894 — Gary Fortune — B 1916, 18 P G-6

1915 — Boston beats Phillies, 2-1, in third game of World Series, played at new park of Boston Nationals before what was then a record World Series crowd of 42,300. Dutch Leonard out pitches Grover Alexander and wins in ninth inning when Duffy Lewis singles with two out to score Harry Hooper with winning run.

1948 — Pitcher Russ Meyer purchased from Chicago Cubs.

1956 — Pitcher Stu Miller traded to New York Giants for pitcher Jim Hearn.

## October 12

1861 — Frank Ringo B 1883-84 C-IF-OF G-86

1890 — Dixie Davis — B 1918 P G-18

1893 — Hank Ritter — B 1912 P G-3

1902 — Stew Bolen — B 1931-32 P G-33

1907 — Al Smith — B 1938-39 P G-42

Phil Weintraub — B 1938 1B G-100

1915 — Lou Novikoff — B 1946 OF G-17

Boston beats Phillies for the third straight time by 2-1 score in fourth

95

World Series game (A). Ernie Shore outpitches George Chalmers, and Duffy Lewis drives in winning run for the second game in a row with double in sixth inning for 2-0 lead.

1976 — Cincinnati scores three runs in ninth inning to beat Phillies, 7-6, in third National League Championship Series game at Riverfront Stadium to win pennant. Phillies hold 6-4 lead in last of ninth inning when George Foster and Johnny Bench hit solo home runs off pitcher Ron Reed to tie the score. Reds then get winning run on Dave Concepcion's single off loser Gene Garber, and two walks and Ken Griffey's infield hit off Tommy Underwood.

## October 13

1858 — Fred Lewis — B 1883 OF G-38

1876 — Wild Bill Donovan — B 1921 MGR

1893 — Dick Spalding — B 1927 OF G-115

1894 — Pickles Dillhoefer — B 1918 C G-8

1915 — Boston beats Phillies, 5-4, in fifth game to win World Series (P). Erskine Mayer, who started for Phillies because Grover Alexander came up with sore arm, is chased in third inning when Red Sox tie score, 2-2. Eppa Rixey relieves and is tagged for runs that tie the score at 4-4 in eighth inning on two-run home run by Duffy Lewis, then loses in ninth when Harry Hooper bounces home run into center field stands, his second of the game. Phillies take 2-0 lead in first inning and 4-2 lead in fourth when Fred Luderus, who batted .438 and drove in six runs in the five games, hit Phillies only World Series homer.

1928 — Shortstop Heinie Sand and cash traded to St. Louis Cardinals for shortstop Tommy Thevenow.

1930 — Pitcher Les Sweetland sold to Chicago Cubs.

1965 — Pitchers Lew Burdette and Ed Roebuck released.

## October 14

1853 — Charlie Waitt — B 1883 OF G-1

1883 — Harry Houston — B 1906 C G-2

1891 — Bert Gallia — B 1920 P G-19

1915 — Ken Heintzelman — B 1947-52 P G-165

1930 — Outfielder Lefty O'Doul and second baseman Fresco Thompson traded to Brooklyn Dodgers for outfielder Hal Lee, pitchers Clise Dudley and Jumbo Elliott and $25,000.

1940 — Bill Sorrell — B 1965 3B G-10

1954 — Mayo Smith, who had been managing in the New York Yankees minor league system, named manager of the Phillies, succeeding Terry Moore.

1977 — Infielder Ron Clark released.

## October 15

1863 — Con Murphy — B 1884 P G-3

1928 — Jim Command — B 1954-55 3B G-14

1956 — Pitcher Ben Flowers sold to Kansas City A's.

1957 — Outfielder Ron Northey released.

1964 — Catcher Bill Heath and pitcher Joel Gibson traded to Chicago White Sox for pitcher Rudy May.

## October 16

1885 — Dan Howley — B 1913 C G-26

1904 — Boom-Boom Beck — B 1939-43 P G-128

1915 — Paul Masterson — B 1940-42 P G-8

1936 — Jack Baldschun — B 1961-65 P G-333

1941 — Tim McCarver — B 1970-72, 75-78 C G-543

1961 — Pitcher Robin Roberts sold to New York Yankees for $25,000.

Outfielder Elmer Valo released.

## October 17

1927 — Johnny Klippstein — B 1963-64 P G-60

1947 — Jim Hutto — B 1970 OF-IF-C G-57

## October 18

1881 — Hans Lobert — B 1911-14, 38, 42 3B-MGR G-497

1884 — Burt Shotton — B 1928-33 MGR

1897 — Tom Sullivan — B 1922 P G-3

1906 — Wally Millies — B 1939-41 C G-111

1910 — Skeeter Newsome — B 1946-47 SS G-207

## October 18 (continued)

1949 — Ed Farmer — B 1974 P G-14

1973 — Pitcher Ken Brett traded to Pittsburgh Pirates for second baseman Dave Cash.

## October 19

1914 — Pat Moran, former reserve catcher who had been a Phillies coach, named manager of Phillies, succeeding Red Dooin, who held the job for five years.

1915 — Sam Nahem — B 1942, 48 P G-63

1930 — Joe Koppe — B 1959-61 SS G-190

1938 — Vic Roznovsky — B 1969 C G-13

1962 — Catcher Sammy White and infielder Billy Klaus released.

## October 20

1864 — Jocko Fields — B 1891 C G-8

1926 — Sutffy McInnis, veteran first baseman who was a member of the Philadelphia A's "Million Dollar Infield" in 1914, named manager of the Phillies.

1928 — Bobby Micelotta — B 1954-55 SS G-17

## October 21

1873 — Fred Abbott — B 1905 C G-42

1909 — Bill Lee — B 1943-45 P G-57

1930 — Valmy Thomas — B 1959 C G-66

## October 22

1863 — Al Myers — B 1885, 89-91 2B G-420

1870 — Kid Carsey — B 1892-97 P G-193

1900 — Jumbo Elliott — B 1931-34 P G-130

1902 — Rusty Yarnall — B 1926 P G-1

1907 — Jimmie Foxx — B 1945 1B-3B-P G-89

1918 — Harry Walker — B 1947-48 OF G-242

1971 — Outfielder Larry Hisle traded to Los Angeles Dodgers for first baseman Tommy Hutton.

## October 23

1886 — Lena Blackburne — B 1919 3B G-72

1890 — Dick Cotter — B 1911 C G-20

1894 — Rube Bressler — B 1932 OF G-27

1907 — Lee Grissom — B 1941 P G-29

1930 — Solly Drake — B 1959 OF G-67

1931 — Jim Bunning — B 1964-67, 70-71 P G-229

1939 — George Williams — B 1961 2B G-17

## October 24

1887 — Eddie Stack — B 1910-11 P G-33

1904 — Harry Smythe — B 1929-30 P G-45

1927 — Jim Greengrass — B 1955-56 OF G-180

1950 — Rawly Eastwick — B 1978 P G-22

1975 — Catcher Larry Cox traded to Minnesota Twins for infielder Sergio Ferrer.

Pitcher Joe Hoerner released.

## October 25

1863 — Bill Shettsline — B 1898-1902 MGR

1869 — Jack Doyle — B 1904 1B G-66

1887 — Oscar M Dugey — B 1915-17 2B G-127

1904 — Andy Cohen — B 1960 MGR

1913 — Gene Corbett — B 1936-38 IF G-37

1923 — Russ Meyer — B 1949-52 P G-134

1974 — Pitchers Frank Linzy and Pete Richert released.

1977 — Pitcher Manny Seoane traded to Chicago Cubs for outfielder-first baseman Jose Cardenal.

## October 26

1866 — Kid Gleason — B 1888-91, 1903-08 P-OF-IF G-769

1904 — Monk Sherlock — B 1930 1B G-92

## October 26 (continued)

1923 — Tommy Glaviano — B 1953 IF G-53

1972 — Pitcher Chris Short released.

## October 27

1858 — Joe Mulvey — B 1883-89, 92 3B G-682

1939 — Catcher Spud Davis sold to Pittsburgh Pirates for $15,000.

1965 — Outfielder Alex Johnson, catcher Pat Corrales, and pitcher Art Mahaffey traded to St. Louis Cardinals for first baseman Bill White, shortstop Dick Groat, and catcher Bob Uecker.

## October 28

1897 — Clarence Huber — B 1925-26 3B G-242

1904 — Joe O'Rourke — B 1929 PH G-3

1910 — George Hennessey — B 1942 P G-5

1916 — Ed Levy — B 1940 PH G-1

## October 29

1891 — Happy Finneran — B 1912-13 P G-17

1897 — Ty Pickup — B 1918 OF G-1

1928 — Outfielder Fred Leach traded to New York Giants for outfielder Lefty O'Doul and $25,000.

1939 — Pete Richert — B 1974 P G-34

1944 — Gary Neibauer — B 1972 P G-9

1968 — Pitcher Dick Hall released.

1969 — Pitcher Jim Bunning signed as free agent after release by Los Angeles Dodgers.

## October 30

1861 — Shadow Pyle — B 1884 P G-1

1867 — Ed Delahanty — B 1888-89, 91-1901 OF G-1555

1878 — Ham Iburg — B 1902 P G-31

1917 — Bobby Bragan — B 1940-42 SS G-395

## October 31

1862 — Hardie Henderson — B 1883 P G-2

1887 — Ed Burns — B 1913-18 C G-320

1910 — Mickey Haslin — B 1933-36 IF G-224

1972 — Third baseman Don Money, infielder John Vukovich, and pitcher Billy Champion traded to Milwaukee Brewers for pitchers Jim Lonborg, Ken Brett, Ken Sanders, and Earl Stephenson.

## NOVEMBER 1

1874 — Red Owens — G 1899 2B G-8

1906 — Pete Rambo — B 1916 P G-1

1922 — Andy Lapihuska — B 1942-43 P G-4

1931 — Vic Power — B 1964 1B G-18

1934 — Shortstop Dick Bartell traded to New York Giants for shortstop Blondy Ryan, third baseman Johnny Vergez, outfielder George Watkins, pitcher Pretzels Pezzullo, and cash.

1972 — Long-time Los Angeles Dodger coach and minor league manager Danny Ozark named manager of the Phillies, succeeding General Manager Paul Owens, who had held the post since July 10.

## November 2

1904 — Lease and effects of Phillies purchased at sheriff's sale by Arthur Newbold and James Potter.

1920 — Dick Sisler — B 1948-51 OF-1B G-508

1928 — Bob Ross — B 1956 P G-3

1942 — Ron Reed — B 1976-78 P G-185

1976 — Infielder Tony Taylor released.

## November 3

1875 — Phil Geier — B 1896-97 OF-IF-C G-109

1917 — Eli Hodkey — B 1946 P G-2

1919 — Mike Goliat — B 1949-51 2B G-241

1921 — Wally Flagler — B 1945 SS G-49

## November 4

1869 — Mike Kilroy — B 1891 P G-3

## November 4 (continued)

1915 — Joe Kracher — B 1939 C G-5

1927 — Carl Sawatski — B 1958-59 C G-134

1930 — Dick Groat — B 1966-67 SS G-165

1933 — Tito Francona — B 1967 1B G-27

1943 — Dick Selma — B 1970-73 P G-144

1969 — Pitcher Dick Farrell released.

## November 5

1891 — Greasy Neale — B 1921 OF G-22

1912 — Les Powers — B 1939 1B G-19

1913 — Jim Tabor — B 1946-47 3B G-199

1927 — Putsy Caballero — B 1944-45, 47-52 IF G-322

## November 6

1893 — Dana Fillingham — B 1925 P G-5

1910 — Chet Covington — B 1944 P G-19

1930 — Shortstop Tommy Thevenow and pitcher Claude Willoughby traded to Pittsburgh Pirates for shortstop Dick Bartell.

## November 7

1857 — The Only Nolan — B 1885 P G-7

1898 — Mike Pasquriello — B 1919 1B G-1

1927 — Burt Shotton, former manager of Syracuse, named manager of Phillies, succeeding Stuffy McInnis, who held the job for one year.

1932 — Dick Stuart — B 1965 1B G-149

1938 — Jim Kaat — B 1976-78 P G-104

1945 — Dave Bennett — B 1964 P G-1

1973 — Pitcher Billy Wilson traded to Milwaukee Brewers from pitcher Frank Linzy.

## November 8

1896 — Bucky Harris — B 1943 MGR

1920 — Wally Westlake — B 1956 PH G-5

## November 9

1857 — Alonzo Breitenstein — B 1883 P G-1

1858 — George Wood — B 1886-89 OF G-422

1897 — Harvey Hendrick — B 1934 OF-IF G-59

1902 — Mike Kelly — B 1926 P G-4

1906 — Fred Brickell — B 1930-33 OF G-236

1920 — Homer Spragins — B 1947 P G-4

1920 — Dick Whitman — B 1950-51 OF G-94

## November 10

1873 — Willie McGill — B 1895-96 P G-32

1930 — Gene Conley — B 1959-60 P G-54

1953 — Larry Christenson — B 1973-78 P G-148

## November 11

1917 — Pitcher Grover Alexander and catcher Bill Killefer traded to Chicago Cubs for pitcher Mike Prendergast, catcher Pickles Dillhoefer, and $60,000.

1933 — Ken Walters — B 1960-61 OF G-210

1940 — Pitcher Kirby Higbe traded to Brooklyn Dodgers for pitchers Vito Tamulis and Bill Crouch, catcher Mickey Livingston, and $100,000.

## November 12

1887 — Ben Froelich — B 1909 C G-1

1924 — Andy Hansen — B 1951-53 P G-97

1927 — Harry Hanebrink — B 1959 IF-OF G-57

1936 — Joe Hoerner — B 1970-72, 75 P G-133

## November 13

1887 — Josh Devore — B 1913-14 OF G-53

1889 — Buck Stanley — B 1911 P G-4

1895 — Ray Steineder — B 1924 P G-9

1917 — Nick Goulish — B 1944-45 OF G-14

1943 — Bobby Pfeil — B 1971 IF-OF-C G-44

1947 — Gene Garber — B 1974-78 P G-250

1972 — Infielder Jose Pagan signed as free agent after being released by Pittsburgh Pirates.

## November 14

1898 — Claude Willoughby — B 1925-30 P G-210

## November 15

1871 — Pete Childs — B 1902 2B G-123

1888 — Pat Ragan — B 1923 P G-1

1899 — Broadway Jones — B 1923 P G-3

1914 — Mickey Livingston — B 1941-43 C G-268

1933 — Infielder Eddie Delker and catcher Spud Davis traded to St. Louis Cardinals for catcher Jimmie Wilson.

1951 — Orlando Gonzalez — B 1978 OF G-26

## November 16

1892 — Gene Steinbrenner — B 1912 2B G-3

1948 — Don Hahn — B 1975 OF G-9

## November 17

1867 — George Stallings — B 1897-98 OF-1B-MGR G-3

1886 — Fred Beck — B 1911 OF G-66

1942 — Catcher Bennie Warren sold to Chicago Cubs.

1969 — Outfielder Johnny Callison traded to Chicago Cubs for outfielder Oscar Gamble and pitcher Dick Selma.

## November 18

1863 — Deacon McGuire — B 1886-88 C G-103

1869 — John Johnson — B 1894 P G-4

1882 — Jack Coombs — B 1919 MGR

1899 — Dutch Ulrich — B 1925-27 P G-98

1912 — Charlie Fuchs — B 1943 P G-17

1925 — Gene Mauch — B 1960-68 MGR

## November 18 (continued)

1926 — Roy Sievers — B 1962-64 1B G-331

## November 19

1840 — Neal Phelps — B 1876 C G-1

1862 — Billy Sunday — B 1890 OF G-31

1930 — Joe Morgan — B 1960 3B G-26

1945 — Bobby Tolan — B 1976-77 1B-OF G-125

1947 — Bob Boone — B 1972-78 C G-789

1956 — Outfielder Del Ennis traded to St. Louis Cardinals for outfielder Rip Repulski and infielder Bobby Morgan.

## November 20

1873 — Tom Fleming — B 1902, 04 OF G-8

1910 — Morrie Arnovich — B 1936-40 OF G-442

1945 — Jay Johnstone — B 1974-78 OF-1B G-462

## November 21

1897 — Andy High — B 1934 3B-2B G-47

1905 — Les Mallon — B 1931-32 2B G-225

1914 — George Scharein — B 1937-40 SS G-388

1924 — Warren Hacker — B 1957-58 P G-29

1933 — Outfielder Chuck Klein traded to Chicago Cubs for pitcher Ted Kleinhans, infielder Mark Koenig, outfielder Harvey Hendrick, and $65,000.

1935 — Catcher Al Todd traded to Pittsburgh Pirates for catcher Earl Grace and pitcher Claude Passeau.

1962 — Catcher Jim Coker sold to Baltimore Orioles.

## November 22

1907 — Dick Bartell — B 1931-34 SS G-587

1914 — Alex Pitko — B 1938 OF G-7

1916 — Ted Cieslak — B 1944 3B G-85

1920 — Pitcher Eppa Rixey traded to Cincinnati Reds for pitcher Jimmy Ring and outfielder Greasy Neale.

## November 22 (continued)

1926 — Lew Burdette — B 1965 P G-19

1946 — Cy Acosta — B 1975 P G-6

1950 — Greg Luzinski — B 1970-78 OF G-1046

1972 — Ruly Carpenter replaces his father, Bob Carpenter, as President of Phillies.

## November 23

1860 — Chief Zimmer — B 1903 C-MGR G-37

1897 — Bubber Jonnard — B 1926-27, 35 C G-73

1897 — Freddy Leach — B 1923-28 OF G-539

1932 — John Anderson — B 1958 P G-5

1934 — John Kennedy — B 1957 SS G-5

1955 — Todd Cruz — B 1978 SS G-3

## November 24

1889 — George Burns — B 1925 OF G-88

## November 25

1880 — Frank Corridon — B 1904-05, 07-09 P G-139

1915 — Bob Finley — B 1943-44 C G-122

1941 — Mike Ryan — B 1968-73 C G-392

1969 — Pitcher Fred Wenz purchased from Boston Red Sox.

## November 26

1866 — Hugh Duffy — B 1904-06 OF-MGR G-34

1909 — Former Philadelphia sports writer Horace Fogel named president of Phillies.

1912 — Alfred D. Wiler named president of Phillies, succeeding Horace Fogel, who was forced out by the National League's Board of Directors after making unfounded charges that the 1912 pennant race was "crooked."

1913 — Garton Del Savio — B 1943 SS G-4

1916 — Eddie Miller — B 1948-49 SS-2B G-215

1923 — Danny Ozark — B 1973-78 MGR

1941 — Hans Lobert, long-time coach with the club, named manager of the Phillies.

1947 — Richie Hebner — B 1977-78 1B G-255

## November 27

1896 — John Singleton — B 1922 P G-22

1903 — Bil Hohman — B 1927 OF G-7

1941 — Al Raffo — B 1969 P G-45

1962 — Pitcher Jim Owens traded to Cincinnati Reds for infielder Cookie Rojas.

## November 28

1883 — Fred Osborn — B 1907-09 OF G-266

1961 — Bill Conway — B 1884 C G-1

Pitcher John Buzhardt and third baseman Charlie Smith traded to Chicago White Sox for first baseman Roy Sievers.

1962 — Outfielder Ted Savage and first baseman Pancho Herrera traded to Pittsburgh Pirates for third baseman Don Hoak.

## November 29

1922 — Lynn Lovenguth — B 1955 P G-14

1964 — Pitcher Dennis Bennett traded to Boston Red Sox for first baseman Dick Stuart.

1965 — Shortstop Ruben Amaro traded to New York Yankees for shortstop Phil Linz.

## November 30

1964 — First baseman Vic Power sold to Los Angeles Angels.

1966 — Pitcher Darold Knowles and cash traded to Washington Senators for outfielder Don Lock.

1972 — Outfielders Oscar Gamble and Roger Freed traded to Cleveland Indians for outfielder Del Unser and infielder Terry Wedgewood.

Pitchers Ken Sanders and Ken Reynolds and outfielder Joe Lis traded to Minnesota Twins for infielder-outfielder Cesar Tovar.

# DECEMBER 1

1904 — Former Phillies Manager Bill Shettsline elected president of Phillies, and Hugh Duffy, a star outfielder with the Boston Nationals for almost a decade, named manager of Phillies.

1921 — Charlie Ripple — B 1944-46 P G-11

1925 — Niles Jordan — B 1951 P G-5

Cal McLish — B 1962-64 P G-67

1952 — Dan Warthen — B 1977 P G-3

1964 — Outfielder-infielder Danny Cater and shortstop Lee Elia traded to Chicago White Sox for pitcher Ray Herbert and first baseman Jeoff Long.

## December 2

1897 — Art Jahn — B 1928 OF G-36

1913 — Glenn Crawford — B 1945-46 OF-IF G-83

1948 — Wayne Simpson — B 1975 P G-7

## December 3

1936 — Clay Dalrymple — B 1960-68 C G-1006

1943 — Jerry Johnson — B 1968-69 P G-49

1958 — Outfielder Chuck Essegian traded to St. Louis Cardinals for shortstop Ruben Amaro.

Pitcher Jack Sanford traded to San Francisco Giants for pitcher Ruben Gomez and catcher Valmy Thomas.

1964 — Pitcher Rudy May and first baseman Costen Shockley traded to Los Angeles Angels for pitcher Bo Belinsky.

1968 — First baseman-third baseman Deron Johnson purchased from Atlanta Braves.

1973 — Pitcher Barry Lersch, infielder Craig Robinson, and first baseman-outfielder Bob Beall traded to Atlanta Braves for pitcher Ron Schueler and infielder Gil Garrido.

1974 — Outfielder Del Unser, catcher John Stearns, and pitcher Mac Scarce traded to New York Mets for pitcher Tug McGraw and outfielders Don Hahn and Dave Schneck.

## December 4

1876 — Henry Krug — B 1902 OF-IF G-53

## December 4 (continued)

1883 — Jim Maroney — B 1910 P G-12

1930 — Harvey Kuenn — B 1966 OF-IF G-86

1941 — Outfielder Lloyd Waner signed as free agent after release by Cincinnati, Reds.

1959 — Catcher Carl Sawatski traded to St. Louis Cardinals for outfielder Bobby Gene Smith and pitcher Billy Smith.

1963 — Outfielder Don Demeter and pitcher Jack Hamilton traded to Detroit Tigers for pitcher Jim Bunning and catcher Gus Triandos.

## December 5

1863 — Bill Shindle — B 1891 3B G-103

1871 — Tom Smith — B 1895 P G-11

1905 — Gus Mancuso — B 1945 C G-70

1911 — Don Padgett — B 1947-48 C G-111

1939 — Outfielder Hub Bates sold to Boston Braves.

1959 — Pitcher Ray Semproch and shortstop Chico Fernandez traded to Detroit Tigers for outfielder Ken Walters and infielders Ted Lepcio and Alex Cosmidis.

1978 — Pete Rose is signed to a multi-year pact which makes him at this time the highest paid player in history.

## December 6

1873 — Harry Wolverton — B 1900-01, 02-04 3B G-453

1882 — Cozy Dolan — B 1912-13 3B G-66

1913 — Bill Kerksieck — B 1939 P G-25

1914 — Turkey Tyson — B 1944 PH G-1

1902 — Gus Niarhos — B 1954-55 C G-10

1927 — Tommy Brown — B 1951-52 OF-IF G-96

1945 — Larry Bowa — B 1970-78 SS G-1342

1957 — Pitcher Harvey Haddix traded to Cincinnati Reds for outfielder Wally Post.

1965 — Pitcher Jack Baldschun traded to Baltimore Orioles for pitcher Darold Knowles and outfielder Jackie Brandt.

## December 6 (continued)

1973 — Infielder Denny Doyle traded to California Angels for pitcher Aurelio Monteagudo and outfielder Chris Coletta, completing August 14 deal in which Phillies got Bill Grabarkewitz.

## December 7

1935 — Don Cardwell — B 1957-60 P G-77

1936 — Bo Belinsky — B 1965-66 P G-40

1938 — First baseman Les Powers purchased from New York Giants.

1942 — Alex Johnson — B 1964-65 OF G-140

1966 — Pitcher Ray Culp and cash traded to Chicago Cubs for pitcher Dick Ellsworth.

1973 — Infielder-outfielder Cesar Tovar sold to Texas Rangers.

Pitcher Eddie Watt purchased from Baltimore Orioles.

## December 8

1877 — Bill Thomas — B 1902 OF-IF G-6

1936 — Infielder Lou Chiozza traded to New York Giants for infielder George Scharein and cash.

1959 — Third baseman Gene Freese traded to Chicago White Sox for outfielder Johnny Callison.

1977 — First baseman Tommy Hutton sold to Toronto Blue Jays.

## December 9

1928 — Billy Klaus — B 1962-63 IF G-113

1941 — Darold Knowles — B 1966 P G-69

1944 — Del Unser — B 1973-74 OF G-278

1946 — Pitcher Dutch Leonard purchased from Washington Senators.

1955 — Outfielder Frankie Baumholtz purchased from Chicago Cubs.

1975 — Outfielder Mike Anderson traded to St. Louis Cardinals for pitcher Ron Reed.

## December 10

1889 — Troy Puckett — B 1911 P G-1

1898 — Spoke Emery — B 1924 OF G-5

1911 — Pretzels Pezzullo — B 1935-36 P G-42

1926 — Leo Cristante — B 1951 P G-10

1937 — Doc Edwards — B 1970 C G-35

1941 — Outfielder Johnny Rizzo sold to Brooklyn Dodgers.

1945 — First baseman Frank McCormick purchased from Cincinnati Reds for $30,000.

1951 — Catcher Andy Seminick, infielder Eddie Pellagrini, outfielder Dick Sisler, and pitcher Niles Jordan traded to Cincinnati Reds for catcher Smoky Burgess, infielder Connie Ryan, and pitcher Howie Fox.

1954 — Phillies purchase Connie Mack Stadium as Philadelphia Athletics prepare to move to Kansas City.

1966 — Pitcher Joe Verbanic and cash traded to New York Yankees for pitcher Pedro Ramos.

1975 — Pitchers Dick Ruthven and Roy Thomas and outfielder Alan Bannister traded to Chicago White Sox for pitcher Jim Kaat and shortstop Mike Buskey.

## December 11

1887 — Petie Behan — B 1921-23 P G-43

1894 — Lou Raymond — B 1919 2B G-1

1909 — Jim Bivin — B 1935 P G-47

1914 — Bill Nicholson — B 1949-53 OF G-317

1927 — John Gray — B 1958 P G-19

1929 — Outfielder Homer Peel and pitcher Bob McGraw traded to St. Louis Cardinals for pitcher Grover Alexander and catcher Harry McCurdy.

1947 — Pitcher Tommy Hughes traded to Cincinnati Reds for infielder-outfielder Bert Haas.

1957 — Outfielder Dave Philley purchased from Detroit Tigers.

1962 — Outfielder Jacke Davis traded to Los Angeles Angels for catcher-outfielder Earl Averill.

## December 12

1864 — Phenomenal Smith — B 1890-91 P G-29

1913 — Bill Webb — B 1943 P G-1

## December 12 (continued)

1915 — Rene Monteagudo — B 1945 OF-P G-114

1922 — First baseman Walter Holke purchased from Boston Braves.

1932 — Outfielder Kiddo Davis traded to New York Giants for outfielder Chick Fullis, first baseman Gus Dugas, and cash.

1942 — Pitcher Rube Melton traded to Brooklyn Dodgers for pitcher Johnny Allen and cash.

1945 — Infielder Skeeter Newsome purchased from Boston Red Sox.

## December 13

1923 — Infielder Cotton Tierney traded to Boston Braves for infielder Hod Ford and outfielder Ray Powell.

1927 — Outfielder Johnny Mokan, infielder Jimmy Cooney, and catcher Bubber Jonnard traded to St. Louis Cardinals for pitcher Jimmy Ring and catcher Johnny Schulte.

1934 — Outfielder Kiddo Davis traded to New York Giants for pitcher Joe Bowman.

1943 — Ferguson Jenkins — B 1965-66 P G-8

1951 — Infielder Jake Schmitt traded to New York Giants for infielder Lucky Lohrke.

## December 14

1870 — Deacon Van Buren — B 1904 OF G-12

1890 — Ben Tincup — B 1914-16, 18 P G-54

1894 — Stan Baumgartner — B 1914, 16, 21-22 P G-71

1908 — Terry Lyons — B 1929 1B G-1

1916 — Paul Erickson — B 1948 P G-4

1948 — Pitchers Dutch Leonard and Monk Dubiel traded to Chicago Cubs for pitcher Hank Borowy and first baseman Eddie Waitkus.

Pitcher Ken Trinkle purchased from New York Giants.

1973 — Darrell Brandon released.

## December 15

1882 — Nig Clarke — B 1919 C G-26

1902 — Frank Watt — B 1931 P G-38

## December 15 (continued)

1919 — Ken Trinkle — B 1949 P G-42

1929 — Ray Herbert — B 1965-66 P G-48

1932 — Pitcher Ray Benge traded to Brooklyn Dodgers for pitcher Austin Moore, second baseman Mickey Finn, and third baseman Jack Warner.

1960 — Pitcher Gene Conley traded to Boston Red Sox for pitcher Frank Sullivan.

1961 — Pitcher Taylor Phillips and infielder Bob Sadowski traded to Chicago White Sox for third baseman Andy Carey and pitcher Frank Barnes. Carey refused to report and on March 24, 1962, Phillies received pitcher Cal McLish in his place.

1966 — Pitcher John Morris traded to Baltimore Orioles for pitcher Dick Hall.

1967 — Pitcher Dick Ellsworth and catcher-first baseman Gene Oliver traded to Boston Red Sox for catcher Mike Ryan and cash.

1976 — Infielder Richie Hebner, selected in re-entry free agent draft, signed.

## December 16

1900 — Tony Kaufmann — B 1927 P G-8

1941 — Adolfo Phillips — B 1964-66 OF G-56

1967 — Pitcher Jim Bunni traded to Pittsburgh Pirates for pitchers Woodie Fryman, Harold Clem, and Bil Laxton, and infielder Don Money.

1970 — Pitcher Grant Jackson, outfielder-infielder Jim Hutto, and outfielder Sam Parrilla traded to Baltimore Orioles for outfielder Roger Freed.

## December 17

1893 — Bert Yeabsley — B 1919 PH G-3

1918 — Dale Jones — B 1941 P G-2

1939 — Third baseman Pinky Whitney released, ending his major league career.

## December 18

1897 — Lance Richbourg — B 1921 2B G-10

1902 — Joe Buskey — B 1926 SS G-5

1906 — Dick Coffman — B 1945 P G-14

1941 — Coaker Triplett — B 1943-45 OF G-309

1898 — Lou Koupal — B 1929-30 P G-28

1935 — Tony Taylor — B 1960-71, 74-75 2B-3B G-1698

1957 — Catcher Andy Seminick released and signed as coach.

1973 — Second baseman Tony Taylor signed after release by Detroit Tigers.

## December 20

1853 — Jack Manning — B 1883-85 OF G-309

1878 — Bob Hall — B 1904 IF G-46

1894 — Butch Henline — B 1921-26 C G-576

1904 — Spud Davis — B 1928-33, 38-39 C G-814

1904 — Pitcher Chick Fraser and third baseman Harry Wolverton traded to Boston Braves for pitcher Togie Pittinger.

Infielder Del Howard traded to Pittsburgh Pirates for first baseman Kitty Bransfield, infielder Otto Krueger, and outfielder Harry McCormick.

1937 — Pitcher Al Smith purchased from St. Louis Cardinals.

1949 — Oscar Gamble — B 1970-72 OF G-254

1976 — Catcher Johnny Oates and pitcher Quency Hill traded to Los Angeles Dodgers for second baseman Ted Sizemore.

## December 21

1887 — Cy Williams — B 1918-30 OF G-1463

1905 — Fred Koster — B 1931 OF G-76

1913 — Heinie Heltzel — B 1944 SS G-11

1925 — Kent Peterson — B 1952-53 P G-18

## December 22

1893 — Jesse Winters — B 1921-23 P G-73

1908 — Ed Fallenstein — B 1931 P G-24

1938 — Tony Curry — B 1960-61 OF G-110

## December 22 (continued)

1944 — Steve Carlton — B 1972-78 P G-262

1953 — Tommy Underwood — B 1974-77 P G-90

1955 — Lonnie Smith — B 1978 OF G-17


## December 23

1869 — Mike Grady — B 1894-97 C-IF G-182

1899 — Tommy Thomas — B 1935 P G-4

1958 — Pitchers Jim Golden and Gene Snyder and outfielder Rip Repulski traded to Los Angeles Dodgers for second basemen Sparky Anderson.


## December 24

1880 — John Breckenridge — B 1904 P G-7

1912 — Dave Coble — B 1939 C G-15


## December 25

1866 — George Haddock — B 1894 P G-10

1892 — Walter Holke — B 1923-25 1B G-334

1904 — Lloyd Brown — B 1940 P G-18

1908 — Ben Chapman — B 1945-48 OF-P-3B-MGR G-25

    Alta Cohen — B 1933 OF G-19

1938 — Jack Hamilton — B 1962-63 P G-60


## December 26

1892 — Lee King — B 1921-22 OF G-83

1899 — Art Gardiner — B 1923 P G-1

1913 — Al Milnar — B 1946 P G-1

1917 — Outfielder Dode Paskert traded to Chicago Cubs for outfielder Cy Williams.

1927 — Stu Miller — B 1956 P G-29

    Danny Schell — B 1954-55 OF G-94

## December 27

1916 — Charlie Brewster — P 1943 SS G-49

1942 — Byron Browne — B 1970-72 OF G-183

## December 28

1887 — Hughie Miller — B 1911 PR G-1

1899 — Bill Kelly — B 1B G-23

1924 — Fred Daniels — B 1945 2B G-76

## December 29

1908 — Phillies first baseman Kitty Bransfield marries Lulu Hoy at Worcester, Mass.

## December 30

1906 — Ray Prim — B 1935 P G-29

1925 — Pitcher Jimmy Ring traded to New York Giants for pitchers Jack Bentley and Wayland Dean.

1931 — Frank Torre — B 1962-63 1B G-200

1943 — Infielder Babe Dahlgren traded to Pittsburgh Pirates for catcher Babe Phelps.

## December 31

1880 — Fred Beebe — B 1911 P G-12

1884 — Bobby Byrne — B 1913-17 3B-2B G-311

1900 — Syl Johnson — B 1934-40 P G-211

1918 — Al Lakeman — B 1947-48 C-1B-P G-87

1931 — Don Erickson — B 1958 P G-9

1947 — Manny Muniz — B 1971 P G-5

# Players With Incomplete Birth Data

| | | | | |
|---|---|---|---|---|
| Hezekiah Allen | No Date | 1884 | C | G-1 |
| Ernie Beam | 1867 | 1895 | P | G-10 |
| Charlie Brady | No Date | 1905 | P | G-2 |
| Willard Brown | 1866 | 1891 | 1B | G-115 |
| Ed Cassian | No Date | 1891 | P | G-6 |
| Pat Cavanaugh | 1900 | 1919 | 3B | G-1 |
| Harry Cheek | No Date | 1910 | C | G-2 |
| Bill Clay | 1875 | 1902 | OF | G-3 |
| John Coleman | No Date | 1890 | P | G-1 |
| Jerry Connors | No Date | 1892 | OF | G-1 |
| Wilbur Coons | No Date | 1876 | OF-C | G-54 |
| Ernie Courtney | 1879 | 1905-08 | 3B | G-461 |
| Henry Croft | No Date | 1899 | 2B | G-2 |
| Pete Curren | No Date | 1876 | C-OF | G-3 |
| Tony Cusick | 1860 | 1884-87 | C | G-84 |
| Jim Devlin | 1867 | 1887 | P | G-2 |
| Joe Donohue | 1869 | 1891 | OF-SS | G-6 |
| Conny Doyle | 1858 | 1883 | OF | G-16 |
| Mike Dupaugher | No Date | 1884 | C | G-4 |
| Ben Ellis | No Date | 1896 | IF | G-4 |
| Jack Fanning | 1863 | 1894 | P | G-5 |
| Harry Felix | 1877 | 1902 | P-3B | G-16 |
| Bob Ferguson | 1845 | 1883 | 2B-MGR | G-86 |
| Bill Fouser | 1855 | 1876 | IF-OF | G-21 |
| Henry Fox | No Date | 1902 | P | G-1 |
| Fletcher Franks | 1891 | 1914 | PH | G-1 |
| Bill Gallagher | No Date | 1883 | OF-P | G-2 |
| Bill Gallagher | 1875 | 1896 | SS | G-14 |
| Gid Gardner | 1859 | 1888 | IF | G-1 |
| Sam Gillen | 1870 | 1897 | SS | G-75 |
| Charlie Girard | 1886 | 1910 | P | G-7 |
| Buck Gladman | 1864 | 1883 | 3B | G-1 |
| Ed Gormley | No Date | 1891 | P | G-1 |
| Lew Graulich | No Date | 1891 | C-1B | G-7 |
| Emil Gross | 1859 | 1883 | C | G-57 |
| Art Hagan | 1863 | 1883 | P | G-17 |
| Jim Haislip | 1890 | 1913 | P | G-1 |
| Bert Hall | 1888 | 1911 | P | G-7 |
| George Hall | 1849 | 1876 | OF | G-60 |
| Roy Hartranft | No Date | 1913 | P | G-1 |
| John Hiland | No Date | 1885 | 2B | G-3 |
| Charlie Hilsey | 1864 | 1883 | P | G-3 |
| George Hodson | 1876 | 1895 | P | G-4 |
| Buster Hoover | 1863 | 1884 | OF-IF | G-10 |
| Tom Johnson | No Date | 1897 | P | G-5 |
| Alex Jones | 1867 | 1894 | P | G-1 |
| Joe Kappel | 1857 | 1884 | C | G-4 |
| Harry Keener | 1869 | 1896 | P | G-16 |
| Charlie Kelly | No Date | 1883 | 3B | G-2 |
| Kick Kelly | 1859 | 1883 | OF | G-1 |
| Phil Knell | 1865 | 1892 | P | G-11 |
| Joe Knight | No Date | 1884 | P | G-6 |
| Tom Lipp | 1871 | 1897 | P | G-1 |

| | | | |
|---|---|---|---|
| Al Lukens | 1872 | 1894 | P | G-3 |
| Harry Lyons | 1866 | 1887 | OF | G-1 |
| George McAvoy | No Date | 1914 | PH | G-1 |
| John McCloskey | No Date | 1906-07 | P | G-12 |
| Jim McElroy | No DAte | 1884 | P | G-14 |
| Gus McGinnis | 1870 | 1893 | P | G-5 |
| Barney McLaughlin | 1857 | 1887 | 2B | G-50 |
| F. Maher | No Date | 1902 | PH | G-1 |
| Tom Maher | No Date | 1902 | PR | G-1 |
| Fergy Malone | 1842 | 1876 | C | G-22 |
| Levi Meyerle | 1849 | 1876 | 3B | G-55 |
| Bert Meyers | No Date | 1900 | 3B | G-7 |
| Bert Miller | No Date | 1897 | 2B | G-3 |
| Doc Miller | 1883 | 1912-13 | OF | G-136 |
| Harry Morelock | No Date | 1891-92 | SS-3B | G-5 |
| Sparrow Morton | No Date | 1884 | P | G-2 |
| John Muller | No Date | 1876 | C | G-1 |
| Dummy Muprhy | 1890 | 1914 | SS | G-9 |
| Tom Murray | 1866 | 1894 | SS | G-1 |
| Paul, * | No Date | 1876 | C | G-3 |
| Dick Pierre | No Date | 1883 | SS | G-5 |
| Togie Pittinger | 1871 | 1905-07 | P | G-82 |
| Blondie Purcell | No Date | 1883-84 | OF-IF-MGR | G-200 |
| Butch Rementer | No Date | 1904 | C | G-1 |
| Jack Remsen | 1851 | 1884 | OF | G-12 |
| E. W. Ritterson | No Date | 1876 | C | G-16 |
| Bill Salisbury | 1876 | 1902 | P | G-2 |
| Hal Savage | No Date | 1912 | 2B | G-2 |
| John Schultze | No Date | 1891 | P | G-6 |
| Frank Shugart | 1867 | 1897 | SS | G-40 |
| Edgar Smith | 1862 | 1883 | P | G-1 |
| Jake Smith | No Date | 1911 | P | G-2 |
| John Strike | No Date | 1886 | P | G-2 |
| John Thornton | 1870 | 1891-92 | P | G-44 |
| Tuck Turner | 1870 | 1893-96 | OF | G-188 |
| Gene Vadeboncoeur | No Date | 1884 | C | G-4 |
| Ben Van Dyke | 1888 | 1909 | P | G-3 |
| John Walsh | No Date | 1903 | 3B | G-1 |
| Jim Ward | March 1855 | 1876 | C | G-1 |
| Fred Warner | 1855 | 1876, 83 | 3B-OF | G-40 |
| Ed Watkins | No Date | 1902 | OF | G-1 |
| Milt Watson | 1893 | 1918-19 | P | G-31 |
| Harry Welchonce | No Date | 1911 | OF | G-26 |
| C.B. White | No Date | 1883 | SS-3B | G-1 |
| Jesse Whiting | No Date | 1902 | P | G-1 |
| Wilsonholm, * | No Date | 1883 | C-OF | G-3 |
| Bill Wolfe | No Date | 1902 | P | G-1 |
| Joe Yingling | 1864 | 1894 | SS | G-1 |

*First names not available.

# TIDBITS

**VET WINS** — Steve Carlton has the Phillies record for most victories in one season at Veterans Stadium, finishing 17-3 in 1977.

## PHILLIES IN FIRST PLACE

| May 1 | June 1 | July 1 | August 1 | September 1 |
|-------|--------|--------|----------|-------------|
| 1953 | 1913 | 1950 | 1915 | 1950 |
| 1964 | 1964 | 1976 | 1950 | 1964 |
| | 1976 | 1978 | 1964 | 1976 |
| | | | 1976 | 1977 |
| | | | 1978 | 1978 |

## PHILLIES PINCH HOMERS
### (Career, Since 1927)

6 Rick Joseph
5 Cy Williams, Bill Nicholson, Gene Freese
4 Bob Bowman, Rip Repulski, Wally Post, Johnny Callison, Ollie Brown
3 Stan Lopata, Deron Johnson, Tony Taylor, Tommy Hutton, Dave Johnson, Jerry Martin

**BIGGEST INNING** — A twelve-run sixth inning against the Chicago Cubs, game one of the July 21, 1923, doubleheader, is the Phillies biggest inning ever.

**100 WINS** — When the Phillies won 101 games in 1976 and 1977, they became the first National League Eastern Division champion to win over 100 in two consecutive years.

**THREE STRAIGHT** — Division championships of 1976-77-78 enabled Phillies to tie the National League record of consecutive division titles set by the Pittsburgh Pirates of 1970-71-72.

**MOST RUNS** — The most runs ever scored by the Phillies in one game was twenty-three, beating Pittsburgh, 23-8, July 13, 1900, and losing to the Chicago Cubs, 26-23, August 25, 1922.

**ONE YEAR PINCH** — Gene Freese holds the Phillies single season record for most homers by a pinch hitter with five in 1959.

**GRAND SLAMS** — Vince DiMaggio holds the Phillies record for most grand slams in one season, belting four in 1945.

**L-O-N-G ONE** — The Phillies longest game was a 2-1 loss to the Cubs in Chicago, July 17, 1918, a twenty-one-inning contest.

**WHIFFS** — Right-hander Art Mahaffey holds the Phillies record for most strikeouts in a nine-inning game when he fanned seventeen Chicago Cubs, April 23, 1961.

**DRAFTED FIRST** — Pitcher Hugh Mulcahy of the Phillies was the first player in the major leagues to be drafted in World War II.

**CHANGE THE NAME** — Owner Horace Fogel in 1910 started a personal campaign with the press to change the name of the Phillies. But, his suggestion of "Live Wires" went for naught with the press.

**LONELY** — In the long history of the Phillies, they've had just one player in their Alumni Club under letter "Q" — right-hand Tommy Qualters, who pitched in 1953 and again in 1957-58.

**BEST EVER** — The Phillies best one-season record against a National League team came in the pennant-winning 1950 season when they took eighteen of twenty-two from Cincinnati.

# TIDBITS
## (continued)

**VET RECORD** — Right-handed sluggers Deron Johnson, Mike Schmidt, and Greg Luzinski share the Veteran's Stadium record for most home runs by a Phillies player in one season. The record is twenty-two with Johnson setting it in 1971, Schmidt tying it in 1975, and Luzinski in 1977.

**THE ENEMY** — The most home runs hit by a visiting player in one season at Veterans Stadium is seven by Montreal's Gary Carter in 1978. The old mark was five by Pittsburgh's Bob Robertson in 1971 and Montreal's Hal Breeden in 1973.

**HOME RUN EVERYWHERE** — The last Phillies player to hit a home run in every National League park in one season was outfielder Wally Post, who performed the feat in 1959.

**OH BROTHER** — The 1930 Phillies hitters set a major league record for one season by collecting 1,783 hits, but their pitchers also set a big league mark by allowing the most runs ever 1,199.

**FEAST OR FAMINE** — Emil Verban of the Phillies holds the National League record for the fewest strikeouts in 150 or more games with eight in 1947. But, Pancho Herrera of the Phils also holds the league mark for most strikeouts for 150-game or more games, 136 in 1960.

**ON BASE RECORD** — Outfielder Lefty O'Doul of the Phillies set a National League record for most times reached base in a season when he got on base 334 times in 1929 on 254 hits (also an NL record), seventy-six walks and four hit-by-pitchers.

**TOP MONTHS** — The most wins the Phillies have achieved in one month is twenty-two, first set in September of 1916 and then matched in July of 1950, July of 1952, May of 1976, and August of 1977.

**TIRED OF SITTING?** — The Phillies hold the National league record for most doubleheaders in one season. The 1943 club played fourty-three, winning eleven, losing fourteen and splitting eighteen.

**GO GET 'EM** — Two-time batting champion Richie Ashburn was also quite a centerfielder. He holds the major league record for most years, 400 or more putouts, with nine.

**HIGH AND LOW** — The Phillies have the dubious distinction of having the lowest team Earned Run Average in National League history, 2.18 in 1915, and also the highest, 6.70 in 1930.

**ROOKIE RECORD** — Right-hander Grover Cleveland Alexander won twenty-eight games as a rookie in 1911, a modern major league record.

**TWO GREAT ONES** — Grover Cleveland Alexander who pitched for the Phillies from 1911-17 and again in 1930 shares the major league record for most games won (373) in a career for a right-hander with Christy Mathewson of the Giants.

**BEST LEFTIES** — Steve Carlton of the Phillies and Sandy Koufax of the Dodgers share the modern National League record for most wins by a left-hander in one season: twenty-seven. Koufax did it in 1966 and Carlton tied the mark six years later.

**FOR OPENERS** — Hall of Famer Robin Roberts holds the National League record for most times pitched the opening game of the season, thirteen. Twelve of those came in his brilliant Phillies career with the other one occurring with the Houston Astros in 1966.

# NICKNAMES

Nicknames have always been a part of baseball lore, and those who have played for the Phillies have had their share of the usual and unusual in monickers. Players and managers are included in this list.

**ACE**
Hal Elliott
Jimmie Wilson

**APPLES**
Andy Lapihuska

**AUGIE**
Gene Freese

**BABE**
Ellsworth Dahlgren
Del Wilber

**BABY**
Ray Semproch

**BAKE**
Arnold McBride

**BAMA**
Carvel Rowell

**BARNEY**
Augustaf Friberg
George Schultz
Burt Shotton
Byron Slaughter

**BEANS**
Harry Keener

**BEAR**
Jim Owens

**THE BEAST**
Jimmie Foxx

**BEAUTY**
Dave Bancroft

**BEVO**
DeWitt LeBourveau

**BITSY**
Elisha Mott

**BLACKIE**
Alvin Dark
Gus Mancuso

**BLIX**
Sylvester Donnelly

**BLONDIE**
William Purcell

**BLONDY**
John Ryan

**BO**
Robert Belinsky

**BOOM-BOOM**
Walter Beck

**BOOTS**
Al Hollingsworth

**BREWERY JACK**
Jack Taylor

**BUBBA**
Emory Church

**BUBBER**
Clarence Jonnard

**BUCK**
John Gladman
Grant Jackson
Baxter Jordan
Frank McCormick
William Washer

**BUCKEYE**
Don Grate

**BUCKSHOT**
Tommy Brown

**BUCKY**
Darrell Brandon
Stanley Harris
John Stanley
William Walters

**BUD**
Charlie Bicknell
John Clancy
Daniel Hafey
Derrel Harrelson
Harry Weiser

**BUDDY**
Robert Blattner

**BULL**
Greg Luzinski
Albert Schroll

**BUSTER**
Elvin Adams
Charles Brown
William Hoover

**BUTCH**
Walter Henline
Willis Rementer
Ed Sanicki

**BUTTERMILK TOMMY**
Thomas Dowd

**BUZ**
Albert Phillips

**BUZZ**
Russell Arlett

**CACTUS**
Clifford Cravath

**CALIFORNIA**
Willard Brown

**CANDY**
Johnny Callison

**CANNONBALL**
Ledell Titcomb

**CAP**
John Clark

**CASEY**
Charles Stengel

**CHARMER, THE**
George Zettlein

**CHESTY**
Chet Covington

**CHICK**
Charles Fraser
Charles Fullis
Walter Keating

**CHICKEN**
Nelson Hawks

**CHICO**
Humberto Fernandez

**CHIEF**
Charles Bender
Johnny Blatnik
Ernie Koy
Euel Moore
Charles Zimmer

**CHILE**
Jose Gomez

**CHOO CHOO**
Clarence Coleman

**CHUCK**
Charles Essegian
Charles Harmon
Charles Hiller
Charles Klein

**COD**
Al Myers

**COLBY JACK**
Jack Coombs

**COLUMBIA GEORGE**
George Smith

**COOKIE**
Octavio Rojas

121

# NICKNAMES

COONSKIN
  Curt Davis
COTTON
  Hughie Miller
  James Tierney
COWBOY
  Ray Harrell
COZY
  Patrick Dolan
CRASH
  Dick Allen
CROSSFIRE
  Earl Moore
CUPID
  Clarence Childs
CURVELESS
WONDER, THE
  Al Orth
CY
  Cecilio Acosta
  Darrell Blanton
  Roy Marshall
  William Moore
  Fred Williams
CYCLONE
  Joseph Miller

DANDY
  George Wood
DAPPER DAN
  Dan Howley
DEACON
  John Donahue
  James McGuire
  Edward Van Buren
DEE
  D. C. Miller
  Duane Pillette
DIRTY JACK
  John Doyle
DIXIE
  Frank Davis
  Douglas Parker
DOC
  Albert Bushong
  Howard Edwards
  Harry Imlay
  Edward Marshall
  Marty Martell
  Roy Miller
  James Prothro
  Fred Wallace
  Guy White

DOCTOR
STRANGEGLOVE
  Dick Stuart
DODE
  Bill Brinker
  George Paskert
DONKEY
  Frank Thomas
DOTS
  John Miller
DOUBLE X
  Jimmie Foxx
DOWNTOWN
  Ollie Brown
DREAMY
  Frank Scanlan
DUKE
  Henry Sedgwick
DUMMY
  Reuben Stephenson
DUSTY
  Allen Cooke
DUT
  George Chalmers
DUTCH
  Jim Bolger
  Lloyd Dietz
  Otto Knabe
  Emil Leonard
  John Rudolph
  Charles Schesler
  Frank Ulrich
  Emil Verban
DYNAMO
  Dino Chiozza

EARACHE
  Benny Meyer
EARL OF SNOHOMISH,
THE
  Earl Torgeson
EE-YAH
  Hughie Jennings
ELI
  Al Hodkey
EPPA JEPTHA
  Eppa Rixey
EPPIE
  Eddie Miller
EVANGELIST, THE
  Billy Sunday

FAT FREDDIE
  Fred Fitzsimmons

FIDDLER
  Frank Corridon
FIDGETY PHIL
  Phil Collins
FIREBALL
  Fred Wenz
FLIP
  Frank Lafferty
FRITZ
  Frank Henrich
  Wilfred Knothe
  Fred Koster
FROSTY BILL
  Bill Duggleby

GABBY
  Glen Stewart
GAVVY
  Clifford Cravath
GENTLEMAN GEORGE
  George Haddock
GENTLEMAN JIM
  Jim Lonborg
GERMANY
  Herman Long
  Joe Schultz
GIANT KILLER, THE
  Harry Covelski
GIBBY
  Gilbert Brack
GID
  Franklin Gardner
GILLY
  Clarence Huber
GIMPY
  Lloyd Brown
GINK
  Harvey Hendrick
GOLDIE
  Joseph Rapp
GOOD KID
  George Susce
GOOSE
  John Easton
GREASY
  Earle Neale
GREEK
  Bobby Del Greco
GRUMP
  Hal Irelan
GUS
  Constantine Niarhos
GYP
  Manny Salvo

# NICKNAMES

HACK
  Lewis Wilson
HACKER
  Richie Hebner
HAIRBREADTH HARRY
  Jack Hamilton
HAM
  Herman Iburg
  Herman Schulte
HANDY ANDY
  Andy High
HANK
  Henry Borowy
  Henry Mason
  William Ritter
HANS
  John Lobert
HAP
  Earl Collard
HAPPY
  Joseph Finneran
  Al Milnar
  Jack Townsend
HARVARD EDDIE
  Eddie Grant
HAT, THE
  Harry Walker
HAWK
  Ken Silvestri
HEINIE
  William Heltzel
  Emmett Mueller
  John Sand
HICK
  Forrest Cady
HICKS
  Lew Moren
HIGHPOCKETS
  Dick Koecher
HOD
  Horace Ford
HODGE
  Joe Berry
HOME RUN
  Charlie Johnson
HONDO
  Stan Hollmig
HONEST JACK
  John Boyle
HOOKS
  Ken Johnson
HORSE
  Harry Anderson

HUCK
  Walter Betts
  Harry Wallace
HUSKY
  Ed Walczak

IGOR
  Jim Command
IRISH
  Emil Meusel
IRON HANDS
  Charles Hiller
IRON MAN
  Wiley Piatt
ITZIE
  Eddie Feinberg

JAY
  John Johnstone
JEEP
  Lee Handley
  Roy Hughes
JESSE
  Jeff James
  Paul Masterson
  Leon Pettit
  Ray Pierce
  Al Porto
  Phil Saylor
  Marshall Scott
JINX
  Jennings Poindexter
JOCKO
  John Fields
  John Thompson
JUG
  Joe Kracher
JUMBO
  Jim Elliott

KAISER
  Irvin Wilhelm
KEWPIE
  Dick Barrett
KICK
  John Kelly
KID
  Wilfred Carsey
  Norman Elberfeld
  William Gleason
  Willie McGill
  George Stutz
KIDDO
  George Davis

KILO
  Frank Watt
KING
  Clarence Lehr
KITTEN
  Harvey Haddix
KITTY
  William Bransfield
  Jim Kaat
KLONDIKE
  William Douglas
  Harry Kane

LARRY
  Napoleon Lajoie
LEFTY
  Roman Bertrand
  Bobby Burke
  Charlie Butler
  Steve Carlton
  Al Gerheauser
  Wilbur Goode
  Howie Gorman
  Lee Grissom
  Frank Hoerst
  Frank O'Doul
  Ben Shields
  Clyde Smoll
  Edward Taber
  Harry Wallace
  Phil Weinert
LIL
  Ulysses Stone
LITTLE PHIL
  Phil Geier
LITTLE POISON
  Lloyd Waner
LONG BOB
  George Ewing
LONG LEVI
  Levi Meyerle
LOSING PITCHER
  Hugh Mulcahy
LUCKY
  Jack Lohrke
LUKE
  Frank Lucchesi

MAC
  Guerrant Scarce
MAD MONK
  Russ Meyer
MAD RUSSIAN, THE
  Lou Novikoff

123

# NICKNAMES

MICKEY
  William Devine
  Michael Doolan
  Cornelius Finn
  Thompson Livingston
  Bob Micelotta
  Frank O'Brien
  Phil Weintraub
MIDGET
  Don Ferrarese
MIKE
  Justin Fitzgerald
  Mel Mazzera
MONEY BAGS
  Tom Qualters
MONK
  Walt Dubiel
  John Sherlock
MOON
  Ford Mullen
MOOSE
  Jack Farrell
  Al Lakeman
  Harry McCormick
MULE
  John Watson
NAP
  John Shea
NIBBLER
  Jim Hearn
NIG
  Jay Clarke
NIPPY
  Vernal Jones
NIXEY
  James Callahan
NUBS
  Dale Jones
OLD PROFESSOR, THE
  Casey Stengel
ONLY, THE
  Edward Nolan
OOM PAUL
  Otto Krueger
OZARK IKE
  Danny Ozark
PADDY
  Adair Mayes
PALM TREES
  Ron Stone
PANCHO
  Francisco Herrera
PATSY
  Martin McGaffigan

PEACHES
  George Graham
PEANUTS
  Harry Lowrey
PECK
  Walt Lerian
PEP
  Otto Deininger
PEPITO
  Cesar Tovar
PETE
  Grover Alexander
  Warren Rambo
  Pedro Ramos
PETIE
  Charles Behan
PHENOMENAL
  John Smith
PICKLES
  William Dillhoefer
PIGGY
  Frank Ward
PINKY
  Merrill May
  Arthur Whitney
PIT
  John Quinn
POCO
  Doug Taitt
POP
  Ray Prim
  Walter Williams
POPE
  Paul Owens
POSSUM
  George Whitted
PRETZELS
  John Pezzullo
PRINCE
  Henry Oana
PRINCETON CHARLIE
  Charles Reilly
PUDDIN' HEAD
  Willie Jones
PUG
  Tony Rensa
PUTSY
  Ralph Caballero
QUIET JACK
  Joe Knight

RABBIT
  Tommy Glaviano
  Jimmy Slagle

RAGS
  James Faircloth
RAWHIDE
  Jim Tabor
RAZZLE DAZZLE
  Con Murphy
RED
  Leon Ames
  Paul Busby
  Howie Camnitz
  Cecil Causey
  Francis Donahue
  Charles Dooin
  John Kleinow
  Clarence Munson
  Albert Nelson
  Thomas Owens
  Don Padgett
REINDEER BILL
  Bill Killefer
RIP
  Eldon Repulski
ROLLIE
  Ralston Hemsley
ROUND MAN, THE
  Ron Northey
ROWDY RICHARD
  Dick Bartell
RUBE
  Raymond Bressler
  Roy Marshall
RUNT
  Jimmy Walsh
RUSTY
  Waldo Yarnall

SAGE
  Roy Hughes
SANDOW
  Sam Mertes
SARGE
  Bob Kuzava
SCHOOLBOY
  Alta Cohen
  Lynwood Rowe
SCRAPPY
  Jesse Purnell
SHAD
  John Barry
  Flint Rhem
SHADOW
  Harry Pyle
SHE
  Charles Donahue

# NICKNAMES

SHERIFF
Fred Blake
Hal Lee
John Singleton
SHORTY
Glenn Crawford
SHOTGUN
John Peters
SHUCKS
Hub Pruett
SID
Bob Sadowski
SILENT CAL
Ray Benge
SILENT JOHN
John Titus
SIR RICHARD
Duff Cooley
SIR TIMOTHY
Tim Keefe
SKEETER
Lamar Newsome
SKINNY
Oran O'Neal
SKIP
Bill Crouch
Gene Mauch
SLATS
Lena Blackburne
SLEEPY
Bill Burns
SLEUTH
Tom Fleming
SLIDING BILLY
William Hamilton
SMILING AL
Al Maul
SMOKY
Forrest Burgess
SNIPE
Roy Hansen
SNITZ
Earl Browne
SNOOKER
Morrie Arnovich

SPARKY
George Anderson
SPARROW
William Morton
SPECS
Lee Meadows
John Podgajny

SPUD
Virgil Davis
SPUNK
Alex Pitko
SQUACK
Ches Crist
SQUIRREL
Roy Sievers
STEEPLE
Howie Schultz
STONE FINGERS
Dick Stuart
STRAWBERRY BILL
William Bernhard
STRETCH
Howie Schultz
STUD
George Myatt
STUFFY
John McInnis
STUMPY
Al Verdel
STYLE
Chris Short
SUDS
Gary Sutherland
SUGAR
Les Sweetland
SUNNY JACK
John Suthoff
SUPERSUB
Phil Linz
SWATS
Carl Sawatski
SWEDE
Elmer Burkhart
Andy Hansen
SWISH
Bill Nicholson

TARZAN
Walter Stephenson
T-BONE
Taylor Phillips
Jesse Winters
TEACH
Earl Caldwell
TED
Henry Baldwin
Thaddeus Cieslak
TEXAS JACK
John Kraus
THREE STAR
George Hennessey

TIGER
Don Hoak
TIOGA
George Burns
TITO
John Francona
TOGIE
Charles Pittinger
TOOTS
Wallace Shultz
TUBBY
Edward Spencer
TUCK
George Stainback
George Turner
TUCKER
Stan Jok
TUG
Frank McGraw
TULLY
Frank Sparks
TURK
Dick Farrell
TURKEY
Cecil Tyson
TY
Clarence Pickup

UNION MAN
Walter Holke

WAGON TONGUE
Bill Keister
WEEPING WILLIE
Claude Willoughby
WHAT'S THE USE
Pearce Chiles
WHITEY
Richie Ashburn
Charles Glazner
Hal Wiltse
WILD BILL
William Donovan
William Hallahan
WILD ELK
Ed Heusser
WILDFIRE
Frank Schulte
WILLIE
Guillermo Montanez
WOODY
Jim Woods

YOUNGIE
John Johnson

# VETERANS STADIUM

Montreal's Boots Day grounds back to pitcher Jim Bunning who tosses to first baseman Deron Johnson for an out and Veterans Stadium is officially opened.

The date was April 10, 1972, and for many Phillies fans, the dream of a new stadium finally became a reality. For years, there was talk of a new stadium to replace ancient Connie Mack Stadium.

But, there were squabbles over the site, then design and costs, but finally Philadelphia had the largest and most attractive multi-purpose sports stadium in the country.

The stadium was bult on seventy-four acres in south Philadelphia, at the corner of Broad and Pattison Streets. Across the street is The Spectrum, home of the Philadelphia Flyers of the National Hockey League and the Philadelphia 76ers of the National Basketball Association. To the rear of the Spectrum, is J. F. Kennedy Stadium. Thus, Philadelphia boasted of the nation's finest sports complex.

Veterans Stadium, named in honor of the men who gave their lives for their country, has a seating capacity of over 58,000 for baseball, largest in the National League. Over 65,000 can be seated for football.

While the stadium looks circular, it really isn't. By architectual terms, it really is an octorad-shaped sports palace. "Octo" is Latin for eight, "Rad" is short for radius. There are eight points of radius on the structure, which is 840 feet in diameter and 160 feet high.

The final cost ranged in the $52 million area.

Baseball is a game of numbers but check out some of the numbers on the stadium: 87,000 cubic yards of concrete were used; 2,720,000 square feet of form work; 7,600 tons of reinforcing steel; 1,440 tons of structural steel and 146,000 square feet of AstroTurf playing surface.

Playing dimensions for baseball are 330 feet to left and right and 408 to dead center.

After sixty-one years of baseball in Shibe Park/Connie Mack Stadium, Philadelphia baseball fans began pouring into Veterans Stadium by the millions as the Phillies became one of the National League's outstanding ball clubs.

# SHIBE PARK/CONNIE MACK STADIUM

Ground-breaking ceremonies for Shibe Park, the home of the Philadelphia Athletics of the American League, took place on April 13, 1908.

One day short of a full year (April 12, 1909), the A's beat Boston, 8-1, before 30,162 in the park's first game, with Eddie Plank getting the victory.

The park was named Shibe Park for Benjamin Shibe, owner of the Athletics. The cost was one-half million dollars. It was located at 21st Street and Lehigh Avenue.

The architecture of the pavilion facade was French Renaissance. The original structure had a seating capacity of 20,000. The outer edges of the outfield were banked to permit 10,000 standees to view the game from behind rope barriers. The original playing dimensions were 378 feet to left, 515 to center, and 340 to right.

The capacity was increased in 1925 when an upper deck was added to the bleacher sections — first base to right field, third base to left, and left to center.

Two seasons later, Baker Bowl, where the Phillies played their games, had a mini-disaster and the Phils moved to Shibe Park for a few games while the repairs could be made to their own ball park. Wooden bleachers gave way and had to be rebuilt.

## SHIBE PARK (continued)

In 1934, Shibe Park's right field fence was raised from twelve feet to fifty feet.

The Phillies moved permanently to Shibe Park on July 4, 1938, after fifty-one years at Baker Bowl, splitting a doubleheader with Boston.

Prior to the 1953 baseball season, Shibe Park became Connie Mack Stadium in honor of the Athletics' great manager-owner. Mack managed the A's for fifty years, a record which will probably never be broken for managers.

On November 4, 1954, the A's were sold and moved to Kansas City. The Phillies, who had been leasing the stadium from the A's, purchased it from the A.L. club.

As the grand old structure entered its final season of baseball in 1970, the capacity was 33,608 and the playing dimensions were 334 feet to left, 447 to center, and 329 to right.

Connie Mack Stadium, for many years, was one of baseball's best parks. Now it's just a memory to thousands of Philadelphia baseball fans.

## BAKER BOWL

Baker Bowl, known as Philadelpha National League Park when it was opened on April 30, 1887, was called the finest in the world when it was built. By the time it was abandoned by the Phillies in mid-season, 1938, it was the most outmoded park in baseball. It was also a hitter's paradise because of the short right field. It was 335 feet to left field, 408 feet to center and only 272 to right, where a 30-foot high fence intercepted many a line drive. Home plate was later moved to make it 341 feet to left and 280 to right. Capacity was a mere 18,800, with 2,000 seats in the left and center field bleachers. In August, 1894, the main stands were destroyed by fire; in 1896, the park was renovated, and in both 1903 and 1927 a portion of the stands collapsed.

## VETERANS STADIUM "FIRSTS"

Game: April 10, 1971, Phillies 4, Montreal Expos 1, before 55,352 fans. Unless otherwise indicated all "firsts" took place during this game.
Winning Pitcher: Jim Bunning
Losing Pitcher: Bill Stoneman
Batter: Boots Day, Expos
Pitch Thrown: Day grounds out, Bunning to Deron Johnson
Hit: Larry Bowa, Phillies; single
Run: Ron Hunt, Expos
Double: Hunt
Triple: Bowa
Home Run: Don Money, Phillies, sixth inning
RBI: Bob Bailey, Expos
Walk: Hunt by Bunning
Strikeout: Stoneman by Bunning
Stolen Base: Hunt
Hit By Pitch: Hunt
Save: Joe Hoerner, Phillies
Assist: Bunning
Putout: D. Johnson
Error: Mack Jones, Expos
Two-Home Runs Game: Earl Williams, Atlanta Braves, April 17, 1971
Three-Home Runs Game: Deron Johnson, Phillies, July 10, 1971

One-Hitter: Steve Renko, Montreal Expos, July 9, 1971
No-Hitter: None yet
Shutout: Ferguson Jenkins, Chicago Cubs, 3-0, May 10, 1971
Ejection: Phillies Manager Frank Lucchesi by Harry Wendelstedt, April 14, 1971
Triple Play: None yet
Inside Park Home Run: Don Hahn, New York Mets, September 5, 1971
Grand Slam Home Run: Roger Freed, Phillies, April 11, 1971 (Off Expos' Howie Reed)
Pinch Hit Home Run: Roberto Clemente, Pittsburgh Pirates, June 27, 1971, second game

## CONNIE MACK STADIUM "LASTS"

Hit — Gamble, Phillies
Run — McCarver, Phillies
Stolen base — McCarver, Phillies
RBI — Gamble, Phillies
Walk — Gamble, Phillies
Extra — base hit — Wine, Expos (double)
Putout — Fairly, Expos
Assist — Reed, Expos
Strikeout (pitcher) — Reed, Expos
Strikeout (batter) — Selma, Phillies
Win — Selma, Phillies
Loss — Reed, Expos
Home run — Bateman, Expos
Walk (pitcher) — Marshall, Expos

## PHILLIES PRESIDENTS/MANAGERS

### Presidents (Fourteen)

| | |
|---|---|
| 1876 | Thomas J. Smith |
| 1883-1902 | Alfred J. Reach |
| 1903-04 | James Potter |
| 1905-08 | William J. Shettsline |
| 1909 | Israel W. Durham |
| 1909-12 | Horace S. Fogel |
| 1912 | Alfred D. Wiler |
| 1913 | William H. Locke |
| 1913-30 | William F. Baker |
| 1931-32 | L. Charles Ruch |
| 1932-42 | Gerald P. Nugent |
| 1943 | William D. Cox |
| 1943-72 | R. R. M. Carpenter, Jr. |
| 1972-78 | R. R. M. Carpenter, 3rd |

## PHILLIES MANAGERS    (Forty-one)
### (With Games Won And Lost)

| | |
|---|---|
| 1876 | Al Wright (14-45) |
| 1883 | Bob Ferguson (4-13) |
| 1883 | Blondie Purcell (13-68) |

## PHILLIES MANAGERS (continued)

| | |
|---|---|
| 1884-93 | Harry Wright (678-589) |
| 1894-95 | Arthur Irwin (149-110) |
| 1896 | Billy Nash (62-68) |
| 1897-98 | George Stallings (74-104) |
| 1898-1902 | Bill Shettsline (367-303) |
| 1903 | Chief Zimmer (49-86) |
| 1904-06 | Hugh Duffy (206-251) |
| 1907-09 | Billy Murray (240-214) |
| 1910-14 | Red Dooin (392-370) |
| 1915-18 | Pat Moran (323-257) |
| 1919 | Jack Coombs (18-44) |
| 1919-20 | Gavvy Cravath (92-137) |
| 1921 | Bill Donovan (31-71) |
| 1921-22 | Kaiser Wilhelm (77-128) |
| 1923-26 | Art Fletcher (231-378) |
| 1927 | Stuffy McInnis (51-103) |
| 1928-33 | Burt Shotton (370-549) |
| 1934-38 | Jimmie Wilson (280-477) |
| 1938 | Hans Lobert (0-2) |
| 1939-41 | Doc Prothro (138-320) |
| 1942 | Hans Lobert (42-109) |
| 1943 | Bucky Harris (40-53) |
| 1943-45 | Freddie Fitzsimmons (102-179) |
| 1945-48 | Ben Chapman (197-277) |
| 1948 | Dusty Cooke (6-5) |
| 1948-52 | Eddie Sawyer (296-293) |
| 1952-54 | Steve O'Neill (182-140) |
| 1954 | Terry Moore (35-42) |
| 1955-58 | Mayo Smith (264-281) |
| 1958-60 | Eddie Sawyer (94-132) |
| 1960 | Andy Cohen (1-0) |
| 1960-68 | Gene Mauch (645-684) |
| 1968 | George Myatt (2-0) |
| 1968-69 | Bob Skinner (92-123) |
| 1969 | George Myatt (19-35) |
| 1970-72 | Frank Lucchesi (166-233) |
| 1972 | Paul Owens (33-47) |
| 1973 | Danny Ozark (529-443) |

## SEASONS IN WHICH PHILLIES WON OR LOST NINETY OR MORE GAMES

### Years Winning Ninety Or More Games

| Year | Won | Lost | Pct. | Finish |
|---|---|---|---|---|
| 1899 | 94 | 58 | .618 | 3 |
| 1915 | 90 | 62 | .592 | 1 |
| 1916 | 91 | 62 | .595 | 2 |
| 1950 | 91 | 63 | .591 | 1 |
| 1964 | 92 | 70 | .568 | t-2 |
| 1976 | 101 | 61 | .623 | 1-x |
| 1977 | 101 | 61 | .623 | 1-x |
| 1978 | 90 | 72 | .556 | 1-x |

## Years Losing Ninety Or More Games

| Year | Won | Lost | Pct. | Finish |
|------|-----|------|------|--------|
| 1904 | 52 | 100 | .342 | 8 |
| 1919 | 47 | 90 | .343 | 8 |
| 1920 | 62 | 91 | .405 | 8 |
| 1921 | 51 | 103 | .331 | 8 |
| 1922 | 57 | 96 | .373 | 7 |
| 1923 | 50 | 104 | .325 | 8 |
| 1924 | 55 | 96 | .364 | 7 |
| 1926 | 58 | 93 | .384 | 8 |
| 1927 | 51 | 103 | .331 | 8 |
| 1928 | 43 | 109 | .283 | 8 |
| 1930 | 52 | 102 | .338 | 8 |
| 1933 | 60 | 92 | .395 | 7 |
| 1934 | 56 | 93 | .376 | 7 |
| 1936 | 54 | 100 | .351 | 8 |
| 1937 | 61 | 92 | .399 | 7 |
| 1939 | 45 | 106 | .298 | 8 |
| 1940 | 50 | 103 | .327 | 8 |
| 1941 | 43 | 111 | .279 | 8 |
| 1942 | 42 | 109 | .278 | 8 |
| 1943 | 64 | 90 | .416 | 7 |
| 1944 | 61 | 92 | .399 | 8 |
| 1945 | 46 | 108 | .299 | 8 |
| 1947 | 62 | 92 | .403 | t-7 |
| 1948 | 45 | 105 | .300 | 8 |
| 1959 | 64 | 90 | .416 | 8 |
| 1960 | 58 | 94 | .383 | 8 |
| 1961 | 47 | 107 | .305 | 8 |
| 1969 | 63 | 99 | .389 | 5-x |
| 1971 | 67 | 95 | .414 | 6-x |
| 1972 | 59 | 97 | .378 | 6-x |
| 1973 | 71 | 91 | .438 | 6-x |

t — tied for position.
x — in Eastern Division.

Note: National League had eight teams, except in 1892 through 1899 (when it had 12), 1962 through 1968 (when it had ten), and 1969 through 1978 (when it had two six-team divisions).

## PHILLIES COACHES (1934-78)

Benny Bengough (1946-59)
Carroll Beringer (1973-78)
Dick Carter (1959-60)
Andy Cohen (1960)
Earle Combs (1954)
Dusty Cooke (1948-52)
Billy DeMars (1968-78)
George Earnshaw (1949-50)

## PHILLIES COACHES (continued)

Doc Edwards (1970-72)
Tom Ferrick (1959)
Don Hoak (1967)
Syl Johnson (1941)
Bubber Jonnard (1935)
Bill Killefer (1942)
Chuck Klein (1942-45)
Bob Lemon (1961)
Hans Lobert (1934-41)
Peanuts Lowrey (1960-66)
Eddie Mayo (1952-54)
Maje McDonnell (1954-57)
Cal McLish (1965-66)
Wally Moses (1955-58)
George Myatt (1964-72)
Bob Oldis (1965-66)
Cy Perkins (1946-54)
Bill Posedel (1958)
Johnny Riddle (1959)
Ray Rippelmeyer (1970-78)
Andy Seminick (1957-58, 1967-69)
Merv Shea (1944-45)
Larry Shepard (1967)
Ken Silvestri (1959-60)
Dick Spalding (1934-36)
Tony Taylor (1977-78)
Al Vincent (1961-63)
Earl Whitehill (1943)
Al Widmar (1962-64, 1968-69)
Bobby Wine (1973-78)
Whit Wyatt (1955-57)

# ARMED FORCES LIST

Men who played with the Phillies and whose careers were interrupted by duty in the Armed Forces during World War I and World War II.

## WORLD WAR I

Gerald Claycomb
Pickles Dillhoefer
Dixie Davis
Patsy McGaffigan

Eppa Rixey
Ben Tincup
Possum Whitted
Frank Woodward

## WORLD WAR II

Bill Burich
Benny Culp
Fred Daniels
Del Ennis
George Eyrich
Ed Freed
Lee Grissom
Granny Hamner

Ray Hamrick
Don Hasenmayer
Eli Hodkey
Frank Hoerst
Tommy Hughes
Si Johnson
Dale Jones
Ernie Koy

## WORLD WAR II (continued)

Tex Kraus
Andy Lapihuska
Charlie Letchas
Tony Lupien
Joe Marty
Pinky May
Rogers McKee
John Miller
Dee Moore
Bitsy Mott
Emmett Mueller
Hugh Mulcahy

Ford Mullen
Ed Murphy
Danny Murtaugh
Sam Nahem
Ron Northey
Lou Novikoff
Ike Pearson
Bill Peterman
Nick Picciuto
Ken Raffensberger
Schoolboy Rowe
Ed Walczak

## PHILLIES LONGEST WINNING AND LOSING STREAKS

| | Winning | | Losing |
|---|---|---|---|
| Games | Years | Games | Year |
| 16 | 1887, 1890, 1892 | 23 | 1961 |
| 13 | 1977 | 14 | 1936 |
| 11 | 1955 | 13 | 1919 (twice), 1942, 1955 |
| 9 | 1969 | 12 | 1922, 1928 (twice), 1944 |
| 8 | 1915, 1929, 1953, 1963, | 11 | 1925, 1930, 1939 |
| | 1967 (twice), 1977, 1978 | 10 | 1928 (twice), 1931, 1948, |
| | | | 1956, 1961, 1964, 1970, |
| | | | 1972 |

## PHILLIES LONGEST WINNING STREAKS

Before baseball's so-called modern era, the Phillies put together three winning streaks which rank as their longest of all time. In each, they won sixteen straight games, but the first of these lasted through seventeen games because a tie intervened between the fifteenth and sixteenth victory. That was in 1887. The other sixteen-game streaks came in 1890 and 1892. a game-by-game rundown of each streak follows:

———— 1887 ————

| Date | Opponent | Score | Date | Opponent | Score |
|---|---|---|---|---|---|
| September 15 | at Indianapolis | 8-4 | September 23 | at Pittsburgh | 5-0 |
| 16 | at Indianapolis | 8-2 | 24 | at Pittsburgh | 12-3 |
| 17 | at Indianapolis | 17-6 | 24 | at Pittsburgh | 8-1 |
| 19 | at Detroit | 10-1 | 26 | Washington | 8-5 |
| 20 | at Detroit | 3-2 | 27 | Washington | 13-1 |
| October 1 | Boston | 13-4 | October 6 | at New York | 6-3 |
| 3 | Boston | 3-0 | 7 | at New York | 5-5* |
| 4 | Boston | 6-3 | 8 | at New York | 6-3 |
| 5 | at New York | 1-0 | | | |

*Nine-inning tie

132

| Date | | Opponent | Score | Date | | Opponent | Score |
|------|---|----------|-------|------|---|----------|-------|
| July | 8 | Cincinnati | 9-4 | July | 17 | Chicago | 7-5 |
| | 9 | Cincinnati | 6-1 | | 18 | Chicago | 7-2 |
| | 10 | Cleveland | 14-9 | | 19 | Chicago | 4-0 |
| | 11 | Cleveland | 10-2 | | 21 | Pittsburgh | 20-7 |
| | 12 | Cleveland | 15-4 | | 22 | Pittsburgh | 10-8* |
| | 14 | Pittsburgh | 17-1 | | 23 | Pittsburgh | 17-6 |
| | 15 | Pittsburgh | 8-4 | | 25 | at Cleveland | 8-5 |
| | 16 | Pittsburgh | 15-3 | | 26 | at Cleveland | 5-2 |

*Fifteen-inning game.
This streak ended July 28 in 12-4 loss at Chicago.

| Date | | Opponent | Score | Date | | Opponent | Score |
|------|---|----------|-------|------|---|----------|-------|
| June | 10 | Cleveland | 7-1 | June | 20 | Brooklyn | 9-6 |
| | 11 | Pittsburgh | 10-3 | | 21 | Baltimore | 9-4 |
| | 13 | Pittsburgh | 11-5 | | 22 | Baltimore | 9-8 |
| | 14 | Pittsburgh | 10-4 | | 22 | Baltimore | 7-3 |
| | 15 | at Boston | 1-0 | | 23 | at New York | 5-2 |
| | 17 | at Boston | 14-3 | | 24 | at New York | 6-3 |
| | 18 | Brooklyn | 6-4 | | 25 | at Washington | 9-2 |
| | 18 | Brooklyn | 4-3 | | 28 | Boston | 8-1 |

This streak ended June 29 in 9-1 loss to Boston at Philadelphia.

## PHILLIES LONGEST MODERN WINNING STREAK (Post-1900)

The Phillies longest winning streak since the turn of the century lasted through thirteen games and helped the club win its second National League Eastern Division title in succession. The game-by-game rundown of the 1977 streak follows:

| Date | | Opponent | Score | Winning Pitcher | Losing Pitcher |
|------|---|----------|-------|-----------------|----------------|
| August | 3 | San Diego | 8-1 | Carlton | Shirley |
| | 4 | San Diego | 2-1 in ten | McGraw | Spillner |
| | 5 | Los Angeles | 8-3 | Garber | Rautzhan |
| | 6 | Los Angeles | 1-0 | Garber | Hooton |
| | 7 | Los Angeles | 3-1 | Carlton | Sutton |
| | 10 | Montreal | 6-1 | Christenson | Rogers |
| | 10 | Montreal | 6-1 | Lonborg | Alcala |
| | 11 | Montreal | 10-5 | Kaat | Brown |
| | 12 | at Chicago | 10-3 | Carlton | R. Reuschel |
| | 13 | at Chicago | 10-7 in eleven | Reed | Giusti |
| | 14 | at Chicago | 10-2 | Christenson | Krukow |
| | 14 | at Chicago | 4-2 | Lonborg | Renko |
| | 16 | at Montreal | 7-5 | Brusstar | Kerrigan |

The streak ended on August 17 in Montreal when the Expos won, 13-0, as Stan Bahnsen beat Steve Carlton.

# PHILLIES LONGEST LOSING STREAK

The longest losing streak in the history of the Phillies lasted through twenty-three games and ranks as the longest in modern (post-1900) major league history. The game-by-game rundown of the 1961 streak follows:

| Date | | Opponent | Score | Winning Pitcher | Losing Pitcher |
|------|---|----------|-------|-----------------|----------------|
| July | 29 | San Francisco | 4-3 | McCormick | Ferrarese |
| | 30 | San Francisco | 5-2 | Sanford | Owens |
| August | 2 | at Cincinnati | 4-2 | O'Toole | Mahaffey |
| | 2 | at Cincinnati | 3-2 | Jay | Short |
| | 3 | at Cincinnati | 7-1 | Johnson | Buzhardt |
| | 4 | at St. Louis | 9-8 | Broglio | Ferrarese |
| | 5 | at St. Louis | 7-0 | Simmons | Brown |
| | 6 | at St. Louis | 3-1 | Sadecki | Sullivan |
| | 6 | at St. Louis | 3-2 | Gibson | Owens |
| | 7 | Pittsburgh | 3-1 | Friend | Buzhardt |
| | 8 | Pittsburgh | 10-2 | Haddix | Mahaffey |
| | 8 | Pittsburgh | 3-2 | Sturdivant | Short |
| | 9 | Cincinnati | 5-0 | Jay | Ferrarese |
| | 11 | at Pittsburgh | 6-0 in seven | Friend | Roberts |
| | 12 | at Pittsburgh | 4-0 | Mizell | Owens |
| | 13 | at Pittsburgh | 13-4 | Sturdivant | Buzhardt |
| | 14 | at Chicago | 9-2 | Ellsworth | Sullivan |
| | 15 | at Chicago | 6-5 | Curtis | Mahaffey |
| | 16 | at Chicago | 9-5 | Cardwell | Short |
| | 17 | at Milwaukee | 7-6 in eleven | Nottebart | Baldschun |
| | 18 | at Milwaukee | 4-1 | Burdette | Owens |
| | 19 | at Milwaukee | 4-3 | Cloninger | Sullivan |
| | 20 | at Milwaukee | 5-2 | Spahn | Short |

The streak ended in the second game of the August 20 doubleheader when the Phillies beat the Braves, 7-4, as John Buzhardt beat Carlton Willey. It was the first complete game by a Phillies pitcher since Buzhardt beat the Giants, 4-3, in the second game of a July 28 doubleheader the night before the losing streak began. Remarkably enough, the starting pitchers were the pitchers of record in every game during the losing streak except on August 17 when Bob Buhl started for the Braves against Robin Roberts.

## LONGEST WINNING AND LOSING STREAKS
## BY PHILLIES PITCHERS

——— Winning ———

| Games | Pitcher | Year | Games | Pitcher | Year |
|-------|---------|------|-------|---------|------|
| 15 | Steve Carlton | 1972 | 8 | Russ Meyer | 1949 |
| 12 | Charles Ferguson | 1886 | 8 | Bob Miller | 1950 |
| 10 | Grover Alexander | 1914 | 8 | Robin Roberts | 1952 |
| 9 | Grover Alexander | 1915 | 8 | Jim Bunning | 1964 |
| 9 | Ken Heintzelman | 1949 | 8 | Jim Bunning | 1966 |
| 9 | Robin Roberts | 1952 | 8 | Chris Short | 1968 |
| 8 | Togie Pittinger | 1905 | 8 | Jim Lonborg | 1976 |
| 8 | Grover Alexander | 1913 | 8 | Larry Christenson | 1977 |
| 8 | Syl Johnson | 1935 | 8 | Jim Lonborg | 1977 |

| Games | Pitcher | Year | Games | Pitcher | Year |
|---|---|---|---|---|---|
| 12 | John Coleman | 1883 | 11 | John Buzhardt | 1960 |
| 12 | Russ Miller | 1928 | 11 | Barry Lersch | 1971 |
| 12 | Hugh Mulcahy | 1940 | 11 | Billy Champion | 1972 |
| 12 | Ken Reynolds | 1972 | 10 | Murry Dickson | 1954 |
| 11 | Lee Grissom | 1941 | 10 | Art Mahaffey | 1961 |

## LONGEST WINNING STREAK BY PHILLIES PITCHER

Steve Carlton won fifteen straight games in 1972 to set a Phillies club record. Carlton won twenty-seven games that season for the Phillies, who won only fifty-nine games and finished sixth and last in the National League's Eastern Division. The game-by-game rundown of the streak follows:

| Date | | Opponent | Score | Losing Pitcher |
|---|---|---|---|---|
| June | 7 | Houston | 3-1 | Reuss |
| | 11 | Atlanta | 3-1 | Reed |
| | 25 | at Montreal | 1-0 | McAnally |
| | 29 | New York | 9-4 | Gentry |
| | | | | |
| July | 3 | San Francisco | 4-2 | Carrithers |
| | 7 | San Diego (1) | 4-2 | Corkins |
| | 11 | Los Angeles | 4-1 | Sutton |
| | 19 | at San Diego | 3-2 in eleven | Kirby |
| | 23 | at Los Angeles | 2-0 | John |
| | 28 | Chicago | -0 | Pappas |
| | | | | |
| August | 1 | at New York (2) | 4-1 | Koosman |
| | 5 | at St. Louis | 5-0 | Cleveland |
| | 9 | at Pittsburgh | 2-0 | Blass |
| | 13 | Montreal (1) | 2-1 | McAnally |
| | 17 | Cincinnati | 9-4 | Grimsley |

Carlton's streak ended August 21 when Atlanta beat the Phillies, 2-1, in eleven innings at Veterans Stadium as both winner Phil Niekro and Carlton pitched complete games. Carlton, who beat every team in the league during his streak, pitched complete games in all but his first victory in the streak.

On June 7, Carlton was removed from a pinch-hitter while leading, 3-1, in the seventh inning because of a muscle pull in his lower back. Darrell Brandon finished with two scoreless innings.

During the streak, Carlton started three games in which he was not involved in the decision. On June 16 at Houston, he pitched ten scoreless innings before being removed for a pinch-hitter in a game the Phillies lost, 1-0, in eleven innings; on June 21 at Atlanta, he was removed for a pinch-hitter in the sixth inning with the Phillies trailing, 5-4, in a game they went on to win, 9-7; on July 15 at San Francisco, he was removed for a pinch-hitter in the sixth inning with the Phillies trailing, 4-0, in a game they went on to win, 11-4, with eleven runs in the seventh inning.

# PHILLIES PINCH-HIT LEADERS (1933-78)

| Year | Name | Pinch-Hits | Year | Name | Pinch-Hits |
|------|------|------------|------|------|------------|
| 1933 | Al Todd | 7 | 1953 | Eddie Waitkus | 7 |
| 1934 | Mickey Haslin | 5 | 1954 | Smoky Burgess | 6 |
| 1935 | Al Todd | 5 | 1955 | Glen Gorbous | 9 |
| 1936 | Jimmie Wilson | 8 | 1956 | Solly Hemus | 9 |
| 1937 | Earl Browne | 7 | 1957 | Ron Northey | 7 |
| | Johnny Moore | 7 | 1958 | Dave Philley | 18 |
| 1938 | Buck Jordan | 5 | 1959 | Dave Philley | 15 |
| 1939 | Emmett Mueller | 8 | 1960 | Bobby Gene Smith | 11 |
| 1940 | Herschel Martin | 4 | 1961 | Tony Gonzalez | 6 |
| | Emmett Mueller | 4 | 1962 | Wes Covington | 9 |
| | Bennie Warren | 4 | 1963 | Wes Covington | 8 |
| 1941 | Chuck Klein | 5 | 1964 | John Herrnstein | 7 |
| | Johnny Rizzo | 5 | 1965 | Alex Johnson | 8 |
| 1942 | Earl Naylor | 6 | 1966 | Doug Clemens | 12 |
| 1943 | Schoolboy Rowe* | 15 | 1967 | Doug Clemens | 11 |
| 1944 | Coaker Triplett | 8 | 1968 | Rick Joseph | 11 |
| 1945 | Rene Monteagudo* | 18 | 1969 | Terry Harmon | 4 |
| 1946 | Lou Novikoff | 6 | 1970 | Rick Joseph | 11 |
| 1947 | Charlie Gilbert | 9 | 1971 | Byron Browne | 7 |
| 1948 | Bama Rowell | 7 | 1972 | Tommy Hutton | 8 |
| | Harry Walker | 7 | 1973 | Mike Rogodzinski* | 16 |
| 1949 | Buddy Blattner | 7 | 1974 | Tony Taylor | 17 |
| 1950 | Dick Whitman* | 12 | 1975 | Tommy Hutton | 11 |
| 1951 | Bill Nicholson | 11 | 1976 | Ollie Brown | 9 |
| 1952 | Bill Nicholson | 8 | 1977 | Tommy Hutton | 10 |
| 1953 | Connie Ryan | 7 | 1978 | Jose Cardenal | 9 |

* — National League leader

# PLAYERS WHO TRAINED WITH BUT DID NOT PLAY
## WITH THE PHILLIES
### (1941-78)

| Year | Name | Year | Name |
|------|------|------|------|
| 1941 | Jim Dillingham, IF | 1948 | Albert Flair, IF |
| | Stan Stuka, C | | Ed Oswald, C |
| 1942 | Dan Reynolds, IF | | Grady Wilson, OF |
| 1943 | Bill Ankse, C | 1949 | Charley Hood, C |
| | Roberto Ortiz, OF | | Don Johnston, P |
| 1944 | Dick Carter, P | | Bill Loos, OF |
| | Warren Fralick, P | | George Thomas, P |
| | Julius Homokay, P | | John Walz, P |
| | Wilbur Reeser, P | | John Werner, P |
| 1945 | Bill Sanders, OF | 1950 | Buzz Bowers, P |
| | Les Scarsella, OF | | Alex Garbowski, IF |
| 1946 | Pat Ambrose, C | | Lou Heyman, C |
| | George Copeland, P | | Bill Koszarek, P |
| | Robert Engle, IF | | Elmer Sexauer, P |
| | Lee Ross, P | | Ed Wright, P |
| 1947 | Bill Pless, P | 1951 | Bill Fogg, OF |
| | Joe Scheldt, OF | | Clarence Hicks, IF |

## Players Who Trained But Did Not Play With The Phillies (continued)

| | | | |
|---|---|---|---|
| 1952 | Con Dempsey, P | | Bob Nash, OF |
| 1953 | Joe Tesauro, OF | | Gary Schlieve, P |
| 1954 | Tom Casagrande, P | 1967 | Ron Allen, IF |
| | Harry Markell, P | | John Penn, P |
| | Mike Sandlock, C | | Gil Torres, OF |
| 1955 | Gerry Clacomb, P | 1968 | Steve Arlin, P |
| | Larry Novak, OF | | Hal Clem, P |
| | Spencer Robbins, IF | | John Parker, P |
| 1956 | John Moskus, IF | 1969 | Pat Bayless, P |
| | Ben Tompkins, IF | | Larry Keener, P |
| 1957 | Henry Bolinda, P | | Bob McLachlin, P |
| | Jim Davis, OF | | Phil Meyer, P |
| | Earl Hunsinger, P | | Pat Skrable, OF |
| | Gene Snyder, P | 1970 | None |
| 1958 | Jim Golden, P | 1971 | Frank DeCastris, OF |
| | Woody Smith, IF | | Wayne Redmond, OF |
| | John Turk, C | 1972 | Steve Cates, P |
| 1959 | Bart Dupon, OF | | Nellie Garcia, OF |
| | Johnny O'Brien, IF | | Blas Santana, IF |
| | Lou Vassie, IF | | Craig Scramuzzo, P |
| 1960 | Larry Cutright, C | 1973 | Mike Bruhert, P |
| | Fred Hopke, 1B | | Rickey Clark, P |
| 1961 | Dick Edwards, IF | | Don Leshnock, P |
| | Bruce Gruber, P | | Mike Martin, P |
| | Jess Hickman, P | | Earl Stephenson, P |
| 1962 | Leo Burke, IF | 1974 | Ed Crosby, IF |
| | Len Clendenin, P | | Jackie Hernandez, IF |
| | Joel Gibson, P | | Chuck Kniffin, P |
| | Bob Lipski, C | | Aurelio Monteagudo, P |
| | Ed Lunsford, P | | Roy Thomas, P |
| | Dwight Siebler, P | 1975 | Jack Bastable, C |
| 1963 | Bob Baillargeon, P | | Jim Chamberlain, P |
| | Dick Beck, P | | Quency Hill, P |
| | Lane Phillips, P | | Larry Kiser, P |
| | Dick Quiroz, P | | Andy Kosco, OF |
| 1964 | Gene Harbeson, C | | Dave Schneck, OF |
| | Jim Miller, P | 1976 | Sergio Ferrer, IF |
| | Dave Roberts, P | | Willie Hernandez, P |
| | Darrell Sutherland, P | | John Hughes, C |
| 1965 | Jack Nutter, P | 1977 | Jim Wright, P |
| | Frank Pollard, P | 1978 | Bobby Brown, OF |
| | Jim Speight, IF | | Orlando Isales, OF |
| | Mike Wegener, P | | Joe Jones, IF |
| 1966 | Bruce Brubaker, P | | Jose Moreno, IF |
| | Mike Everett, P | | John Poff, IF |
| | Warren Halverson, IF | | Steve Waterbury, P |
| | Jerry Messerly, P | | |

# "SPORTING NEWS" ALL STARS

## PHILLIES PLAYERS NAMED TO "SPORTING NEWS" MAJOR LEAGUE ALL-STAR TEAM
### (Selected from 1925 through 1960)

| | | | |
|---|---|---|---|
| 1932 | Chuck Klein, OF | 1953 | Robin Roberts, P |
| 1933 | Chuck Klein, OF | 1954 | Robin Roberts, P |
| 1950 | Jim Konstanty, P | 1955 | Robin Roberts, P |
| 1952 | Robin Roberts, P | | |

## PHILLIES PLAYERS NAMED TO "SPORTING NEWS" NATIONAL LEAGUE ALL-STAR TEAM
### (Selected from 1961 through 1978)

| | | | |
|---|---|---|---|
| 1964 | Jim Bunning, P | | Mike Schmidt, 3B |
| 1972 | Steve Carlton, P | 1977 | Steve Carlton, P |
| 1974 | Mike Schmidt, 3B | | Greg Luzinski, OF |
| 1975 | Larry Bowa, SS | | Mike Schmidt, 3B |
| | Greg Luzinski, OF | 1978 | Larry Bowa, SS |
| 1976 | Bob Boone, C | | |

## PHILLIES PLAYERS NAMED TO "SPORTING NEWS" ALL-STAR FIELDING TEAM
### (Gold Glove Winners, 1963-78)

| | | | |
|---|---|---|---|
| 1963 | Bobby Wine, SS | | Mike Schmidt, 3B |
| 1964 | Ruben Amaro, SS | 1977 | Jim Kaat, P |
| | Bobby Shantz, P | | Garry Maddox, OF |
| 1966 | Bill White, 1B | | Mike Schmidt, 3B |
| 1972 | Larry Bowa, SS | 1978 | Bob Boone, C |
| 1975 | Garry Maddox, OF | | Larry Bowa, SS |
| 1976 | Jim Kaat, P | | Garry Maddox, OF |
| | Garry Maddox, OF | | Mike Schmidt, 3B |

## CHUCK KLEIN — QUITE A CAREER

Charles (Chuck) Herbert Klein spent seventeen years in the major leagues, fifteen with the Phillies, and had an outstanding career.

However, the native of Indianapolis, Indiana, isn't a member of baseball's prestigious Hall of Fame. His critics claim the short right field fence (280 feet) was largely instrumental in the impressive career compiled by the left-handed hitting outfielder.

Maybe that's true, but Klein's records and heavy stats were compiled in the major leagues against big league pitchers. His career is much more impressive than that of a lot of players who have been elected to the Hall of Fame.

And, his first five full seasons with the Phillies were perhaps the greatest years of ANY hitter in the history of baseball. During those years his totals were:

| AB | R | H | 2b | 3b | HR | RBI | AVE |
|---|---|---|---|---|---|---|---|
| 3114 | 658 | 1118 | 232 | 46 | 180 | 693 | .359 |

# CHUCK KLEIN (continued)

Some of Klein's other records and statistics:

**MAJOR LEAGUE RECORD:**
Most Games, One or More Hits, Season — 135 (1930)

**MAJOR LEAGUE RECORD TIED:**
Most Consecutive Years Leading League in Total Bases ( 4 (1930-31-32-33)

**NATIONAL LEAGUE RECORDS**
Most Consecutive Years, 200 or More Hits—5, from 1929-33
Most Years, 400 or More Total Bases — 3 (1929-30-32)
Most Consecutive Years, 400 or More Total Bases — 2 (1929-30)
Most Long Hits — 107 (1930; 59 doubles, 8 triples, 40 homers)
Most Runs, Doubleheader, eighteen innings — 8 (August 21, 1935)
Most Assists, Outfielder, Season, Since 1900 — 44 (1930)
Most Years 150 or More Runs, Since 1900 — 2 (1930-32)
Most Runs, Season, Since 1900 — 158 (1930)
Most RBI, Left-Handed Hitter, Season — 170 (1930)
Most Total Bases, Left-Handed Hitter, Season — 445 (1930)

**NATIONAL LEAGUE RECORDS TIED:**
Most Consecutive Batting Streaks (Twenty or More Games), Season — 4
    (1930 twice; 1931, 39)
Most Consecutive Years Leading League in Runs — 3 (1930-31-32)
Most Total Bases, Extra Inning Game — 16 (July 10, 1936)
Most Home Runs, Ten Innings — 4 (July 10, 1936)

**PHILLIES CLUB RECORDS, SEASON:**
Most Runs — 158 (1930)
Most Doubles — 59 (1930)
Most Home Runs — 43 (1929)
Most Total Bases — 445 (1930)
Most Extra Base Hits — 107 (1930)
Most RBI — 170 (1930)
Highest Slugging Average — .687 (1930)
Longest Hitting Streaks — 26 (1930, twice)

**PHILLIES CLUB RECORD, SEASON, TIED:**
Fewest Grounded Into Double Plays — 3 (152 games, 1933)

**NATIONAL LEAGUE LEADER, SEASON:**
Batting Champion — .368 (1933)
Runs Scored — 158 (1930)
              121 (1931)
              152 (1932)
Hits — 226 (1932)
       223 (1933)
Doubles — 59 (1930)
          44 (1933)
Home Runs — 43 (1929)
            31 (1931)
            38 (1932)
            28 (1933)

# CHUCK KLEIN (continued)

Total Bases — 445 (1930)
           347 (1931)
           420 (1932)
           365 (1933)
RBI — 121 (1931)
     120 (1933)
Stolen Bases — 20 (1932)
Slugging Average — .584 (1931)
                .646 (1932)
                .602 (1933)

CAREER TOTALS, Phillies Stats in ():
GAMES — 1,753 (1,405)
AT BATS — 6,486 (5,238)
RUNS — 1,168 (963)
HITS — 2,076 (1,705)
DOUBLES — 398 (336)
TRIPLES — 74 (64)
HOME RUNS — 300 (243)
RBI — 1,201 (983)
TOTAL BASES — 3,522 (2,898)
SLUGGING AVERAGE — .543 (.553)
TWO HOMERS, GAME — 28 (23)
AVERAGE — .320 (.326)

Klein was born in Indianapolis on October 7, 1904, and died there on March 28, 1958. He was an even 6-feet, weighed 185 pounds, batted left and threw right.

## BATTING RECORDS
## PHILLIES CLUB RECORD FOR HOME RUNS IN ONE SEASON
### Forty-three by Chuck Klein in 1929

| Home Run No. | Team Game No. | Date | Opponent | Score |
|---|---|---|---|---|
| 1 | 8 | April 27 | at Brooklyn | 8-3 |
| 2 | 12 | May 4 (2) | Chicago | 7-9 |
| 3 | 17 | 10 | Pittsburgh | 13-14 |
| 4 | 18 | 11 | Pittsburgh | 11-6 |
| 5 | 18 | 11 | | |
| 6 | 22 | 17 | Brooklyn | 13-14 |
| 7 | 23 | 18 (1) | Brooklyn | 16-20 |
| 8 | 24 | 18 (2) | Brooklyn | 8-6 |
| 9 | 28 | 25 | at Brooklyn | 3-5 |
| 10 | 35 | 30 (2) | Boston | 11-5 |
| 11 | 35 | 30 (2) | | |
| 12 | 36 | 31 | at Pittsburgh | 10-7 |
| 13 | 37 | June 1 | at Pittsburgh | 9-4 |
| 14 | 40 | 5 | at Cincinnati | 4-21 |
| 15 | 45 | 10 | at St. Louis | 9-10 |
| 16 | 49 | 15 | at Chicago | 7-8 in ten |
| 17 | 51 | 18 | Boston | 4-2 |
| 18 | 52 | 19 (1) | New York | 14-15 in eleven |

## BATTING RECORDS (continued)

| Home Run No. | Team Game No. | Date | Opponent | Score |
|---|---|---|---|---|
| 19 | 68 | 30 (2) | at New York | 4-2 |
| 20 | 71 | July 5 | St. Louis | 10-9 |
| 21 | 72 | 6 (1) | St. Louis | 10-6 |
| 22 | 76 | 10 | Pittsburgh | 9-15 |
| 23 | 79 | 13 | Pittsburgh | 2-10 |
| 24 | 80 | 15 (1) | Chicago | 6-9 |
| 25 | 81 | 15 (2) | Chicago | 6-7 |
| 26 | 81 | 15 (2) | | |
| 27 | 82 | 16 | Chicago | 6-5 |
| 28 | 82 | 16 | | |
| 29 | 85 | 20 (1) | Cincinnati | 9-4 |
| 30 | 90 | 25 | at St. Louis | 3-10 |
| 31 | 91 | 26 | at Chicago | 10-13 |
| 32 | 96 | 30 | at Pittsburgh | 13-5 |
| 33 | 97 | 31 | at Pittsburgh | 6-2 |
| 34 | 123 | August 30 | at Boston | 9-5 |
| 35 | 124 | 31 | at Boston | 9-5 |
| 36 | 125 | September 1 (1) | at Brooklyn | 15-2 |
| 37 | 127 | 2 (1) | at New York | 4-11 |
| 38 | 135 | 11 | at Chicago | 2-5 |
| 39 | 136 | 12 | at Chicago | 7-1 |
| 40 | 146 | 25 (1) | Brooklyn | 10-9 |
| 41 | 147 | 25 (2) | Brooklyn | 8-5 |
| 42 | 149 | 27 | Boston | 11-5 |
| 43 | 153 | October 5 (1) | New York | 5-4 |

Home runs: home, 25; away, 18.

## PHILLIES CLUB RECORD FOR RUNS BATTED IN FOR ONE MONTH
### Forty-one By Del Ennis in July 1950

| Date | | Opponent | Score | AB | R | H | RBI |
|---|---|---|---|---|---|---|---|
| July | 1 | Brooklyn | 6-4 | 4 | 1 | 1 | 1 |
| | 2 | Brooklyn | 6-4 | 3 | 0 | 0 | 1 |
| | 2 | Brooklyn | 8-8 in ten | 4 | 2 | 2 | 1 |
| | 3 | Boston | 1-3 | 4 | 0 | 1 | 0 |
| | 4 | Boston | 14-5 | 4 | 2 | 1 | 3 |
| | 4 | Boston | 9-12 | 3 | 1 | 1 | 0 |
| | 5 | New York | 10-3 | 5 | 1 | 2 | 3 |
| | 5 | New York | 9-7 | 3 | 2 | 2 | 3 |
| | 6 | New York | 9-6 | 3 | 0 | 0 | 0 |
| | 7 | at Brooklyn | 7-2 | 4 | 2 | 2 | 0 |
| | 8 | at Brooklyn | 4-1 | 4 | 0 | 0 | 0 |
| | 9 | at Brooklyn | 3-7 | 1 | 0 | 0 | 0 |
| | 13 | at St. Louis | 3-2 | 4 | 0 | 1 | 0 |
| | 14 | at St. Louis | 2-4 | 4 | 0 | 1 | 0 |
| | 15 | at St. Louis | 6-8 | 4 | 0 | 1 | 1 |
| | 16 | at Chicago | 0-8 | 4 | 0 | 0 | 0 |
| | 16 | at Chicago | 3-10 | 4 | 0 | 0 | 0 |
| | 18 | at Chicago | 2-5 | 4 | 1 | 2 | 1 |
| | 18 | at Chicago | 8-3 | 5 | 1 | 1 | 1 |
| | 19 | at Pittsburgh | 3-2 in eleven | 5 | 0 | 3 | 1 |
| | 19 | at Pittsburgh | 2-4 | 4 | 0 | 1 | 0 |
| | 20 | at Pittsburgh | 8-10 | 5 | 1 | 2 | 1 |
| | 21 | at Pittsburgh | 4-1 | 4 | 0 | 1 | 0 |
| | 22 | at Cincinnati | 2-0 | 3 | 0 | 0 | 0 |

# BATTING RECORDS (continued)

| Date | Opponent | Score | RBIs | Player | Year | Month |
|------|----------|-------|------|--------|------|-------|
| 22 | at Cincinnati | 1-6 | 4 | 0 | 1 | 0 |
| 23 | at Cincinnati | 12-4 | 5 | 1 | 3 | 3 |
| 23 | at Cincinnati | 7-4 | 4 | 0 | 0 | 0 |
| 24 | at Pittsburgh | 1-2 in six | 3 | 0 | 1 | 0 |
| 25 | Chicago | 7-0 | 4 | 1 | 2 | 3 |
| 25 | Chicago | 1-0 | 4 | 0 | 0 | 0 |
| 26 | Chicago | 6-4 | 4 | 1 | 2 | 1 |
| 27 | Chicago | 13-3 | 5 | 1 | 2 | 7 |
| 28 | Pittsburgh | 4-1 | 4 | 0 | 2 | 1 |
| 29 | Pittsburgh | 4-7 | 4 | 1 | 1 | 2 |
| 30 | Pittsburgh | 10-0 | 5 | 2 | 3 | 5 |
| 30 | Pittsburgh | 4-2 | 4 | 1 | 1 | 2 |
| | | Totals . . . . . . | 142 | 22 | 43 | 41 | Average .303 |

## LONGEST HITTING STREAKS BY PHILLIES PLAYERS

| Games | Player | Year | Games | Player | Year |
|-------|--------|------|-------|--------|------|
| 36 | Billy Hamilton | 1894 | 17 | Richie Ashburn | 1950 |
| 26 | Chuck Klein | 1930 | 17 | Mel Clark | 1952 |
| 26 | Chuck Klein | 1930 | 17 | Willie Jones | 1956 |
| 24 | Willie Montanez | 1974 | 17 | Tony Gonzalez | 1962 |
| 23 | Goldie Rapp | 1921 | 16 | Lefty O'Doul | 1929 |
| 23 | Richie Ashburn | 1948 | 16 | Richie Ashburn | 1953 |
| 22 | Chuck Klein | 1931 | 16 | Solly Hemus | 1958 |
| 22 | Chick Fullis | 1933 | 16 | Rick Joseph | 1969 |
| 21 | Dany Litwhiler | 1940 | 16 | Larry Bowa | 1975 |
| 20 | Chuck Klein | 1932 | 15 | Lefty O'Doul | 1929 |
| 20 | Richie Ashburn | 1951 | 15 | Richie Ashburn | 1949 |
| 20 | Pancho Herrera | 1961 | 15 | Granny Hamner | 1954 |
| 20 | Garry Maddox | 1978 | 15 | Richie Ashburn | 1958 |
| 19 | Gavvy Cravath | 1917 | 15 | Lee Walls | 1961 |
| 19 | Del Ennis | 1947 | 15 | Dick Allen | 1969 |
| 18 | Gene Paulette | 1920 | 15 | Greg Luzinski | 1973 |
| 18 | Richie Ashburn | 1955 | 15 | Garry Maddox | 1975 |
| 18 | Larry Bowa | 1970 | 15 | Jay Johnstone | 1976 |
| 17 | Chuck Klein | 1931 | 15 | Garry Maddox | 1976 |

## MOST RUNS BATTED IN BY PHILLIES PLAYER BY POSITION

### IN ONE SEASON

| Position | Name | Year | RBIs |
|----------|------|------|------|
| C | Stan Lopata | 1956 | 95 |
| 1B | Don Hurst | 1932 | 143 |
| 2B | Granny Hamner | 1953 | 92 |
| 3B | Pinky Whitney | 1932 | 124 |
| SS | Granny Hamner | 1952 | 87 |
| LF | Greg Luzinski | 1977 | 130 |
| CF | Cy Williams | 1923 | 114 |
| RF | Chuck Klein | 1930 | 170 |

# MOST RUNS BATTED IN BY PHILLIES PLAYER IN ONE MONTH
## (1928-78)

| RBIs | Player | Year | Month | RBIs | Player | Year | Month |
|---|---|---|---|---|---|---|---|
| 41 | Del Ennis | 1950 | July | 32 | Don Hurst | 1932 | May |
| 40 | Chuck Klein | 1929 | July | 32 | Chuck Klein | 1932 | May |
| 38 | Pinky Whitney | 1932 | July | 32 | Del Ennis | 1954 | May |
| 36 | Chuck Klein | 1930 | July | 32 | Mike Schmidt | 1974 | June |
| 35 | Chuck Klein | 1930 | June | 32 | Greg Luzinski | 1977 | July |
| 34 | Don Hurst | 1929 | July | 31 | Chuck Klein | 1930 | May |
| 34 | Dick Allen | 1966 | June | 31 | Dolf Camilli | 1934 | July |
| 33 | Chuck Klein | 1929 | May | 31 | Don Demeter | 1962 | August |
| 33 | Chuck Klein | 1932 | June | 30 | Chuck Klein | 1933 | May |
| 33 | Johnny Moore | 1934 | July | 30 | Del Ennis | 1949 | June |
| 33 | Greg Luzinski | 1973 | June | 30 | Del Ennis | 1955 | July |

# MOST RUNS BATTED IN BY PHILLIES PLAYER IN EACH MONTH
## (1928-78)

| Month | Player | Year | Month |
|---|---|---|---|
| April | Mike Schmidt | 1976 | 20 |
| May | Chuck Klein | 1929 | 33 |
| June | Chuck Klein | 1930 | 35 |
| July | Del Ennis | 1950 | 41 |
| August | Don Demeter | 1962 | 31 |
| September | Chuck Klein | 1930 | 29 |

# PHILLIES WITH 100 OR MORE RUNS BATTED IN
## DURING ONE SEASON

| RBIs | Player | Year | RBIs | Player | Year |
|---|---|---|---|---|---|
| 170 | Chuck Klein | 1930 | 116 | Mike Schmidt | 1974 |
| 145 | Chuck Klein | 1929 | 115 | Pinky Whitney | 1929 |
| 143 | Don Hurst | 1932 | 114 | Cy Williams | 1923 |
| 137 | Chuck Klein | 1932 | 110 | Del Ennis | 1949 |
| 130 | Greg Luzinski | 1977 | 110 | Dick Allen | 1966 |
| 129 | Gavvy Cravath | 1913 | 107 | Del Ennis | 1952 |
| 126 | Del Ennis | 1950 | 107 | Don Demeter | 1962 |
| 125 | Don Hurst | 1929 | 107 | Mike Schmidt | 1976 |
| 125 | Del Ennis | 1953 | 104 | Chuck Klein | 1936 |
| 124 | Pinky Whitney | 1932 | 104 | Ron Northey | 1944 |
| 122 | Lefty O'Doul | 1929 | 104 | John Callison | 1964 |
| 121 | Chuck Klein | 1931 | 103 | Pinky Whitney | 1928 |
| 120 | Chuck Klein | 1933 | 103 | Bill White | 1966 |
| 120 | Del Ennis | 1955 | 102 | Dolf Camilli | 1936 |
| 120 | Greg Luzinski | 1975 | 101 | Sherry Magee | 1914 |
| 119 | Del Ennis | 1954 | 101 | John Callison | 1965 |
| 118 | Gavvy Cravath | 1915 | 101 | Mike Schmidt | 1977 |
| 117 | Pinky Whitney | 1930 | 101 | Greg Luzinski | 1978 |
| 116 | Sherry Magee | 1910 | 100 | Gavvy Cravath | 1914 |

# MOST RUNS BATTED IN BY PHILLIES PLAYER IN ONE GAME

| RBIs | Player | Date | Opponent |
|------|--------|------|----------|
| 8 | Kitty Bransfield | July 11, 1910 | at Pittsburgh |
| 8 | Gavvy Cravath | August 18, 1915 | Pittsburgh |
| 8 | Willie Jones | August 20, 1958 | at St. Louis |
| 8 | Mike Schmidt | April 17, 1976 | at Chicago |
| 7 | Ed Delahanty | July 13, 1894 | at Chicago |
| 7 | Dolf Camilli | April 19, 1935 | New York |
| 7 | Lee King | April 28, 1922 | at Brooklyn |
| 7 | Cy Williams | May 20, 1927 | Cincinnati |
| 7 | Granny Hamner | July 17, 1948 | at St. Louis |
| 7 | Del Ennis | July 27, 1950 | Chicago |
| 7 | Del Ennis | July 23, 1955 | St. Louis |
| 7 | Don Demeter | September 12, 1961 | at Los Angeles |
| 7 | Dick Allen | September 29, 1968 | at New York |
| 7 | Greg Luzinski | June 11, 1977 | at Atlanta |
| 6 | Barney Friberg | April 30, 1929 | at Brooklyn |
| 6 | George Watkins | June 26, 1935 | Cincinnati |
| 6 | Chuck Klein | July 10, 1936 | at Pittsburgh |
| 6 | Johnny Moore | July 22, 1936 | Pittsburgh |
| 6 | Danny Litwhiler | September 2, 1940 | at Boston |
| 6 | Vince DiMaggio | June 14, 1945 | at Boston |
| 6 | Del Ennis | July 30, 1953 | at Cincinnati |
| 6 | Don Demeter | May 11, 1962 | at Chicago |
| 6 | Wes Covington | August 24, 1964 | at Milwaukee |
| 6 | Dick Stuart | September 5, 1965 | at Cincinnati |
| 6 | Deron Johnson | June 20, 1971 | at New York |
| 6 | Mike Schmidt | August 14, 1977 | at Chicago |

# LARRY BOWA HAS NO PEER

When comparing the best defensive shortstops in baseball history, the Phillies Larry Bowa stands alone at the top. And the facts back him up.

Bowa's lifetime fielding percentage increased .001 to an amazing .981 following the 1978 season. No one in baseball history is close to that figure.

Mark Belanger of the Baltimore Orioles holds the American League mark, .976, for shortstops who have played over 1,000 games in the big leagues.

Belanger was the leader with a .974 mark until Bowa became qualified in games played and passed him with a .979 figure after the 1976 season.

Others who have been league leaders include Dal Maxvill, .973 (St. Louis, Pittsburgh, 1962-74); Lou Boudreau, .974 (Cleveland, Boston Red Sox, 1938-52); Eddie Miller, .972 (Cincinnati, Boston Braves, Phillies, St. Louis Cardinals, 1936-50) and Roy McMillan, .972 (Cincinnati, Milwaukee Braves, 1951-66).

In addition to the highest lifetime fielding average, Bowa also holds the National League record for the fewest errors with nine in 1972 and the highest fielding percentage for a season, .987, set in 1971 and matched the next year.

Four times he's led National League shortstops in fielding for one year, 1971, 1972, 1976, and 1978.

His career fielding stats:

|      | PO    | A     | E   | Pct. |
|------|-------|-------|-----|------|
| 1970 | 202   | 418   | 13  | .979 |
| 1971 | 272   | 560   | 11  | .987 |
| 1972 | 212   | 494   | 9   | .987 |
| 1973 | 191   | 361   | 12  | .979 |
| 1974 | 256   | 462   | 12  | .984 |
| 1975 | 227   | 403   | 25  | .962 |
| 1976 | 180   | 492   | 17  | .975 |
| 1977 | 222   | 518   | 13  | .983 |
| 1978 | 224   | 502   | 10  | .986 |
| TOTALS | 1,986 | 4,210 | 122 | .981 |

## LEAGUE LEADERS, HITTING

### AVERAGE
| 1891 | Billy Hamilton  | .340 |
|------|-----------------|------|
| 1893 | Billy Hamilton  | .380 |
| 1899 | Ed Delahanty    | .410 |
| 1910 | Sherry Magee    | .331 |
| 1929 | Lefty O'Doul    | .398 |
| 1933 | Chuck Klein     | .368 |
| 1947 | Harry Walker    | .363 |
| 1955 | Richie Ashburn  | .338 |
| 1958 | Richie Ashburn  | .350 |

### RUNS
| 1890 | Billy Hamilton  | 141  |
|------|-----------------|------|
| 1894 | Billy Hamilton  | 192  |
| 1895 | Billy Hamilton  | 166  |
| 1896 | Ed Delahanty    | 126  |
| 1900 | Roy Thomas      | 132  |
| 1910 | Sherry Magee    | 110  |
| 1915 | Gavvy Cravath   | 89   |
| 1930 | Chuck Klein     | 158  |
| 1931 | Chuck Klein     | 121* |
| 1932 | Chuck Klein     | 152  |
| 1964 | Dick Allen      | 125  |

### HITS
| 1890 | Sam Thompson    | 172  |
|------|-----------------|------|
| 1891 | Billy Hamilton  | 179  |
| 1893 | Sam Thompson    | 222  |
| 1893 | Ed Delahanty    | 238  |
| 1913 | Gavvy Cravath   | 179  |
| 1914 | Sherry Magee    | 171  |
| 1929 | Lefty O'Doul    | 254  |
| 1932 | Chuck Klein     | 226  |
| 1933 | Chuck Klein     | 223  |
| 1951 | Richie Asbhurn  | 221  |
| 1953 | Richie Ashburn  | 205  |
| 1958 | Richie Ashburn  | 15   |
| 1975 | Dave Cash       | 213  |

### DOUBLES
| 1890 | Sam Thompson     | 41  |
|------|------------------|-----|
| 1893 | Sam Thompson     | 37  |
| 1895 | Ed Delahanty     | 49  |
| 1896 | Ed Delahanty     | 44  |
| 1898 | Nap Lajoie       | 43  |
| 1899 | Nap Lajoie       | 55  |
| 1901 | Nap Lajoie       | 38  |
| 1914 | Sherry Magee     | 39  |
| 1916 | Bery Niehoff     | 42  |
| 1930 | Chuck Klein      | 59  |
| 1933 | Chuck Klein      | 44  |
| 1934 | Ethan Allen      | 42* |
| 1966 | Johnny Callison  | 40  |
| 1972 | Willie Montanez  | 39  |

### TRIPLES
| 1892 | Ed Delahanty     | 21  |
|------|------------------|-----|
| 1947 | Harry Walker     | 16  |
| 1950 | Richie Ashburn   | 14  |
| 1958 | Richie Ashburn   | 13  |
| 1962 | Johnny Callison  | 10* |
| 1964 | Dick Allen       | 13* |
| 1965 | Johnny Callison  | 16  |
| 1972 | Larry Bowa       | 13  |
| 1976 | Dave Cash        | 12  |

### HOME RUNS
| 1889 | Sam Thompson     | 20  |
|------|------------------|-----|
| 1893 | Ed Delahanty     | 19  |
| 1895 | Sam Thompson     | 18  |
| 1913 | Gavvy Cravath    | 19  |
| 1914 | Gavvy Cravath    | 19  |
| 1915 | Gavvy Cravath    | 24  |
| 1917 | Gavvy Cravath    | 12* |
| 1918 | Gavvy Cravath    | 8   |
| 1919 | Gavvy Cravath    | 12  |

## LEAGUE LEADERS HITTING continued

### HOME RUNS

| | | |
|---|---|---|
| 1920 | Cy Williams | 15 |
| 1923 | Cy Williams | 41 |
| 1927 | Cy Williams | 30* |
| 1929 | Chuck Klein | 43 |
| 1931 | Chuck Klein | 31 |
| 1932 | Chuck Klein | 38* |
| 1933 | Chuck Klein | 28 |
| 1974 | Mike Schmidt | 36 |
| 1975 | Mike Schmidt | 38 |
| 1976 | Mike Schmidt | 38 |

### RUNS BATTED IN

| | | |
|---|---|---|
| 1893 | Ed Delahanty | 146 |
| 1895 | Sam Thompson | 165 |
| 1896 | Sam Thompson | 126 |
| 1898 | Nap Lajoie | 127 |
| 1899 | Ed Delahanty | 137 |
| 1900 | Elmer Flock | 110 |
| 1910 | Sherry Magee | 116 |
| 1913 | Gavvy Cravath | 118 |
| 1914 | Sherry Magee | 101 |
| 1915 | Gavvy Cravath | 118 |
| 1931 | Chuck Klein | 121 |
| 1932 | Don Hurst | 143 |
| 1933 | Chuck Klein | 120 |
| 1950 | Del Ennis | 126 |
| 1975 | Greg Luzinski | 120 |

### STOLEN BASES

| | | |
|---|---|---|
| 1889 | Jim Fogarty | 99 |
| 1890 | Billy Hamilton | 102 |
| 1891 | Billy Hamilton | 111 |
| 1894 | Billy Hamilton | 98 |
| 1895 | Billy Hamilton | 97 |
| 1898 | Ed Delahanty | 58 |
| 1932 | Chuck Klein | 20 |

*Tied for Lead

| | | |
|---|---|---|
| 1941 | Danny Murtaugh | 18 |
| 1948 | Richie Ashburn | 32 |

### TOTAL BASES

| | | |
|---|---|---|
| 1893 | Ed Delahanty | 347 |
| 1895 | Sam Thompson | 352 |
| 1897 | Nap Lajoie | 310 |
| 1899 | Ed Delahanty | 338 |
| 1910 | Sherry Magee | 263 |
| 1913 | Gavvy Cravath | 298 |
| 1914 | Sherry Magee | 279 |
| 1915 | Gavvy Cravath | 266 |
| 1930 | Chuck Klein | 445 |
| 1931 | Chuck Klein | 347 |
| 1932 | Chuck Klein | 420 |
| 1933 | Chuck Klein | 365 |
| 1964 | Dick Allen | 352 |
| 1975 | Greg Luzinski | 322 |
| 1976 | Mike Schmidt | 306 |

### SLUGGING AVERAGE

| | | |
|---|---|---|
| 1892 | Ed Delahanty | .495 |
| 1893 | Ed Delahanty | .583 |
| 1895 | Sam Thompson | .654 |
| 1896 | Ed Delahanty | .631 |
| 1897 | Nap Lajoie | .569 |
| 1899 | Ed Delahanty | .582 |
| 1910 | Sherry Magee | .507 |
| 1913 | Gavvy Cravath | .568 |
| 1914 | Sherry Magee | .513 |
| 1915 | Gavvy Cravath | .510 |
| 1926 | Cy Williams | .568 |
| 1931 | Chuck Klein | .584 |
| 1932 | Chuck Klein | .646 |
| 1933 | Chuck Klein | .602 |
| 1966 | Dick Allen | .632 |
| 1974 | Mike Schmidt | .546 |

## PHILLIES PITCHERS WINNING FIFTEEN OR MORE GAMES IN ONE SEASON

| | | |
|---|---|---|
| 1884 | Charley Ferguson | 21 |
| 1885 | Ed Daily | 26 |
| | Charley Ferguson | 26 |
| 1886 | Charley Ferguson | 30 |
| | Dan Casey | 24 |
| | Ed Daily | 16 |
| 1887 | Dan Casey | 28 |
| | Charley Ferguson | 22 |
| | Charlie Buffington | 21 |

| | | |
|---|---|---|
| 1888 | Charlie Buffinton | 28 |
| | Ben Sanders | 19 |
| 1889 | Charlie Buffinton | 27 |
| | Ben Sanders | 19 |
| 1890 | Kid Gleason | 38 |
| | Tom Vickery | 24 |
| 1891 | Kid Gleason | 24 |
| | Duke Esper | 20 |
| | John Thornton | 15 |

# Phillies Pitchers Winning Fifteen Or More Games In One Season (continued)

| | | | | | | |
|------|------------------|----|------|--------------------|----|
| 1892 | Gus Weyhing | 32 | 1917 | Grover Alexander | 30 |
| | Tim Keefe | 20 | | Joe Oeschger | 16 |
| | Kid Carsey | 19 | | Eppa Rixey | 16 |
| 1893 | Gus Weyhing | 23 | 1920 | Lee Meadows | 16 |
| | Kid Carsey | 20 | 1923 | Jimmy Ring | 18 |
| 1894 | Jack Taylor | 23 | 1926 | Hal Carlson | 17 |
| | Kid Carsey | 18 | 1929 | Claude Willoughby | 15 |
| | Gus Weyhing | 16 | 1930 | Phil Collins | 16 |
| 1895 | Jack Taylor | 26 | 1931 | Jumbo Elliott | 19 |
| | Kid Carsey | 24 | 1934 | Curt Davis | 19 |
| 1896 | Jack Taylor | 20 | 1935 | Curt Davis | 16 |
| | Al Orth | 15 | 1937 | Wayne LaMaster | 15 |
| 1897 | Jack Taylor | 16 | 1947 | Dutch Leonard | 17 |
| 1898 | Wiley Piatt | 24 | 1949 | Ken Heintzelman | 17 |
| | Red Donahue | 17 | | Russ Meyer | 17 |
| | Al Orth | 15 | | Robin Roberts | 15 |
| 1899 | Wiley Piatt | 23 | 1950 | Robin Roberts | 20 |
| | Red Donahue | 21 | | Curt Simmons | 17 |
| | Chick Fraser | 21 | | Jim Konstanty | 16 |
| 1900 | Chick Fraser | 16 | 1951 | Robin Roberts | 21 |
| | Bill Bernhard | 15 | | Bubba Church | 15 |
| | Red Donahue | 15 | 1952 | Robin Roberts | 28 |
| 1901 | Red Donahue | 22 | 1953 | Robin Roberts | 23 |
| | Al Orth | 20 | | Curt Simmons | 16 |
| | Bill Duggleby | 16 | 1954 | Robin Roberts | 23 |
| 1902 | Doc White | 16 | 1955 | Robin Roberts | 23 |
| 1903 | Bill Duggleby | 15 | 1956 | Robin Roberts | 19 |
| 1905 | Togie Pittinger | 23 | | Curt Simmons | 15 |
| | Bill Duggleby | 18 | 1957 | Jack Sanford | 19 |
| 1906 | Tully Sparks | 19 | 1958 | Robin Roberts | 17 |
| | John Lush | 18 | 1959 | Robin Roberts | 15 |
| 1907 | Tully Sparks | 21 | 1962 | Art Mahaffey | 19 |
| | Frank Corridon | 19 | 1964 | Jim Bunning | 19 |
| 1908 | George McQuillan | 23 | | Chris Short | 17 |
| | Tully Sparks | 16 | 1965 | Jim Bunning | 19 |
| 1909 | Earl Moore | 18 | | Chris Short | 18 |
| | Lew Moren | 16 | 1966 | Chris Short | 20 |
| 1910 | Earl Moore | 21 | | Jim Bunning | 19 |
| | Bob Ewing | 16 | | Larry Jackson | 15 |
| 1911 | Grover Alexander | 28 | 1967 | Jim Bunning | 17 |
| | Earl Moore | 15 | 1968 | Chris Short | 19 |
| 1912 | Grover Alexander | 19 | 1969 | Rick Wise | 15 |
| | Tom Seaton | 16 | 1971 | Rick Wise | 17 |
| 1913 | Tom Seaton | 27 | 1972 | Steve Carlton | 27 |
| | Grover Alexander | 22 | 1974 | Jim Lonborg | 17 |
| 1914 | Grover Alexander | 27 | | Steve Carlton | 16 |
| | Erskine Mayer | 21 | 1975 | Steve Carlton | 15 |
| 1915 | Grover Alexander | 31 | 1976 | Steve Carlton | 20 |
| | Erskine Mayer | 21 | | Jim Lonborg | 18 |
| 1916 | Grover Alexander | 33 | 1977 | Steve Carlton | 23 |
| | Eppa Rixey | 22 | | Larry Christenson | 19 |
| | Al Demaree | 19 | 1978 | Steve Carlton | 16 |

# LEAGUE LEADERS — PITCHING

## GAMES
| | | |
|---|---|---|
| 1927 | Jack Scott | 48* |
| 1930 | Hal Elliott | 48 |
| 1931 | Jumbo Elliott | 52 |
| 1934 | Curt Davis | 51 |
| 1935 | Orville Jorgens | 53 |
| 1937 | Hugh Mulcahy | 56 |
| 1945 | Andy Karl | 67 |
| 1950 | Jim Konstanty | 74 |
| 1961 | Jack Baldschun | 65 |
| 1975 | Gene Garber | 71 |

## COMPLETE GAMES
| | | |
|---|---|---|
| 1911 | Grover Alexander | 31 |
| 1914 | Grover Alexander | 32 |
| 1915 | Grover Alexander | 36 |
| 1916 | Grover Alexander | 38 |
| 1917 | Grover Alexander | 35 |
| 1952 | Robin Roberts | 30 |
| 1953 | Robin Roberts | 33 |
| 1954 | Robin Roberts | 29 |
| 1955 | Robin Roberts | 26 |
| 1956 | Robin Roberts | 22 |
| 1972 | Steve Carlton | 30 |
| 1963 | Steve Carlton | 18* |

## WINS
| | | |
|---|---|---|
| 1911 | Grover Alexander | 28 |
| 1913 | Tom Seaton | 27 |
| 1914 | Grover Alexander | 27* |
| 1915 | Grover Alexander | 31 |
| 1916 | Grover Alexander | 33 |
| 1917 | Grover Alexander | 30 |
| 1931 | Jumbo Elliott | 19* |
| 1952 | Robin Roberts | 28 |
| 1953 | Robin Roberts | 23* |
| 1954 | Robin Roberts | 23 |
| 1955 | Robin Roberts | 23 |
| 1972 | Steve Carlton | 27 |
| 1977 | Steve Carlton | 23 |

## SHUTOUTS
| | | |
|---|---|---|
| 1887 | Dan Casey | 4 |
| 1898 | Wiley Piatt | 6* |
| 1901 | Al Orth | 6* |
| 1911 | Grover Alexander | 7 |
| 1913 | Grover Alexander | 9 |
| 1915 | Grover Alexander | 12 |
| 1916 | Grover Alexander | 16 |
| 1917 | Grover Alexander | 8 |
| 1925 | Hal Carlson | 4* |

| | | |
|---|---|---|
| 1936 | Bucky Walters | 4* |
| 1949 | Ken Heintzelman | 5* |
| 1950 | Robin Roberts | 5* |
| 1952 | Curt Simmons | 6* |
| 1966 | Jim Bunning | 5* |
| 1966 | Larry Jackson | 5* |
| 1967 | Jim Bunning | 6 |

## INNINGS PITCHED
| | | |
|---|---|---|
| 1911 | Grover Alexander | 367 |
| 1912 | Grover Alexander | 310* |
| 1913 | Tom Seaton | 322 |
| 1914 | Grover Alexander | 355 |
| 1915 | Grover Alexander | 376 |
| 1916 | Grover Alexander | 389 |
| 1917 | Grover Alexander | 388 |
| 1937 | Claude Passeau | 292 |
| 1951 | Robin Roberts | 315 |
| 1952 | Robin Roberts | 330 |
| 1953 | Robin Roberts | 347 |
| 1954 | Robin Roberts | 337 |
| 1955 | Robin Roberts | 305 |
| 1967 | Jim Bunning | 302 |
| 1972 | Steve Carlton | 346 |
| 1973 | Steve Carlton | 293* |

## STRIKEOUTS
| | | |
|---|---|---|
| 1910 | Earl Moore | 185 |
| 1912 | Grover Alexander | 195 |
| 1913 | Tom Seaton | 168 |
| 1914 | Grover Alexander | 214 |
| 1915 | Grover Alexander | 241 |
| 1916 | Grover Alexander | 167 |
| 1917 | Grover Alexander | 201 |
| 1939 | Claude Passeau | 137* |
| 1940 | Kirby Higbe | 137 |
| 1953 | Robin Roberts | 198 |
| 1954 | Robin Roberts | 185 |
| 1957 | Jack Sanford | 188 |
| 1967 | Jim Bunning | 253 |
| 1972 | Steve Carlton | 310 |
| 1974 | Steve Carlton | 240 |

## EARNED RUN AVERAGE
| | | |
|---|---|---|
| 1886 | Charles Ferguson | 1.98 |
| 1887 | Dan Casey | 2.86 |
| 1889 | Al Orth | 2.49 |
| 1910 | George McQuillan | 1.60 |
| 1915 | Grover Alexander | 1.22 |
| 1916 | Grover Alexander | 1.55 |
| 1917 | Grover Alexander | 1.86 |
| 1972 | Steve Carlton | 1.98 |

*Tied

148

# PHILLIES CAREER GAMES

## By Position

**FIRST BASE**

| | | |
|---|---|---|
| Fred Luderus | 1910-20 | 1,298 |
| Sid Farrar | 1883-89 | 816 |
| Don Hurst | 1928-34 | 815 |
| Kitty Bransfield | 1905-11 | 781 |
| Eddie Waitkus | 1949-53; 55 | 585 |

**SHORTSTOP**

| | | |
|---|---|---|
| Larry Bowa | 1970- | 1,335 |
| Mickey Doolan | 1905-13 | 1,297 |
| Granny Hamner | 1944-59 | 924 |
| Heinie Sand | 1923-28 | 772 |
| Dave Bancroft | 1915-20 | 670 |

**OUTFIELD**

| | | |
|---|---|---|
| Richie Ashburn | 1948-59 | 1,785 |
| Del Ennis | 1946-56 | 1,610 |
| Sherry Magee | 1904-14 | 1,415 |
| Johnny Callison | 1960-69 | 1,379 |
| Cy Williams | 1918-30 | 1,324 |
| Chuck Klein | 1928-33; 36-44 | 1,284 |
| Roy Thomas | 1899-1908; 10-11 | 1,257 |
| John Titus | 1903-12 | 1,185 |
| Ed Delahanty | 1888-89; 1891-1901 | 1,175 |
| Tony Gonzalez | 1960-68 | 1,054 |
| Sam Thompson | 1889-98 | 1,033 |
| Gavvy Cravath | 1889-98 | 995 |
| Greg Luzinski | 1970- | 991 |

**SECOND BASE**

| | | |
|---|---|---|
| Tony Taylor | 1960-71; 74-76 | 1,003 |
| Otto Knabe | 1907-13 | 931 |
| Bill Hallman | 1888-89; 1892-97 1901-1903 | 779 |
| Cookie Rojas | 1963-69 | 617 |
| Kid Gleason | 1888-91; 1903-08 | 572 |

**THIRD BASE**

| | | |
|---|---|---|
| Willie Jones | 1947-59 | 1,495 |
| Pinky Whitney | 1928-33; 36-39 | 1,076 |
| Mike Schmidt | 1972- | 898 |
| Joe Mulvey | 1883-89; 92 | 682 |
| Pinky May | 1939-43 | 646 |

**CATCHER**

| | | |
|---|---|---|
| Red Dooin | 1902-14 | 1,124 |
| Jack Clements | 1884-97 | 953 |
| Clay Dalrymple | 1960-68 | 944 |
| Andy Seminick | 1943-51; 55-57 | 917 |
| Bob Boone | 1972- | 765 |

# PHILLIES DEFENSIVE LEAGUE LEADERS
## By Percentage (Since 1963)

| | | | | | | |
|---|---|---|---|---|---|---|
| 1963 | Chris Short, p | 1.000 | | 1971 | Larry Bowa, ss | .9869 |
| 1963 | Don Demeter, of | 1.000 | | 1972 | Don Money, 3b | .978 |
| 1963 | Tony Taylor, 2b | .986 | | 1972 | Larry Bowa, ss | .9874 |
| 1964 | Tony Gonzalez, of | .996 | | 1973 | Ken Brett, p | 1.000 |
| 1966 | Bill White, 1b | .994 | | 1973 | Greg Luzinski, of | .993 |
| 1967 | Tony Gonzalez, of | .993 | | 1974 | Larry Bowa, ss | .984 |
| 1967 | Bobby Wine, ss | .980 | | 1976 | Dave Cash, 2b | .988 |
| 1968 | Larry Jackson, p | 1.000 | | 1978 | Bob Boone, c | .991 |
| 1968 | John Callison, of | 1.000 | | 1978 | Bake McBride, of | .996 |
| 1968 | Cookie Rojas, 2b | .987 | | 1978 | Larry Bowa, ss | .986 |
| 1971 | Rick Wise, p | 1.000 | | | | |

# PHILLIES PITCHING RECORDS
## INDIVIDUAL SEASON (Since 1900)

| | Player | Record | Year |
|---|---|---|---|
| Games, RH | Konstanty | 74 | 1950 |
| Games, LH | Knowles | 69 | 1966 |
| Games Started, RH | Alexander | 45 | 1916 |
| Games Started, LH | Carlton | 41 | 1972 |
| Complete Games, RH | Alexander | 38 | 1916 |
| Complete Games, LH | Carlton | 30 | 1972 |
| Games Finished | Konstanty | 62 | 1950 |
| Wins, RH | Alexander | 33 | 1916 |
| Wins, LH | Carlton | 27 | 1972 |
| Losses, RH | Fraser | 24 | 1904 |
| Losses, LH | Rixey | 22 | 1920 |
| Shutouts, RH | Alexander | 16 | 1916 |
| Shutouts, LH | Carlton | 8 | 1972 |
| 1-0 Shutouts, Won | Alexander | 4 | 1916 |
| 1-0 Shutouts, Lost | McQuillan | 5 | 1908 |
| | Bunning | 5 | 1967 |
| Shutouts, Lost | McQuillan | 8 | 1908 |
| Innings, Pitched, RH | Alexander | 399 | 1916 |
| Innings, Pitched, LH | Carlton | 346 | 1972 |
| Hits, RH | Passeau | 348 | 1937 |
| Hits, LH | Carlton | 293 | 1973 |
| Runs, RH | Benge | 175 | 1930 |
| Runs, LH | Sweetland | 164 | 1930 |
| Earned Runs, RH | Roberts | 147 | 1956 |
| Earned Runs, LH | Sweetland | 143 | 1930 |
| Walks, RH | Moore | 164 | 1911 |
| Walks, LH | Carlton | 136 | 1974 |
| Strike Outs, RH | Bunning | 268 | 1965 |
| Strike Outs, LH | Carlton | 310 | 1972 |
| Hit Batters, RH | Mitchell | 19 | 1903 |
| | Bunning | 19 | 1966 |
| Hit Batters, LH | Lush | 16 | 1906 |
| Wild Pitches, RH | Hamilton | 22 | 1962 |
| Wild Pitches, LH | Short | 14 | 1961 |

## PHILLIES PITCHING RECORDS (Continued)

| | Player | Record | Year |
|---|---|---|---|
| Home Runs, RH | Roberts | 46 | 1956 |
| Home Runs, LH | Carlton | 30 | 1978 |
| Earned Run Average, RH | Alexander | 1.22 | 1915 |
| Earned Run Average, LH | Rixey | 1.85 | 1916 |
| Percentage, RH | Roberts (28-7) | .800 | 1952 |
| Percentage, LH | Carlton (20-7) | .741 | 1976 |
| Saves, RH | Konstanty | 22 | 1950 |
| | Selma | 22 | 1970 |
| Saves, LH | McGraw | 14 | 1975 |
| Longest Winning Streak | Carlton | 15 | 1972 |
| Longest Losing Streak | Miller | 12 | 1928 |
| | Mulcahy | 12 | 1940 |
| | Reynolds | 12 | 1972 |

# CLUB HITTING RECORDS

**SEASON (Since 1883)**

Most Games .............162 ('63-64-65-66-67-68-69-71-73-74-75-76-77-78)
Most At Bats .................................5667 in 1930 (156 games)
Most Runs .................................944 in 1930 (156 games)
Fewest Runs...............................394 in 1942 (151 games)
Most Hits ...................................1783 in 1930 (156 games)
Fewest Hits ...............................1113 in 1907 (149 games)
Most Singles ..............................1268 in 1930 (156 games)
Most Doubles ...............................345 in 1930 (156 games)
Most Triples ................................82 in 1905 (155 games)
Most Homers ................................186 in 1977 (162 games)
Most Homers, Pinch Hitters ..............................11 in 1958
Most Homers, Bases Filled .....................7 in 1925, 1929, 1976
Most Consecutive Games, One Home Run, or more ...................13
(16 homers), 1964
Most Consecutive Games, No Home Runs .................12 in 1960, 1961
Most Total Bases .............................2594 in 1930 (156 games)
Most Stolen Bases............................200 in 1908 (155 games)
Most Walks...................................652 in 1955 (154 games)
Most Strikeouts ............................1130 in 1969 (162 games)
Fewest Strikeouts............................452 in 1924 (152 games)
Most Hit By Pitcher ..........................53 in 1962 (161 games)
Most Runs Batted in ..........................884 in 1930 (156 games)
Highest Batting Average .......................315 in 1930 (156 games)
Lowest Batting Average .......................232 in 1942 (151 games)
Highest Slugging Percentage ...................467 in 1929 (154 games)
Lowest Slugging Percentage ...................305 in 1907 (149 games)
Most Grounded Into Double Play .................144 in 1950 (157 games)
Fewest Grounded Into Double Play ...............91 in 1935 (156 games)
91 in 1973 (162 games)
Most Left On Base ...........................1272 in 1975 (162 games)
Fewest Left On Bases .........................991 in 1920 (153 games)

# CLUB FIELDING RECORDS

## Season (Since 1883)

Most Errors .................................. 403 in 1904 (155 games)
Fewest Errors ................................. 104 in 1978 (162 games)
Most Errorless Games .......................... 89 in 1966 (162 games)
Most Consecutive Errorless Games ..................... 11 in 1967
Most Double Plays ............................ 179 in 1961 (155 games)
                  179 in 1973 (162 games)
Fewest Double Plays .......................... 117 in 1955 (154 games)
                  117 in 1957 (156 games)
Most Consecutive Games, 1 or More DPs ............. 16 (29 DPs) in 1961
Most Passed Balls ............................. 27 in 1971 (162 games)
                  27 in 1947 (155 games)
Fewest Passed Balls ........................... 3 in 1952 (154 games)
                  3 in 1956 (154 games)
Most Putouts ................................ 4406 in 1965 (162 games)
Fewest Putouts .............................. 3887 in 1907 (149 games)
Most Assists ................................ 2176 in 1921 (154 games)
Fewest Assists .............................. 1437 in 1957 (156 games)
Most Total Chances .......................... 6440 in 1913 (159 games)
Fewest Total Chances ........................ 5545 in 1955 (154 games)
Highest Fielding Percentage .................... .983 in 1978 (162 games)
Lowest Fielding Percentage .................... .936 in 1904 (155 games)

# PHILLIES HITTING RECORDS

## INDIVIDUAL — SEASON (Since 1900)

| | Player (Games Played) | Record | Year |
|---|---|---|---|
| Games, LH | Callison (162 games) | 162 | 1964 |
| Games, RH | R. Allen (162 games) | 162 | 1964 |
| | Bowa (162 games) | 162 | 1974 |
| | Cash (162 games) | 162 | 1974 |
| | Schmidt (162 games) | 162 | 1974 |
| | Cash (162 games) | 162 | 1975 |
| At Bats, LH | Ashburn (154 games) | 662 | 1949 |
| At Bats, RH | Cash (162 games) | 699 | 1975 |
| At Bats, SW | Bowa (162 games) | 696 | 1974 |
| Runs, LH | Klein (156 games) | 158 | 1930 |
| Runs, RH | R. Allen (162 games) | 125 | 1964 |
| Hits, LH | O'Doul (154 games) | 254 | 1929 |
| Hits, RH | Cash (162 games) | 213 | 1975 |
| Singles, LH | O'Doul (154 games) | 181 | 1929 |
| | Ashburn (154 games) | 181 | 1951 |
| Singles, RH | Cash (162 games) | 166 | 1975 |
| Doubles, LH | Klein (156 games) | 59 | 1930 |
| Doubles, RH | E. Allen (154 games) | 46 | 1935 |
| Triples, LH | Flick (138 games) | 17 | 1901 |
| Triples, RH | Magee (155 games) | 17 | 1905, 1910 |
| Home Runs, LH | Klein (149 games) | 43 | 1929 |

152

## PHILLIES HITTING RECORDS (Continued)

| Player (Games Played) | Record | Year |
|---|---|---|
| Home Runs, RH .......... R. Allen (141 games) | 40 | 1966 |
| Home Runs, Rookie, LH .... Montanez (158 games) | 30 | 1971 |
| Home Runs, Rookie, RH .... R. Allen (162 games) | 29 | 1964 |
| Home Runs, Home, LH ..... Williams (136 games) | 23 | 1923 |
| Home Runs, Home, RH ..... Johnson (158 games) | 22 | 1971 |
| Schmidt (162 games) | 22 | 1975 |
| Luzinski (149 games) | 22 | 1977 |
| Home Runs, Month, LH ..... Williams (May) | 15 | 1923 |
| Home Runs, Month, RH .... Schmidt (June) | 14 | 1977 |
| Home Runs, Pinch Hitter .... Freese | 5 | 1959 |
| Total Bases, LH .......... Klein (156 games) | 445 | 1930 |
| Total Bases, RH .......... R. Allen (162 games) | 352 | 1964 |
| Extra Base Hits, LH ........ Klein (156 games) | 107 | 1930 |
| Extra Base Hits, RH ....... R. Allen (162 games) | 80 | 1964 |
| Sacrifices .............. Gleason (155 games) | 43 | 1905 |
| Stolen Bases, LH .......... Slagle (141 games) | 38 | 1900 |
| Bowa (162 games) | 39 | 1974 |
| Stolen Bases, RH .......... Magee (154 games) | 55 | 1906 |
| Walks, LH .............. Ashburn (153 games) | 125 | 1954 |
| Walks, RH .............. Schmidt (162 games) | 106 | 1974 |
| Strike Outs, LH ........... Callison (160 games) | 118 | 1965 |
| Strike Outs, RH ........... Schmidt (162 games) | 180 | 1975 |
| Fewest Strike Outs, LH ..... O'Doul (154 games) | 19 | 1929 |
| Fewest Strike Outs, RH .... Verban (155 games) | 18 | 1947 |
| Hit By Pitch, LH .......... Bouchee (154 games) | 14 | 1957 |
| Hit By Pitch, RH .......... Taylor (162 games) | 13 | 1964 |
| Runs Batted in, LH ....... Klein (154 games) | 170 | 1930 |
| Runs Batted in, RH ....... Luzinski (149 games) | 130 | 1977 |
| Average, LH ............. O'Doul (154 games) | 398 | 1929 |
| Average, RH ............. Delahanty (139 games) | 357 | 1901 |
| Slugging Percentage, LH .... Klein (156 games) | 687 | 1930 |
| Slugging Percentage, RH .... R. Allen (141 games) | 632 | 1966 |
| Hitting Streak ........... Klein (twice) | 26 | 1930 |
| Montanez | 24 | 1974 |
| Hitting Streak, Rookie ...... Ashburn | 23 | 1948 |
| Rapp | 23 | 1921 |
| Grounded Into Double Plays . Ennis (153 games) | 25 | 1950 |
| Sizemore (152 games) | 25 | 1977 |
| Fewest GI DP ............ Klein (152 games) | 3 | 1933 |
| Ashburn (156 games) | 3 | 1953 |
| Ashburn (153 games) | 3 | 1954 |

# PHILLIES MAJOR LEAGUE ALL-STAR GAME SELECTIONS

| | | | | |
|---|---|---|---|---|
| 1933 | Dick Bartell, SS | | 1940 | Kirby Higbe, P |
| | Chuck Klein, OF | | | Pinky May, 3B |
| 1934 | None | | | Hugh Mulcahy, P |
| 1935 | Jimmie Wilson, C | | | Doc Prothro, Coach |
| 1936 | Pinky Whitney, 3B | | 1941 | Cy Blanton, P |
| 1937 | Bucky Walters, P | | 1942 | Danny Litwhiler, OF |
| 1938 | Herschel Martin, OF | | 1943 | Babe Dahlgren, 1B |
| 1939 | Morrie Arnovich, OF | | 1944 | Ken Raffensberger, P |

# PHILLIES MAJOR LEAGUE ALL—STAR GAME (Continued)

|      |                          |      |                          |
|------|--------------------------|------|--------------------------|
|      | Freddie Fitzsimmons, Coach | 1959 | Gene Conley, P          |
| 1945 | No Game                  |      | Eddie Sawyer, Coach      |
| 1946 | Frank McCormick, 1B      | 1960 | Tony Taylor, 2B          |
|      | Del Ennis, OF            | 1961 | Art Mahaffey, P          |
|      | Emil Verban, 2B          |      | Gene Mauch, Coach        |
| 1947 | Schoolboy Rowe, P        | 1962 | Johnny Callison, OF      |
|      | Emil Verban, 2B          |      | Art Mahaffey, P          |
|      | Harry Walker, OF         | 1963 | Ray Culp, P              |
|      | Ben Chapman, Coach       |      | Gene Mauch, Coach        |
| 1948 | Richie Ashburn, OF       | 1964 | Jim Bunning, P           |
| 1949 | Andy Seminick, C         |      | Johnny Callison, OF      |
|      | Eddie Waitkus, 1B        |      | Chris Short, P           |
| 1950 | Willie Jones, 3B         | 1965 | Richie Allen, 3B         |
|      | Jim Konstanty, P         |      | Johnny Callison, OF      |
|      | Robin Roberts, P         |      | Cookie Rojas, 2B         |
|      | Dick Sisler, OF          |      | Gene Mauch, Manager      |
| 1951 | Richie Ashburn, OF       | 1966 | Richie Allen, OF         |
|      | Del Ennis, OF            |      | Jim Bunning, P           |
|      | Willie Jones, 3B         | 1967 | Richie Allen, 3B         |
|      | Robin Roberts, P         |      | Chris Short, P           |
|      | Eddie Sawyer, Manager    | 1968 | Woodie Fryman, P         |
|      | Benny Bengough, Coach    | 1969 | Grant Jackson, P         |
|      | Dusty Cooke, Coach       | 1970 | Joe Hoerner, P           |
|      | Cy Perkins, Coach        | 1971 | Rick Wise, P             |
| 1952 | Granny Hamner, SS        | 1972 | Steve Carlton, P         |
|      | Robin Roberts, P         | 1973 | Wayne Twitchell, P       |
|      | Curt Simmons, P          | 1974 | Larry Bowa, SS           |
| 1953 | Richie Ashburn, OF       |      | Steve Carlton, P         |
|      | Granny Hamner, SS        |      | Dave Cash, 2B            |
|      | Robin Roberts, P         |      | Mike Schmidt, 3B         |
|      | Curt Simmons, P          | 1975 | Larry Bowa, SS           |
| 1954 | Smoky Burgess, C         |      | Dave Cash, 2B            |
|      | Granny Hamner, 2B        |      | Greg Luzinski, OF        |
|      | Robin Roberts, P         |      | Tug McGraw, P            |
| 1955 | Del Ennis, OF            | 1976 | Bob Boone, C             |
|      | Robin Roberts, P         |      | Larry Bowa, SS           |
|      | Mayo Smith, Coach        |      | Dave Cash, 2B            |
| 1956 | Stan Lopata, C           |      | Greg Luzinski, OF        |
|      | Robin Roberts, P         |      | Mike Schmidt, 3B         |
| 1957 | Jack Sanford, P          | 1977 | Steve Carlton, P         |
|      | Curt Simmons, P          |      | Greg Luzinski, OF        |
| 1958 | Richie Ashburn, OF       |      | Mike Schmidt, 3B         |
|      | Dick Farrell, P          | 1978 | Bob Boone, C             |
|      | Mayo Smith, Coach        |      | Larry Bowa, SS           |
|      |                          |      | Greg Luzinski, OF        |

# SPRING TRAINING
## PHILLIES SPRING TRAINING SITES

| 1902 | Washington, D.C.   | 1906-08 | Savannah, Georgia               |
|------|--------------------|---------|---------------------------------|
| 1903 | Richmond, Virginia | 1909-10 | Southern Pines, North Carolina  |
| 1904 | Savannah, Georgia  | 1911    | Birmingham, Alabama             |
| 1905 | Augusta, Georgia   | 1912    | Hot Springs, Arkansas           |

## PHILLIES SPRING TRAINING SITES (Continued)

| | | | |
|---|---|---|---|
| 1913 | Southern Pines, North Carolina | 1928-37 | Winter Haven, Florida |
| 1914 | Wilmington, North Carolina | 1938 | Biloxi, Mississippi |
| 1915-18 | St. Petersburg, Florida | 1939 | New Braunfels, Texas |
| 1919 | Charlotte, North Carolina | 1940-42 | Miami Beach, Florida |
| 1920 | Birmingham, Alabama | 1943 | Hershey, Pensylvania |
| 1921 | Gainesville, Florida | 1944-45 | Wilmington, Delaware |
| 1922-24 | Leesburgh, Florida | 1946 | Miami Beach, Florida |
| 1925-27 | Bradenton, Florida | 1947-78 | Clearwater, Florida |

## PHILLIES EXHIBITION SEASON RECORD (1948-78))

| Year | Won-Lost | Year | Won-Lost | Year | Won-Lost |
|---|---|---|---|---|---|
| 1948 | 12-20 | 1959 | 11-14 | 1969 | 14-11 |
| 1949 | 12-11 | 1960 | 7-13 | 1970 | 14-10 |
| 1950 | 12-11 | 1961 | 14-11 | 1971 | 11-14 |
| 1951 | 16-15 | 1962 | 7-14 | 1972 | 9-10 |
| 1952 | 17-15 | 1963 | 11-15 | 1973 | 11-13 |
| 1953 | 15-15 | 1964 | 12-14 | 1974 | 12-10 |
| 1954 | 12-20 | 1965 | 13-13 | 1975 | 17-10 |
| 1955 | 14-11 | 1966 | 10-16 | 1976 | 8-7 |
| 1956 | 14-18 | 1967 | 9-20 | 1977 | 16-9 |
| 1957 | 18-14 | 1968 | 14-14 | 1978 | 14-11 |
| 1958 | 14-16 | | | | |

# PHILLIES SEASON .300 HITTERS

### (Minimum 400 at bats)

| | | | | | | |
|---|---|---|---|---|---|---|
| 1887 | Ed Andrews | .325 | 1897 | Ed Delahanty | .377 |
| 1890 | Billy Hamilton | .325 | | Nap Lajoie | .361 |
| | Sam Thompson | .325 | | Duff Cooley | .329 |
| 1891 | Billy Hamilton | .340 | 1898 | Ed Delahanty | .334 |
| | Jack Clements | .310 | | Nap Lajoie | .328 |
| 1892 | Billy Hamilton | .330 | | Elmer Flick | .313 |
| | Ed Delahanty | .306 | | Duff Cooley | .312 |
| | Sam Thompson | .305 | 1899 | Ed Delahanty | .410 |
| 1893 | Billy Hamilton | .380 | | Elmer Flick | .342 |
| | Sam Thompson | .370 | | Roy Thomas | .325 |
| | Ed Delahanty | .368 | 1900 | Elmer Flick | .378 |
| | Bill Hallman | .307 | | Nap Lajoie | .337 |
| 1894 | Ed Delahanty | .407 | | Ed Delahanty | .323 |
| | Billy Hamilton | .404 | | Roy Thomas | .316 |
| | Sam Thompson | .404 | 1901 | Ed Delahanty | .354 |
| | Lave Cross | .386 | | Elmer Flick | .336 |
| | Bill Hallman | .309 | | Roy Thomas | .309 |
| | Jack Boyle | .301 | 1903 | Roy Thomas | .327 |
| 1895 | Ed Delahanty | .404 | | Bill Keister | .320 |
| | Sam Thompson | .392 | | Harry Wolverton | .308 |
| | Billy Hamilton | .389 | 1905 | Roy Thomas | .317 |
| | Bill Hallman | .314 | | John Titus | .308 |
| 1896 | Ed Delahanty | .397 | 1907 | Sherry Magee | .328 |
| | Bill Hallman | .320 | 1908 | Kitty Bransfield | .304 |

155

## PHILLIES SEASON .300 SERIES (Continued)

| | | | | |
|---|---|---|---|---|
| 1910 | Sherry Magee ......331 | | Spud Davis .........349 |
| | Johnny Bates ......305 | | Chick Fullis ........309 |
| 1911 | Fred Luderus ......301 | 1934 | Johnny Moore .....343 |
| 1912 | Dode Paskert ......315 | | Ethan Allen ........330 |
| | Sherry Magee ......306 | | Dick Bartell .......310 |
| 1913 | Gavvy Cravath .....341 | | Lou Chiozza ......304 |
| | Sherry Magee ......306 | 1935 | Johnny Moore .....323 |
| | Hans Lobert ........300 | | Ethan Allen ........307 |
| 1914 | Beals Becker ......325 | 1936 | Johnny Moore .....328 |
| | Sherry Magee ......314 | | Dolf Camilli ........315 |
| 1915 | Fred Luderus ......315 | | Chuck Klein ........309 |
| 1919 | Irish Meusel .......305 | 1937 | Pinky Whitney .....341 |
| 1920 | Cy Williams .......325 | | Dolf Camilli ........339 |
| | Irish Meusel .......309 | | Chuck Klein .......325 |
| 1921 | Cy Williams .......320 | 1939 | Morrie Arnovich ....324 |
| 1922 | Curt Walker .......337 | 1941 | Nick Etten ........311 |
| | Cliff Lee ..........322 | | Danny Litwhiler ....305 |
| | Butch Henline .....316 | 1945 | Jimmy Wasdell .....300 |
| | Cy Williams .......308 | 1946 | Del Ennis .........313 |
| 1923 | Cotton Tierney ....317 | 1947 | Harry Walker ......371 |
| | Johnny Mokan .....313 | 1948 | Richie Ashburn ....333 |
| | Walter Holke ......311 | 1949 | Del Ennis .........302 |
| 1924 | Cy Williams .......328 | 1950 | Del Ennis .........311 |
| | Walter Holke ......300 | | Richie Ashburn ....303 |
| 1925 | George Harper .....349 | 1951 | Richie Ashburn ....344 |
| | Lew Fonseca ......319 | 1953 | Richie Ashburn ....330 |
| 1926 | Freddy Leach .....329 | 1954 | Richie Ashburn ....313 |
| | Johnny Mokan .....303 | 1955 | Richie Ashburn ....338 |
| 1927 | Freddy Leach .....306 | 1956 | Richie Ashburn .....303 |
| | Russ Wrightstone ...306 | 1958 | Richie Ashburn ....350 |
| | Fresco Thompson ....303 | | Harry Anderson ....301 |
| 1928 | Freddy Leach .....304 | 1962 | Don Demeter ......307 |
| | Pinky Whitney .....301 | | Tony Gonzalez ....302 |
| 1929 | Lefty O'Doul ......398 | | Johnny Callison ....300 |
| | Chuck Klein .......356 | 1963 | Tony Gonzalez ....306 |
| | Pinky Whitney .....327 | 1964 | Richie Allen .......318 |
| | Fresco Thompson ....324 | 1965 | Cookie Rojas ......303 |
| | Don Hurst ........304 | | Richie Allen .......302 |
| | Barney Friberg .....301 | 1966 | Richie Allen .......317 |
| 1930 | Chuck Klein .......386 | 1967 | Tony Gonzalez ....339 |
| | Lefty O'Doul ......383 | | Richie Allen .......307 |
| | Pinky Whitney .....342 | 1970 | Tony Taylor ......301 |
| | Don Hurst ........327 | 1974 | Willie Montanez .....304 |
| 1931 | Chuck Klein .......337 | | Dave Cash ........300 |
| | Buzz Arlett .......313 | 1975 | Larry Bowa ........305 |
| | Don Hurst ........305 | | Dave Cash ........305 |
| 1932 | Chuck Klein .......348 | | Greg Luzinski .....300 |
| | Don Hurst ........339 | 1976 | Garry Maddox .....330 |
| | Spud Davis ........336 | | Jay Johnstone .....318 |
| | Kiddo Davis .......309 | | Greg Luzinski .....304 |
| | Dick Bartell .......308 | 1977 | Bake McBride ......316 |
| | Hal Lee ..........303 | | Greg Luzinski ......309 |
| 1933 | Chuck Klein .......368 | | |

# MAJOR HONORS AWARDED PHILLIES PERSONNEL

### MOST VALUABLE PLAYER AWARD
Baseball Writers Association

| | |
|---|---|
| 1932 | Chuck Klein, OF |
| 1950 | Jim Konstanty, P |

### CY YOUNG MEMORIAL AWARD
Baseball Writers Association

| | |
|---|---|
| 1972 | Steve Carlton |
| 1977 | Steve Carlton |

### ROOKIE OF THE YEAR
Baseball Writers Association

| | |
|---|---|
| 1957 | Jack Sanford, P |
| 1964 | Richie Allen, 3B |

### MAJOR LEAGUE PLAYER OF YEAR
"The Sporting News"

| | |
|---|---|
| 1952 | Robin Roberts, P |

### MAJOR LEAGUE MANAGER OF YEAR
"The Sporting News"

| | |
|---|---|
| 1976 | Danny Ozark |

### MAJOR LEAGUE EXECUTIVE OF YEAR
"The Sporting News"

| | |
|---|---|
| 1950 | R.R.M. Carpenter, Jr. |

### MOST VALUABLE PLAYER AWARD
"The Sporting News"

| | |
|---|---|
| 1931 | Chuck Klein, OF |
| 1932 | Chuck Klein, OF |

### PLAYER, PITCHER OF THE YEAR
"The Sporting News"

| | |
|---|---|
| 1950 | Jim Konstanty, P |
| 1952 | Robin Roberts, P |
| 1955 | Robin Roberts, P |
| 1972 | Steve Carlton, P |
| 1977 | Steve Carlton, P |

### ROOKIE AWARD
"The Sporting News

| | |
|---|---|
| 1946 | Del Ennis, OF |
| 1948 | Richie Ashburn, OF |
| 1957 | Ed Bouchee, 1B |
| | Jack Sanford, P |
| 1963 | Ray Culp, P |
| 1964 | Richie Allen, 3B |

157

# PHILLIES IN HALL OF FAME
## PLAYERS

| Name | Years with Phillies | Year Selected |
|------|---------------------|---------------|
| Dave Bancroft | 1915-20 | 1971 |
| Dan Brouthers | 1896 | 1945 |
| Roger Connor | 1892 | 1976 |
| Ed Delahanty | 1888-89, 1891-1901 | 1945 |
| Hugh Duffy* | 1904-06 | 1945 |
| Johnny Evers | 1917 | 1946 |
| Elmer Flick | 1898-1902 | 1963 |
| Jimmie Foxx | 1945 | 1951 |
| Billy Hamilton | 1890-95 | 1961 |
| Hughie Jennings | 1901-02 | 1945 |
| Nap Lajoie | 1896-1900 | 1937 |
| Tommy McCarthy | 1886-87 | 1946 |
| Casey Stengel | 1920-21 | 1966 |
| Sam Thompson | 1889-98 | 1974 |
| Lloyd Waner | 1942 | 1967 |

### Pitchers

| | | |
|------|---------------------|---------------|
| Grover Alexander | 1911-17 | 1938 |
| Chief Bender | 1916-17 | 1953 |
| Tim Keefe | 1891-93 | 1964 |
| Kid Nichols | 1905-06 | 1949 |
| Eppa Rixey | 1912-17, 1919-20 | 1963 |
| Robin Roberts | 1948-61 | 1976 |

### Managers

| | | |
|------|---------------------|---------------|
| Bucky Harris | 1943 | 1974 |
| Harry Wright | 1884-93 | 1953 |

*player-manager

# ATTENDANCE
## TOP FIFTEEN YEARS — HOME ATTENDANCE

| Year | Attendance | Finish | Year | Attendance | Finish |
|------|-----------|--------|------|-----------|--------|
| 1977 | 2,700,007 | 1-x | 1972 | 1,343,329 | 6-x |
| 1978 | 2,583,389 | 1-x | 1950 | 1,217,035 | 1 |
| 1976 | 2,480,150 | 1-x | 1965 | 1,166,376 | 6 |
| 1975 | 1,909,233 | 2-x | 1957 | 1,146,230 | 5 |
| 1974 | 1,808,648 | 3-x | 1966 | 1,108,201 | 4 |
| 1971 | 1,511,223 | 6-x | 1946 | 1,045,247 | 5 |
| 1973 | 1,475,934 | 6-x | 1951 | 937,658 | 5 |
| 1964 | 1,425,891 | t-2 | | | |

t-tied for position. x-in Eastern Division. Note: 1971 through 1978, Phillies played at Veterans Stadium; mid-season, 1938 through 1970 at Shibe Park-Connie Mack Stadium.

## TOP FIVE YEARS ATTENDANCE AT BAKER BOWL

| Year | Attendance | Finish | Year | Attendance | Finish |
|------|-----------|--------|------|-----------|--------|
| 1916 | 515,365 | 2 | 1908 | 420,660 | 4 |
| 1913 | 470,000 | 2 | 1911 | 416,000 | 4 |
| 1915 | 449,898 | 1 | | | |

# WORLD SERIES AND CHAMPIONSHIP SERIES GAMES

## World Series — 1915

| Date | Place | Score | Winning Pitcher | Losing Pitcher |
|---|---|---|---|---|
| October 8 | Philadelphia | Phillies 3, Boston 1 | Grover Alexander | Ernie Shore |
| 9 | Philadelphia | Boston 2, Phillies 1 | George Foster | Erskine Mayer |
| 11 | Boston | Boston 2, Phillies 1 | Dutch Leonard | Grover Alexander |
| 12 | Boston | Boston 2, Phillies 1 | Ernie Shore | George Chalmers |
| 13 | Philadelphia | Boston 5, Phillies 4 | George Foster | Eppa Rixey |

## World Series — 1950

| Date | Place | Score | Winning Pitcher | Losing Pitcher |
|---|---|---|---|---|
| October 4 | Philadelphia | New York 1, Phillies 0 | Vic Raschi | Jim Konstanty |
| 5 | Philadelphia | New York 2, Phillies 1* | Allie Reynolds | Robin Roberts |
| 6 | New York | New York 3, Phillies 2 | Tom Ferrick | Russ Meyer |
| 7 | New York | New York 5, Phillies 2 | Whitey Ford | Bob Miller |

*Ten Innings

## PHILLIES LEADING BATTERS IN WORLD SERIES

| Year | Player | G | AB | R | H | 2B | 3B | HR | RBI | Pct. |
|---|---|---|---|---|---|---|---|---|---|---|
| 1915 | Fred Luderus | 5 | 16 | 1 | 7 | 2 | 0 | 1 | 6 | .438 |
| 1950 | Granny Hamner | 4 | 14 | 1 | 6 | 2 | 1 | 0 | 0 | .429 |

# PHILLIES WORLD SERIES HOME RUN

In 1915, Fred Luderus hit the only World Series home run by a Phillies player. It came in the fourth inning with no one on base off Boston Red Sox righthander George Foster and gave the Phillies a 3-2 lead.

## National League Championship Series — 1976

| Date | Place | Score | Winning Pitcher | Losing Pitcher |
|---|---|---|---|---|
| October 9 | Philadelphia | Cincinnati 6, Phillies 3 | Don Gullett | Steve Carlton |
| 10 | Philadelphia | Cincinnati 6, Phillies 2 | Pat Zachry | Jim Lonborg |
| 12 | Cincinnati | Cincinnati 7, Phillies 6 | Rawly Eastwick | Gene Garber |

## National League Championship Series — 1977

| Date | Place | Score | Winning Pitcher | Losing Pitcher |
|---|---|---|---|---|
| October 4 | Los Angeles | Phillies 7, Los Angeles 5 | Gene Garber | Elias Sosa |
| 5 | Los Angeles | Los Angeles 7, Phillies 1 | Don Sutton | Jim Lonborg |
| 7 | Philadelphia | Los Angeles 6, Phillies 5 | Lance Rautzhan | Gene Garber |
| 8 | Philadelphia | Los Angeles 4, Phillies 1 | Tommy John | Steve Carlton |

## National League Championship Series — 1978

| Date | Place | Score | Winning Pitcher | Losing Pitcher |
|---|---|---|---|---|
| October 4 | Philadelphia | Los Angeles 9, Phillies 5 | Bob Welch | Larry Christenson |
| 5 | Philadelphia | Los Angeles 4, Phillies 0 | Tommy John | Dick Ruthven |
| 6 | Los Angeles | Phillies 9, Los Angeles 4 | Steve Carlton | Don Sutton |
| 7 | Los Angeles | Los Angeles 4, Phillies 3* | Terry Forster | Tug McGraw |

*Ten Innings.

## PHILLIES LEADING BATTERS IN NATIONAL LEAGUE CHAMPIONSHIP SERIES

| Year | Player | G | AB | R | H | 2B | 3B | HR | RBl | Pct. |
|------|--------|---|----|---|---|----|----|----|----|------|
| 1976 | Jay Johnstone | 3 | 9 | 1 | 7 | 1 | 1 | 0 | 2 | .778 |
| 1976 | Dave Cash | 3 | 13 | 1 | 4 | 1 | 0 | 0 | 1 | .308 |
| 1976 | Mike Schmidt | 3 | 13 | 1 | 4 | 2 | 0 | 0 | 2 | .308 |
| 1977 | Garry Maddox | 2 | 7 | 1 | 3 | 0 | 0 | 0 | 2 | .429 |
| 1977 | Bob Boone | 4 | 10 | 1 | 4 | 0 | 0 | 0 | 0 | .400 |
| 1977 | Richie Hebner | 4 | 14 | 2 | 5 | 2 | 0 | 0 | 0 | .357 |
| 1978 | Ted Sizemore | 4 | 13 | 3 | 5 | 0 | 1 | 0 | 1 | .385 |
| 1978 | Greg Luzinski | 4 | 16 | 3 | 6 | 0 | 1 | 2 | 3 | .375 |
| 1978 | Larry Bowa | 4 | 18 | 2 | 6 | 0 | 0 | 0 | 0 | .333 |

## PHILLIES PLAYERS APPEARING IN WORLD SERIES AND NATIONAL LEAGUE CHAMPIONSHIP SERIES GAMES

### World Series — 1915

Grover Alexander, P
Dave Bancroft, SS
Beals Becker, CF
Ed Burns, C
Bobby Byrne, PH
George Chalmers, P

Gavvy Cravath, RF
Oscar Dugey, PR
Bill Killefer, PH
Fred Luderus, 1B
Erskine Mayer, P
Bert Niehoff, 2B

Dode Paskert, CF
Eppa Rixey, P
Milt Stock 3B
Possum Whitted, LF-1B

### World Series — 1950

Richie Ashburn, CF
Jimmie Bloodworth, 2B
Putsy Caballero, PR-PH
Del Ennis, RF
Mike Goliat, 2B
Granny Hamner, SS
Ken Heintzelman, P

Ken Johnson, P
Willie Jones, 3B
Jim Konstanty, P
Stan Lopata, C-PH
Jack Mayor, LF
Russ Meyer, P
Bob Miller, P

Robin Roberts, P
Andy Seminick, C
Ken Silvestri, C
Dick Sisler, LF
Eddie Waitkus, 1B
Dick Whitman, PH

### Championship Series — 1976

Dick Allen, 1B
Bob Boone, C
Larry Bowa, SS
Ollie Brown, RF
Steve Carlton, P
Dave Cash, 2B
Gene Garber, P
Terry Harmon, PR

Tommy Hutton, PH
Jay Johnstone, RF-PH
Jim Kaat, P
Jim Lonborg, P
Greg Luzinski, LF
Tim McCarver, C-PH
Tug McGraw, P
Garry Maddox, CF

Jerry Martin, LF-PH
Johnny Oates, C
Ron Reed, P
Mike Schmidt, 3B
Bobby Tolan, LF-1B -PH
Tommy Underwood, P

### Championship Series — 1977

Bob Boone, C
Larry Bowa, SS
Ollie Brown, PH
Warren Brusstar, P
Steve Carlton, P
Larry Christenson, P
Gene Garber, P

Richie Hebner, 1B-PH
Tommy Hutton, 1B-PH
Dave Johnson, 1B
Jay Johnstone, RF-PH
Jim Lonborg, P
Greg Luzinski, LF
Bake McBride, CF-RF

Tim McCarver, C-PH
Tug McGraw, P
Garry Maddox, CF
Jerry Martin, RF-PH
Ron Reed, P
Mike Schmidt, 3B
Ted Sizemore, 2B

### Championship Series — 1978

Bob Boone, C
Larry Bowa, SS
Warren Brusstar, P
Jose Cardenal, 1B
Steve Carlton, P
Larry Christenson, P
Rawly Eastwick, P
Barry Foote, PH

Orlando Gonzalez, PH
Richie Hebner, 1B-PH
Randy Lerch, P
Greg Luzinski, LF
Bake McBride, RF-PH
Tim McCarver, C-PH
Tug McGraw, P

Garry Maddox, CF
Jerry Martin, RF-PH
Jim Morrison, PH
Ron Reed, P
Dick Ruthven, P
Mike Schmidt, 3B
Ted Sizemore, 2B

## TEAM HITTING, PITCHING, FIELDING

| | HITTING | | | PITCHING | | FIELDING | | |
|---|---|---|---|---|---|---|---|---|
| | R | HR | B.A./RANK | CG | ERA/RANK | E | DP | F.A./RANK |
| 1876 | 378 | 7 | .271-2 | 53 | 3.22-7 | 456 | 32 | .839-7 |
| 1883 | 437 | 4 | .240-8 | 91 | 5.33-8 | 639 | 62 | .858-8 |
| 1884 | 549 | 14 | .234-7 | 106 | 3.93-8 | 536 | 67 | .888-6 |
| 1885 | 513 | 20 | .229-6 | 108 | 2.39-3 | 447 | 66 | .925-3 |
| 1886 | 621 | 26 | .240-5 | 110 | 2.45-1 | 393 | 46 | .920-3 |
| 1887 | 901 | 47 | .274-4 | 119 | 3.47-2 | 471 | 76 | .912-5 |
| 1888 | 535 | 16 | .225-7 | 125 | 2.38-3 | 424 | 70 | .923-3 |
| 1889 | 742 | 44 | .266-4 | 106 | 4.00-5 | 466 | 92 | .915-7 |
| 1890 | 827 | 25 | .269-1 | 122 | 3.32-6 | 398 | 122* | .928-5 |
| 1891 | 756 | 21 | .252.6 | 105 | 3.73-7 | 443 | 108 | .925-5 |
| 1892 | 860 | 50 | .262-1** | 131 | 2.93-3 | 393 | 128 | .939-1** |
| 1893 | 1011* | 79* | .301-1 | 107 | 4.68-7 | 318 | 121 | .943-1 |
| 1894 | 1143 | 40 | .349-1 | 102 | 5.63-10 | 338 | 111 | .935-2** |
| 1895 | 1068* | 61* | .330-1 | 106 | 5.47-7 | 369 | 93 | .933-5 |
| 1896 | 890 | 49* | .295-5 | 107 | 5.20-11 | 313 | 112 | .940-6 |
| 1897 | 752 | 40 | .293-6 | 115 | 5.60-9** | 296 | 72 | .944-5 |
| 1898 | 823 | 33 | .280-3 | 129 | 3.72-8 | 379 | 102 | .937-9 |
| 1899 | 916* | 30 | .301-1 | 129 | 3.48-7 | 379 | 110 | .940-6 |
| 1900 | 810 | 29 | .290-3 | 116 | 4.12-8 | 330 | 125* | .945-3 |
| 1901 | 668 | 23 | .266-4 | 125 | 2.87-2 | 262* | 65 | .954-1 |
| 1902 | 484 | 4 | .247-7 | 118 | 3.50-8 | 305 | 81 | .946-4** |
| 1903 | 618 | 12 | .268-5 | 126** | 3.97-8 | 300 | 76 | .947-2** |
| 1904 | 571 | 23 | .248-5** | 131 | 3.40-7 | 403 | 93* | .936-8 |

## TEAM HITTING, PITCHING, FIELDING

| | HITTING | | | PITCHING | | FIELDING | | |
|---|---|---|---|---|---|---|---|---|
| | R | HR | B.A./RANK | CG | ERA/RANK | E | DP | F.A./RANK |
| 1905 | 708 | 16 | .260-4 | 119 | 2.81-3 | 275 | 99 | .956-4** |
| 1906 | 532 | 13 | .241-4 | 108 | 2.58-3 | 271 | 83 | .955-6 |
| 1907 | 514 | 12 | .236-6 | 110 | 2.43-5 | 256 | 104 | .957-6 |
| 1908 | 503 | 11 | .244-4 | 116 | 2.11-1 | 238 | 75 | .963-3 |
| 1909 | 514 | 12 | .244-5 | 88 | 2.44-4 | 240 | 97 | .960-2** |
| 1910 | 655 | 33 | .266-3 | 73 | 2.83-3 | 245 | 102 | .960-3** |
| 1911 | 658 | 60* | .259-5 | 90 | 3.30-5 | 231* | 113 | .962-1 |
| 1912 | 670 | 42 | .267-7 | 82 | 3.25-3 | 231 | 98 | .962-2 |
| 1913 | 693 | 73* | .265-3 | 77 | 3.15-6 | 214* | 112 | .967-1 |
| 1914 | 652 | 63* | .263-3 | 85 | 3.06-8 | 324 | 81 | .949-8 |
| 1915 | 589 | 58* | .247-5 | 98* | 2.17-1 | 216 | 99 | .965-2** |
| 1916 | 581 | 42 | .250-4 | 97* | 2.36-3 | 234 | 119 | .963-5 |
| 1917 | 578 | 38 | .248-4 | 103 | 2.46-2 | 212 | 112 | .967-2 |
| 1918 | 431 | 26 | .244-6** | 85 | 3.15-8 | 211 | 91 | .960-8 |
| 1919 | 510 | 42* | .251-7 | 93 | 4.17-8 | 219 | 112** | .962-7** |
| 1920 | 565 | 64* | .263-6 | 77 | 3.63-8 | 232 | 135 | .964-6 |
| 1921 | 617 | 88* | .284-6 | 82 | 4.48-8 | 295 | 127 | .954-8 |
| 1922 | 738 | 116* | .282-7 | 73 | 4.64-8 | 225 | 152 | .965-6** |
| 1923 | 748 | 112* | .278-7 | 68 | 5.30-8 | 217 | 172* | .965-5** |
| 1924 | 676 | 94 | .275-7 | 59 | 4.87-8 | 175 | 168* | .972-2 |
| 1925 | 812 | 100 | .295-4 | 69 | 5.02-8 | 211 | 147 | .965-5** |
| 1926 | 687 | 75 | .281-4 | 68 | 5.19-8 | 224 | 153 | .964-7 |
| 1927 | 678 | 57 | .280-4 | 81 | 5.35-8 | 169 | 152 | .972-2 |

# TEAM HITTING, PITCHING, FIELDING

| | HITTING | | PITCHING | | | FIELDING | | |
|---|---|---|---|---|---|---|---|---|
| | R | HR | B.A./RANK | CG | ERA/RANK | E | DP | F.A./RANK |
| 1928 | 660 | 85 | .267-7 | 42 | 5.52-8 | 181 | 171 | .970-5 |
| 1929 | 897 | 153* | .309-1 | 45 | 6.13-8 | 191 | 153 | .969-6 |
| 1930 | 944 | 126 | .315-2 | 54 | 6.71-8 | 239 | 169 | .962-8 |
| 1931 | 684 | 81 | .279-4 | 60 | 4.58-8 | 210 | 149 | .965-8 |
| 1932 | 844* | 122* | .292-1 | 59 | 4.47-8 | 194 | 133 | .968-7** |
| 1933 | 607 | 60 | .274-3 | 52 | 4.34-8 | 183 | 156 | .969-8 |
| 1934 | 675 | 56 | .284-3 | 52 | 4.76-8 | 197 | 140 | .965-8 |
| 1935 | 685 | 92 | .269-6 | 53 | 4.76-7 | 228 | 145 | .962-8 |
| 1936 | 726 | 103* | .281-2** | 51 | 4.64-8 | 252 | 144 | .959-8 |
| 1937 | 724 | 103 | .273-5 | 59 | 5.06-8 | 184 | 157* | .970-5** |
| 1938 | 550 | 40 | .254-7 | 68 | 4.93-8 | 201 | 135 | .965-8 |
| 1939 | 553 | 49 | .261-8 | 67 | 5.17-8 | 171 | 133 | .970-5** |
| 1940 | 494 | 75 | .238-8 | 66 | 4.40-8 | 181 | 136 | .970-4** |
| 1941 | 501 | 64 | .244-8 | 35 | 4.50-8 | 187 | 147 | .969-6** |
| 1942 | 394 | 44 | .232-7 | 51 | 4.12-8 | 194 | 147 | .967-8 |
| 1943 | 571 | 66 | .249-6 | 66 | 3.79-6 | 189 | 143 | .969-8 |
| 1944 | 539 | 55 | .251-7 | 66 | 3.64-5 | 177 | 138 | .971-3 |
| 1945 | 548 | 56 | .246-8 | 31 | 4.64-8 | 234 | 150 | .961-8 |
| 1946 | 552 | 60 | .250-7 | 61 | 3.72-6 | 184 | 127 | .969-8 |
| 1947 | 589 | 60 | .258-8 | 70 | 3.96-4 | 152 | 140 | .974-5** |
| 1948 | 591 | 91 | .259-6 | 61 | 4.08-6 | 210 | 126 | .964-8 |
| 1949 | 662 | 122 | .254-8 | 58 | 3.89-4 | 156 | 141 | .973-6 |
| 1950 | 722 | 125 | .265-2 | 57 | 3.50-1 | 151 | 155 | .975-5** |
| 1951 | 648 | 108 | .260-4** | 57 | 3.81-3 | 138 | 146 | .976-3** |
| 1952 | 657 | 93 | .260-4 | 80* | 3.07-1 | 150 | 145 | .975-4** |
| 1953 | 716 | 115 | .265-5 | 76* | 3.80-2 | 147 | 161 | .974-5** |
| 1954 | 659 | 102 | .267-3 | 78* | 3.59-3 | 145 | 133 | .975-5 |
| 1955 | 675 | 132 | .255-6 | 58 | 3.93-4 | 110* | 117 | .980-1 |
| 1956 | 668 | 121 | .252-6 | 57 | 4.20-8 | 144 | 140 | .974-7 |
| 1957 | 623 | 117 | .250-7 | 54 | 3.80-4 | 136 | 117 | .976-5 |
| 1958 | 664 | 124 | .266-1** | 51 | 4.32-7 | 129 | 136 | .977-3** |
| 1959 | 599 | 113 | .242-8 | 54 | 4.27-6 | 154 | 132 | .973-8 |
| 1960 | 546 | 99 | .239-8 | 45 | 4.01-7 | 155 | 129 | .973-7 |
| 1961 | 584 | 103 | .243-8 | 29 | 4.61-8 | 146 | 179 | .976-4 |
| 1962 | 705 | 142 | .260-6 | 43 | 4.28-8 | 138 | 167 | .977-3** |
| 1963 | 642 | 126 | .252-3 | 45 | 3.09-3 | 142 | 147 | .977-2** |
| 1964 | 693 | 130 | .258-4 | 37 | 3.36-4 | 157 | 150 | .974-4** |
| 1965 | 654 | 144 | .250-6 | 50 | 3.53-5 | 157 | 153 | .975-7 |
| 1966 | 696 | 117 | .258-4 | 52** | 3.57-4 | 113* | 147 | .982-1 |
| 1967 | 612 | 103 | .242-7 | 46 | 3.10-4 | 137 | 174 | .978-2 |
| 1968 | 543 | 100 | .233-7 | 42 | 3.36-8 | 127 | 163* | .979-3** |
| 1969 | 645 | 137 | .241-9 | 47 | 4.14-10 | 137 | 157 | .977-5** |
| 1970 | 594 | 101 | .238-11 | 24 | 4.17-7 | 114* | 134 | .981-1 |
| 1971 | 558 | 123 | .233-11** | 31 | 3.71-9 | 122 | 158 | .981-3** |
| 1972 | 503 | 98 | .236-9 | 43 | 3.66-8 | 116 | 142 | .981-2 |
| 1973 | 642 | 134 | .249-9 | 49* | 3.99-10 | 134 | 179* | .979-5 |
| 1974 | 676 | 95 | .261-5 | 46 | 3.91-10 | 148 | 168 | .976-5** |
| 1975 | 735 | 125 | .269-3 | 33 | 3.82-9 | 152 | 156 | .976-4** |
| 1976 | 770 | 110 | .272-2 | 34 | 3.08-3 | 115 | 148 | .981-2 |
| 1977 | 847* | 186 | .279-1 | 31 | 3.71-4 | 120 | 168 | .981-2** |
| 1978 | 708 | 133 | .258-3** | 38 | 3.33-4 | 104* | 155 | .983-1 |

\* Led League
\*\* Tied

162

## SEASONAL LEADERS

| Year | Games | | At Bats | | Runs | | Hits | | Total Bases | | Doubles | | Triples | |
|---|---|---|---|---|---|---|---|---|---|---|---|---|---|---|
| 1876 | Hall Force | 60 | Force | 284 | Hall | 51 | Hall | 98 | Hall | 146 | Fisler | 15 | Hall | 13 |
| 1883 | Farrar | 99 | Purcell | 425 | Purcell | 70 | Purcell | 114 | Manning | 153 | Manning | 31 | Coleman | 8 |
| 1884 | Farrar | 111 | McClellan | 450 | Andrews | 74 | McClellan | 116 | Manning | 167 | Manning | 29 | Purcell | 7 |
| 1885 | Farrar Fogarty | 111 | Manning | 445 | Andrews | 77 | Mulvey | 119 | Mulvey | 174 | Mulvey | 25 | Mulvey | 6 |
| 1886 | Farrar | 118 | Wood | 450 | Andrews | 93 | Wood | 123 | Wood | 183 | Wood | 18 | Wood | 15 |
| 1887 | Fogarty | 126 | Fogarty | 495 | Wood | 118 | Wood | 142 | Wood | 244 | Fogarty | 26 | Wood | 19 |
| 1888 | Farrar | 131 | Andrews | 528 | Andrews | 75 | Andrews | 126 | Farrar | 165 | Farrar | 24 | Wood | 6 |
| 1889 | Farrar | 130 | Mulvey | 544 | Fogarty | 107 | Thompson | 158 | Thompson | 262 | Thompson | 36 | Fogarty | 17 |
| 1890 | Allen | 133 | Thompson | 549 | Hamilton | 141 | Thompson | 172 | Thompson | 246 | Thompson | 41 | Burke | 11 |
| 1891 | Myers | 135 | Thompson | 554 | Hamilton | 133 | Hamilton | 179 | Thompson | 230 | Clements | 29 | Thompson | 10 |
| 1892 | Connor | 155 | Thompson | 609 | Hamilton | 132 | Thompson | 186 | Thompson | 263 | Delahanty | 30 | Delahanty | 21 |
| 1893 | Delahanty Hallman | 132 | Thompson | 600 | Delahanty | 145 | Thompson | 222 | Delahanty | 347 | Thompson | 37 | Delahanty | 18 |
| 1894 | Hamilton | 129 | Hamilton | 544 | Hamilton | 192 | Hamilton | 220 | Thompson | 297 | Delahanty | 39 | Thompson | 27 |

# SEASONAL LEADERS

| Year | Home Runs | | RBI | | Walks | | Strikeouts | | Stolen Bases | | Average | |
|---|---|---|---|---|---|---|---|---|---|---|---|---|
| 1876 | Hall | 5 | Hall | 45 | Hall | 8 | Fisler | 4 | Meyerle | 3 | Hall | .366 |
| 1883 | Farrar McClellan | 1 | Not Available | | Manning | 20 | Coleman | 39 | Not Available | | Purcell | .268 |
| 1884 | Manning | 5 | Not Available | | Manning | 40 | Manning | 67 | Not Available | | Manning | .271 |
| 1885 | Mulvey | 6 | Not Available | | Manning | 37 | Bastian | 82 | Not Available | | Mulvey | .269 |
| 1886 | Farrar | 5 | Mulvey | 53 | Fogarty | 42 | Wood | 76 | Not Available | | Wood | .273 |
| 1887 | Wood | 14 | Ferguson | 85 | Fogarty | 82 | Wood | 51 | Fogarty | 102 | Andrews | .325 |
| 1888 | Wood | 6 | Farrar | 53 | Fogarty | 53 | Fogarty | 66 | Fogarty | 58 | Farrar | .244 |
| 1889 | Thompson | 20 | Thompson | 111 | Fogarty | 65 | Fogarty | 60 | Fogarty | 99 | Thompson | .296 |
| 1890 | Clements | 7 | Thompson | 103 | Allen | 87 | Allen | 54 | Hamilton | 102 | Hamilton | .325 |
| 1891 | Thompson | 8 | Thompson | 90 | Hamilton | 102 | Delahanty | 50 | Hamilton | 111 | Hamilton | .340 |
| 1892 | Connor | 12 | Thompson | 104 | Connor | 116 | Allen | 60 | Hamilton | 57 | Hamilton | .330 |
| 1893 | Delahanty | 19 | Delahanty | 146 | Allen | 71 | Allen | 40 | Hamilton | 43 | Hamilton | .380 |
| 1894 | Thompson | 13 | Thompson | 141 | Hamilton | 126 | Boyle | 26 | Hamilton | 98 | Delahanty | .407 |

SEASONAL LEADERS

| Year | Games | | At Bats | | Runs | | Hits | | Total Bases | | Doubles | | Triples | |
|---|---|---|---|---|---|---|---|---|---|---|---|---|---|---|
| 1895 | Boyle | 133 | Boyle | 565 | Hamilton | 166 | Thompson | 211 | Thompson | 352 | Delahanty | 49 | Thompson | 21 |
| 1896 | Delahanty | 123 | Thompson | 517 | Delahanty | 126 | Delahanty | 198 | Delahanty | 315 | Delahanty | 44 | Delahanty | 17 |
| 1897 | Cooley | 133 | Cooley | 566 | Cooley | 124 | Delahanty | 200 | Lajoie | 310 | Delahanty Lajoie | 40 | Lajoie | 23 |
| 1898 | Cross | 149 | Cooley | 629 | Cooley | 123 | Lajoie | 200 | Lajoie | 280 | Lajoie | 43 | Flick | 14 |
| 1899 | Cross | 154 | Lauder | 583 | Thomas | 137 | Delahanty | 238 | Delahanty | 338 | Delahanty | 55 | Flick | 14 |
| 1900 | Slagle | 141 | Slagle | 574 | Thomas | 132 | Flick | 207 | Flick | 297 | Delahanty | 32 | Delahanty | 10 |
| 1901 | M. Cross | 139 | Flick | 542 | Flick | 111 | Delahanty | 192 | Delahanty | 286 | Delahanty | 38 | Flick | 17 |
| 1902 | Barry Thomas | 138 | Barry | 543 | Thomas | 89 | Barry | 156 | Barry | 192 | Barry | 20 | Hulswitt | 7 |
| 1903 | Barry Hulswitt | 138 | Barry | 550 | Thomas | 88 | Thomas | 156 | Barry Wolverton | 189 | Keister | 27 | Wolverton | 12 |
| 1904 | Gleason | 153 | Gleason | 587 | Thomas | 92 | Gleason | 161 | Gleason | 196 | Titus | 25 | Magee | 12 |
| 1905 | Courtney Gleason Magee | 155 | Gleason | 608 | Thomas | 118 | Magee | 180 | Magee | 253 | Titus | 36 | Magee | 5 |
| 1906 | Doolan Magee | 154 | Magee | 563 | Thomas | 81 | Magee | 159 | Magee | 230 | Magee | 36 | Magee | 8 |
| 1907 | Doolan | 145 | Titus | 523 | Magee | 75 | Magee | 165 | Magee | 229 | Magee | 28 | Magee Titus | 12 |

## SEASONAL LEADERS

| Year | Home Runs | | RBI | | Walks | | Strikeouts | | Stolen Bases | | Average | |
|---|---|---|---|---|---|---|---|---|---|---|---|---|
| 1895 | Thompson | 18 | Thompson | 165 | Hamilton | 96 | Delahanty | 31 | Hamilton | 97 | Delahanty | .404 |
| 1896 | Delahanty | 13 | Delahanty | 126 | Delahanty | 62 | Hallman | 23 | Delahanty | 37 | Delahanty | .397 |
| 1897 | Lajoie | 9 | Lajoie | 127 | Delahanty Nash | 60 | Not Available | | Cooley | 31 | Delahanty | .377 |
| 1898 | Flick | 7 | Lajoie | 127 | Flick | 86 | Not Available | | Delahanty | 58 | Delahanty | .334 |
| 1899 | Delahanty | 9 | Delahanty | 127 | Thomas | 115 | Not Available | | Thomas | 42 | Delahanty | .410 |
| 1900 | Flick | 11 | Flick | 110 | Thomas | 115 | Not Available | | Thomas | 37 | Flick | .378 |
| 1901 | Delahanty | 8 | Delahanty | 108 | Thomas | 100 | Not Available | | Flick | 30 | Delahanty | .354 |
| 1902 | Barry | 2 | Barry | 57 | Thomas | 107 | Not Available | | Thomas | 17 | Barry | .287 |
| 1903 | Keister | 3 | Keister | 63 | Thomas | 107 | Not Available | | Barry | 26 | Thomas | .327 |
| 1904 | Dooin | 6 | Magee | 57 | Thomas | 102 | Not Available | | Thomas | 28 | Titus | .294 |
| 1905 | Magee | 5 | Magee | 98 | Thomas | 93 | Not Available | | Magee | 48 | Thomas | .317 |
| 1906 | Magee | 7 | Magee | 69 | Thomas | 107 | Not Available | | Magee | 55 | Magee | .282 |
| 1907 | Magee | 4 | Magee | 85 | Thomas | 83 | Not Available | | Magee | 46 | Magee | .328 |

## SEASONAL LEADERS

| Year | Games | | At Bats | | Runs | | Hits | | Total Bases | | Doubles | | Triples | |
|---|---|---|---|---|---|---|---|---|---|---|---|---|---|---|
| 1908 | Osborn | 152 | Grant | 598 | Magee | 79 | Bransfield | 160 | Magee | 208 | Magee | 30 | Magee | 16 |
| 1909 | Grant | 153 | Grant | 629 | Grant | 75 | Grant | 170 | Magee | 208 | Magee | 33 | Magee | 14 |
| 1910 | Magee | 154 | Grant | 579 | Magee | 110 | Magee | 172 | Magee | 263 | Magee | 39 | Magee | 17 |
| 1911 | Paskert | 153 | Paskert | 560 | Paskert | 96 | Luderus | 166 | Luderus | 260 | Magee | 32 | Luderus | 11 |
| 1912 | Luderus | 148 | Luderus | 572 | Paskert | 102 | Paskert | 170 | Paskert | 221 | Paskert | 38 | Cravath Magee | 9 |
| 1913 | Luderus | 155 | Luderus | 588 | Lobert | 98 | Cravath | 179 | Cravath | 298 | Magee | 36 | Cravath | 14 |
| 1914 | Cravath | 149 | Magee | 544 | Magee | 96 | Magee | 171 | Magee | 279 | Magee | 39 | Magee | 11 |
| 1915 | Bancroft | 153 | Bancroft | 563 | Cravath | 89 | Luderus | 157 | Cravath | 266 | Luderus | 36 | Cravath Luderus | 7 |
| 1916 | Paskert | 149 | Paskert | 555 | Paskert | 82 | Paskert | 155 | Paskert | 223 | Niehoff | 42 | Whitted | 12 |
| 1917 | Luderus | 154 | Whitted | 553 | Paskert | 78 | Whitted | 155 | Cravath | 238 | Cravath | 29 | Cravath | 16 |
| 1918 | Bancroft Luderus | 125 | Bancroft | 499 | Bancroft | 69 | Luderus | 135 | Meusel | 181 | Cravath | 27 | Meusel | 6 |
| 1919 | Luderus | 138 | Meusel | 521 | Meusel | 65 | Meusel | 159 | Meusel | 214 | Luderus | 30 | Bancroft Meusel | 7 |
| 1920 | Williams | 148 | Williams | 590 | Williams | 88 | Williams | 192 | Williams | 293 | Williams | 36 | Williams | 10 |

167

## SEASONAL LEADERS

| Year | Home Runs | | RBI | | Walks | | Strikeouts | | Stolen Bases | | Average | |
|---|---|---|---|---|---|---|---|---|---|---|---|---|
| 1908 | Bransfield | 3 | Bransfield | 71 | Titus | 53 | Not Available | | Magee | 40 | Bransfield | .304 |
| 1909 | Titus | 3 | Magee | 66 | Titus | 66 | Not Available | | Magee | 38 | Bransfield | .291 |
| 1910 | Magee | 6 | Magee | 123 | Magee | 94 | Doolan | 56 | Magee | 49 | Magee | .331 |
| 1911 | Luderus | 16 | Luderus | 99 | Knabe | 94 | Luderus | 76 | Lobert | 40 | Luderus | .301 |
| 1912 | Cravath | 11 | Cravath | 70 | Paskert | 91 | Cravath | 77 | Paskert | 36 | Paskert | .315 |
| 1913 | Cravath | 19 | Cravath | 128 | Paskert | 65 | Paskert | 69 | Lobert | 41 | Cravath | .341 |
| 1914 | Cravath | 19 | Cravath | 100 | Cravath | 83 | Cravath | 72 | Lobert | 31 | Becker | .325 |
| 1915 | Cravath | 24 | Cravath | 115 | Cravath | 86 | Cravath | 77 | Whitted | 24 | Luderus | .315 |
| 1916 | Cravath | 11 | Cravath | 70 | Bancroft | 74 | Cravath | 89 | Whitted | 29 | Cravath | .283 |
| 1917 | Cravath | 12 | Cravath | 83 | Cravath | 70 | Paskert | 63 | Stock | 25 | Cravath Whitted | .280 |
| 1918 | Cravath | 8 | Luderus | 67 | Bancroft Cravath | 54 | Cravath | 46 | Stock | 20 | Luderus | .288 |
| 1919 | Cravath | 12 | Meusel | 59 | Luderus | 54 | Luderus | 48 | Meusel | 24 | Meusel | .305 |
| 1920 | Williams | 15 | Williams | 72 | Stengel | 38 | Williams | 45 | Williams | 18 | Williams | .325 |

## SEASONAL LEADERS

| Year | Games | | At Bats | | Runs | | Hits | | Total Bases | | Doubles | | Triples | |
|---|---|---|---|---|---|---|---|---|---|---|---|---|---|---|
| 1921 | Williams | 146 | Williams | 562 | Williams | 67 | Williams | 180 | Meusel | 302 | Williams | 28 | Meusel | 7 |
| 1922 | Williams | 151 | Williams | 584 | Walker | 102 | Walker | 196 | Williams | 300 | Walker | 36 | Walker | 11 |
| 1923 | Holke | 147 | Holke | 562 | Williams | 98 | Holke | 175 | Williams | 308 | Holke | 31 | Wrightstone | 7 |
| 1924 | Holke Williams | 148 | Holke | 563 | Williams | 101 | Williams | 183 | Williams | 308 | Williams | 31 | Williams | 11 |
| 1925 | Sand | 148 | Sand | 496 | Harper | 86 | Harper | 173 | Harper | 276 | Harper | 35 | Harper Sand | 7 |
| 1926 | Sand | 149 | Sand | 567 | Sand | 99 | Leach | 162 | Leach | 232 | Sand | 30 | Leach Huber | 7 |
| 1927 | F. Thompson | 153 | F. Thompson | 597 | Sand | 87 | F. Thompson | 181 | Williams | 247 | F. Thompson | 32 | F. Thompson | 14 |
| 1928 | F. Thompson | 152 | F. Thompson | 634 | F. Thompson | 99 | F. Thompson | 182 | Leach | 276 | Leach | 36 | Leach F. Thompson | 11 |
| 1929 | Hurst O'Doul Whitney | 154 | O'Doul | 638 | O'Doul | 152 | O'Doul | 254 | Klein | 405 | Klein | 45 | Whitney | 14 |
| 1930 | Klein Thevenow | 156 | Klein | 648 | Klein | 158 | Klein | 250 | Klein | 445 | Klein | 59 | Klein | 8 |
| 1931 | Klein | 148 | Klein | 594 | Klein | 121 | Klein | 200 | Klein | 347 | Bartell | 43 | Klein | 10 |
| 1932 | Bartell Klein Whitney | 154 | Klein | 650 | Klein | 152 | Klein | 226 | Klein | 420 | Klein | 50 | Klein | 15 |
| 1933 | Bartell Klein | 152 | Fullis | 647 | Klein | 101 | Klein | 223 | Klein | 365 | Klein | 44 | Hurst | 8 |

## SEASONAL LEADERS

| Year | Home Runs | | RBI | | Walks | | Strikeouts | | Stolen Bases | | Average | |
|---|---|---|---|---|---|---|---|---|---|---|---|---|
| 1921 | Williams | 18 | Williams | 75 | Williams | 30 | Parkinson | 81 | Meusel | 8 | Williams | .320 |
| 1922 | Williams | 26 | Williams | 92 | Williams | 74 | Parkinson | 93 | Walker Williams | 11 | Walker | .337 |
| 1923 | Williams | 41 | Williams | 114 | Sand | 82 | Williams | 57 | Walker | 12 | Holke | .311 |
| 1924 | Williams | 24 | Williams | 93 | Williams | 67 | Sand | 57 | Harper | 10 | Williams | .328 |
| 1925 | Harper | 18 | Harper | 97 | Sand | 64 | Sand | 65 | Harper | 10 | Harper | .349 |
| 1926 | Williams | 18 | Leach | 71 | Sand | 66 | Friberg | 77 | Huber | 9 | Williams | .345 |
| 1927 | Williams | 30 | Williams | 98 | Williams | 61 | Sand | 59 | F. Thompson | 19 | Leach | .306 |
| 1928 | Hurst | 19 | Whitney | 108 | Hurst | 68 | Sothern | 53 | F. Thompson | 19 | Leach | .304 |
| 1929 | Klein | 43 | Klein | 145 | Hurst | 80 | Klein | 61 | F. Thompson | 16 | O'Doul | .398 |
| 1930 | Klein | 40 | Klein | 170 | O'Doul | 63 | Klein | 50 | F. Thompson | 7 | Klein | .386 |
| 1931 | Klein | 31 | Klein | 121 | Hurst | 64 | Klein | 49 | Hurst | 8 | Klein | .337 |
| 1932 | Klein | 38 | Hurst | 143 | Hurst | 65 | Whitney | 66 | Klein | 20 | Klein | .348 |
| 1933 | Klein | 28 | Klein | 120 | Bartell Klein | 56 | Bartell | 46 | Fullis | 18 | Klein | .368 |

## SEASONAL LEADERS

| Year | Games | | At Bats | | Runs | | Hits | | Total Bases | | Doubles | | Triples | |
|---|---|---|---|---|---|---|---|---|---|---|---|---|---|---|
| 1934 | Bartell | 146 | Bartell | 604 | Bartell | 102 | Allen | 192 | Allen | 272 | Allen | 42 | J. Moore | 6 |
| 1935 | Allen Camilli | 156 | Allen | 645 | Allen | 90 | Allen | 198 | J. Moore | 290 | Allen | 46 | Chiozza | 6 |
| 1936 | Norris | 154 | Norris | 581 | Camilli | 106 | Chiozza | 170 | Camilli | 308 | Chiozza | 32 | Camilli | 13 |
| 1937 | Scharein | 146 | Martin | 579 | Martin | 102 | Whitney | 166 | Camilli | 279 | Martin | 35 | Camilli Martin | 7 |
| 1938 | Arnovich | 139 | Arnovich | 502 | Martin | 58 | Martin | 139 | Martin | 196 | Martin | 36 | Martin | 6 |
| 1939 | May | 135 | Arnovich | 491 | Arnovich | 68 | Arnovich | 159 | Arnovich | 203 | Martin | 28 | Marty | 6 |
| 1940 | Mahan | 146 | Mahan | 544 | May | 58 | May | 147 | Marty | 199 | Mahan May | 24 | Marty | 8 |
| 1941 | Bragan | 154 | Litwhiler | 590 | Etten | 78 | Litwhiler | 180 | Litwhiler | 275 | Litwhiler | 29 | Benjamin | 7 |
| 1942 | Litwhiler | 151 | Litwhiler | 591 | Litwhiler | 59 | Litwhiler | 160 | Litwhiler | 230 | Litwhiler | 25 | Litwhiler | 9 |
| 1943 | Northey | 147 | Northey | 586 | Northey | 72 | Northey | 163 | Northey | 252 | Northey | 31 | Adams | 7 |
| 1944 | Lupien | 153 | Lupien | 597 | Adams | 86 | Lupien | 169 | Northey | 283 | Adams Northey | 35 | Lupien Northey | 9 |
| 1945 | Wasdell | 134 | Antonelli | 504 | Wasdell | 65 | Wasdell | 150 | Wasdell | 206 | Antonelli | 27 | Wasdell | 8 |
| 1946 | Wyrostek | 145 | Wyrostek | 545 | Wyrostek | 73 | Ennis | 169 | Ennis | 262 | Ennis Wyrostek | 30 | Ennis Northey | 6 |

## SEASONAL LEADERS

| Year | Home Runs | | RBI | | Walks | | Strikeouts | | Stolen Bases | | Average | |
|---|---|---|---|---|---|---|---|---|---|---|---|---|
| 1934 | Camilli | 12 | J. Moore | 93 | Bartell | 64 | Camilli | 69 | Bartell | 13 | J. Moore | .343 |
| 1935 | Camilli | 25 | J. Moore | 93 | Camilli | 65 | Camilli | 113 | Camilli | 9 | J. Moore | .323 |
| 1936 | Camilli | 28 | Camilli | 102 | Camilli | 116 | Camilli | 84 | Chiozza | 17 | J. Moore | .328 |
| 1937 | Camilli | 27 | Camilli | 80 | Camilli | 90 | Camilli | 82 | Scharein | 13 | Whitney | .341 |
| 1938 | Klein | 8 | Arnovich | 72 | Mueller Weintraub | 64 | Martin | 48 | Martin | 8 | Weintraub | .311 |
| 1939 | Marty Mueller | 9 | Arnovich | 67 | Arnovich | 58 | Scharein | 40 | Arnovich | 7 | Arnovich | .324 |
| 1940 | Rizzo | 20 | Rizzo | 53 | May | 58 | Marty | 50 | Mahan | 4 | May | .293 |
| 1941 | Litwhiler | 18 | Etten | 79 | Etten | 82 | Benjamin | 81 | Murtaugh | 18 | Etten | .311 |
| 1942 | Litwhiler | 9 | Litwhiler | 56 | Etten | 67 | Litwhiler | 42 | Etten Glossop May | 3 | Litwhiler | .271 |
| 1943 | Northey | 16 | Northey | 68 | Murtaugh | 57 | Adams | 67 | Wasdell | 6 | Dahlgren | .287 |
| 1944 | Northey | 22 | Northey | 104 | Northey | 67 | Adams | 74 | Lupien | 18 | Northey | .288 |
| 1945 | DiMaggio | 19 | DiMaggio | 84 | DiMaggio | 43 | DiMaggio | 91 | DiMaggio | 12 | Wasdell | .300 |
| 1946 | Ennis | 17 | Ennis | 73 | Wyrostek | 70 | Seminick | 86 | Wyrostek | 7 | Ennis | .313 |

## SEASONAL LEADERS

| Year | Games | | At Bats | | Runs | | Hits | | Total Bases | | Doubles | | Triples | |
|---|---|---|---|---|---|---|---|---|---|---|---|---|---|---|
| 1947 | Verban | 155 | Ennis | 541 | Walker | 79 | Walker | 181 | Walker | 244 | Walker | 28 | Walker | 16 |
| 1948 | Ennis | 152 | Ennis | 589 | Ennis | 86 | Ennis | 171 | Ennis | 309 | Ennis | 40 | Blatnik | 8 |
| 1949 | Ashburn Ennis Hamner | 154 | Ashburn Hamner | 662 | Ennis | 92 | Ashburn | 188 | Ennis | 320 | Ennis | 39 | Ennis Ashburn | 11 |
| 1950 | Hamner Jones | 157 | Waitkus | 641 | Waitkus | 102 | Ennis | 185 | Ennis | 328 | Ennis | 34 | Ashburn | 14 |
| 1951 | Ashburn | 154 | Ashburn | 643 | Ashburn | 92 | Ashburn | 221 | Ashburn | 274 | Ashburn | 31 | Hamner | 7 |
| 1952 | Ashburn Ryan | 154 | Ashburn | 613 | Ashburn | 93 | Ashburn | 173 | Ennis | 281 | Ashburn | 31 | Ennis | 10 |

| Year | Home Runs | | RBI | | Walks | | Strikeouts | | Stolen Bases | | Average | |
|---|---|---|---|---|---|---|---|---|---|---|---|---|
| 1947 | Seminick | 13 | Ennis | 81 | Wyrostek | 61 | Schultz | 70 | Walker | 13 | Walker | .371 |
| 1948 | Ennis | 30 | Ennis | 95 | Ashburn | 60 | Seminick | 68 | Ashburn | 32 | Ashburn | .333 |
| 1949 | Ennis | 25 | Ennis | 110 | Seminick | 69 | Seminick | 74 | Ashburn | 9 | Ennis | .302 |
| 1950 | Ennis | 31 | Ennis | 126 | Seminick | 68 | Goliat | 75 | Ashburn | 14 | Ennis | .311 |
| 1951 | Jones | 22 | Jones | 81 | Ennis | 68 | Seminick | 67 | Ashburn | 29 | Ashburn | .344 |
| 1952 | Ennis | 20 | Ennis | 107 | Ryan | 69 | Ryan | 72 | Ashburn | 16 | Burgess | .296 |

## SEASONAL LEADERS

| YEAR | GAMES | | AT BAT | | RUNS | | HITS | | TOTAL BASES | | DOUBLES | |
|------|-------|---|--------|---|------|---|------|---|-------------|---|---------|---|
| 1953 | Ashburn | 156 | Ashburn | 622 | Ashburn | 110 | Ashburn | 205 | Ennis | 280 | Hamner | 30 |
| 1954 | Ashburn | 153 | Hamner | 596 | Ashburn | 111 | Hamner | 178 | Hamner | 278 | Hamner | 39 |
| 1955 | Ennis Jones | 146 | Ennis | 564 | Ashburn | 91 | Ashburn | 180 | Ennis | 292 | Ashburn | 32 |
| 1956 | Ashburn | 154 | Ennis | 630 | Lopata | 96 | Ashburn | 190 | Lopata | 286 | Lopata | 33 |
| 1957 | Ashburn | 156 | Ashburn | 626 | Ashburn | 93 | Ashburn | 186 | Bouchee | 270 | Bouchee | 35 |
| 1958 | Ashburn | 152 | Ashburn | 615 | Ashburn | 98 | Ashburn | 215 | Ashburn | 271 | Anderson | 34 |
| 1959 | Ashburn | 153 | Ashburn | 564 | Ashburn | 86 | Ashburn | 150 | Bouchee | 224 | Bouchee | 29 |
| 1960 | Herrera | 145 | Herrera | 512 | Taylor | 66 | Taylor | 145 | Herrera | 233 | Herrera | 26 |
| 1961 | Callison | 138 | Callison | 455 | Callison | 74 | Callison | 121 | Callison | 190 | Callison | 20 |
| 1962 | Callison | 157 | Taylor | 625 | Callison | 107 | Callison | 181 | Callison | 296 | Callison | 26 |
| 1963 | Callison Taylor | 157 | Taylor | 640 | Taylor | 102 | Taylor | 180 | Callison | 314 | Callison Gonzalez | 36 |
| 1964 | Allen Callison | 162 | Callison | 654 | Allen | 125 | Allen | 201 | Allen | 352 | Allen | 38 |
| 1965 | Allen | 161 | Callison Allen | 619 | Callison Allen | 93 | Allen | 187 | Callison | 315 | Allen | 31 |
| 1966 | White | 159 | Rojas | 626 | Allen | 112 | Callison | 169 | Allen | 331 | Callison | 40 |
| 1967 | Callison Gonzalez | 149 | Callison | 556 | Allen | 89 | Gonzalez | 172 | Allen | 262 | Allen | 31 |
| 1968 | Allen Rojas | 152 | Rojas | 621 | Allen | 87 | Rojas | 144 | Allen | 271 | Taylor | 20 |
| 1969 | Hisle | 145 | Taylor | 557 | Allen | 79 | Taylor | 146 | Allen | 251 | Callison | 29 |
| 1970 | Johnson | 159 | Johnson | 574 | Taylor | 74 | Johnson | 147 | Johnson | 262 | Johnson | 28 |
| 1971 | Bowa | 159 | Bowa | 650 | Montanez | 78 | Bowa | 162 | Johnson | 285 | Johnson | 29 |
| 1972 | Bowa Money | 152 | Bowa | 579 | Bowa | 67 | Luzinski | 158 | Luzinski | 255 | Montanez | 39 |
| 1973 | Luzinski | 161 | Luzinski | 610 | Luzinski | 76 | Luzinski | 174 | Luzinski | 295 | B. Robinson | 32 |
| 1974 | Bowa Cash Schmidt | 162 | Cash | 687 | Schmidt | 108 | Cash | 206 | Schmidt | 310 | Montanez | 33 |
| 1975 | Cash | 162 | Cash | 699 | Cash | 111 | Cash | 213 | Luzinski | 322 | Cash | 40 |
| 1976 | Cash Schmidt | 160 | Cash | 666 | Schmidt | 112 | Cash | 189 | Schmidt | 306 | Johnstone | 38 |
| 1977 | Bowa Schmidt | 154 | Bowa | 624 | Schmidt | 114 | Bowa | 175 | Luzinski | 329 | Luzinski | 35 |
| 1978 | Bowa | 156 | Bowa | 654 | Schmidt | 93 | Bowa | 192 | | | Maddox | 34 |

# SEASONAL LEADERS

| YEAR | TRIPLES | HOME RUNS | RBI | WALKS | STRIKE OUTS | STOLEN BASES | AVERAGE |
|---|---|---|---|---|---|---|---|
| 1953 | Ashburn 9 | Ennis 29 | Ennis 125 | Jones 85 | Torgeson 57 | Ashburn 14 | Ashburn .330 |
| 1954 | Hamner 11 | Ennis 25 | Ennis 119 | Ashburn 125 | B. Morgan 68 | Ashburn 11 | Ashburn .313 |
| 1955 | Ashburn 9 | Ennis 29 | Ennis 120 | Ashburn 105 | B. Morgan 72 | Ashburn 12 | Ashburn .338 |
| 1956 | Ashburn 8 | Lopata 32 | Ennis 95 Lopata | Jones 92 | Lopata 93 | Ashburn 10 | Ashburn .303 |
| 1957 | Ashburn 8 Bouchee | Lopata 18 | Bouchee 76 | Ashburn 94 | Bouchee 91 | Ashburn 13 | Ashburn .297 |
| 1958 | Ashburn 13 | Anderson 23 | Anderson 97 | Ashburn 97 | Anderson 95 | Ashburn 30 | Ashburn .350 |
| 1959 | Anderson 6 | Freese 23 | Post 94 | Ashburn 79 | Post 101 | Ashburn 9 | Bouchee .285 |
| 1960 | Gonzalez 6 Herrera | Herrera 17 | Herrera 71 | DelGreco 54 | Herrera 136 | Taylor 24 | Taylor .284 |
| 1961 | Callison 11 | Herrera 13 | Gonzalez 58 | Callison 69 | Herrera 120 | Gonzalez 15 | Gonzalez .277 |
| 1962 | Callison 10 | Demeter 29 | Demeter 107 | Dalrymple 70 | Callison 96 | Taylor 28 | Demeter .307 |
| 1963 | Gonzalez 12 | Callison 26 | Demeter 83 | Gonzalez 53 | Callison 111 | Taylor 23 | Gonzalez .306 |
| 1964 | Allen 13 | Callison 31 | Callison 104 | Allen 67 | Allen 138 | Taylor 13 | Allen .318 |
| 1965 | Callison 16 | Callison 32 | Callison 101 | Allen 73 | Allen 150 | Allen 15 | Rojas .303 |
| 1966 | Allen 10 | Allen 40 | Allen 110 | White 68 Allen | Allen 136 | White 16 | Allen .317 |
| 1967 | Allen 10 | Allen 23 | Allen 77 | Allen 75 | Allen 117 | Allen 20 | Gonzalez .339 |
| 1968 | Allen 9 | Allen 33 | Allen 90 | Allen 74 | Allen 160 | Taylor 22 | Gonzalez .264 |
| 1969 | Callison 5 Hisle Taylor | Allen 32 | Allen 89 | Allen 64 Briggs | Hisle 152 | Taylor 19 | Allen .288 |
| 1970 | Taylor 9 | Johnson 27 | Johnson 93 | Johnson 72 | Hisle 138 | Bowa 24 | Taylor .301 |
| 1971 | Money 8 | Johnson 34 | Montanez 99 | Johnson 72 | Johnson 146 | Bowa 28 | McCarver .278 |
| 1972 | Bowa 13 | Luzinski 18 | Luzinski 68 | Montanez 58 | Luzinski 114 | Bowa 17 | Luzinski .281 |
| 1973 | Montanez 5 | Luzinski 29 | Luzinski 97 | Schmidt 62 | Schmidt 136 | Bowa 10 | Luzinski .285 |
| 1974 | Cash 11 | Schmidt 36 | Schmidt 116 | Schmidt 106 | Schmidt 138 | Bowa 39 | Cash .300 |
| 1975 | Bowa 9 | Schmidt 38 | Luzinski 120 | Schmidt 101 | Schmidt 180 | Schmidt 29 | Bowa .305 Cash |
| 1976 | Cash 12 | Schmidt 38 | Schmidt 107 | Schmidt 100 | Schmidt 149 | Bowa 30 | Maddox .330 |
| 1977 | Schmidt 11 | Luzinski 39 | Luzinski 130 | Schmidt 104 | Luzinski 140 | Bowa 32 | Luzinski .309 |
| 1978 | Bowa 5 | Luzinski 35 | Luzinski 101 | Luzinski 100 | Luzinski 135 | Maddox 33 | Bowa .294 |

## REGULARS AT EACH POSITION SINCE 1876

| Year | 1b | 2b | SS | 3b | C | OF | OF | OF |
|---|---|---|---|---|---|---|---|---|
| 1876 | Sutton .297 | Fouser .135 | Force .230 | Meyerle .340 | Malone .229 | Fisler .288 | Hall .366 | Coons .227 |
| 1883 | Farrar .233 | Ferguson .258 | McClellan .230 | Warner .227 | Gross .307 | Purcell .268 | Lewis .250 | Manning .267 |
| 1884 | Farrar .245 | Andrews .221 | McClellan .258 | Mulvey .229 | Crowley .244 | Fogarty .212 | Purcell .252 | Manning .271 |
| 1885 | Farrar .245 | Myers .204 | Bastian .167 | Mulvey .269 | Clements .191 | Fogarty .232 | Andrews .266 | Manning .256 |
| 1886 | Farrar .248 | Bastian .217 | Irwin .233 | Mulvey .267 | Clements .205 | Fogarty .293 | Andrews .249 | Wood .273 |
| 1887 | Farrar .282 | McLaughlin .220 | Irwin .254 | Mulvey .287 | Clements .280 | Fogarty .261 | Andrews .325 | Wood .289 |
| 1888 | Farrar .244 | Bastian .193 | Irwin .219 | Mulvey .216 | Clements .245 | Fogarty .236 | Andrews .239 | Wood .229 |
| 1889 | Farrar .268 | Myers .269 | Hallman .253 | Mulvey .289 | Clements .284 | Fogarty .259 | Thompson .296 | Wood .251 |
| 1890 | McCauley .244 | Myers .277 | Allen .226 | Mayer .242 | Clements .315 | Hamilton .325 | Burke .263 | Thompson .313 |
| 1891 | W. Brown .243 | Myers .230 | Allen .221 | Shindle .210 | Clements .310 | Hamilton .340 | Delahanty .243 | Thompson .294 |
| 1892 | Connor .294 | Hallman .292 | Allen .227 | Reilly .196 | Clements .264 | Delahanty .306 | Hamilton .330 | Thompson .305 |
| 1893 | Boyle .286 | Hallman .307 | Allen .268 | Reilly .245 | Clements .285 | Delahanty .368 | Hamilton .380 | Thompson .370 |
| 1894 | Boyle .301 | Hallman .309 | Sullivan .352 | L. Cross .386 | Clements .346 | Delahanty .407 | Hamilton .404 | Thompson .404 |

REGULARS AT EACH POSITION SINCE 1876

| Year | 1b | 2b | SS | 3b | C | OF | OF | OF |
|---|---|---|---|---|---|---|---|---|
| 1895 | Boyle .253 | Hallman .314 | Sullivan .338 | L. Cross .271 | Clements .394 | Delahanty .404 | Hamilton .389 | Thompson .392 |
| 1896 | Brouthers .344 | Hallman .320 | Hulen .265 | Nash .247 | Grady .318 | Delahanty .397 | Cooley .307 | Thompson .298 |
| 1897 | Lajoie .361 | L. Cross .259 | Gillen .259 | Nash .258 | Boyle .253 | Delahanty .377 | Cooley .329 | Dowd .292 |
| 1898 | Douglas .258 | Lajoie .328 | M. Cross .257 | Lauder .263 | McFarland .282 | Delahanty .334 | Cooley .312 | Flick .313 |
| 1899 | Cooley .276 | Lajoie .378 | M. Cross .257 | Lauder .268 | McFarland .333 | Delahanty .410 | Thomas .325 | Flick .342 |
| 1900 | Delahanty .323 | Lajoie .337 | M. Cross .202 | Wolverton .282 | McFarland .305 | Slagle .287 | Thomas .316 | Flick .378 |
| 1901 | Jennings .262 | Hallman .184 | M. Cross .197 | Wolverton .309 | McFarland .285 | Delahanty .354 | Thomas .309 | Flick .336 |
| 1902 | Jennings .272 | Childs .194 | Hulswitt .272 | Hallman .248 | Dooin .231 | Barry .287 | Thomas .286 | Browne .260 |
| 1903 | Douglas .255 | Gleason .284 | Hulswitt .247 | Wolverton .308 | Roth .273 | Barry .276 | Thomas .327 | Keister .300 |
| 1904 | Doyle .220 | Gleason .274 | Hulswitt .244 | Wolverton .266 | Dooin .242 | Magee .277 | Thomas .290 | Titus .294 |
| 1905 | Bransfield .259 | Gleason .247 | Doolan .254 | Courtney .275 | Dooin .250 | Magee .299 | Thomas .317 | Titus .308 |
| 1906 | Bransfield .275 | Gleason .227 | Doolan .230 | Courtney .236 | Dooin .245 | Magee .282 | Thomas .254 | Titus .267 |
| 1907 | Bransfield .233 | Knabe .255 | Doolan .204 | Courtney .243 | Dooin .211 | Magee .328 | Thomas .243 | Titus .275 |

## REGULARS AT EACH POSITION SINCE 1876

| Year | 1b | | 2b | | SS | | 3b | | C | | OF | | OF | | OF | |
|---|---|---|---|---|---|---|---|---|---|---|---|---|---|---|---|---|
| 1908 | Bransfield | .304 | Knabe | .218 | Doolan | .234 | Grant | .244 | Dooin | .248 | Magee | .283 | Osborn | .267 | Titus | .286 |
| 1909 | Bransfield | .291 | Knabe | .235 | Doolan | .220 | Grant | .270 | Dooin | .225 | Magee | .270 | Bates | .295 | Titus | .270 |
| 1910 | Bransfield | .239 | Knabe | .261 | Doolan | .263 | Grant | .268 | Dooin | .242 | Magee | .331 | Bates | .305 | Titus | .241 |
| 1911 | Luderus | .301 | Knabe | .237 | Doolan | .238 | Lobert | .285 | Dooin | .328 | Magee | .288 | Paskert | .273 | Titus | .284 |
| 1912 | Luderus | .257 | Knabe | .282 | Doolan | .258 | Lobert | .327 | Killefer | .224 | Magee | .306 | Paskert | .315 | Cravath | .284 |
| 1913 | Luderus | .262 | Knabe | .263 | Doolan | .218 | Lobert | .300 | Killefer | .244 | Magee | .306 | Paskert | .262 | Cravath | .341 |
| 1914 | Luderus | .248 | Byrne | .272 | Martin | .253 | Lobert | .275 | Killefer | .234 | Becker | .325 | Paskert | .264 | Cravath | .298 |
| 1915 | Luderus | .315 | Niehoff | .238 | Bancroft | .254 | Byrne | .209 | Killefer | .238 | Whitted | .281 | Paskert | .244 | Cravath | .285 |
| 1916 | Luderus | .281 | Niehoff | .243 | Bancroft | .212 | Stock | .281 | Killefer | .217 | Whitted | .281 | Paskert | .279 | Cravath | .283 |
| 1917 | Luderus | .261 | Niehoff | .255 | Bancroft | .243 | Stock | .264 | Killefer | .274 | Whitted | .280 | Paskert | .251 | Cravath | .280 |
| 1918 | Luderus | .288 | Pearce | .244 | Bancroft | .265 | Stock | .274 | Adams | .176 | Williams | .276 | Meusel | .279 | Cravath | .232 |
| 1919 | Luderus | .293 | Paulette | .259 | Bancroft | .272 | Blackburne | .199 | Adams | .233 | Williams | .278 | Meusel | .305 | Callahan | .230 |
| 1920 | Paulette | .288 | Rawlings | .234 | Fletcher | .296 | R. Miller | .219 | Wheat | .226 | Williams | .325 | Meusel | .309 | Stengel | .292 |

REGULARS AT EACH POSITION SINCE 1876

| Year | 1b | 2b | SS | 3b | C | OF | OF | OF |
|---|---|---|---|---|---|---|---|---|
| 1921 | Konetchy .321 | J. Smith .231 | Parkinson .253 | Wrightstone .296 | Bruggy .310 | LeBourveau .281 | Meusel .353 | Williams .320 |
| 1922 | Leslie .271 | Parkinson .275 | Fletcher .280 | Rapp .253 | Henline .316 | C. Lee .322 | W. Walker .337 | Williams .308 |
| 1923 | Holke .311 | Tierney .317 | Sand .228 | Wrightstone .273 | Henline .324 | Mokan .313 | W. Walker .321 | Williams .293 |
| 1924 | Holke .300 | Ford .272 | Sand .245 | Wrightstone .307 | Henline .284 | Harper .294 | Mokan .260 | Williams .328 |
| 1925 | Hawks .322 | Fonseca .319 | Sand .278 | Huber .284 | Wilson .328 | Harper .349 | Burns .292 | Williams .331 |
| 1926 | Wrightstone .307 | Friberg .268 | Sand .272 | Huber .245 | Wilson .305 | Leach .329 | Mokan .303 | Williams .345 |
| 1927 | Wrightstone .306 | Thompson .303 | Sand .299 | Friberg .233 | Wilson .275 | Spalding .296 | Leach .306 | Williams .274 |
| 1928 | Hurst .285 | Thompson .287 | Sand .211 | Whitney .301 | Lerian .272 | Leach .304 | Southern .285 | Klein .360 |
| 1929 | Hurst .304 | Thompson .324 | Thevenow .227 | Whitney .327 | Lerian .223 | O'Doul .398 | Southern .306 | Klein .356 |
| 1930 | Hurst .327 | Thompson .282 | Thevenow .286 | Whitney .342 | Davis .313 | O'Doul .383 | Southern .280 | Klein .386 |
| 1931 | Hurst .305 | Mallon .309 | Bartell .289 | Whitney .287 | Davis .326 | Arlett .313 | Brickell .253 | Klein .337 |
| 1932 | Hurst .339 | Mallon .259 | Bartell .308 | Whitney .298 | Davis .336 | Lee .303 | Davis .309 | Klein .348 |
| 1933 | Hurst .267 | Warner .224 | Bartell .271 | McLeod .194 | Davis .349 | Schulmerich .334 | Fullis .309 | Klein .368 |

179

REGULARS AT EACH POSITION SINCE 1876

| Year | 1b | 2b | SS | 3b | C | OF | OF | OF |
|---|---|---|---|---|---|---|---|---|
| 1934 | Camilli .265 | Chiozza .304 | Bartell .310 | Walters .260 | Todd .218 | Allen .330 | Davis .293 | Moore .343 |
| 1935 | Camilli .261 | Chiozza .284 | Haslin .265 | Vergez .249 | Todd .290 | Watkins .270 | Allen .307 | Moore .323 |
| 1936 | Camilli .315 | Gomez .232 | Norris .265 | Whitney .294 | Grace .249 | Chiozza .297 | Moore .328 | Klein .309 |
| 1937 | Camilli .339 | Young .194 | Scharein .241 | Whitney .341 | Atwood .244 | Arnovich .290 | Martin .283 | Klein .325 |
| 1938 | Weintraub .311 | Meuller .250 | Young .229 | Whitney .277 | Atwood .196 | Arnovich .275 | Martin .298 | Klein .247 |
| 1939 | Suhr .318 | Hughes .228 | Scharein .238 | May .287 | Davis .307 | Arnovich .324 | Marty .254 | Brack .289 |
| 1940 | Mahan .244 | Schulte .236 | Bragan .222 | May .293 | Warren .246 | Rizzo .292 | Marty .270 | Klein .218 |
| 1941 | Etten .311 | Murtaugh .219 | Bragan .251 | May .267 | Warren .215 | Litwhiler .305 | Marty .268 | Benjamin .235 |
| 1942 | Etten .264 | Murtaugh .241 | Bragan .218 | May .238 | Warren .209 | Litwhiler .271 | Waner .261 | Northey .251 |
| 1943 | Wasdell .261 | Murtaugh .273 | Stewart .211 | May .282 | Livingston .249 | Triplett .272 | Adams .256 | Northey .278 |
| 1944 | Lupien .283 | Mullen .267 | Hamrick .205 | Stewart .220 | Finley .249 | Wasdell .277 | Adams .283 | Northey .288 |
| 1945 | Wasdell .300 | Daniels .200 | Mott .221 | Antonelli .256 | Seminick .239 | Triplett .240 | DiMaggio .257 | Dinges .287 |
| 1946 | McCormick .284 | Verban .275 | Newsome .232 | Tabor .268 | Seminick .264 | Ennis .313 | Wyrostek .281 | Northey .249 |

## REGULARS AT EACH POSITION SINCE 1876

| Year | 1b | 2b | SS | 3b | C | OF | OF | OF |
|---|---|---|---|---|---|---|---|---|
| 1947 | Schultz .223 | Verban .285 | Newsome .229 | Handley .253 | Seminick .252 | Ennis .275 | Wyrostek .273 | Walker .371 |
| 1948 | Sisler .274 | Hamner .260 | Miller .246 | Caballero .245 | Seminick .225 | Ennis .290 | Ashburn .333 | Blatnik .260 |
| 1949 | Sisler .289 | Miller .207 | Hamner .263 | Jones .244 | Seminick .243 | Ennis .302 | Ashburn .284 | Nicholson .234 |
| 1950 | Waitkus .284 | Goliat .234 | Hamner .270 | Jones .267 | Seminick .288 | Ennis .311 | Ashburn .303 | Sisler .296 |
| 1951 | Waitkus .257 | Pellagrini .234 | Hamner .255 | Jones .285 | Seminick .223 | Ennis .267 | Ashburn .344 | Sisler .287 |
| 1952 | Waitkus .289 | Ryan .241 | Hamner .275 | Jones .250 | Burgess .296 | Ennis .289 | Ashburn .282 | Wyrostek .265 |
| 1953 | Torgeson .274 | Hamner .276 | Kazanski .217 | Jones .225 | Burgess .292 | Ennis .285 | Ashburn .330 | Wyrostek .271 |
| 1954 | Torgeson .271 | Hamner .299 | Morgan .262 | jones .271 | Burgess .368 | Ennis .261 | Ashburn .313 | Schell .283 |
| 1955 | Blaylock .208 | Morgan .232 | Smalley .196 | Jones .258 | Seminick .246 | Ennis .296 | Ashburn .338 | Greengrass .254 |
| 1956 | Blaylock .254 | Kazanski .211 | Hamner .224 | Jones .277 | Lopata .267 | Ennis .260 | Ashburn .303 | Valo .289 |
| 1957 | Bouchee .257 | Hamner .227 | Fernandez .262 | Jones .218 | Lopata .237 | H. Anderson .268 | Ashburn .297 | Repulski .260 |
| 1958 | Bouchee .257 | Hemus .284 | Fernandez .230 | Jones .271 | Lopata .248 | H. Anderson .301 | Ashburn .350 | Post .282 |
| 1959 | Bouchee .285 | G. Anderson .218 | Koppe .261 | Freese .268 | Sawatski .293 | H. Anderson .240 | Ashburn .266 | Post .254 |

## REGULARS AT EACH POSITION SINCE 1876

| Year | 1b | 2b | SS | 3b | C | OF | OF | OF |
|---|---|---|---|---|---|---|---|---|
| 1960 | Herrera .281 | Taylor .284 | Amaro .231 | Dark .265 | Coker .214 | Walters .239 | DelGreco .237 | Callison .260 |
| 1961 | Herrera .258 | Taylor .250 | Amaro .257 | Smith .248 | Dalrymple .220 | Demeter .251 | Gonzalez .277 | Callison .268 |
| 1962 | Sievers .262 | Taylor .259 | Wine .244 | Demeter .307 | Dalrymple .276 | Covington .283 | Gonzalez .302 | Callison .300 |
| 1963 | Sievers .240 | Taylor .281 | Wine .215 | Hoak .231 | Dalrymple .252 | Gonzalez .306 | Demeter .258 | Callison .284 |
| 1964 | Herrnstein .234 | Taylor .251 | Wine .212 | Allen .318 | Dalrymple .238 | Covington .280 | Gonzalez .278 | Callison .274 |
| 1965 | Stuart .234 | Taylor .229 | Wine .228 | Allen .302 | Dalrymple .213 | A. Johnson .294 | Gonzalez .295 | Callison .262 |
| 1966 | White .276 | Rojas .268 | Groat .260 | Allen .317 | Dalrymple .245 | Briggs .282 | Gonzalez .286 | Callison .276 |
| 1967 | White .250 | Rojas .259 | Wine .190 | Allen .307 | Dalrymple .172 | Gonzalez .339 | Lock .252 | Callison .261 |
| 1968 | White .239 | Rojas .232 | Pena .260 | Taylor .250 | Ryan .179 | Allen .263 | Gonzalez .264 | Callison .244 |
| 1969 | Allen .288 | Rojas .228 | Money .229 | Taylor .262 | Ryan .204 | D. Johnson .255 | Hisle .266 | Callison .265 |
| 1970 | D. Johnson .256 | Doyle .208 | Bowa .250 | Money .295 | McCarver .287 | Briggs .270 | Hisle .205 | Stone .262 |
| 1971 | D. Johnson .265 | Doyle .231 | Bowa .249 | Money .223 | McCarver .278 | Gamble .221 | Montanez .255 | Freed .221 |
| 1972 | D. Johnson .213 | Doyle .249 | Bowa .250 | Money .222 | Bateman .224 | Luzinski .281 | Montanez .247 | Hutton .260 |
| 1973 | Montanez .263 | Doyle .273 | Bowa .211 | Schmidt .196 | Boone .261 | Luzinski .285 | Unser .289 | Robinson .288 |
| 1974 | Montanez .304 | Cash .300 | Bowa .275 | Schmidt .282 | Boone .242 | Luzinski .272 | Unser .264 | Anderson .251 |
| 1975 | Allen .233 | Cash .305 | Bowa .305 | Schmidt .249 | Boone .246 | Luzinski .300 | Maddox .272 | Johnstone .329 |
| 1976 | Allen .268 | Cash .284 | Bowa .248 | Schmidt .262 | Boone .271 | Luzinski .304 | Maddox .330 | Johnstone .318 |
| 1977 | Hebner .285 | Sizemore .281 | Bowa .280 | Schmidt .274 | Boone .284 | Luzinski .309 | Maddox .292 | McBride .316 |
| 1978 | Hebner .283 | Sizemore .219 | Bowa .294 | Schmidt .251 | Boone .283 | Luzinski .265 | Maddox .288 | McBride .269 |

# PITCHING LEADERS

| Year | Games | | Games Started | | Complete Games | | Wins | | Losses | | Shutouts | |
|------|-------|---|---------------|---|----------------|---|------|---|--------|---|----------|---|
| 1876 | Knight | 32 | Knight | 32 | Knight | 27 | Knight | 10 | Knight | 22 | Zettlein | 4 |
| 1883 | Coleman | 65 | Coleman | 61 | Coleman | 59 | Coleman | 12 | Coleman | 48 | Coleman | 3 |
| 1884 | Ferguson | 50 | Ferguson | 47 | Ferguson | 46 | Ferguson | 21 | Ferguson | 25 | Ferguson | 2 |
| 1885 | Daily | 50 | Daily | 50 | Daily | 49 | Daily Ferguson | 26 | Daily | 23 | Daily | 4 |
| 1886 | Ferguson | 48 | Ferguson | 45 | Ferguson | 43 | Ferguson | 30 | Casey | 18 | Casey Ferguson | 4 |
| 1887 | Casey | 45 | Casey | 45 | Casey | 43 | Casey | 28 | Bluffinton | 17 | Casey | 4 |
| 1888 | Bluffinton | 46 | Bluffinton | 46 | Bluffinton | 43 | Bluffinton | 29 | Bluffinton | 17 | Sanders | 4 |
| 1889 | Bluffinton | 47 | Bluffinton | 43 | Bluffinton | 37 | Bluffinton | 28 | Sanders | 18 | Bluffinton | 2 |
| 1890 | Gleason | 60 | Gleason | 55 | Gleason | 54 | Gleason | 38 | Vickery | 22 | Gleason | 6 |
| 1891 | Gleason | 53 | Gleason | 44 | Gleason | 40 | Gleason | 24 | Gleason | 22 | Espen Gleason Thornton | 1 |
| 1892 | Weyhing | 59 | Weyhing | 49 | Weyhing | 46 | Weyhing | 32 | Weyhing | 21 | Weyhing | 6 |
| 1893 | Weyhing | 42 | Weyhing | 40 | Weyhing | 33 | Weyhing | 23 | Weyhing | 16 | Weyhing | 2 |
| 1894 | Taylor | 41 | Taylor Weyhing | 34 | Taylor | 31 | Taylor | 23 | Weyhing | 14 | Weyhing | 2 |

PITCHING LEADERS

| Year | Innings Pitched | | Hits | | Walks | | Strikeouts | | ERA | |
|---|---|---|---|---|---|---|---|---|---|---|
| 1876 | Knight | 282 | Knight | 383 | Knight | 34 | Knight | 12 | Knight | 2.62 |
| 1883 | Coleman | 538 | Coleman | 722 | Coleman | 48 | Coleman | 159 | Coleman | 4.87 |
| 1884 | Ferguson | 417 | Ferguson | 443 | Ferguson | 93 | Ferguson | 194 | Vinton | 2.23 |
| 1885 | Daily | 440 | Daily | 370 | Daily | 90 | Daily | 140 | Daily | 2.21 |
| 1886 | Ferguson | 396 | Casey | 326 | Casey | 104 | Ferguson | 212 | Ferguson | 1.98 |
| 1887 | Casey | 390 | Casey | 377 | Casey | 115 | Bluffinton | 160 | Casey | 2.86 |
| 1888 | Bluffinton | 400 | Bluffinton | 324 | Bluffinton | 59 | Bluffinton | 199 | Sanders | 1.90 |
| 1889 | Bluffinton | 380 | Sanders | 406 | Bluffinton | 121 | Bluffinton | 153 | Bluffinton | 3.24 |
| 1890 | Gleason | 506 | Gleason | 479 | Vickery | 184 | Gleason | 222 | Gleason | 2.63 |
| 1891 | Gleason | 418 | Gleason | 431 | Gleason | 165 | Espen | 108 | Gleason | 3.51 |
| 1892 | Weyhing | 470 | Weyhing | 411 | Weyhing | 168 | Weyhing | 202 | Keefe | 2.36 |
| 1893 | Weyhing | 345 | Weyhing | 399 | Weyhing | 145 | Weyhing | 101 | Taylor | 4.24 |
| 1894 | Taylor | 298 | Weyhing | 365 | Weyhing | 116 | Weyhing | 81 | Taylor | 4.08 |

PITCHING LEADERS

| Year | Games | | Games Started | | Complete Games | | Wins | | Losses | | Shutouts | |
|---|---|---|---|---|---|---|---|---|---|---|---|---|
| 1895 | Carsey | 44 | Carsey | 40 | Carsey | 35 | Taylor | 26 | Carsey | 16 | Taylor | 1 |
| 1896 | Taylor | 45 | Taylor | 41 | Taylor | 35 | Taylor | 20 | Taylor | 21 | Taylor | 1 |
| 1897 | Taylor | 40 | Taylor | 37 | Taylor | 35 | Taylor | 16 | Taylor | 20 | Orth Taylor | 2 |
| 1898 | Piatt | 39 | Piatt | 37 | Donahue Piatt | 33 | Piatt | 24 | Donahue | 17 | Piatt | 6 |
| 1899 | Piatt | 39 | Piatt | 38 | Piatt | 31 | Piatt | 23 | Piatt | 15 | Donahue Fraser | 4 |
| 1900 | Orth | 33 | Orth | 30 | Orth | 24 | Bernhard Donahue Fraser | 15 | Orth | 14 | Donahue | 4 |
| 1901 | Donahue | 35 | Donahue Duggleby | 34 | Donahue | 34 | Donahue | 22 | Donahue | 13 | Orth | 6 |
| 1902 | White | 36 | White | 35 | White | 34 | White | 14 | White | 20 | Fraser White | 3 |
| 1903 | Duggleby | 36 | Duggleby | 30 | Duggleby | 28 | Duggleby | 15 | Duggleby | 18 | Duggleby | 3 |
| 1904 | Fraser | 42 | Fraser | 36 | Fraser | 32 | Fraser | 14 | Fraser | 24 | Sparks | 3 |
| 1905 | Pittinger | 46 | Pittinger | 37 | Pittinger | 29 | Pittinger | 23 | Duggleby | 17 | Pittinger | 4 |
| 1906 | Duggleby Sparks | 42 | Sparks | 37 | Sparks | 29 | Sparks | 19 | Duggleby | 19 | Sparks | 6 |
| 1907 | Corridon Moren | 37 | Corridon | 32 | Sparks | 24 | Sparks | 21 | Moren | 18 | Moren Sparks Corridon | 3 |

**PITCHING LEADERS**

| Year | Innings Pitched | | Hits | | Walks | | Strikeouts | | ERA | |
|------|-----------|-----|----------|-----|----------|-----|-----------|-----|---------|------|
| 1895 | Carsey | 342 | Carsey | 460 | Carsey | 118 | Taylor | 93 | Taylor | 4.49 |
| 1896 | Taylor | 359 | Taylor | 459 | Taylor | 112 | Taylor | 97 | Orth | 4.41 |
| 1897 | Taylor | 317 | Taylor | 376 | Orth | 82 | Taylor | 88 | Wheeler | 3.96 |
| 1898 | Piatt | 306 | Donahue | 327 | Piatt | 97 | Piatt | 121 | Piatt | 3.18 |
| 1899 | Piatt | 305 | Piatt | 323 | Piatt | 86 | Piatt | 89 | Orth | 2.49 |
| 1900 | Orth | 262 | Orth | 302 | Fraser | 93 | Orth | 68 | Fraser | 3.14 |
| 1901 | Donahue | 304 | Donahue | 307 | Donahue | 60 | Duggleby | 94 | Orth | 2.27 |
| 1902 | White | 306 | Duggleby | 301 | Fraser | 97 | White | 185 | White | 2.53 |
| 1903 | Duggleby | 264 | Duggleby | 318 | Mitchell | 102 | Fraser | 104 | Sparks | 2.72 |
| 1904 | Fraser | 302 | Fraser | 287 | Fraser | 100 | Fraser | 127 | Sparks | 2.65 |
| 1905 | Pittinger | 337 | Pittinger | 311 | Pittinger | 104 | Pittinger | 136 | Sparks | 2.18 |
| 1906 | Sparks | 317 | Sparks | 244 | Lush | 119 | Lush | 151 | Sparks | 2.16 |
| 1907 | Corridon | 274 | Corridon | 228 | Moren | 101 | Corridon | 131 | Sparks | 2.00 |

| Year | Games | Games Started | Complete Games | Wins | Losses | Shutouts |
|---|---|---|---|---|---|---|
| 1908 | McQuillan 48 | McQuillan 42 | McQuillan 32 | McQuillan 23 | McQuillan 17 | McQuillan 7 |
| 1909 | McQuillan 41 | Moore 38 | Moore 24 | Moore 18 | McQuillan 16 | McQuillan Moore 4 |
| 1910 | Moore 46 | Moore 35 | Moore 19 | Moore 21 | Moore 15 | Moore 6 |
| 1911 | Alexander 48 | Alexander 37 | Alexander 31 | Alexander 28 | Moore 19 | Alexander 7 |
| 1912 | Alexander 46 | Alexander 34 | Alexander 26 | Alexander 19 | Alexander 17 | Alexander 3 |
| 1913 | Seaton 52 | Alexander Seaton 35 | Alexander 23 | Seaton 27 | Brennan Seaton 12 | Alexander 9 |
| 1914 | Mayer 48 | Alexander Mayer 39 | Alexander 32 | Alexander 27 | Mayer 19 | Alexander 6 |
| 1915 | Alexander 49 | Alexander 42 | Alexander 36 | Alexander 31 | Mayer 15 | Alexander 12 |
| 1916 | Alexander 48 | Alexander 45 | Alexander 38 | Alexander 33 | Demaree 14 | Alexander 16 |
| 1917 | Alexander 45 | Alexander 44 | Alexander 35 | Alexander 30 | Rixey 21 | Alexander 8 |
| 1918 | Prendergast 33 | Prendergast 30 | Prendergast 20 | Hogg Prendergast 13 | Deschger 18 | Jacobs Hogg 3 |
| 1919 | Smith 31 | Smith 20 | Meadows 15 | Meadows 8 | Hogg Rixey 12 | Meadows 3 |
| 1920 | Smith 43 | Meadows Rixey 33 | Rixey 25 | Meadows 16 | Rixey 22 | Meadows 3 |

PITCHING LEADERS

| Year | Innings Pitched | Hits | Walks | Strikeouts | ERA | |
|------|-----------------|------|-------|------------|-----|---|
| 1908 | McQuillan 360 | McQuillan 263 | McQuillan 91 | McQuillan 114 | McQuillan 1.53 | |
| 1909 | Moore 300 | Moore 238 | Moore 108 | Moore 173 | Moore 2.10 | |
| 1910 | Moore 283 | Moore 228 | Moore 121 | Moore 185 | McQuillan 1.60 | |
| 1911 | Alexander 367 | Alexander 285 | Moore 64 | Alexander 227 | Alexander 2.57 | |
| 1912 | Alexander 310 | Alexander 289 | Alexander 105 | Alexander 195 | Alexander 1.86 | |
| 1913 | Seaton 322 | Alexander 288 | Seaton 136 | Seaton 168 | Seaton 2.60 | |
| 1914 | Alexander 355 | Alexander 327 | Mayer 91 | Alexander 214 | Alexander 2.38 | |
| 1915 | Alexander 376 | Alexander 253 | Alexander 64 | Alexander 241 | Alexander 1.22 | |
| 1916 | Alexander 389 | Alexander 323 | Rixey 74 | Alexander 167 | Alexander 1.55 | |
| 1917 | Alexander 388 | Alexander 336 | Oeschger 72 | Alexander 201 | Alexander 1.86 | |
| 1918 | Prendergast 252 | Prendergast 257 | Oeschger 83 | Hogg 81 | Hogg 2.53 | |
| 1919 | Smith 185 | Smith 194 | Hogg 55 | Meadows 88 | Meadows 2.48 | |
| 1920 | Rixey 284 | Rixey 288 | Meadows 90 | Rixey 109 | Meadows 2.84 | |

## PITCHING LEADERS

| Year | Games | | Games Started | | Complete Games | | Wins | | Losses | | Shutouts | |
|---|---|---|---|---|---|---|---|---|---|---|---|---|
| 1921 | Smith | 39 | Hubbell Ring | 30 | Ring | 21 | Meadows | 11 | Smith | 20 | Meadows | 2 |
| 1922* | Smith | 42 | Meadows Ring | 33 | Meadows | 19 | Meadows Ring | 12 | Meadows Ring | 18 | Meadows | 2 |
| 1923 | Ring | 39 | Ring | 36 | Ring | 23 | Ring | 18 | Weinert | 17 | Glazner | 3 |
| 1924 | Carlson | 38 | Ring | 31 | Ring | 16 | Hubbell Ring | 10 | Carlson | 17 | Glazner Hubbell | 2 |
| 1925 | Ring | 38 | Ring | 37 | Ring | 21 | Ring | 14 | Mitchell | 17 | Carlson | 4 |
| 1926 | Willoughby | 47 | Carlson | 34 | Carlson | 20 | Carlson | 17 | Dean | 16 | Carlson | 3 |
| 1927 | Scott | 48 | Ferguson | 31 | Scott | 17 | Scott | 9 | Scott | 21 | Pruett Scott Ulrich | 1 |
| 1928 | Benge | 40 | Benge | 28 | Benge | 12 | Benge | 8 | Benge | 18 | Benge Ferguson Willoughby | 1 |
| 1929 | Willoughby | 49 | Willoughby | 35 | Willoughby | 14 | Willoughby | 15 | Benge | 15 | Benge Sweetland | 2 |
| 1930 | H. Elliott | 48 | Benge | 29 | Collins | 17 | Collins | 16 | Willoughby | 17 | Collins Willoughby | 1 |
| 1931 | Elliott | 52 | Benge | 31 | Benge Collins | 16 | J. Elliott | 19 | Benge | 18 | Benge J. Elliott | 2 |
| 1932 | Collins | 43 | Holley | 30 | Holley | 16 | Collins | 14 | Holley | 14 | Benge Holley | 2 |
| 1933 | Collins | 42 | Holley | 28 | Holley | 12 | Holley | 13 | Holley | 15 | Holley Moore | 3 |

PITCHING LEADERS

| Year | Innings Pitched | | Hits | | Walks | | Strikeouts | | ERA | |
|------|------|------|------|------|------|------|------|------|------|------|
| 1921 | Ring | 246 | Smith | 303 | Ring | 88 | Ring | 88 | Ring | 4.24 |
| 1922 | Ring | 249 | Ring | 292 | Ring | 103 | Ring | 116 | Weinert | 3.40 |
| 1923 | Ring | 313 | Ring | 336 | Ring | 115 | Ring | 112 | Ring | 3.76 |
| 1924 | Ring | 215 | Carlson | 267 | Ring | 108 | Ring | 72 | Ring | 3.97 |
| 1925 | Ring | 270 | Ring | 325 | Ring | 119 | Ring | 93 | Carlson | 4.23 |
| 1926 | Carlson | 267 | Carlson | 293 | Dean | 89 | Carlson | 55 | Carlson | 3.23 |
| 1927 | Scott | 233 | Scott | 304 | Pruett | 89 | Pruett | 90 | Ulrich | 3.17 |
| 1928 | Benge | 202 | Benge | 219 | Ring | 103 | Ring | 72 | Benge | 4.55 |
| 1929 | Willoughby 243 | | Willoughby 288 | | Willoughby 108 | | Benge | 78 | Willoughby 4.99 | |
| 1930 | Collins | 239 | Benge | 305 | Collins | 86 | Collins | 87 | Collins | 4.78 |
| 1931 | J. Elliott | 249 | J. Elliott | 288 | Collins J. Elliott | 83 | Benge | 117 | Benge | 3.17 |
| 1932 | Holley | 228 | Benge Holley | 247 | Collins | 65 | Benge | 89 | Hansen | 3.72 |
| 1933 | Holley | 207 | Holley | 219 | Holley | 62 | Holley | 56 | Holley | 3.53 |

PITCHING LEADERS

| Year | Games | | Games Started | | Complete Games | | Wins | | Losses | | Shutouts | |
|---|---|---|---|---|---|---|---|---|---|---|---|---|
| 1934 | Davis | 51 | Collins | 32 | Davis | 18 | Davis | 19 | Collins | 18 | Davis Johnson | 3 |
| 1935 | Jorgens | 53 | Davis | 27 | Davis | 19 | Davis | 16 | Jorgens | 15 | Davis | 3 |
| 1936 | Passeau | 49 | Walters | 33 | Walters | 15 | Passeau Walters | 11 | Walters | 21 | Davis | 4 |
| 1937 | Mulcahy | 56 | Passeau Walters | 34 | Passeau | 18 | LaMaster | 15 | LaMaster | 19 | Walters | 3 |
| 1938 | Mulcahy | 46 | Mulcahy | 34 | Mulcahy Passeau | 15 | Passeau | 11 | Mulcahy | 20 | Walters | 3 |
| 1939 | Mulcahy | 38 | Mulcahy | 31 | Mulcahy | 14 | Higbe | 10 | Mulcahy | 16 | Hollingsworth 1 | |
| 1940 | Higbe | 41 | Higbe Mulcahy | 36 | Mulcahy | 21 | Higbe | 14 | Mulcahy | 22 | Higbe Mulcahy | 1 |
| 1941 | Pearson | 46 | Blanton | 25 | Podgajny | 8 | Hughes Podgajny | 9 | Hughes Pearson | 14 | Mulcahy | 3 |
| 1942 | Podgajny | 43 | Hughes | 31 | Hughes | 19 | Hughes | 12 | Melton | 20 | Hughes | 2 |
| 1943 | Gerheauser 38 | | Gerheauser | 31 | Gerheauser Rowe | 11 | Rowe | 14 | Gerheauser 19 | | Johnson Melton | 1 |
| 1944 | Schanz | 40 | Raffensberger 31 | | Raffensberger 18 | | Raffensberger 13 Schanz | | Raffensberger 20 | | Rowe | 3 |
| 1945 | Karl | 67 | Barrett | 30 | Barrett | 8 | Karl | 9 | Barrett | 20 | Lee Raffensberger | 3 |
| 1946 | Karl Raffensberger | 39 | Judd | 24 | Raffensberger 14 | | Judd Rowe | 11 | Raffensberger 15 | | Raffensberger 2 Rowe | |

## PITCHING LEADERS

| Year | Innings Pitched | | Hits | | Walks | | Strikeouts | | ERA | |
|------|------------------|--|------|--|-------|--|------------|--|-----|--|
| 1934 | Davis | 274 | Davis | 283 | Collins | 87 | Davis | 99 | Davis | 2.95 |
| 1935 | Davis | 231 | Davis | 264 | Jorgens | 96 | Johnson | 89 | Johnson | 3.56 |
| 1936 | Walters | 258 | Walters | 284 | Walters | 115 | Passeau | 85 | Passeau | 3.48 |
| 1937 | Passeau | 292 | Passeau | 348 | Mulcahy | 97 | LaMaster Passeau | 135 | Passeau | 4.34 |
| 1938 | Mulcahy | 267 | Mulcahy | 294 | Mulcahy | 120 | Passeau | 100 | Passeau | 4.52 |
| 1939 | Mulcahy | 226 | Mulcahy | 246 | Higbe | 123 | Higbe | 95 | Higbe | 4.67 |
| 1940 | Higbe | 283 | Mulcahy | 283 | Higbe | 121 | Higbe | 137 | Mulcahy | 3.60 |
| 1941 | Podgajny | 181 | Johnson | 207 | Hughes | 82 | Johnson | 80 | Pearson | 3.57 |
| 1942 | Hughes | 253 | Hughes | 224 | Melton | 114 | Melton | 107 | Hughes | 3.06 |
| 1943 | Gerheauser | 215 | Gerheauser | 222 | Gerheauser | 70 | Gerheauser | 92 | Rowe | 2.94 |
| 1944 | Raffensberger | 259 | Raffensberger | 257 | Schanz | 103 | Raffensberger | 136 | Raffensberger | 3.06 |
| 1945 | Barrett | 191 | Barrett | 216 | Barrett | 92 | Barrett | 72 | Karl | 2.99 |
| 1946 | Raffensberger | 196 | Raffensberger | 203 | Judd | 90 | Raffensberger | 73 | Judd | 3.53 |

# PITCHING LEADERS

| Year | Games | Games Started | Complete Games | Wins | Losses | Shutouts |
|---|---|---|---|---|---|---|
| 1947 | Donnelly 38 | Leonard 29 | Leonard 19 | Leonard 17 | Judd 15 | Leonard 3 |
| 1948 | Dubiel 37 | Leonard 31 | Leonard 16 | Leonard 12 | Leonard 17 | Dubiel 2 / Heintzelman |
| 1949 | Konstanty 53 | Heintzelman 32 | Heintzelman 15 | Heintzelman 17 / R. Meyer | Roberts 15 | Heintzelman 5 |
| 1950 | Konstanty 74 | Roberts 39 | Roberts 21 | Roberts 20 | R. Meyer 11 / Roberts | Roberts 5 |
| 1951 | Konstanty 58 | Roberts 39 | Roberts 22 | Roberts 21 | Roberts 15 | Roberts 6 |
| 1952 | Hansen 43 | Roberts 37 | Roberts 30 | Roberts 28 | Drews 15 | Simmons 6 |
| 1953 | Konstanty 48 | Roberts 41 | Roberts 33 | Roberts 23 | Roberts 16 | Roberts 5 |
| 1954 | Roberts 45 | Roberts 38 | Roberts 29 | Roberts 23 | Dickson 20 | Dickson 4 / Roberts |
| 1955 | J. Meyer 50 | Roberts 38 | Roberts 26 | Roberts 23 | Roberts 14 | Dickson 4 |
| 1956 | R. Miller 49 | Roberts 37 | Roberts 22 | Roberts 19 | Roberts 18 | Haddix 2 |
| 1957 | Farrell 52 | Sanford 33 | Sanford 15 | Sanford 19 | Roberts 22 | Roberts 5 |
| 1958 | Farrell 54 | Roberts 34 | Roberts 21 | Roberts 17 | Roberts 14 / Simmons | Sanford 2 / Semproch |
| 1959 | J. Meyer 47 | Roberts 35 | Roberts 19 | Roberts 15 | Roberts 17 | Conley 3 |

## PITCHING LEADERS

| Year | Innings Pitched | | Hits | | Walks | | Strikeouts | | ERA | |
|------|------------|-----|-------------|-----|-------------|-----|---------------------|-----|-------------|------|
| 1947 | Leonard | 235 | Rowe | 232 | Judd | 69 | Leonard | 103 | Leonard | 2.68 |
| 1948 | Leonard | 226 | Leonard | 226 | Simmons | 108 | Leonard | 92 | Leonard | 2.51 |
| 1949 | Heintzelman | 250 | Heintzelman | 239 | Heintzelman | 93 | Roberts | 95 | Heintzelman | 3.02 |
| 1950 | Roberts | 304 | Roberts | 282 | Simmons | 88 | Roberts Simmons | 146 | Konstanty | 2.66 |
| 1951 | Roberts | 315 | Roberts | 284 | Church | 90 | Roberts | 127 | Roberts | 3.03 |
| 1952 | Roberts | 330 | Roberts | 292 | Simmons | 70 | Roberts | 148 | Roberts | 2.59 |
| 1953 | Roberts | 347 | Roberts | 342 | Lindell | 139 | Roberts | 198 | Roberts | 2.75 |
| 1954 | Roberts | 337 | Roberts | 289 | Simmons | 98 | Roberts | 185 | Simmons | 2.81 |
| 1955 | Roberts | 305 | Roberts | 292 | Dickson | 82 | Roberts | 160 | Roberts | 3.28 |
| 1956 | Roberts | 297 | Roberts | 328 | Simmons | 65 | Roberts | 157 | Simmons | 3.36 |
| 1957 | Roberts | 250 | Roberts | 246 | Sanford | 94 | Sanford | 188 | Sanford | 3.08 |
| 1958 | Roberts | 270 | Roberts | 270 | Sanford | 81 | Roberts | 130 | Roberts | 3.24 |
| 1959 | Roberts | 257 | Roberts | 267 | Owens | 73 | Roberts | 137 | Conley | 3.00 |

## PITCHING LEADERS

| Year | Games | Games Started | Complete Games | Wins | Losses | Shutouts |
|---|---|---|---|---|---|---|
| 1960 | Farrell 59 | Roberts 33 | Roberts 13 | Roberts 12 | Buzhardt 16<br>Roberts | Conley 2<br>Roberts |
| 1961 | Baldschun 65 | Mahaffey 32 | Mahaffey 12 | Mahaffey 11 | Mahaffey 19 | Mahaffey 3 |
| 1962 | Baldschun 67 | Mahaffey 39 | Mahaffey 20 | Mahaffey 19 | Mahaffey 14 | Mahaffey 2 |
| 1963 | Baldschun 65 | McLish 32 | Culp 10<br>McLish | Culp 14 | Short 12 | Culp 5 |
| 1964 | Baldschun 71 | Bunning 39 | Bunnins 13 | Bunnins 19 | Bennett 14 | Bunning 5 |
| 1965 | Baldschun 65 | Short 40 | Bunning 15 | Bunning 19 | Short 11 | Bunning 7 |
| 1966 | Knowles 69 | Bunning 41 | Short 19 | Short 20 | Bunning 14 | Bunning 5<br>L. Jackson |
| 1967 | Farrell 50 | Bunning 40 | Bunning 16 | Bunning 17 | Bunning 15<br>L. Jackson | Bunning 6 |
| 1968 | Farrell 54 | Short 36 | L. Jackson 12 | Short 19 | L. Jackson 17 | Fryman 5 |
| 1969 | Boozer 46<br>Farrell | Fryman 35<br>G. Jackson | Wise 14 | Wise 15 | G. Jackson 18 | G. Jackson 4<br>Wise |
| 1970 | Selma 73 | Short 34<br>Wise | Short 7 | Wise 13 | Short 16 | Fryman 3 |
| 1971 | Brandon 52 | Wise 37 | Wise 17 | Wise 17 | Lersch 14<br>Short<br>Wise | Wise 4 |
| 1972 | Twitchell 49 | Carlton 41 | Carlton 30 | Carlton 27 | Reynolds 15 | Carlton 8 |

## PITCHING LEADERS

| Year | Innings Pitched | Hits | Walks | Strikeouts | ERA | |
|---|---|---|---|---|---|---|
| 1960 | Roberts 237 | Roberts 256 | Buzhardt 68 | Roberts 122 | Farrell 2.70 | |
| 1961 | Mahaffey 219 | Mahaffey 205 | Mahaffey 70 | Mahaffey 158 | Farrell 3.69 | |
| 1962 | Mahaffey 274 | Mahaffey 253 | Hamilton 107 | Mahaffey 177 | Baldschun 2.97 | |
| 1963 | McLish 210 | Short 185 | Culp 102 | Culp 176 | Klippstein 1.93 | |
| 1964 | Bunning 284 | Bunning 248 | Mahaffey 82 | Bunning 219 | Short 2.20 | |
| 1965 | Short 297 | Short 260 | Short 89 | Bunning 268 | Bunning 2.60 | |
| 1966 | Bunning 314 | Bunning 260 | Short 68 | Bunning 252 | Bunning 2.41 | |
| 1967 | Bunning 302 | L. Jackson 242 | Short 74 | Bunning 253 | Hall 2.20 | |
| 1968 | Short 270 | Short 236 | Short 81 | Short 202 | L. Jackson 2.77 | |
| 1969 | G. Jackson 253 | Fryman 243 | G. Jackson 92 | G. Jackson 180 | Wise 3.23 | |
| 1970 | Wise 220 | Wise 253 | Short 66 | Selma 153 | Bunning 4.11 | |
| 1971 | Wise 272 | Wise 261 | Reynolds 82 | Wise 155 | Wise 2.88 | |
| 1972 | Carlton 346 | Carlton 257 | Carlton 87 | Carlton 310 | Carlton 1.98 | |

| Year | Games | Games Started | Complete Games | Wins | Losses | Shutouts |
|---|---|---|---|---|---|---|
| 1973 | Scarce 52 | Carlton 40 | Carlton 18 | Brett<br>Carlton<br>Lonborg 13 | Carlton 20 | Twitchell 5 |
| 1974 | Scarce 58 | Carlton<br>Lonborg 39 | Carlton 17 | Lonborg<br>Twitchell 17 | Schueler 16 | Lonborg 3 |
| 1975 | Garber 71 | Carlton 37 | Carlton 14 | Carlton 15 | Carlton 14 | Carlton 3 |
| 1976 | Garber<br>Reed 59 | Carlton<br>Kaat 35 | Carlton 13 | Carlton 20 | Kaat 14 | Carlton 2 |
| 1977 | Garber 64 | Carlton 36 | Carlton 17 | Carlton 23 | Kaat 11 | Carlton 2 |
| 1978 | Reed 66 | Carlton 34 | Carlton 12 | Carlton 16 | Christenson 14 | Carlton<br>Christenson 3 |

## PITCHING LEADERS

| Year | Innings Pitched | Hits | Walks | Strikeouts | ERA | |
|---|---|---|---|---|---|---|
| 1973 | Carlton 293 | Carlton 293 | Carlton 113 | Carlton 223 | Twitchell 2.54 | |
| 1974 | Carlton 291 | Lonborg 280 | Carlton 136 | Carlton 240 | Lonborg 3.21 | |
| 1975 | Carlton 255 | Underwood 221 | Carlton 104 | Carlton 192 | Carlton 3.56 | |
| 1976 | Carlton 253 | Kaat 241 | Carlton 72 | Carlton 195 | Lonborg 3.08 | |
| 1977 | Carlton 283 | Carlton 229 Christenson | Carlton 89 | Carlton 198 | Carlton 2.64 | |
| 1978 | Carlton 247 | Carlton 228 | Lerch 70 | Carlton 161 | Carlton 2.84 | |

# 25TH ANNIVERSARY OF THE 1950 WHIZ KIDS

On August 16, 1975, the Silver Anniversary reunion of the Whiz Kids was held at Veterans Stadium. Here is a recap of their glory, followed by notes on what each of the members of the team was doing 25 years after their pennant.

The Brooklyn Dodgers had just beaten the Phillies, 9-7 in 10 innings at Connie Mack Stadium to win the National League championship by a game over the St. Louis Cardinals. The date was Oct. 2, 1949, the final game of that season.

But, during the second half of that season the Phils had proved they had arrived as a contender in the tough National League. Eddie Sawyer's young club won 32 and lost 24 after July 29 that year to finish a strong third, the Phillies' highest finish since 1917.

"After that last game, players were milling around, saying their good-byes," recalls Richie Ashburn, then a 22-year-old who had just completed his sophomore season in the biggies. "Sawyer got everyone together and made a short talk, 'Boys, come back here next year ready to play. We're gonna win it.'"

"We had a bunch of kids who had gone through their indoctrination period in the major leagues," remembers Sawyer. "The glory of being in the majors had worn off. They proved they could play and win and to me it looked like we had a pretty good shot in '50. I just wanted them to be ready to go from the start in spring training next year."

364 days after that little speech, Sawyer's prophecy came true and he reigned as manager of the National League champions. It was the first N.L. pennant for Philadelphia in 35 years.

A former science professor at Ithaca College, Eddie can undoubtedly attribute some of his grey hair to the 1950 championship season. Bouncing around between first and third places, the Whiz Kids moved into first place a good 25 years ago by sweeping a home doubleheader from the Chicago Cubs, 7-0 and 1-0, on July 25th. Bubba Church and Robin Roberts were authors of the two shutouts.

By September 20th, the Phillies had built their lead up to 7½ games and a pennant appeared to be a shoo-in. But, the club was having troubles as Sawyer recalls: "We lost Curt (Simmons) to the service, (Bob) Miller and (Bubba) Church were injured so our pitching was thin. Our hitters weren't hitting and we couldn't score runs. Fortunately, we had a lead big enough to coast a little bit." The Phils lost their last two homes games to the Dodgers seeing their lead cut to five, as they departed for the final road trip — nine games in Boston, New York and Brooklyn.

Winning two out of three in Boston, the Phils headed for New York with a five-game lead and only six games left to play. The situation got worse, instead of better. The Giants won back-to-back doubleheaders from the Phillies in the Polo Grounds sending the Whiz Kids across New York City for the final two games of the season and a two-game margin over the second-place Brooklyn Dodgers.

Exactly, one year after the Dodgers had beaten the Phils for the 1949 pennant, they cut the deficit to one game with a 7-3 decision over Bob Miller. The Phillies were down to their last ray of hope, the finale of a long 1950 season. Sawyer, who was relying heavily on Roberts and bullpen ace Jim Konstanty down the stretch, decided to go with Robbie, who was making his fourth start in the last nine games.

Two-out singles by Dick Sisler, Del Ennis and Willie Jones off Don Newcombe had given Roberts and the Phils a 1-0 lead in the top of the sixth inning in that crucial final game, Oct. 1, 1950. In the Dodgers' half of the same inning, the Phillies must have thought their luck had ended as shortstop Pee Wee Reese sent a two-out drive deep to right field. The ball hit the screen above the fence and dropped down to a one-foot coping. To the Phils' disgust and the Dodgers' delight, the ball stayed on top of the coping and Reese circled the bases to tie the game.

Still tied, 1-1, Roberts began that historic 9th inning by walking Cal Abrams, the second walk issued by the Phillies' workhorse in the game.

Reese was the next hitter and Roberts jumped ahead of him in the count, no balls and two strikes, as the Dodger shortstop failed in two bunt attempts. Reese then singled sharply to left field. Broadcaster Gene Kelly describes the action at this point:

"... Here comes Sawyer to the mound. The batter due is Duke Snider ... Runner at first, Reese; runner at second, Abrams ... Snider, who is hitless in the game, is the next batter due. It was he of course who hit the homer off Konstanty yesterday ... However, Sawyer is leaving him in, Roberts stays ... Two men on, nobody out ... Last half of the ninth, score tied, 1-1, what represents the winning run is at second in Abrams ... Infield moves in to look for the bunt ... Roberts stretches, throws, Snider takes a full cut, line-drive to center-field ... Ashburn races in with the ball and here comes the throw from center field ... he is - - - - OUT!"

On the play, Reese takes third and Snider second and Roberts is still in a jam. Following another mound conference, the Phils decide to walk Jackie Robinson intentionally, loading the bases. Carl Furillo is the next hitter in the awesome Dodger attack. Furillo swings at the first pitch and fouls to the late Eddie Waitkus for the second out. The pressure doesn't ease as Gil Hodges, a dangerous clutch hitter, follows Furillo. Roberts has a 1-1 count on the late Brooklyn first baseman. Back to Gene Kelly:

"... 1-1 count, throwing, swinging, a fly ball hits towards right field, Ennis moving way, way back, under it, makes it ... It's a ten-inning game ... What an inning by Roberts, no runs, two hits, no errors, three men left ... We move into overtime."

After such a gutty performance by Roberts, the worm had to turn for the Phillies and it did. Roberts, himself, began the winning rally in the top of the tenth with a ground-ball base-hit through the middle. Waitkus huddled with Sawyer over the bunt possibility but swung away on a 1-1 pitch and looped a Texas-league single to center, sending Roberts to second. Ashburn was the next hitter:

"... Richie's 0 for 4 ... Infielders move in for the bunt ... the pitch, a bunt along the third-base line ... Newcombe up with it, throw to third ... in time ... Roberts made a head-long slide but he's out ... One away, runners on first and second ... Sisler coming up, he has three singles in four trips."

Newcombe got two quick strikes, wasted a pitch and Sisler then fouled off the next pitch:

"... Count 1 and 2 on Dick Sisler ... Score tied 1-1, top of 10th, man at first and second ... Now Newcombe decides to call time, a real tough moment for this big right-hander, course Roberts had one too in that last of the ninth ... One ball, two strikes, now Newcombe's set, in the stretch, delivering, swinging, a fly ball, very, very deep to left field, moving back Abrams, way, way back, he can't get it — it's a home run ... WOW! ... A home run for Dick Sisler, the Phillies lead, 4-1 ... One out and Sisler gets a left-field home run, his 13th of the season. It just cleared the barrier in left field 350 feet from home plate. Pandemonium breaks loose at Ebbets Field."

In the last of the 10th, Roberts gets Roy Campanella for the first out and strikes out pinch-hitter Jimmy Russell for the second out. Back to Gene Kelly:

"... Phillies are one out away from the 1950 National League pennant ... and Tommy Brown is the one hurdle in their way righ now. He's

200

*hitting for Newcombe and batting .294 ... That was Roberts' second strikeout victim ... He hadn't registered a strikeout since the third inning ... Brown bats righthanded ... Throwing, swinging, a foul back to the screen ... Most of the fans, except the Phils fans of course, are beginning to leave the ball park ... Nothing and one ... If you had told most Phils fans last night that they would do it, they would smile weakly, say gee we hope so ... Now the 0-1 pitch, change, fouled off, in play, first base side, Waitkus under, the Phillies win the pennant!"*

The hectic last week seemed to take its toll with the young Phils. They went into the World Series against the New York Yankees, and were swept, four games to none. The first two were at Connie Mack Stadium, Jim Konstanty a surprise starter in the opener. He lost, 1-0, to Vic Raschi, with Jerry Coleman's fly ball producing the lone run. Game 2, Joe DiMaggio's 10th inning homer off Roberts gave Yanks a 2-1 win. Games 3, 3-2, Tom Ferrick beating Russ Meyer and game 4, 5-2, Whitey Ford over Bob Miller.

## 24 EDDIE SAWYER
### Manager

Former science professor at Ithaca College lives in Valley Forge, Pa. He's 64 years old and a distributor for the Plymouth Golf Ball Company. "That last game was something. Robbie was great. They weren't going to score much off him but the question was whether we could score. Our hitting wasn't too good down the stretch and the pitching was thin with Simmons in the service, Church and Miller hurting ... On Sisler's home run, you were never too sure in Brooklyn. The fans used to reach out for the balls and it seemed like the visiting team would wind up with doubles because the fans would touch the ball. When the Dodgers hit the ball, they wouldn't interfere and it was a home run for them."

## 40 MAJE McDONNELL
### Coach

Resident of Philadelphia, Pa., now 54 years old. "We had a big win in St. Louis at the end of August, I believe. We came from behind several times and won, Whitman tripled in the winning run. I had a feeling then, we were gonna win it. That was the time we took our only plane ride of the season. Carpenter chartered a plane and flew the club to Boston in four hours rather than take the 28-hour train ride."

## FRANK WIECHEC
### Trainer

Served as the Phillies trainer for 15 years, 1948 through 1963. Now 60, he lives in Blue Bell, Pa., and is a physical therapist at Einstein Medical Center, Willowcrest Division. "I'll never forget Waitkus and I working all winter after the 1949 season. He was shot during that season and Carpenter sent us to Clearwater, Fla., for the winter. He had no endurance, lost a lot of strength and was very short of breath. We did a lot of running, rowing a boat, treatment and by next spring training he was ready to play, a surprise to everyone. Then there was Seminick with the bad ankle in September. I had to give him novocain shots daily and wrap the ankle every day too. He played the rest of the season and the series in an awful lot of pain."

# 1 RICHIE ASHBURN
## Centerfielder

"Putt-putt" is now 48 years old, lives in Gladwyne, Pa., and is a Phillies broadcaster and sports columnist for the Evening Bulletin. "Actually, Snider's hit to me and the out at home plate in the 9th was a routine play. It was a key play but it wouldn't have meant anything had the Dodgers scored after it and won. Roberts really did some outstanding pitching. Something else sticks in my mind from that season — Konstanty made the point how valuable a relief pitcher is to the game. He was the first to bring importance to relief pitching."

# JIMMY BLOODWORTH
## Infielder

Jimmy turned 58 last month. He lives in Apalachicola, Fla., and works as a carpenter for the St. Joe paper company. "It was the greatest year. No one knows what it's like to be on a championship club unless you can live it. I was just glad to be part of that club."

# 3 RALPH "PUTSY" CABALLERO
## Infielder

57 years old; owner of a pest control company in New Orleans, La. "Getting into the world series. That stands out in my mind because that's the goal of every ball player. It was a real thrill."

# 18 MILO CANDINI
## Pitcher

Now 58, he lives in Manteca, Calif., where he is the owner of a liquor store. "Sisler's home run was a bit painful, as I remember. The dugouts in Ebbetts Field were low. I jumped up when Dick hit that ball and conked myself on the head pretty good. I also remember how difficult it was to win. Robbie and Jim (Konstanty) did a great job for us down the stretch."

# 23 EMORY "BUBBA" CHURCH
## Pitcher

A manufacturer's representative for medical surgical supplies, Bubba, now 50, lives in Birmingham, Ala. "Getting hit in the face by the line-drive from Kluszewski. I remember seeing Ennis pick up the ball in right field. It scared me to death. But, I was determined to come back. Maje and I went in the outfield after I got out of the hospital and I had him hit the ball at me as hard as he could to get over any fear . . . It was a great club, complete unity with everyone pulling for everybody. Nobody had a chance to get down."

# 30 SYLVESTER "BLIX" DONNELLY
## Pitcher

61-year-old from Olivia, Minn., where he's semi-retired from his anhydrous ammonia business of the past 20 years. "I was part of the Fizz-Kids, Heintzelman and me, the old grey-beards trying to help the Whiz Kids win. I guess my biggest contribution was winning a game in Boston the last week when we were scuffling. It kept us in the running."

## 14 DEL ENNIS
Outfielder

50 years old, lives in Jenkinton, Pa., and operates a bowling alley. "The play I remember well was Hodges' last out in the 9th inning the day we won it. Gene Kelly said it was a fly ball hit to me in right. It wasn't that easy because it was a line-drive. I lost it in the sun and didn't see it too good until I caught it chest high."


## 9 MIKE GOLIAT
Second baseman

50-year-old from Seven Hills, O., where he's in the trucking business. "It was a big year for me. I got married and we won the pennant. I remember the first game of that season, had a homer, double and two singles off Newcombe. For some reason, I had a lot of luck against him. He was a fast-ball pitcher and I was a fast-ball hitter and everything just seemed to find the holes against him."


## 2 GRANNY HAMNER
Shortstop

48 years old now, lives in Clearwater, Fla., an infield instructor in the Phillies minor league system. "I felt we had it cinched when we had that great western trip (8-2 record) in late August. The last game of that trip was in St. Louis and we came from way behind to win it. We were behind three times in the game and still won. It was a big victory."


## 6 WILLIE "PUDDIN' HEAD" JONES
Third Baseman

The native South Carolinean now resides in Cincinnati. "What a great feeling to see that last out in the 10th when we beat them in the last game. I was in a slump toward the end, actually concerned about myself from the all-star game on. We had a big doubleheader — back-to-back doubleheaders — with the Giants in New York the last week and I must have left a dozen men in scoring position."


## 27 KEN HEINTZELMAN
Pitcher

Resident of St. Peter, Mo., where the 59-year-old lefty works for McDonnell Douglas. "The game that sticks out in my mind was taking over for Bubba after he was hit and winning the game. The entire season, though, was a really big thrill, we had a lot of fun."

## 17 STAN HOLLMIG
### Outfielder

Resides in New Braunfels, Tex., and scouts for the Houston Astros. Now 49 years old. "I can still see Sisler's ball go out. It was quite a thrill, fantastic and the older you get the more you appreciate the thrill."


## 35 JIM KONSTANTY
### Pitcher

Most valuable player in the National League 25 years ago, now retired, living in Worcester, NY. "It's been a long time since '50 and things are kind of cloudy. But, I remember pitching 10 innings of relief, giving up 2 runs, against the Reds. I left the game, we scored the next inning and won. I thought I deserved some kind of credit for the win so I jotted down a "save" in my little note book next to that game." Note: Jim passed away on June 11, 1976.


## 29 STAN LOPATA
### Catcher

"Big Stash" lives in Abington, Pa., and is a salesman for J.D.M. materials company, dealing in redi-mix concrete. "I was in the last game when we beat the Dodgers. With Ashburn's throw coming in and Abrams coming home, the thought crossed my mind all I have to do is miss the ball. But, we got him by plenty, 20-25 feet. I was really surprised they sent him but I was glad they did. Instead of the bases loaded and no one out, we had one out and a better chance to get out of it."


## 15 JACK MAYO
### Outfielder

From Youngstown, O., where he's a land developer — real estate broker. Age: 49. "I was a line-drive type hitter, definitely not a home-run hitter. I did hit a homer late in September that looked like it might help us only to have it washed out by rain. Because of the illness to Nick (Nicholson), I was placed on the World Series eligibility list, which was an honor."


## 34 RUSS MEYER
### Pitcher

51-year-old resident of Gary, Ind., where he's the general manager and part-owner of a bowling alley. "1949 was a big year for me, 17 wins, lowest ERA among righthanders in the league. Spring training next year, I hurt my arm and didn't win many that season. But I won three the last five weeks, two over Brooklyn. I remember one game in Philadelphia late in the season. I hadn't pitched for 3-4 weeks when Eddie came up and told me 'you're it tomorrow.' We won the game, a big one at the time."

## 19 BOB MILLER
Pitcher

Born and raised in Detroit, Mich., where he's an insurance agent and baseball coach for the U. of Detroit. "Beating Boston, 2-1, in April for my first big league win sticks out in my mind. Then, there's that last game. Robbie just pitched fantastically."


## 12 BILL NICHOLSON
Outfielder

60 years old; semi-retired from his 120-acre farm in Chestertown, Md. "Our hitting fell off a little the last month and maybe I could have helped a little bit. But I came down with diabetes on Labor Day and missed the rest of the season. My big thrill was being allowed out of the hospital to see the first World Series game."


## 36 ROBIN ROBERTS
Pitcher

Resides in Ft. Washington, Pa., is color man on radio when Phils televise at home; also writes a sports column once a week for Wilmington News-Journal. "Ashburn's throw and Sisler's home run have high priorities in my memory of 1950. We were all kind of surprised Sisler's ball carried into the seats. The ball was hit on a low trajectory but it made it."


## 21 ANDY SEMINICK
Catcher

Popular ex-Phil lives in Melbourne, Fla., where he does some scouting for the Phillies. He'll be 55 next month. "Everyone remembers the fight with the Giants. Eddie Stanky started it by jumping up and down at second base while I was batting. It aggravated me so damn much I couldn't sleep that night wondering what was going to happen the next day. I was ready for anything and it happened. Stanky was thrown out for doing the same thing. I had run into Thompson (Hank, Giants' third baseman) pretty good. Later, I slid hard into (Bill) Rigney, who had replaced Stanky, and all hell broke loose. We were a close bunch of guys and it seemed that this incident made us much more together the rest of the way."


## 25 KEN SILVESTRI
Catcher

59-year-old bullpen coach for the Atlanta Braves. Resides in Tallahassee, Fla. "We had lost a doubleheader late in September and everyone was really down. Sawyer came in and said 'One day does not constitute a season.' It was the greatest picker-up I've ever heard from a manager."

## 28 CURT SIMMONS
Pitcher

Manager of Limekiln Golf Course. Lives in Meadowbrook, Pa. 46 years old. "I was in the National Guard unit doing two weeks of summer camp at Indiantown Gap. I got a pass for one night and was flown to Philadelphia to pitch against the Reds. I'd been out in the field on maneuvers all day and was really tired. I didn't last very long in the game, either. Then, later the unit was activated and I missed the last couple weeks of the season. I'm not complaining. It was just one of those things that happens."

## 8 DICK SISLER
Outfielder

54-year-old batting coach with the San Diego Padres, resides in Nashville, Tenn. "I remember the pitch from Newcombe before the big homer. It was a fast ball but outside a little. The next pitch was in closer and I was fortunate enough that it carried. Earlier in the game I hit a fly ball out the same way but it didn't carry; I didn't know it was going all the way until after I had rounded first base. It was a great feeling and actually the World Series seemed kind of anti-climatic after that final game."

## 33 JOHN "JOCKO" THOMPSON
Pitcher

Occupation: sales manager for General Binding Sales Corporation; Residence: Rockville, Md. Age: 55. "It was just like a dream you dream all your life actually coming true. I had played in Toronto with most of the Phils. My roommate there was Konstanty and he and I roomed again when I was called up by the Phils late that year."

## 4 EDDIE WAITKUS
First Baseman

Born Sept. 4, 1919; died, Sept. 15, 1972, in Boston, Mass. Played in major leagues from 1941 through 1955, seeing service with Chicago Cubs, Phillies, Baltimore Orioles and Phils again. Was with Phillies, 1949 through 1953 and ended career with 33 games here in 1955. Line-drive type hitter who compiled a .285 lifetime average. Missed much of 1949 season after being shot in chest by a woman in Chicago. Came back to play in 154 games during the championship season, hitting .284.

## 37 DICK WHITMAN
Outfielder

From Campbell, Calif., Dick is 54 and the maintenance manager at the San Jose water works. "I came from the Dodgers organization so it was a thrill beating that club. I can remember Ashburn's great throw and then seeing Roberts swell up that right arm and just throw the ball by the rest of them after that play."

206

## THE 1950 WHIZ KIDS

| Pitchers | Age | Bats | Throws | G. | IP. | H. | BB. | SO. | W. | L. | PC. |
|---|---|---|---|---|---|---|---|---|---|---|---|
| Candini, Milo | 32 | Right | Right | 18 | 30 | 32 | 15 | 9 | 1 | 0 | 1.000 |
| Church, Bubba | 24 | Right | Right | 31 | 142 | 113 | 56 | 51 | 8 | 6 | .571 |
| Donnelly, Blix | 35 | Right | Right | 14 | 21 | 30 | 10 | 11 | 2 | 4 | .333 |
| Heintzelman, Ken | 34 | Right | Left | 23 | 126 | 122 | 54 | 39 | 3 | 9 | .250 |
| Johnson, Ken | 27 | Left | Left | 16 | 63 | 61 | 46 | 32 | 4 | 1 | .800 |
| Konstanty, Jim | 33 | Right | Right | 74 | 151 | 109 | 51 | 54 | 16 | 7 | .696 |
| Meyer, Russ | 26 | Both | Right | 33 | 161 | 193 | 66 | 74 | 9 | 11 | .450 |
| Miller, Bob | 23 | Right | Right | 35 | 174 | 190 | 57 | 46 | 11 | 6 | .647 |
| Roberts, Robin | 23 | Left | Right | 40 | 304 | 283 | 76 | 146 | 20 | 11 | .645 |
| Curt Simmons | 20 | Left | Left | 31 | 215 | 178 | 87 | 146 | 17 | 8 | .680 |
| Thompson, Jocko | 30 | Left | Left | 2 | 4 | 1 | 4 | 2 | 0 | 0 | .000 |

| Catchers | Age | Bats | Throws | G. | AB. | R. | H. | HR. | RBI. | PC. |
|---|---|---|---|---|---|---|---|---|---|---|
| Lopata, Stan | 24 | Right | Right | 58 | 130 | 10 | 26 | 1 | 11 | .200 |
| Seminick, Andy | 29 | Right | Right | 130 | 393 | 55 | 113 | 24 | 68 | .288 |
| Silvestri, Ken | 33 | Both | Right | 11 | 20 | 2 | 5 | 0 | 4 | .250 |

| Infielders | Age | Bats | Throws | G. | AB. | R. | H. | HR. | RBI. | PC. |
|---|---|---|---|---|---|---|---|---|---|---|
| Bloodworth, Jimmy | 32 | Right | Right | 58 | 110 | 7 | 25 | 0 | 13 | .227 |
| Caballero, Ralph | 22 | Right | Right | 46 | 24 | 12 | 4 | 0 | 0 | .167 |
| Goliat, Mike | 24 | Right | Right | 145 | 483 | 49 | 113 | 13 | 65 | .234 |
| Hamner, Granny | 22 | Right | Right | 157 | 638 | 78 | 172 | 11 | 80 | .270 |
| Jones, Willie | 24 | Right | Right | 157 | 610 | 100 | 162 | 25 | 88 | .266 |
| Waitkus, Eddie | 29 | Left | Left | 154 | 641 | 102 | 182 | 2 | 43 | .284 |

| Outfielders | Age | Bats | Throws | G. | AB. | R. | H. | HR. | RBI. | PC. |
|---|---|---|---|---|---|---|---|---|---|---|
| Ashburn, Richie | 23 | Left | Right | 151 | 594 | 84 | 180 | 2 | 39 | .303 |
| Ennis, Del | 24 | Right | Right | 153 | 595 | 91 | 186 | 31 | 125 | .313 |
| Hollmig, Stan | 24 | Right | Right | 11 | 12 | 1 | 3 | 0 | 1 | .250 |
| Nicholson, Bill | 34 | Left | Right | 40 | 58 | 3 | 13 | 3 | 10 | .224 |
| Sisler, Dick | 29 | Left | Right | 141 | 523 | 79 | 156 | 13 | 83 | .298 |
| Whitman, Dick | 29 | Left | Right | 75 | 132 | 21 | 33 | 0 | 12 | .250 |
| Mayo, Jack | 23 | Left | Right | 18 | 36 | 1 | 8 | 0 | 3 | .222 |

## THE 1950 NATIONAL LEAGUE RACE MONTH-BY-MONTH

| May 1 | W. | L. | PC. | GB. |
|---|---|---|---|---|
| Brooklyn | 7 | 3 | .700 | — |
| Chicago | 3 | 2 | .600 | 1½ |
| Pittsburgh | 6 | 5 | .545 | 1½ |
| St. Louis | 6 | 5 | .545 | 1½ |
| Boston | 6 | 6 | .500 | 2 |
| PHILLIES | 6 | 6 | .500 | 2 |
| Cincinnati | 4 | 6 | .400 | 3 |
| New York | 1 | 6 | .143 | 4½ |
| **June 1** | | | | |
| Brooklyn | 23 | 14 | .622 | — |
| St. Louis | 23 | 14 | .622 | — |
| PHILLIES | 23 | 15 | .605 | ½ |
| Boston | 20 | 16 | .556 | 2½ |
| Chicago | 18 | 17 | .514 | 4 |
| Pittsburgh | 16 | 24 | .400 | 8½ |
| New York | 13 | 21 | .382 | 8½ |
| Cincinnati | 11 | 26 | .297 | 12 |

| July 1 | | | | |
|---|---|---|---|---|
| PHILLIES | 37 | 26 | .587 | — |
| St. Louis | 38 | 27 | .585 | — |
| Brooklyn | 35 | 27 | .565 | 1½ |
| Boston | 35 | 29 | .547 | 2½ |
| New York | 32 | 31 | .508 | 5 |
| Chicago | 31 | 31 | .500 | 5½ |
| Pittsburgh | 23 | 41 | .359 | 14½ |
| Cincinnati | 22 | 41 | .349 | 15 |
| **August 1** | | | | |
| PHILLIES | 59 | 40 | .586 | — |
| St. Louis | 54 | 41 | .568 | 3 |
| Brooklyn | 52 | 40 | .565 | 3½ |
| Boston | 53 | 41 | .564 | 3½ |
| New York | 45 | 47 | .489 | 10½ |
| Chicago | 41 | 51 | .446 | 14½ |
| Cincinnati | 39 | 56 | .411 | 18 |
| Pittsburgh | 34 | 61 | .358 | 23 |

## THE 1950 NATIONAL LEAGUE RACE MONTH-BY-MONTH (continued)

| September 1 | | | | | October 1 (Final) | | | | |
|---|---|---|---|---|---|---|---|---|---|
| PHILLIES | 79 | 47 | .627 | — | PHILLIES | 91 | 63 | .591 | — |
| Brooklyn | 69 | 51 | .575 | 7 | Brooklyn | 89 | 65 | .578 | 2 |
| Boston | 68 | 55 | .553 | 9½ | New York | 86 | 68 | .558 | 5 |
| New York | 66 | 57 | .537 | 11½ | Boston | 83 | 71 | .539 | 8 |
| St. Louis | 65 | 58 | .528 | 12½ | St. Louis | 78 | 75 | .510 | 12½ |
| Chicago | 54 | 70 | .435 | 24 | Cincinnati | 66 | 87 | .431 | 24½ |
| Cincinnati | 49 | 73 | .402 | 28 | Chicago | 64 | 89 | .418 | 26½ |
| Pittsburgh | 43 | 82 | .344 | 35½ | Pittsburgh | 57 | 96 | .373 | 33½ |

Statistical Notes . . .

Jim Konstanty. In addition to his 16-7 won-lost record for seventy-four appearances, Jim also saved twenty-two games that season. He had one unbelievable spell, allowing no runs in 22.1 innings and giving up just seven hits, spanning a month, July 23 to Aug. 23.

Game Winning Hits: Mike Goliat led with thirteen followed by eleven each for Del Ennis, Andy Seminick, and Willie Jones; Dick Sisler nine, Granny Hamner five, Richie Ashburn four, and Eddie Waitkus three.

Longest winning streak: six games, while the club lost five in a row three different times.

---

## BOX SCORES
### MAJOR LEAGUE SHUTOUT RECORD
Philadelphia at Providence, August 21, 1883.

| Provid'ce | Ab | R | H | PO | A | Phila. | Ab | R | H | PO | A |
|---|---|---|---|---|---|---|---|---|---|---|---|
| Hines, cf | 7 | 3 | 1 | 2 | 1 | Purcell, lf | 4 | 0 | 1 | 0 | 1 |
| Farrell, 2b | 7 | 4 | 4 | 1 | 3 | Manning, rf | 4 | 0 | 2 | 0 | 0 |
| Start, 1b | 7 | 4 | 4 | 12 | 0 | Gross, c | 4 | 0 | 0 | 3 | 2 |
| Radb'rne, p | 7 | 3 | 4 | 0 | 4 | McClell'd, ss | 4 | 0 | 0 | 5 | 3 |
| Irwin, ss | 6 | 2 | 2 | 2 | 4 | Coleman, cf | 4 | 0 | 2 | 3 | 1 |
| Carroll, lf | 6 | 2 | 3 | 2 | 0 | Fergus'n 2b | 4 | 0 | 0 | 4 | 1 |
| Denny, 3b | 5 | 4 | 3 | 3 | 2 | Warner, 3b | 3 | 0 | 0 | 1 | 1 |
| Cassidy, rf | 5 | 3 | 2 | 0 | 0 | Farrar, 1b | 3 | 0 | 0 | 7 | 1 |
| Gilligan, c | 3 | 3 | 3 | 5 | 0 | Hagan, p | 3 | 0 | 1 | 1 | 1 |
| Totals | 53 | 28 | 26 | 27 | 14 | Totals | 33 | 0 | 6 | 24 | 10 |

Errors — Philadelphia 27: Hagan 11, Gross 8, McClelland 3, Warner 2, Manning 1, Coleman 1, Ferguson 1. Providence 4: Radbourne 1, Irwin 1, Carroll 1, Gilligan 1.

| Providence | 7 | 2 | 2 | 0 | 1 | 8 | 1 | 7 | x—28 |
|---|---|---|---|---|---|---|---|---|---|
| Philadelphia | 0 | 0 | 0 | 0 | 0 | 0 | 0 | 0 | 0—0 |

Earned runs: Providence 7. Two base hits: Start 2, Carroll 2, Farrell, Radbourne, Coleman, Hagan, Irwin, Denny. Home run: Denny. Struck out, by Radbourne 2, by Hagan 3. Wild pitch: Hagan 5. Double plays: Irwin to Farrell. Passed balls, Gilligan 1, Gross 2. Left on bases: Providence 5, Philadelphia 5. Time 2:00. Umpire: Furlong.

## MOST HITS — GAME — CLUB MAJOR LEAGUE RECORD
### Philadelphia At Louisville August 17, 1894.

| Phila. | Ab | R | H | PO | A | Louisville | Ab | R | H | PO | A |
|---|---|---|---|---|---|---|---|---|---|---|---|
| Hamilton, cf | 7 | 3 | 5 | 1 | 0 | Brown, cf | 4 | 1 | 1 | 3 | 0 |
| Boyle, 1b | 8 | 3 | 3 | 9 | 2 | Clarke, lf | 3 | 2 | 2 | 3 | 0 |
| Cross, 3b | 8 | 1 | 1 | 2 | 5 | Grim, 2b | 4 | 1 | 1 | 4 | 4 |
| Delehanty, | | | | | | Flaherty, 3b | 4 | 0 | 1 | 1 | 4 |
| lf, 2b | 7 | 5 | 4 | 4 | 3 | Smith, rf | 4 | 0 | 1 | 4 | 1 |
| Thompsn rf | 7 | 4 | 6 | 0 | 0 | Lutenberg, 1b | 4 | 0 | 0 | 9 | 4 |
| Hallman, 2b | 1 | 2 | 1 | 1 | 2 | Richdsn, ss | 4 | 0 | 1 | 1 | 3 |
| Buckley, c | 1 | 1 | 1 | 0 | 0 | Weaver, c | 1 | 0 | 0 | 1 | 0 |
| Sullivan, ss | 7 | 4 | 5 | 3 | 0 | Wadswth, p | 4 | 0 | 1 | 1 | 1 |
| Carsey, p | 7 | 3 | 4 | 3 | 0 | Zahner, c | 2 | 0 | 0 | 0 | 0 |
| Grady, c | 6 | 3 | 5 | 3 | 0 | | | | | | |
| Turner, lf | 5 | 0 | 1 | 1 | 0 | | | | | | |
| Totals | 64 | 29 | 36 | 27 | 12 | Totals | 34 | 4 | 8 | 27 | 17 |

Errors — Philadelphia 1: Cross. Louisville 4: Grimm 2, Clarke, Weaver.

| Philadelphia | 6 | 0 | 6 | 2 | 3 | 1 | 5 | 2 | 4—29 |
|---|---|---|---|---|---|---|---|---|---|
| Louisville | 0 | 0 | 0 | 2 | 0 | 2 | 0 | 0 | 0—4 |

Two base hits: Carsey, Boyle, Thompson, Grady, Sullivan, Brown. Three base hit: Thompson. Home runs: Thompson, Cross, Grim. Stolen bases: Boyle 3, Hamilton, Delehanty. Double plays: Cross, Hallman to Boyle; Grim to Lutenberg. Base on balls: off Carsey 3, off Wadsworth 2. Struck out: by Carsey 1, by Wadsworth 1. Wild pitch: Wadsworth. Passed balls: Weaver 2. Umpire: Keefe. Time of game, 2:05.

## ED DELAHANTY'S FOUR HOMERS:
### July 13, 1896,
### At Chicago

| PHILADELPHIA | ab | r | h | o | a | CHICAGO | ab | r | h | o | a |
|---|---|---|---|---|---|---|---|---|---|---|---|
| Cooley, lf | 3 | 1 | 1 | 1 | 0 | Everett, 3b | 3 | 1 | 2 | 1 | 3 |
| Hulen, ss | 4 | 1 | 1 | 1 | 4 | Dahlen, ss | 2 | 2 | 0 | 0 | 0 |
| Mertes, cf | 5 | 1 | 0 | 1 | 0 | Lange, cf | 4 | 2 | 2 | 4 | 0 |
| Delahanty, 1b | 5 | 4 | 5 | 9 | 0 | Anson, 1b | 3 | 0 | 1 | 12 | 2 |
| Thompson, rf | 5 | 0 | 1 | 2 | 0 | Ryan, rf | 4 | 1 | 1 | 2 | 0 |
| Hallman | 4 | 1 | 1 | 5 | 3 | Decker, lf | 4 | 1 | 1 | 0 | 0 |
| Clements, c | 2 | 0 | 0 | 5 | 3 | Pfeffer, 2b | 4 | 0 | 2 | 1 | 4 |
| Nash, 3b | 4 | 0 | 0 | 0 | 3 | Terry, p | 4 | 1 | 2 | 2 | 3 |
| Garvin, p | 4 | 0 | 0 | 0 | 1 | Donohue, c | 3 | 1 | 0 | 5 | 0 |
| Total | 36 | 8 | 9 | 24 | 14 | Total | 31 | 9 | 11 | 27 | 12 |

| Philadelphia | 2 | 0 | 0 | 1 | 3 | 0 | 1 | 0 | 1—8 |
|---|---|---|---|---|---|---|---|---|---|
| Chicago | 1 | 0 | 4 | 0 | 1 | 0 | 0 | 3 | x—9 |

Errors — Nash, Ryan, Decker. Two-base hits: Thompson, Lange, Decker, Terry. Three-base hits: Lange, Pfeffer. Home run: Delahanty 4. Left on base: Philadelphia 6, Chicago 4. Bases on balls: off Terry 3, Garver 4. Struck out: by Terry 5, Garver 4. Double plays: Hulen, Hall, and Delahanty. Wild pitch: Garvin. Umpire: Emslie. Time, 2:15. Attendance, 1,100.

## PHILLIES WIN PENNANT
### Philadelphia at Boston
### Sept. 29, 1915

### PHILLIES

| | ab | r | bh | tb | sh | sb | po | a | e |
|---|---|---|---|---|---|---|---|---|---|
| Stock, 3b | 4 | 0 | 0 | 0 | 1 | 0 | 2 | 4 | 0 |
| Bancroft, ss | 5 | 2 | 2 | 2 | 0 | 0 | 2 | 2 | 0 |
| Paskert, cf | 4 | 1 | 1 | 3 | 0 | 0 | 6 | 0 | 0 |
| Cravath, rf | 4 | 2 | 2 | 6 | 0 | 0 | 0 | 1 | 1 |
| Luderus, 1b | 4 | 0 | 1 | 1 | 0 | 0 | 11 | 0 | 0 |
| Whitted, lf | 4 | 0 | 1 | 1 | 0 | 0 | 1 | 0 | 0 |
| Niehoff, 2b | 4 | 0 | 1 | 1 | 0 | 0 | 1 | 2 | 0 |
| Burns, c | 4 | 0 | 0 | 0 | 0 | 0 | 4 | 0 | 0 |
| Alexander, p | 4 | 0 | 2 | 3 | 0 | 0 | 0 | 2 | 0 |
| Totals | 37 | 5 | 10 | 17 | 1 | 0 | 27 | 11 | 1 |

### BOSTON

| | ab | r | bh | tb | sh | sb | po | a | e |
|---|---|---|---|---|---|---|---|---|---|
| Moran, rf | 3 | 0 | 0 | 0 | 0 | 0 | 1 | 0 | 0 |
| Evers, 2b | 4 | 0 | 0 | 0 | 0 | 0 | 4 | 3 | 0 |
| Compton, cf | 4 | 0 | 0 | 0 | 0 | 0 | 3 | 0 | 0 |
| Magee, 1b | 3 | 0 | 1 | 1 | 0 | 0 | 0 | 1 | 0 |
| Smith, 3b | 3 | 0 | 0 | 0 | 0 | 0 | 0 | 3 | 2 |
| Connally, lf | 3 | 0 | 0 | 0 | 0 | 0 | 2 | 1 | 0 |
| Maranville, ss | 3 | 0 | 0 | 0 | 0 | 0 | 0 | 3 | 0 |
| Gowdy, c | 3 | 0 | 0 | 0 | 0 | 0 | 7 | 0 | 0 |
| Rudolph, p | 3 | 0 | 0 | 0 | 0 | 0 | 1 | 2 | 0 |
| Totals | 29 | 0 | 1 | 1 | 0 | 0 | 27 | 13 | 2 |

| | | | | | | | | | |
|---|---|---|---|---|---|---|---|---|---|
| Phillies | 3 | 0 | 0 | 1 | 0 | 0 | 1 | 0 | 0—5 |
| Boston | 0 | 0 | 0 | 0 | 0 | 0 | 0 | 0 | 0—0 |

Two-base hits: Alexander, Cravath. Three-base hit: Paskert. Home run: Cravath. Left on bases: Phils 7, Boston 3. First base on errors: Phils 2, Boston 1. Bases on balls: Alexander 1, Rudolph 1. Strikeouts: Alexander 4, Rudolph 6. Umpires: Rigler and O'Day. Time, 1:28.

---

### 1915 WORLD SERIES
### Friday, October 8 — At Philadelphia

| Boston (A.L.) | AB. | R. | H. | O. | A. | E. |
|---|---|---|---|---|---|---|
| Hooper, rf | 5 | 0 | 1 | 0 | 0 | 0 |
| Scott, ss | 3 | 0 | 1 | 2 | 2 | 0 |
| Speaker, cf | 2 | 1 | 0 | 1 | 0 | 0 |
| Hoblitzel, 1b | 4 | 0 | 1 | 12 | 0 | 0 |
| Lewis, lf | 4 | 0 | 2 | 2 | 0 | 0 |
| Gardner, 3b | 3 | 0 | 1 | 0 | 1 | 0 |
| Barry, 2b | 4 | 0 | 1 | 4 | 4 | 0 |
| Cady, c | 2 | 0 | 0 | 3 | 2 | 0 |
| *Henriksen | 1 | 0 | 0 | 0 | 0 | 0 |
| Shore, p | 3 | 0 | 1 | 0 | 4 | 1 |
| †Ruth | 1 | 0 | 0 | 0 | 0 | 0 |
| Totals | 32 | 1 | 8 | 24 | 13 | 1 |

| Phila'phia (N.L.) | AB. | R. | H. | O. | A. | E. |
|---|---|---|---|---|---|---|
| Stock, 3b | 3 | 1 | 0 | 0 | 2 | 0 |
| Bancroft, ss | 4 | 1 | 1 | 4 | 1 | 0 |
| Paskert, cf | 3 | 1 | 1 | 1 | 0 | 0 |
| Cravath, rf | 2 | 0 | 0 | 1 | 0 | 0 |
| Luderus, 1b | 4 | 0 | 1 | 10 | 0 | 1 |
| Whitted, lf | 2 | 0 | 1 | 3 | 0 | 0 |
| Neihoff, 2b | 3 | 0 | 0 | 1 | 4 | 0 |
| Burns, c | 3 | 0 | 0 | 7 | 0 | 0 |
| Alexander, p | 3 | 0 | 1 | 0 | 5 | 0 |
| Totals | 27 | 3 | 5 | 27 | 12 | 1 |

| | | | | | | | | | | |
|---|---|---|---|---|---|---|---|---|---|---|
| Boston | 0 | 0 | 0 | 0 | 0 | 0 | 0 | 1 | 0—1 |
| Philadelphia | 0 | 0 | 0 | 1 | 0 | 0 | 0 | 2 | *—3 |

*Reached first on Luderus' error for Cady in ninth. †Grounded out for Shore in ninth. Runs batted in: Lewis, Cravath, Luderus, Whitted. Sacrifice hits: Scott, Gardner, Cady, Cravath. Stolen bases: Whitted, Hoblitzel. Left on bases: Boston 9, Philadelphia 5. Earned runs: Philadelphia 3, Boston 1. Struck out: By Alexander 6, by Shore 2. Bases on balls: Off Alexander 2, off Shore 4. Umpires: Klem (N.L.), O'Loughlin (A.L.), Evans (A.L.), and Rigler (N.L.) Time, 1:58. Attendance, 19,343.

---

## Saturday, October 9 — At Philadelphia

| Boston (A.L.) | AB. | R. | H. | O. | A. | E. |
|---|---|---|---|---|---|---|
| Hooper, rf | 3 | 1 | 1 | 2 | 0 | 0 |
| Scott, ss | 3 | 0 | 0 | 0 | 3 | 0 |
| *Henriksen | 1 | 0 | 0 | 0 | 0 | 0 |
| Cady, c | 0 | 0 | 0 | 3 | 0 | 0 |
| Speaker, cf | 4 | 0 | 1 | 3 | 0 | 0 |
| Hoblitzel, 1b | 4 | 0 | 1 | 8 | 3 | 0 |
| Lewis, lf | 4 | 0 | 1 | 1 | 0 | 0 |
| Gardner, 3b | 4 | 1 | 2 | 0 | 2 | 0 |
| Barry, 2b | 4 | 0 | 1 | 0 | 3 | 0 |
| Thomas, c | 3 | 0 | 0 | 6 | 0 | 0 |
| Janvrin, ss | 1 | 0 | 0 | 1 | 0 | 0 |
| Foster, p | 4 | 0 | 3 | 3 | 0 | 0 |
| Totals | 35 | 2 | 10 | 27 | 11 | 0 |
| Phila'phia (N.L.) | AB. | R. | H. | O. | A. | E. |
| Stock, 3b | 4 | 0 | 0 | 0 | 2 | 0 |
| Bancroft, ss | 4 | 0 | 1 | 2 | 2 | 0 |
| Paskert, cf | 4 | 0 | 0 | 1 | 0 | 0 |
| Cravath, rf | 3 | 1 | 1 | 1 | 0 | 0 |
| Luderus, 1b | 3 | 0 | 1 | 9 | 1 | 0 |
| Whitted, lf | 3 | 0 | 0 | 3 | 0 | 0 |
| Niehoff, 2b | 3 | 0 | 0 | 4 | 1 | 0 |
| Burns, c | 3 | 0 | 0 | 6 | 3 | 1 |
| Mayer, p | 3 | 0 | 0 | 1 | 3 | 0 |
| Totals | 30 | 1 | 3 | 27 | 12 | 1 |

| | | | | | | | | | | |
|---|---|---|---|---|---|---|---|---|---|---|
| Boston | 1 | 0 | 0 | 0 | 0 | 0 | 0 | 0 | 1—2 |
| Philadelphia | 0 | 0 | 0 | 0 | 1 | 0 | 0 | 0 | 0—1 |

*Popped out for Scott in seventh. Two-base hits: Foster, Cravath, Luderus. Runs batted in: Foster, Luderus. Left on bases: Boston 8, Philadelphia 2. Earned runs: Boston 1. Philadelphia 1. Struck out: By Foster 8, by Mayer 7. Bases on balls: Off Mayer 2. Umpires: Rigler (N.L.) Evans (A.L.), O'Loughlin (A.L.) and Klem (N.L.). Time, 2:05. Attendance, 20,306.

| Phila'phia (N.L.) | AB. | R. | H. | O. | A. | E. |
|---|---|---|---|---|---|---|
| Stock, 3b | 3 | 0 | 1 | 1 | 0 | 0 |
| Bancroft, ss | 3 | 0 | 1 | 4 | 1 | 0 |
| Paskert, cf | 4 | 0 | 0 | 7 | 0 | 0 |
| Cravath, rf | 4 | 0 | 0 | 2 | 0 | 0 |
| Luderus, 1b | 3 | 0 | 0 | 3 | 1 | 0 |
| Whitted, lf | 3 | 0 | 0 | 2 | 0 | 0 |
| Neihoff, 2b | 3 | 0 | 0 | 0 | 2 | 0 |
| Burns, c | 3 | 1 | 1 | 5 | 2 | 0 |
| Alexander, p | 2 | 0 | 0 | 2 | 0 | 0 |
| Totals | 28 | 1 | 3* | 26 | 6 | 0 |

| Boston (A.L.) | AB. | R. | H. | O. | A. | E. |
|---|---|---|---|---|---|---|
| Hooper, rf | 4 | 1 | 1 | 2 | 0 | 0 |
| Scott, ss | 3 | 0 | 0 | 2 | 1 | 0 |
| Speaker, cf | 3 | 1 | 2 | 2 | 0 | 0 |
| Hoblitzel, 1b | 3 | 0 | 0 | 9 | 0 | 1 |
| Lewis, lf | 4 | 0 | 3 | 1 | 0 | 0 |
| Gardner, 3b | 3 | 0 | 0 | 1 | 6 | 0 |
| Barry, 2b | 3 | 0 | 0 | 2 | 1 | 0 |
| Carrigan, c | 2 | 0 | 0 | 8 | 0 | 0 |
| Leonard, p | 3 | 0 | 0 | 0 | 2 | 0 |
| Totals | 28 | 2 | 6 | 27 | 10 | 1 |

| | | | | | | | | |
|---|---|---|---|---|---|---|---|---|
| Philadelphia | 0 | 0 | 1 | 0 | 0 | 0 | 0 | 0—1 |
| Boston | 0 | 0 | 0 | 1 | 0 | 0 | 0 | 1—2 |

*Two out when winning run scored. Two-base hit: Stock. Three-base hit: Speaker. Runs batted in: Bancroft, Hoblitzel, Lewis. Sacrifice hits: Bancroft, Alexander, Stock, Scott. Sacrifice fly: Hoblitzel. Double play: Burns, Bancroft and Luderus. Left on bases: Boston 4, Philadelphia 3. Earned runs: Boston 2, Philadelphia 1. Struck out: By Leonard 6, by Alexander 4. Bases on balls: Off Alexander 2. Umpires: O'Loughlin (A.L.) Klem (N.L.), Rigler (N.L.), and Evans (A.L.). Time, 1:48. Attendance, 42,300.

---

| Phila'phia (N.L.) | AB. | R. | H. | O. | A. | E. |
|---|---|---|---|---|---|---|
| Stock, 3b | 4 | 0 | 1 | 0 | 3 | 0 |
| Bancroft, ss | 2 | 0 | 0 | 0 | 0 | 0 |
| Paskert, cf | 4 | 0 | 0 | 5 | 0 | 0 |
| Cravath, rf | 4 | 1 | 1 | 0 | 0 | 0 |
| Luderus, 1b | 4 | 0 | 3 | 5 | 0 | 0 |
| *Dugey | 0 | 0 | 0 | 0 | 0 | 0 |
| Becker, lf | 0 | 0 | 0 | 0 | 0 | 0 |
| Whitted, lf-1b | 3 | 0 | 0 | 4 | 0 | 0 |
| Niehoff, 2b | 3 | 0 | 0 | 3 | 1 | 0 |
| Burns, c | 3 | 0 | 1 | 7 | 2 | 0 |
| Chalmers, p | 3 | 0 | 1 | 0 | 4 | 0 |
| †Byrne | 1 | 0 | 0 | 0 | 0 | 0 |
| Totals | 31 | 1 | 7 | 24 | 10 | 0 |

| Boston (A.L.) | AB. | R. | H. | O. | A. | E. |
|---|---|---|---|---|---|---|
| Hooper, rf | 4 | 0 | 1 | 2 | 0 | 0 |
| Scott, ss | 4 | 0 | 0 | 2 | 4 | 0 |
| Speaker, cf | 3 | 0 | 1 | 1 | 0 | 0 |
| Hoblitzel, 1b | 4 | 1 | 3 | 5 | 2 | 0 |
| Lewis, lf | 2 | 0 | 1 | 6 | 1 | 0 |
| Gardner, 3b | 4 | 0 | 0 | 2 | 2 | 0 |
| Barry, 2b | 2 | 1 | 0 | 3 | 1 | 0 |
| Cady, c | 3 | 0 | 2 | 6 | 1 | 0 |
| Shore, p | 2 | 0 | 0 | 0 | 1 | 0 |
| Totals | 28 | 2 | 8 | 27 | 12 | 1 |

| | | | | | | | | | |
|---|---|---|---|---|---|---|---|---|---|
| Philadelphia | 0 | 0 | 0 | 0 | 0 | 0 | 0 | 1 | 0— 1 |
| Boston | 0 | 0 | 1 | 0 | 0 | 1 | 0 | 0 | *— 2 |

*Ran for Luderus in eighth. †Flied out for Chalmers in ninth. Two-base hit: Lewis. Three-base hit: Cravath. Runs batted in: Luderus, Hooper, Lewis. Stolen base: Dugey. Sacrifice hits: Whitted, Shore, Lewis. Left on bases: Philadelphia 8, Boston 7. Earned runs: Boston 2, Philadelphia 1. Double plays: Scott, Barry, Hoblitzel and Barry; Chalmers, Burns and Whitted. Struck out: By Shore 4, by Chalmers 6. Bases on balls: Off Shore 4, off Chalmers 3. Umpires: Evans (A.L.), Rigler (N.L.), O'Loughlin (A.L.), and Klem (N.L.). Time, 2:05. Attendance, 41,096.

## Wednesday, October 13 — At Philadelphia

| Phila'phia (N.L.) | AB | R. | H. | O. | A. | E. |
|---|---|---|---|---|---|---|
| Stock, 3b | 3 | 0 | 0 | 1 | 1 | 0 |
| Bancroft, ss | 4 | 1 | 2 | 3 | 6 | 1 |
| Paskert, cf | 4 | 1 | 2 | 3 | 0 | 0 |
| Cravath, rf | 3 | 0 | 0 | 1 | 0 | 0 |
| †Dugey | 0 | 0 | 0 | 0 | 0 | 0 |
| Becker, rf | 0 | 0 | 0 | 0 | 0 | 0 |
| Luderus, 1b | 2 | 1 | 2 | 13 | 2 | 0 |
| Whitted, lf | 4 | 0 | 0 | 2 | 0 | 0 |
| Niehoff, 2b | 4 | 1 | 1 | 1 | 2 | 0 |
| Burns, c | 4 | 0 | 1 | 2 | 2 | 0 |
| Mayer, p | 1 | 0 | 0 | 1 | 0 | 0 |
| Rixey, p | 2 | 0 | 1 | 0 | 1 | 0 |
| †Killefer | 1 | 0 | 0 | 0 | 0 | 0 |
| Totals | 32 | 4 | 9 | 27 | 14 | 1 |

| Boston (A.L.) | AB. | R. | H. | O. | A. | E. |
|---|---|---|---|---|---|---|
| Hooper, rf | 4 | 2 | 3 | 2 | 0 | 1 |
| Scott, ss | 5 | 0 | 0 | 2 | 2 | 0 |
| Speaker, cf | 5 | 0 | 1 | 3 | 0 | 0 |
| Hoblitzel, 1b | 1 | 0 | 0 | 1 | 0 | 0 |
| *Gainor, 1b | 3 | 1 | 1 | 9 | 0 | 0 |
| Lewis, lf | 4 | 1 | 1 | 0 | 0 | 0 |
| Gardner, 3b | 3 | 1 | 1 | 2 | 3 | 0 |
| Barry, 2b | 4 | 0 | 1 | 1 | 0 | 0 |
| Thomas, c | 2 | 0 | 1 | 4 | 3 | 0 |
| Cady, c | 1 | 0 | 0 | 2 | 1 | 0 |
| Foster, p | 4 | 0 | 1 | 1 | 3 | 0 |
| Totals | 36 | 5 | 10 | 27 | 12 | 1 |

| | | | | | | | | | |
|---|---|---|---|---|---|---|---|---|---|
| Boston | 0 | 1 | 1 | 0 | 0 | 0 | 0 | 2 | 1—5 |
| Philadelphia | 2 | 0 | 0 | 2 | 0 | 0 | 0 | 0 | 0—4 |

*Hit into double play for Hoblitzel in third inning. †Ran for Cravath in eighth. ‡Grounded out for Rixey in ninth. Two-base hit: Luderus. Three-base hit: Gardner. Home runs: Hooper, 2, Lewis, Luderus. Runs batted in: Luderus 3, Hooper 2, Lewis 2, Barry. Double plays: Foster, Thomas and Hoblitzel; Bancroft and Luderus. Left on bases: Boston 7, Philadelphia 5. Earned runs: Boston 5, Philadelphia 3. Struck out: By Foster 5, by Rixey 2. Bases on balls: Off Foster 2, off Rixey 2. Hit by pitcher: by Foster (Stock, Luderus), by Rixey (Hooper). Hits: Off Mayer 6 in 21/3 innings, off Rixey 4 in 62/3 innings. Losing pitcher: Rixey. Umpires: Klem (N.L.), O'Loughlin (A.L.), Evans (A.L.), and Rigler (N.L.). Time, 2:15. Attendance, 20,306.

---

## LONGEST PHILLIES GAME
### Philadelphia at Chicago
### July 17, 1918,
### Twenty-one Innings

| PHILLIES | AB | R | H | TB | SB | PO | A | E |
|---|---|---|---|---|---|---|---|---|
| Bancroft, ss | 9 | 0 | 2 | 2 | 0 | 6 | 0 | 0 |
| Williams, cf | 9 | 1 | 1 | 1 | 0 | 6 | 13 | 0 |
| Stock, 3b | 9 | 0 | 3 | 3 | 0 | 2 | 4 | 0 |
| Luderus, 1b | 9 | 0 | 3 | 3 | 0 | 24 | 2 | 0 |
| Meusel, cf | 9 | 0 | 0 | 0 | 0 | 7 | 0 | 0 |
| Cravath, rf | 7 | 0 | 2 | 2 | 2 | 3 | 0 | 0 |
| Hemingway, 2b | 8 | 0 | 2 | 3 | 0 | 5 | 10 | 0 |
| Adams, c | 7 | 0 | 2 | 2 | 0 | 5 | 1 | 0 |
| Burns, c | 1 | 0 | 0 | 0 | 0 | 2 | 0 | 0 |
| Watson, p | 8 | 0 | 0 | 0 | 0 | 0 | 0 | 0 |
| Totals | 76 | 1 | 13 | 14 | 2 | x60 | 30 | 0 |

| CHICAGO | AB | R | H | TB | SB | PO | A | E |
|---|---|---|---|---|---|---|---|---|
| Flack, rf | 8 | 1 | 5 | 5 | 1 | 5 | 0 | 0 |
| Hollocher, ss | 7 | 0 | 2 | 3 | 0 | 1 | 0 | 0 |
| Mann, lf | 9 | 0 | 1 | 1 | 0 | 6 | 40 | 0 |
| Merkle, 1b | 9 | 0 | 3 | 3 | 0 | 28 | 1 | 0 |
| Paskert, cf | 7 | 0 | 1 | 1 | 0 | 7 | 2 | 0 |
| Deal, 3b | 9 | 0 | 1 | 1 | 0 | 3 | 6 | 0 |
| Zeider, 2b | 8 | 0 | 0 | 0 | 0 | 2 | 10 | 0 |
| Killefer, c | 8 | 0 | 2 | 2 | 0 | 7 | 1 | 0 |
| Tyler, p | 8 | 0 | 2 | 2 | 0 | 4 | 7 | 0 |
| *Barber | 1 | 1 | 1 | 1 | 0 | 0 | 0 | 0 |
| †McCabe | 1 | 0 | 1 | 1 | 0 | 0 | 0 | 0 |
| Totals | 75 | 2 | 19 | 20 | 1 | 63 | 30 | 0 |

x None out when winning run scored.
*Batted for Zeider in twenty-first.
†Batted for Tyler in twenty-first.

Phillies  0 0 0 1 0 0 0 0 0 0 0 0 0 0 0 0 0 0 0 0 0—1
Chicago   1 0 0 0 0 0 0 0 0 0 0 0 0 0 0 0 0 0 0 0 1—2

Two-base hits: Hollocher, Hemingway. Stolen bases: Cravath 2, Flack. Sacrifice hits: Paskert, Hollocher. Double play: Bancroft to Hemingway to Luderus. Left on bases: Philadelphia 13, Chicago 20. First base on errors: Phillies 1. Bases on balls: Off Watson 4, Tyler 1. Hit by pitcher: By Watson, Killefer. Balk: Watson. Struck out: By Watson 5, Tyler 8.

# THE FASTEST MAJOR LEAGUE GAME EVER
### Philadelphia at New York
### September 28, 1919
### (First Game)

The New York Giants beat the Phillies, 6-1, in the first game of a doubleheader in the Polo Grounds on the last day of the 1919 season. The game lasted just fifty-one minutes, which still stands as the fastest game in the major leagues.

| Philadelphia Phils | AB | R | H | RBI |
|---|---|---|---|---|
| LeBourveau, lf | 4 | 0 | 0 | 0 |
| Blackburne, 3b | 4 | 1 | 1 | 0 |
| Williams, cf | 4 | 0 | 0 | 0 |
| Meusel, rf | 4 | 0 | 0 | 1 |
| Luderus, 1b | 4 | 0 | 2 | 0 |
| Bancroft, ss | 4 | 0 | 1 | 0 |
| Paulette, 2b | 3 | 0 | 0 | 0 |
| Adams, c | 3 | 0 | 0 | 0 |
| Meadows, p | 3 | 0 | 1 | 0 |
| Totals | 33 | 1 | 5 | 1 |

| New York Giants | AB | R | H | RBI |
|---|---|---|---|---|
| Burns, lf | 2 | 1 | 1 | 1 |
| Youngs, rf | 3 | 1 | 1 | 0 |
| Kauff, cf | 4 | 1 | 1 | 2 |
| Doyle, 2b | 4 | 1 | 2 | 0 |
| Fletcher, ss | 4 | 0 | 2 | 0 |
| Frisch, 3b | 4 | 0 | 1 | 1 |
| Kelly, 1b | 4 | 1 | 3 | 1 |
| Smith, c | 3 | 0 | 1 | 1 |
| J. Barnes, p | 4 | 1 | 1 | 0 |
| Totals | 32 | 6 | 13 | 6 |

| | | | | | | | | | |
|---|---|---|---|---|---|---|---|---|---|
| Philadelphia Phillies | 1 | 0 | 0 | 0 | 0 | 0 | 0 | 0 | 0—1 |
| New York Giants | 0 | 1 | 3 | 0 | 0 | 2 | 0 | 0 | x—6 |

Error: Fletcher. Double plays: Philadelphia 2. Left on base: Philadelphia 6, New York 7. Two-base hits: Blackburne, Burns, Youngs, Fletcher, Kelly, J. Barnes. Stolen base: Burns. Sacrifice hit: Barnes. Sacrifice fly: Burns.

### Pitching Summary

| | IP | H | R | ER | BB | SO |
|---|---|---|---|---|---|---|
| Meadows (L 12-20) | 8 | 13 | 6 | 6 | 3 | 1 |
| J. Barnes (W 25-9) | 9 | 5 | 1 | 1 | 0 | 2 |

Time — 0:51

# MOST RUNS, GAME, BOTH CLUBS MAJOR LEAGUE RECORD
### Philadelphia At Chicago
### August 25, 1922

| Chicago | AB | R | H | PO | A |
|---|---|---|---|---|---|
| Heathc'te cf | 5 | 5 | 5 | 4 | 0 |
| Holl'chr ss | 5 | 2 | 3 | 5 | 2 |
| Kelleher ss | 1 | 0 | 0 | 0 | 0 |
| Terry, 2b | 5 | 2 | 2 | 2 | 2 |
| Friberg, 2b | 1 | 0 | 1 | 0 | 0 |
| Grimes, 1b | 4 | 2 | 2 | 7 | 1 |
| Call'ghn, rf | 6 | 3 | 2 | 2 | 0 |
| Miller, lf | 5 | 3 | 4 | 1 | 0 |
| Krug, 3b | 5 | 4 | 4 | 1 | 1 |
| O'Farrell, c | 3 | 3 | 2 | 1 | 1 |
| Hartnett, c | 0 | 0 | 0 | 4 | 0 |
| Kaufmn, p | 2 | 0 | 0 | 0 | 1 |
| Stueland, p | 1 | 0 | 0 | 0 | 0 |
| Eubanks, p | 0 | 0 | 0 | 0 | 1 |
| Morris, p | 0 | 0 | 0 | 0 | 0 |
| Osborne p | 0 | 0 | 0 | 0 | 0 |
| †Barber | 1 | 2 | 0 | 0 | 0 |
| ††Maisel | 1 | 0 | 0 | 0 | 0 |
| Totals | 45 | 26 | 25 | 27 | 9 |

| Phillies | AB | R | H | PO | A |
|---|---|---|---|---|---|
| Wright- stone, 3b | 7 | 3 | 4 | 0 | 2 |
| Park'nsn, 2b | 4 | 1 | 2 | 3 | 7 |
| Williams, cf | 3 | 1 | 0 | 2 | 0 |
| Lebour- veau, cf | 4 | 2 | 3 | 0 | 0 |
| Walker, rf | 6 | 2 | 4 | 2 | 0 |
| Mokan, lf | 4 | 2 | 3 | 1 | 0 |
| Fletcher, ss | 3 | 1 | 0 | 0 | 2 |
| Smith, ss | 4 | 2 | 1 | 1 | 2 |
| Leslie, lb | 1 | 1 | 0 | 4 | 0 |
| Lee, 1b | 4 | 4 | 3 | 7 | 0 |
| Henline, c | 2 | 1 | 2 | 3 | 0 |
| Withrow, c | 3 | 1 | 2 | 1 | 0 |
| Ring, p | 2 | 0 | 1 | 0 | 1 |
| Weinert, p | 4 | 2 | 1 | 0 | 1 |
| *Rapp | 0 | 0 | 0 | 0 | 0 |
| Totals | 51 | 23 | 26 | 24 | 15 |

*Batted for Weinert in ninth.
†Batted for Kaufmann in fourth.
††Batted for Steuland in seventh.

| | | | | | | | | | |
|---|---|---|---|---|---|---|---|---|---|
| Phillies | 0 | 3 | 2 | 1 | 3 | 0 | 0 | 8 | 6 —23 |
| Chicago | 1 | 10 | 0 | 14 | 0 | 1 | 0 | 0 | x —26 |

Errors — Chicago 5: Heathcote, Hollocher, Callahan, Krug, Hartnett. Philadelphia 5: Wrightstone, Parkinson, Walker, Williams, Lee.

Two base hits: Terry, Krug 2, Mokan, Hollocher, Heathcote 2, Grimes, Parkinson, Withrow, Friberg, Walker. Three base hits: Walker, Wrightstone. Home runs: Miller 2, O'Farrell. Stolen bases: Hollocher, Weinert. Sacrifice hits: Leslie, O'Farrell, Hollocher, Parkinson, Walker. Bases on balls: off Kaufmann 4, off Ring 5, off Weinert 5, off Stueland 2, off Eubanks 3, off Morris 2, of Osborne 2. Struck out: by Ring 2, by Weinert 2, by Stueland 1, by Morris 1, by Osborne 2. Hit by pitched ball: Grimes (by Weinert). Wild pitch: Stueland. Double plays: Smith to Parkinson to Lee 2; Wrightstone to Parkinson to Lee. Left on bases: Chicago 9, Phillies 16. Umpires: Hart and Rigler. Time, 3:01.

---

## MAJOR LEAGUE RECORD
### Ten Home Runs Made in One Game
### St. Louis at Philadelphia, May 1, 1923

| Phila. | Ab | R | H | PO | A | St. Louis | Ab | R | H | PO | A |
|---|---|---|---|---|---|---|---|---|---|---|---|
| Mokan, lf | 4 | 3 | 3 | 2 | 0 | Smith, cf | 6 | 3 | 3 | 2 | 0 |
| Sand, 3b | 5 | 2 | 1 | 0 | 1 | Dyer, lf | 3 | 2 | 2 | 1 | 0 |
| Williams, cf | 5 | 4 | 3 | 5 | 0 | Mann, lf | 3 | 2 | 2 | 0 | 0 |
| Walker, rf | 4 | 2 | 1 | 0 | 1 | Toporcer 2b | 5 | 1 | 1 | 3 | 1 |
| Holke, 1b | 4 | 1 | 1 | 8 | 1 | Bottmly, 1b | 6 | 1 | 4 | 7 | 2 |
| Parknsn, 2b | 5 | 1 | 3 | 4 | 7 | Stock, 3b | 6 | 1 | 3 | 1 | 1 |
| Wright- | | | | | | Myers, cf | 5 | 0 | 1 | 2 | 0 |
| stone, ss | 4 | 3 | 2 | 5 | 2 | Freigau, ss | 3 | 0 | 1 | 3 | 3 |
| Henline, c | 3 | 3 | 2 | 2 | 1 | Ainsmith, c | 3 | 1 | 1 | 4 | 1 |
| Behan, p | 1 | 1 | 1 | 1 | 0 | McCurdy, c | 1 | 0 | 0 | 0 | 1 |
| Weinert, p | 1 | 0 | 0 | 0 | 1 | Haines, p | 1 | 0 | 1 | 1 | 0 |
| Meadows, p | 1 | 0 | 1 | 0 | 0 | Sherdel, p | 1 | 1 | 1 | 0 | 2 |
| | | | | | | Barfoot, p | 0 | 0 | 0 | 0 | 0 |
| | | | | | | *Flack | 1 | 1 | 1 | 0 | 0 |
| | | | | | | Stuart, p | 0 | 0 | 0 | 0 | 0 |
| | | | | | | North, p | 1 | 0 | 0 | 0 | 0 |
| | | | | | | **Blades | 1 | 1 | 1 | 0 | 0 |
| Totals | 37 | 20 | 18 | 27 | 14 | Totals | 46 | 14 | 22 | 24 | 12 |

*Batted for Barfoot in the fifth inning.
**Batted for North in the ninth inning.

| | | | | | | | | | |
|---|---|---|---|---|---|---|---|---|---|
| Philadelphia | 0 | 0 | 5 | 3 | 4 | 2 | 3 | 3 | x —20 |
| St. Louis | 1 | 1 | 1 | 3 | 0 | 3 | 0 | 3 | 2 —14 |

Errors — Freigau, Myers. Two base hits: Bottomley, Sand, Stock, Blades, Smith, Flack. Three base hit: Stock. HOME RUNS: Mokan 2, Williams 3, Sherdel, Dyer, Parkinson, Mann 2. Stolen bases: Smith, Dyer, Wrightstone, Mokan. Sacrifice hits: Freigau, Holke, Behan 2. Double play: Wrightstone, Parkinson and Holke. Left on bases: St. Louis 9, Philadelphia 5. Bases on balls: off Haines 2, off Sherdel 1, off Stuart 2, off North 4, off Behan 3. Struck out: by Sherdel 1, by North 1, by Meadows 2. Hits: off Haines, 3 in 2 1/3 innings; off

Sherdel, 7 in 2 innings; off Barfoot, 2 in 2/3 inning; off Stuart, none in no inning (none out in sixth); off Behan, 11 in 5 innings; off Weinert, 7 in 2 1/3 innings; off Meadows, 4 in 1 2/3 innings; off North, 6 in 3 innings. Wild pitch: Behan. Winning pitcher: Behan. Losing pitcher: Sherdel. Umpires: Klem and Hart. Time of game, 2:20.

---

## FIRST UNASSISTED TRIPLE PLAY IN THE NATIONAL LEAGUE
### Philadelphia at Boston
### October 6, 1923, Second Game

| Boston | Ab | R | H | PO | A | Phila. | Ab | R | H | PO | A |
|---|---|---|---|---|---|---|---|---|---|---|---|
| Emer'ck, cf | 1 | 0 | 0 | 2 | 0 | Sand, ss | 3 | 0 | 1 | 2 | 3 |
| Felix, lf | 3 | 1 | 1 | 3 | 0 | Mokan, cf | 2 | 0 | 0 | 1 | 0 |
| McInnis, 1b | 1 | 0 | 1 | 0 | 1 | Walker, rf | 2 | 0 | 0 | 3 | 0 |
| Carney, 1b | 1 | 0 | 1 | 2 | 0 | Tierney, 2b | 2 | 0 | 1 | 2 | 2 |
| Herman, 3b | 2 | 0 | 1 | 1 | 1 | Lee, lf | 2 | 0 | 1 | 0 | 0 |
| Padgett, ss | 2 | 1 | 1 | 4 | 0 | Holke, 1b | 2 | 0 | 1 | 5 | 0 |
| Conlon, 2b | 2 | 1 | 1 | 2 | 2 | Woehr, 3b | 2 | 0 | 1 | 1 | 1 |
| Cousmell, c | 2 | 1 | 2 | 0 | 0 | Wilson, c | 1 | 0 | 0 | 1 | 0 |
| Batch'rl'r, p | 1 | 0 | 0 | 1 | 0 | Parker, c | 1 | 0 | 0 | 0 | 0 |
| | | | | | | Weinert, p | 0 | 0 | 0 | 0 | 0 |
| | | | | | | Head, p | 1 | 1 | 1 | 0 | 0 |
| | | | | | | x-Henline | 0 | 0 | 0 | 0 | 0 |
| Totals | 18 | 4 | 8 | 15 | 4 | Totals | 18 | 1 | 6 | 15 | 6 |

Game called on account of darkness.
Errors — Lee 1
x — batted for Head in fifth

| | | | | | |
|---|---|---|---|---|---|
| Boston | 1 | 3 | 0 | 0 | x —4 |
| Philadelphia | 0 | 0 | 1 | 0 | 0 —1 |

Two base hit: Sand. Three base hit: McInnis. Sacrifice hit: Moken. Double play: Sand, Tierney to Holke. TRIPLE PLAY, PADGETT (unassisted). Base on balls: Off Weinert 2, off Head 1. Strikeouts: by Weinert 1. Hits: off Weinert, 5 in 2 innings; off Head, 3 in 2 innings. Time, 45 minutes. Umpires: Hart, McCormick.

---

## FIRST LEGAL SUNDAY GAME IN PHILADELPHIA
### Brooklyn at Philadelphia
### April 29, 1934

| PHILLIES | ab | r | h | Brooklyn | ab | r | h |
|---|---|---|---|---|---|---|---|
| Bartell, ss | 4 | 2 | 3 | Frey, ss-3b | 4 | 1 | 1 |
| Ruble, rf | 5 | 1 | 2 | Bucher, 3b | 4 | 0 | 0 |
| Oanam, lf | 5 | 1 | 2 | Taylor, cf | 3 | 0 | 1 |
| Hurst, lf | 3 | 1 | 1 | Frederick, rf | 5 | 0 | 1 |
| Allen, cf | 4 | 1 | 0 | L. Wilson, lf | 4 | 0 | 0 |
| J. Wilson, c | 4 | 0 | 3 | Leslie, 1b | 4 | 2 | 1 |
| Jeffries, 2b | 4 | 1 | 3 | Cuccinello, 2b | 2 | 2 | 1 |
| Chiozza, ph | 1 | 0 | 0 | Lopez, c | 1 | 0 | 0 |
| Hopkins, | 4 | 0 | 0 | Sukeforth, c | 4 | 1 | 1 |
| Schulmerich, ph | 1 | 0 | 0 | Beck, p | 0 | 0 | 0 |
| Moore, p | 3 | 0 | 0 | Carroll, p | 1 | 0 | 0 |
| Davis, p | 0 | 0 | 0 | Boyle, ph | 0 | 1 | 0 |

# FIRST LEGAL SUNDAY GAME IN PHILADELPHIA (continued)

| PHILLIES | | | | Brooklyn | | | |
|---|---|---|---|---|---|---|---|
| Hansen, p | 1 | 0 | 0 | Lucas, p | 0 | 0 | 0 |
| Pearce, p | 0 | 0 | 0 | Chapman, ph | 0 | 0 | 0 |
| Hendrick, ph | 0 | 0 | 0 | Page, p | 0 | 0 | 0 |
| | | | | Jordan, ss | 2 | 1 | 2 |
| | | | | Leonard, p | 0 | 0 | 0 |
| Totals | 39 | 7 | 14 | Totals | 34 | 8 | 8 |

| | | | | | | | | | | |
|---|---|---|---|---|---|---|---|---|---|---|
| Brooklyn | 0 | 0 | 0 | 0 | 4 | 0 | 0 | 4 | 0 — 8 |
| Phillies | 0 | 6 | 0 | 0 | 1 | 0 | 0 | 0 | 0 — 7 |

Errors: Bucher. Runs batted in: Bartell 1, Oana 1, Allen, 1, Wilson 2, Jeffries 1, Hurst 1, Boyle 1, Frey 3, Taylor 1, Frederick 1, Jordan 2. Two base hits: Jeffries, Ruble, Taylor. Double Plays: Bartell to Jeffries to Hurst; Hopkins to Jeffries to Hurst; Sukeforth to Frey. Left on base: Phillies 12, Brooklyn 11. Base on balls: off Moore 6, off Davis 2, off Hansen 3, off Pearce 1, off Beck 2, off Carroll 2, off Leonard 1. Struck out: by Moore 1, by Carroll 1, by Page 2, by Pearce 1. Hits: off Moore 2 in 4 innings (none out in 5th); off Davis 0 in 1/3 inning (pitched to three men); off Hansen, 3 in 3 innings; off Pearce 3 in 1 2/3 innings; off Leonard 1 in 2 innings; off Beck 7 in 1 2/3 innings; off Carroll 3 in 2 1/3 innings; off Lucas 1 in 1 inning; off Page 2 in 2 innings. Hit By pitch: by Beck (Allen); by Lucas (Bartell). Winning pitcher: Page. Losing pitcher: Pearce. Umpires: Stark, Stewart, and Bigler. Time 2:43.

---

# FIRST NIGHT GAME IN MAJOR LEAGUES
## Philadelphia at Cincinnati
### May 24, 1935

| PHILADELPHIA | ab | r | h | o | a | CINCINNATI | ab | r | h | o | a |
|---|---|---|---|---|---|---|---|---|---|---|---|
| Chiozza, 2b | 4 | 0 | 0 | 1 | 3 | Myers, ss | 3 | 1 | 1 | 2 | 3 |
| Allen, cf | 4 | 0 | 1 | 0 | 0 | Riggs, 3b | 4 | 0 | 0 | 0 | 2 |
| Moore, rf | 4 | 0 | 1 | 0 | 0 | Goodman, rf | 3 | 0 | 0 | 3 | 0 |
| Camilli, 1b | 4 | 0 | 1 | 15 | 0 | Sullivan, 1b | 3 | 1 | 2 | 8 | 2 |
| Vergez, 3b | 4 | 0 | 1 | 0 | 4 | Pool, lf | 3 | 0 | 1 | 0 | 0 |
| Todd, c | 3 | 1 | 1 | 3 | 0 | Campbell, c | 3 | 0 | 0 | 5 | 0 |
| Watkins, lf | 3 | 0 | 0 | 5 | 0 | Byrd, cf | 3 | 0 | 0 | 4 | 0 |
| Haslin, ss | 3 | 0 | 1 | 0 | 5 | Kampouris, 2b | 3 | 0 | 0 | 4 | 3 |
| Bowman, p | 2 | 0 | 0 | 0 | 2 | Derringer, p | 3 | 0 | 0 | 1 | 2 |
| a Wilson | 1 | 0 | 0 | 0 | 0 | | | | | | |
| Bivin, p | 0 | 0 | 0 | 0 | 0 | | | | | | |
| Total | 32 | 1 | 6 | 24 | 14 | Total | 28 | 2 | 4 | 27 | 12 |

a Batted for Bowman in eighth.

| | | | | | | | | | | |
|---|---|---|---|---|---|---|---|---|---|---|
| Philadelphia | 0 | 0 | 0 | 0 | 1 | 0 | 0 | 0 | 0 — 1 |
| Cincinnati | 1 | 0 | 0 | 1 | 0 | 0 | 0 | 0 | x — 2 |

Errors: none. Runs batted in: Sullivan, Campbell, Haslin. Two-base hits: Myers. Stolen base: Vergez, Myers, Bowman. Left on base: Philadelphia 4, Cincinnati 3. Double play: Riggs, Kampouris, and Sullivan. Bases on balls: Bowman 1. Struck out: Derringer 3, Bowman 1, Bivin 1. Hits off: Bowman 4 in 7; Bivin 0 in 1. Loser: Bowman. Time, 1:55. Umpires: Klem, Sears, and Pinelli. Attendance, 20,422.

# BABE RUTH'S LAST GAME
## Boston at Philadelphia
### May 30, 1935, First game

Babe Ruth's last game in the major leagues came against the Phillies in Baker Bowl, the first game of a May 30 doubleheader.

| Boston | ab | r | h |
|---|---|---|---|
| Urbanski, ss | 4 | 0 | 2 |
| Thompson, rf | 4 | 1 | 0 |
| Ruth, lf | 1 | 0 | 0 |
| Lee, lf | 4 | 1 | 3 |
| Berger, cf | 5 | 1 | 1 |
| R. Moore, 1b | 4 | 2 | 2 |
| Mallon, 2b | 3 | 1 | 2 |
| Mowry, ph | 1 | 0 | 0 |
| Whitney, 3b | 5 | 0 | 3 |
| Spohrer, c | 5 | 0 | 0 |
| Frankhouse, p | 4 | 0 | 1 |
| Cantwell, p | 0 | 0 | 0 |
| TOTALS | 40 | 6 | 14 |

| PHILLIES | ab | r | h |
|---|---|---|---|
| Allen, cf | 4 | 1 | 0 |
| Watkins, lf | 5 | 1 | 1 |
| J. Moore, rf | 3 | 2 | 1 |
| Camilli, 1b | 3 | 3 | 2 |
| Haslin, ss | 4 | 2 | 3 |
| Chiozza, 2b | 4 | 0 | 3 |
| Todd, c | 5 | 1 | 1 |
| Vergez, 3b | 3 | 1 | 0 |
| Bivin, p | 2 | 0 | 0 |
| Boland, ph | 1 | 0 | 0 |
| Jorgens, p | 0 | 0 | 0 |
| Wilson, ph | 1 | 0 | 1 |
| C. Davis, p | 0 | 0 | 0 |
| TOTALS | 35 | 11 | 12 |

| | | | | | | | | | |
|---|---|---|---|---|---|---|---|---|---|
| Boston | 0 | 1 | 1 | 0 | 2 | 1 | 1 | 0 | 0 — 6 |
| Phillies | 3 | 0 | 0 | 1 | 0 | 0 | 0 | 7 | 0 — 11 |

Errors: Urbanski, Berger, Mallon, Chiozza, Todd. Runs batted in: Berger, 1, R. Moore 2, Whitney 1, Haslin 3, Chiozza 4, Wilson 1, Watkins 1, Cammilli 1. Two-base hits: Urbanski, Whiteney, Lee, Haslin 2, Watkins. Three-base hits: Chiozza, R. Moore. Home Runs: Berger, R. Moore. Sacrifices: Haslin, Mallon. Left on base: Boston 11, Phillies 8. Base on balls: off Bivin 2, Jorgens 1, Frankhouse 6, Cantwell 1. Struck out: by Bivin 3, Frankhouse 1. Hits: off Bivin 10 in 6 innings; off Jorgens 3 in 2 innings; off C. Davis 1 in 1 inning; off Frankhouse 11 in 7 2/3 innings; off Cantwell 1 in 1/3 inning. Winning pitcher: Jorgens. Losing pitcher: Cantwell. Umpires: Quigley, Pfirman, and Moran. Time, 2:25.

# CHUCK KLEIN'S FOUR HOMERS
## Philadelphia at Pittsburgh
### July 10, 1936

| PHILLIES | ab | r | h |
|---|---|---|---|
| Sulik, cf | 5 | 1 | 1 |
| J. Moore, lf | 5 | 1 | 1 |
| Klein, rf | 5 | 4 | 4 |
| Camilli, 1b | 4 | 2 | 1 |
| Atwood, c | 4 | 0 | 1 |
| Wilson, c | 0 | 1 | 0 |
| Chiozza, 3b | 5 | 0 | 2 |
| Norris, ss | 4 | 0 | 1 |
| Gomez, 2b | 5 | 0 | 0 |
| Passeau, p | 4 | 0 | 1 |
| Walters, p | 0 | 0 | 0 |
| TOTALS | 41 | 9 | 12 |

| PITTSBURGH | ab | r | h |
|---|---|---|---|
| Jensen, lf | 4 | 1 | 1 |
| L. Waner, cf | 4 | 1 | 1 |
| P. Waner, rf | 4 | 2 | 2 |
| Vaughan, ss | 5 | 0 | 1 |
| Suhr, 1b | 4 | 0 | 2 |
| Brubaker, 3b | 5 | 0 | 0 |
| Young, 2b | 3 | 0 | 1 |
| Lavagetto, 2b | 1 | 1 | 0 |
| Todd, c | 2 | 0 | 0 |
| Padden, c | 2 | 1 | 0 |
| Weaver, p | 1 | 0 | 0 |
| Lucas, ph | 1 | 0 | 0 |
| Brown, p | 1 | 0 | 0 |
| Schulte, ph | 1 | 0 | 1 |
| Finney, pr | 0 | 0 | 0 |
| Swith, p | 0 | 0 | 0 |
| TOTALS | 38 | 6 | 9 |

| Phillies | 4 | 0 | 0 | 0 | 1 | 0 | 1 | 0 | 0 | 3 — 9 |
|----------|---|---|---|---|---|---|---|---|---|-------|
| Pittsburgh | 0 | 0 | 0 | 1 | 0 | 3 | 0 | 0 | 2 | 0 — 6 |

Errors: Norris 2, L. Waner, Vaughan 2, Young. Runs batted in: Klein 6, Norris 2, Suhr, P. Waner, Vaughan, Schulte, L. Waner, Chiozza. Two-base hit: Camilli. Three-base hit: Suhr. Home Runs: Klein 4. Sacrifices: Atwood, Norris. Double plays: Chiozza, Gomez, and Camilli; Norris and Camilli; Vaughan, Lavagetto, and Suhr; Walters, Gomez, and Camilli. Left on base: Phillies 5, Pittsburgh 7. Bases on balls: off Weaver 1; off Passeau 1; off Brown 1. Hits: off Weaver 6 in 5 innings; off Passeau, 8 in 8 2/3 innings; off Swift 4 in 1 inning; off Brown 2 in 4 innings; off Walters 1 in 1 1/3 innings. Winning pitcher: Walters. Losing pitcher: Swift. Umpires: Sears, Klem, and Ballanfant. Time of game, 2:15.

---

## AN UNUSUAL GAME
### Brooklyn at Philadelphia
#### April 19, 1938

An unusual game in that the Phillies' Emmett Mueller homered in his first at bat in the major leagues and Brooklyn's Ernie Koy came right back to duplicate the feat in the Dodgers' first inning.

| BROOKLYN | ab | r | h | | PHILLIES | ab | r | h |
|----------|----|----|----|---|----------|----|----|----|
| Rosen, cf | 3 | 0 | 0 | | Mueller, 2b | 3 | 3 | 2 |
| Brack, rf | 2 | 0 | 1 | | Martin, cf | 4 | 1 | 0 |
| Cuyler, rf-cf | 4 | 1 | 1 | | Klein, rf | 3 | 1 | 2 |
| Koy, lf | 5 | 2 | 3 | | Browne, lf | 4 | 0 | 2 |
| Lavagetto, 3b | 5 | 2 | 3 | | Arnovich, lf | 5 | 0 | 2 |
| Camilli, lf | 3 | 3 | 1 | | Whitney, 3b | 5 | 0 | 0 |
| Hudson, 2b | 5 | 1 | 3 | | Scharein, ss | 5 | 0 | 1 |
| Durocher, ss | 4 | 2 | 2 | | Atwood, c | 4 | 0 | 1 |
| Chervinko, c | 3 | 0 | 1 | | LaMaster, p | 3 | 0 | 1 |
| Winsett, pf | 0 | 1 | 0 | | Mulcahy, p | 0 | 0 | 0 |
| Spencer, c | 1 | 0 | 0 | | Smith, p | 0 | 0 | 0 |
| Mungo, p | 2 | 0 | 0 | | Rebel, ph | 1 | 0 | 0 |
| Hamlin, p | 2 | 0 | 0 | | Sivess, p | 0 | 0 | 0 |
| TOTALS | 39 | 12 | 15 | | TOTALS | 37 | 5 | 11 |

| Brooklyn | 1 | 0 | 0 | 3 | 0 | 0 | 0 | 6 | 2 — 12 |
|----------|---|---|---|---|---|---|---|---|--------|
| Phillies | 1 | 0 | 1 | 0 | 2 | 0 | 0 | 0 | 1 — 5 |

Runs batted in: Koy 1, Camilli 2, Chervinko 1, Lavagetto 2, Hudson 1, Durocher 1, Hamlin 1, LeMaster 1, Klein 2, Arnovich 2, Brack 2, Spencer 1. Home runs: Koy, Mueller, Klein, Camilli, Lavagetto. Stolen bases: Atwood. Double plays: Durocher to Hudson to Camilli. Left on base: Brooklyn 6, Phillies 10. Base on balls: off Mungo 5, off LaMaster 2, Mulcahy, 1, Smith 1, Sivess 2, Hamlin 1. Struck out: by Mungo 3, Hamlin 5, LaMaster 5, Smith. Hits: off LaMaster 11 in 7 2/3 innings; off Mulcahy 1 in 0 inning (pitched to two men); off Smith 1 in 1/3 inning; off Sivess 2 in 1 inning; off Mungo 6 in 4 innings (4 runs); off Hamlin 5 in 5 innings. Wild pitch: Mungo. Winning pitcher: Hamlin. Losing pitcher: LaMaster. Umpires: Stark, Barr, Stewart. Time, 2:45.

# THE LAST GAME AT BAKER BOWL
## New York at Philadelphia
### June 30, 1938

| NEW YORK | ab | r | h | | PHILADELPHIA | ab | r | h |
|---|---|---|---|---|---|---|---|---|
| Seeds, lf | 6 | 1 | 1 | | Mueller, 2b | 2 | 0 | 0 |
| Danning, c | 6 | 2 | 3 | | Martin, cf | 3 | 1 | 1 |
| Ripple, rf | 6 | 1 | 2 | | Klein, rf | 2 | 0 | 1 |
| Ott, 3b | 3 | 3 | 2 | | Stainback, rf | 2 | 0 | 0 |
| Leiber, cf | 6 | 3 | 4 | | Weintraub, lf | 3 | 0 | 1 |
| Leslie, lf | 6 | 2 | 5 | | Arnovich, lf | 4 | 0 | 0 |
| Bartell, ss | 4 | 2 | 2 | | Whitney, 3b | 4 | 0 | 3 |
| Kampouris, 2b | 5 | 0 | 0 | | Scharein, ss | 4 | 0 | 0 |
| Castleman, p | 4 | 0 | 0 | | Atwood, c | 2 | 0 | 0 |
| | | | | | Clark, c | 2 | 0 | 0 |
| | | | | | Passeau, p | 1 | 0 | 0 |
| | | | | | Smith, p | 0 | 0 | 0 |
| | | | | | Hallahan, p | 2 | 0 | 1 |
| TOTALS | 46 | 14 | 19 | | TOTALS | 31 | 1 | 7 |

| | | | | | | | | | | |
|---|---|---|---|---|---|---|---|---|---|---|
| New York | 0 | 3 | 9 | 0 | 1 | 0 | 1 | 0 | 0 — 14 |
| Philadelphia | 0 | 0 | 0 | 1 | 0 | 0 | 0 | 0 | 0 — 1 |

Errors: Phillies 2 (Weinstrab, Scharein). Runs batted in: Bartell 1, Leiber 5, Leslie , Seeds 1, Danning 1, Ripple 1, Ott 1, Klein 1. Two-base hit: Ripple, Leiber 2, Leslie 3, Danning, Bartell, Martin, Klein, Whitney. Home Run: Leiber. Sacrifice: Martin. Double-plays: Leiber to Bartell; Bartell to Kampouris to Leslie. Left on base: Phillies 7, New York 10. Base on balls: off Castleman 3, off Passeau 2, off Hallahan 3. Struck out: by Passeau 2, by Smith 1, by Castleman 3. Hits: off Passeau 7 in 2 innings; off Smith 3 in 2/3 inning; off Hallahan, 9 in 6 1/3 innings. Losing pitcher: Passeau. Umpires: Klem, Sears, and Ballanfant. Time of game, 2:17.

---

# FIRST HOME NIGHT GAME FOR PHILLIES
## Pittsburgh at Philadelphia
### June 1, 1939

| PITTSBURGH | ab | r | h | rbi | | PHILLIES | ab | r | h | rbi |
|---|---|---|---|---|---|---|---|---|---|---|
| P. Waner, rf | 3 | 2 | 0 | 0 | | Martin, cf | 4 | 0 | 2 | 0 |
| Vaughan, ss | 4 | 2 | 1 | 0 | | Mueller, 2b | 4 | 0 | 0 | 0 |
| Rizzo, lf | 5 | 0 | 2 | 1 | | Brack, lf | 4 | 1 | 1 | 1 |
| Bell, cf | 3 | 0 | 1 | 1 | | Arnovich, lf | 4 | 1 | 2 | 0 |
| Brubaker, 2b | 5 | 1 | 1 | 1 | | May, 3b | 3 | 0 | 1 | 0 |
| Suhr, lf | 4 | 0 | 1 | 0 | | Scott, rf | 4 | 0 | 1 | 0 |
| Handley, 3b | 5 | 0 | 1 | 0 | | Young, ss | 3 | 0 | 1 | 1 |
| Berres, c | 2 | 0 | 0 | 0 | | Milles, c | 3 | 0 | 2 | 0 |
| Sewell, p | 3 | 0 | 0 | 0 | | Higbe, p | 2 | 0 | 0 | 0 |
| | | | | | | Powers, ph | 1 | 0 | 0 | 0 |
| TOTALS | 34 | 5 | 7 | 3 | | TOTALS | 32 | 2 | 10 | 2 |

| | | | | | | | | | | |
|---|---|---|---|---|---|---|---|---|---|---|
| Pittsburgh | 2 | 0 | 0 | 0 | 0 | 0 | 0 | 1 | 2 — 5 |
| Phillies | 0 | 1 | 0 | 0 | 0 | 1 | 0 | 0 | x — 2 |

Errors: Scott, May. Two-base hit: Vaughan. Home runs: Brack, Brubaker. Stolen base: Handley. Sacrifices: Young, May, Higbe. Double plays: Vaughan to Suhr. Left on base: Pittsburgh 11, Phillies 6. Bases on balls: off Higbe 6. Struck out: by Higbe 8, Sewell 3. Hit by pitch: by Higbe (Berres). Wild pitch: Higbe. Winning pitcher: Sewell 6-3. Losing pitcher: Higbe 2-2. Umpires: Stark, Magerkurth, and Stewart. Time, 1:55.

## ROBIN ROBERTS' FIRST GAME
### Pittsburgh at Philadelphia
### June 18, 1948

| PITTSBURGH | ab | r | h | rbi | PHILLIES | ab | r | h | rbi |
|---|---|---|---|---|---|---|---|---|---|
| Rojek, ss | 3 | 0 | 1 | 0 | Ashburn, cf | 3 | 0 | 0 | 0 |
| Gustine, 3b | 3 | 0 | 0 | 1 | Hamner, 2b | 4 | 0 | 1 | 0 |
| Hopp, cf | 4 | 0 | 0 | 0 | Heusser, p | 0 | 0 | 0 | 0 |
| Kiner, lf | 4 | 0 | 1 | 0 | Blatnik, lf | 4 | 0 | 1 | 0 |
| Westlake, rf | 4 | 1 | 2 | 1 | Sisler, lf | 4 | 0 | 0 | 0 |
| Stevens, 1b | 4 | 0 | 0 | 0 | Ennis, rf | 4 | 0 | 0 | 0 |
| Murtaugh, 2b | 3 | 0 | 0 | 0 | Haas, 3b | 4 | 0 | 1 | 0 |
| FitzGerald, c | 3 | 1 | 1 | 0 | Miller, ss | 4 | 0 | 1 | 0 |
| Riddle, p | 2 | 0 | 0 | 0 | Lakeman, c | 4 | 0 | 0 | 0 |
| | | | | | Roberts, p | 1 | 0 | 0 | 0 |
| | | | | | Walker, ph | 1 | 0 | 1 | 0 |
| Totals | 30 | 2 | 5 | 2 | Totals | 33 | 0 | 5 | 0 |

| | | | | | | | | | |
|---|---|---|---|---|---|---|---|---|---|
| Pittsburgh | 0 | 0 | 1 | 0 | 0 | 0 | 1 | 0 | 0— 2 |
| Phillies | 0 | 0 | 0 | 0 | 0 | 0 | 0 | 0 | 0— 0 |

Errors: Rojek, Gustine, FitzGerald. Two-base hit: Blatnik. Home run: Westlake. Double plays: Rojek-Murtaugh and Stevens. Left on base: Pittsburgh 4, Phillies 8. Base on balls: off Roberts 2, Riddle 2. Struck out: by Roberts 2, Riddle 6. Hits: off Roberts 5 in 8 innings; Heusser 0 in 1 inning. Winning pitcher: Riddle (8-2). Losing Pitcher: Roberts (0-1). Umpires: Barr, Ballanfant and Barlick. Time, 2:09. Attendance, 13,501.

## FIVE HOMERS IN ONE INNING
### Cincinnati at Philadelphia
### June 2, 1949

The Phillies tied a National League record by hitting five home runs in a ten-run eighth inning at Shibe Park. The homers were hit by Del Ennis, Andy Seminick, Nippy Jones, Schoolboy Rowe, and Seminick again.

| CINCINNATI | ab | r | h | rbi | PHILLIES | ab | r | h | rbi |
|---|---|---|---|---|---|---|---|---|---|
| Adams, 3b | 4 | 0 | 1 | 0 | Ashburn, cf | 3 | 1 | 0 | 0 |
| Baumholtz, rf | 4 | 0 | 1 | 1 | Hamner, ss | 5 | 2 | 3 | 0 |
| Stallcup, ss | 4 | 0 | 0 | 0 | Waitkus, lf | 5 | 1 | 0 | 0 |
| Bloodworth, 2b | 4 | 0 | 1 | 0 | Ennis, lf | 4 | 2 | 2 | 2 |
| Kluszewski, 1b | 4 | 0 | 0 | 0 | Seminick, c | 4 | 3 | 3 | 5 |
| Kitwhiler, lf | 3 | 1 | 1 | 0 | Hollmig, rf | 4 | 1 | 1 | 1 |
| Mueller, c | 4 | 1 | 2 | 0 | Mayo, rf | 0 | 0 | 0 | 0 |
| Wyrostek, cf | 4 | 1 | 1 | 1 | Jones, 3b | 5 | 1 | 2 | 2 |
| Raffensberger, p | 3 | 0 | 1 | 1 | Miller, 2b | 5 | 0 | 0 | 0 |
| Dobernic, p | 0 | 0 | 0 | 0 | Simmons, p | 2 | 0 | 0 | 0 |
| Peterson, p | 0 | 0 | 0 | 0 | Lopata, ph | 0 | 0 | 0 | 0 |
| Kress, ph | 1 | 0 | 0 | 0 | Rowe, p | 1 | 1 | 1 | 1 |
| Totals | 35 | 3 | 8 | 3 | Totals | 38 | 12 | 12 | 11 |

| | | | | | | | | | |
|---|---|---|---|---|---|---|---|---|---|
| Cincinnati | 0 | 0 | 0 | 0 | 2 | 0 | 1 | 0 | 0— 3 |
| Phillies | 0 | 1 | 0 | 0 | 0 | 1 | 0 | 10 | x—12 |

Errors: Adams, Kluszewski 2, Ennis. Two-base hit: Bloodworth, Adams, Mueller, Raffensberger, Hamner. Three-base hit: Jones. Home run: Seminick 3, Ennis, Jones, Rowe. Left on base: Cincinnati 6, Phillies 8. Base on balls: Raffensberger 4, Peterson 1, Rowe 1. Strikeouts: Simmons 6, Raffensberger 4, Peterson 1, Rowe 1. Hits: off Simmons 8 in 7 innings; Rowe 0 in 2; Raffensberger 6 in 7; Dobernic 2 in 2-3; Peterson 4 in 1-3. Hit by pitcher: by Peterson (Hollmig). Winni pitcher: Simmons (2-3). Losing pitcher: Raffensberger (6-4). Umpires: Barr, Ballanfant, and Barlick. Time, 2:39. Attendance, 10,549.

# PHILLIES WIN PENNANT
## October 1, 1950

| PHILADELPHIA | ab | r | h | o | a |
|---|---|---|---|---|---|
| Waitkus, lb | 5 | 1 | 1 | 18 | 0 |
| Ashburn, cf | 5 | 1 | 0 | 2 | 1 |
| Sisler, lf | 5 | 2 | 1 | 0 | 0 |
| Mayo, lf | 0 | 0 | 0 | 1 | 0 |
| Ennis, rf | 5 | 0 | 2 | 2 | 0 |
| Jones, 3b | 5 | 0 | 1 | 0 | 3 |
| Hamner, ss | 4 | 0 | 0 | 1 | 2 |
| Seminick, c | 3 | 0 | 1 | 3 | 1 |
| a Caballero | 0 | 0 | 0 | 0 | 0 |
| Lopata, c | 0 | 0 | 0 | 1 | 0 |
| Goliat, 2b | 4 | 0 | 1 | 1 | 3 |
| Roberts, p | 2 | 0 | 1 | 1 | 6 |
| Totals | 38 | 4 | 11 | 30 | 16 |

| BROOKLYN | ab | r | h | o | a |
|---|---|---|---|---|---|
| Abrams, lf | 2 | 0 | 0 | 2 | 0 |
| Reese, ss | 4 | 1 | 3 | 3 | 3 |
| Snider, cf | 4 | 0 | 1 | 3 | 0 |
| Robinson, 2b | 3 | 0 | 0 | 4 | 3 |
| Furillo, rf | 4 | 0 | 0 | 3 | 0 |
| Hodges, 1b | 4 | 0 | 0 | 9 | 3 |
| Campanella, c | 4 | 0 | 1 | 2 | 4 |
| Cox, 3b | 3 | 0 | 0 | 1 | 2 |
| b Russell | 1 | 0 | 0 | 0 | 0 |
| Newcombe, p | 3 | 0 | 0 | 3 | 2 |
| c Brown | 1 | 0 | 0 | 0 | 0 |
| Totals | 33 | 1 | 5 | 30 | 17 |

a Ran for Seninick in ninth.
b Struck out for Cox in tenth.
c Fouled out for Newcombe in tenth.

| | | | | | | | | | | |
|---|---|---|---|---|---|---|---|---|---|---|
| Philadelphia | 0 | 0 | 0 | 0 | 0 | 1 | 0 | 0 | 0 | 3—4 |
| Brooklyn | 0 | 0 | 0 | 0 | 0 | 1 | 0 | 0 | 0 | 0—1 |

Errors: none. Runs batted in: Jones, Reese, Sisler 3. Two-base hits: Reese. Home runs: Reese, Sisler. Sacrifice: Roberts. Double plays: Reese, Robinson, and Hodges; Roberts and Waitkus. Left on base: Philadelphia 7, Brooklyn 5. Bases on balls: Roberts 3, Newcombe 2. Struck out: Roberts 2, Newcombe 3. Umpires: Goetz, Dascoli, Jorda, and Donatelli. Time, 2:35. Attendance, 35,073.

---

# 1950 WORLD SERIES
## Wednesday, October 4 — At Philadelphia

| New York (A.L.) | AB. | R. | H. | O. | A. | E. |
|---|---|---|---|---|---|---|
| Woodling, lf | 3 | 0 | 1 | 1 | 0 | 0 |
| Rizzuto, ss | 3 | 0 | 1 | 0 | 2 | 0 |
| Berra, c | 4 | 0 | 0 | 7 | 0 | 0 |
| DiMaggio, cf | 4 | 0 | 0 | 3 | 0 | 0 |
| Mize, 1b | 4 | 0 | 0 | 7 | 0 | 0 |
| Hopp, 1b | 0 | 0 | 0 | 3 | 0 | 0 |
| Brown, 3b | 4 | 1 | 1 | 0 | 0 | 0 |
| Johnson, 3b | 0 | 0 | 0 | 0 | 0 | 0 |
| Bauer, rf | 4 | 0 | 1 | 5 | 0 | 0 |
| Coleman, 2b | 4 | 0 | 0 | 1 | 2 | 0 |
| Raschi, p | 3 | 0 | 1 | 0 | 3 | 0 |
| Totals | 31 | 1 | 5 | 27 | 7 | 0 |

| Phila'phia (N.L.) | AB. | R. | H. | O. | A. | E. |
|---|---|---|---|---|---|---|
| Waitkus, 1b | 3 | 0 | 0 | 9 | 2 | 0 |
| Ashburn, cf | 4 | 0 | 0 | 2 | 0 | 0 |
| Sisler, lf | 4 | 0 | 0 | 3 | 0 | 0 |
| Ennis, rf | 3 | 0 | 0 | 4 | 0 | 0 |
| Jones, 3b | 3 | 0 | 1 | 4 | 3 | 1 |
| Hamner, ss | 3 | 0 | 0 | 0 | 1 | 0 |
| Seminick, c | 3 | 0 | 1 | 1 | 1 | 0 |
| Goliat, 2b | 3 | 0 | 0 | 3 | 2 | 0 |
| Konstanty, p | 2 | 0 | 0 | 1 | 0 | 0 |
| *Whitman | 1 | 0 | 0 | 0 | 0 | 0 |
| Meyer, p | 0 | 0 | 0 | 0 | 1 | 0 |
| Totals | 29 | 0 | 2 | 27 | 10 | 1 |

| | | | | | | | | | | |
|---|---|---|---|---|---|---|---|---|---|---|
| New York | 0 | 0 | 0 | 1 | 0 | 0 | 0 | 0 | 0—1 |
| Philadelphia | 0 | 0 | 0 | 0 | 0 | 0 | 0 | 0 | 0—0 |

*Flied out for Konstanty in eighth. Two base hit: Brown. Run batted in: Coleman. Sacrifice hits: Rizzuto, Raschi. Bases on balls: Off Konstanty 4, off Raschi 1. Struck out: By Raschi 5. Pitching record: Konstanty 4 hits, 1 run in 8 innings; Meyer 1 hit, 0 runs in 1 inning. Earned runs: New York 1. Left on bases: New York 9, Philadelphia 3. Winning pitcher: Raschi. Losing pitcher: Konstanty. Umpires: Conlan (N.L.), McGowan (A.L.), Boggess (N.L.), Berry (A.L.), Barlick (N.L.), McKinley (A.L.). Time, 2:17. Attendance, 30,746.

| New York (A.L.) | AB. | R. | H. | O. | A. | E. |
|---|---|---|---|---|---|---|
| Woodling lf | 5 | 0 | 2 | 2 | 0 | 0 |
| Rizzuto, ss | 4 | 0 | 0 | 2 | 1 | 0 |
| Berra, c | 5 | 0 | 1 | 7 | 0 | 0 |
| DiMaggio, cf | 5 | 1 | 1 | 3 | 0 | 0 |
| Mize, 1b | 4 | 0 | 1 | 6 | 0 | 0 |
| Johnson, 3b | 1 | 0 | 0 | 0 | 2 | 0 |
| Brown, 3b | 4 | 0 | 2 | 0 | 0 | 0 |
| †Hopp, 1b | 1 | 0 | 0 | 3 | 0 | 0 |
| Bauer, rf | 5 | 0 | 1 | 1 | 0 | 0 |
| Coleman, 2b | 3 | 1 | 1 | 5 | 6 | 0 |
| Reynolds, p | 3 | 0 | 1 | 1 | 2 | 0 |
| Totals | 40 | 2 | 10 | 30 | 11 | 0 |

| Phila'phia (N.L.) | AB. | R. | H. | O. | A. | E. |
|---|---|---|---|---|---|---|
| Waitkus, 1b | 4 | 0 | 2 | 8 | 0 | 0 |
| Ashburn, cf | 5 | 0 | 2 | 4 | 0 | 0 |
| Sisler, lf | 5 | 0 | 0 | 3 | 0 | 0 |
| Ennis, rf | 4 | 0 | 0 | 1 | 0 | 0 |
| Jones, 3b | 4 | 0 | 0 | 3 | 0 | 0 |
| Hamner, ss | 3 | 0 | 2 | 2 | 2 | 0 |
| Seminick, c | 2 | 0 | 0 | 5 | 0 | 0 |
| *Caballero | 0 | 0 | 0 | 0 | 0 | 0 |
| Silvestri, c | 0 | 0 | 0 | 1 | 0 | 0 |
| †Whitman | 0 | 0 | 0 | 0 | 0 | 0 |
| Lopata, c | 0 | 0 | 0 | 1 | 0 | 0 |
| Goliat, 2b | 4 | 1 | 1 | 2 | 2 | 0 |
| Roberts, p | 2 | 0 | 0 | 0 | 0 | 0 |
| *Mayo | 0 | 0 | 0 | 0 | 0 | 0 |
| Totals | 33 | 1 | 7 | 30 | 4 | 0 |

| | | | | | | | | | | |
|---|---|---|---|---|---|---|---|---|---|---|
| New York | 0 | 1 | 0 | 0 | 0 | 0 | 0 | 0 | 1— | 2 |
| Philadelphia | 0 | 0 | 0 | 0 | 1 | 0 | 0 | 0 | 0— | 1 |

*Ran for Seminick in seventh. †Ran for Brown in eighth. †Intentionally walked for Silvestri in ninth. ††Walked for Roberts in tenth. Two-base hits — Ashburn, Waitkus, Coleman, Hamner. Three-base hit — Hamner. Home run: DiMaggio. Runs batted in: Woodling, Ashburn, DiMaggio. Sacrifice hits: Roberts, Waitkus. Stolen base: Hamner. Double plays: Johnson, Coleman and Hopp; Rizzuto, Coleman and Hopp. Bases on balls: Off Roberts 3, off Reynolds 4. Struck out: By Reynolds 6, by Roberts 5. Earned runs: New York 2. Philadelphia 1. Left on bases: New York 11, Philadelphia 8. Winning pitcher: Reynolds. Losing pitcher: Roberts. Umpires: McGowan (A.L.), Boggess (N.L.), Berry (A.L.), Conlan (N.L.), McKinley (A.L.) and Barlick (N.L.). Time, 3:06. Attendance, 32.660.

---

| Phila'phia (N.L.) | AB. | R. | H. | O. | A. | E. |
|---|---|---|---|---|---|---|
| Waitkus, 1b | 5 | 0 | 1 | 8 | 0 | 0 |
| Ashburn, cf | 4 | 0 | 1 | 0 | 0 | 0 |
| Jones, 3b | 3 | 0 | 1 | 1 | 2 | 0 |
| Ennis, rf | 4 | 1 | 1 | 3 | 0 | 0 |
| Sisler, lf | 4 | 0 | 1 | 2 | 1 | 0 |
| Mayo, lf | 0 | 0 | 0 | 1 | 0 | 0 |
| Hamner, ss | 4 | 1 | 3 | 2 | 2 | 1 |
| Seminick, c | 2 | 0 | 1 | 5 | 0 | 1 |
| Goliat, 2b | 3 | 0 | 1 | 4 | 1 | 0 |
| ††Caballero | 0 | 0 | 0 | 0 | 0 | 0 |
| Bloodworth, 2b | 0 | 0 | 0 | 0 | 0 | 0 |
| Heintzelman, p | 2 | 0 | 0 | 0 | 2 | 0 |
| Konstanty, p | 0 | 0 | 0 | 0 | 0 | 0 |
| x Whitman | 1 | 0 | 0 | 0 | 0 | 0 |
| Meyer, p | 0 | 0 | 0 | 0 | 0 | 0 |
| Totals | 32 | 2 | 10y | 26 | 8 | 2 |

| New York (A.L.) | AB. | R. | H. | O. | A. | E. |
|---|---|---|---|---|---|---|
| Rizzuto, ss | 3 | 1 | 1 | 1 | 1 | 0 |
| Coleman, 2b | 4 | 1 | 3 | 3 | 1 | 0 |
| Berra, c | 2 | 0 | 0 | 6 | 1 | 0 |
| DiMaggio, cf | 3 | 0 | 1 | 1 | 0 | 0 |
| Bauer, lf | 3 | 0 | 0 | 1 | 0 | 0 |
| †Brown | 1 | 0 | 0 | 0 | 0 | 0 |
| †Jensen | 0 | 0 | 0 | 0 | 0 | 0 |
| Ferrick, p | 0 | 0 | 0 | 0 | 0 | 0 |
| Mize, 1b | 4 | 0 | 0 | 9 | 2 | 0 |
| Collins, 1b | 0 | 0 | 0 | 1 | 1 | 0 |
| Johnson, 3b | 4 | 0 | 0 | 1 | 3 | 0 |
| Mapes, rf | 4 | 0 | 0 | 3 | 0 | 0 |
| Lopat, p | 2 | 0 | 1 | 1 | 4 | 0 |
| *Woodling, lf | 2 | 1 | 1 | 0 | 0 | 0 |
| Totals | 32 | 3 | 7 | 27 | 13 | 0 |

| | | | | | | | | | | |
|---|---|---|---|---|---|---|---|---|---|---|
| Philadelphia | 0 | 0 | 0 | 0 | 0 | 1 | 1 | 0 | 0— | 2 |
| New York | 0 | 0 | 1 | 0 | 0 | 0 | 0 | 1 | 1— | 3 |

*Popped out for Lopat in eighth. †Safe on error for Bauer in eighth. †† Ran for Brown in eighth. †† Ran for Goliat in ninth. x Batted for Konstanty in ninth and was safe on fielder's choice. y Two out when winning run scored. Two-base hits: Ennis, Hamner, Runs batted in: Coleman 2, Sisler, Goliat. Stolen

224

base: Rizzuto. Sacrifice hits: Seminick 2, Heintzelman, Jones. Double play: Hamner and Waitkus. Bases on balls: Off Heintzelman 6, off Ferrick 1. Struck out: By Heintzelman 3, by Meyer 1, by Lopat 5. Pitching record: Lopat 9 hits, 2 runs in 8 innings; Ferrick 1 hit, 0 runs in 1 inning; Heintzelman 4 hits, 2 4uns in 7 2/3 innings; Konstanty 0 hits 0 runs in 1/3 inning; Meyer 3 hits, 1 run in 2/3 inning. Left on bases: Philadelphia 8, New York 9. Earned runs: Philadelphia 2, New York 2. Winning pitcher: Ferr:ck. Losing pitcher: Meyer. Umpires: Boggess (N.L.). Berry (A.L.), Conlan (N.L.), McGowan (A.L.), Barlick (N.L.) and McKinley (A.L.). Time, 2:35. Attendance, 64,505.

---

### Saturday, October 7 — At New York

| Phila'phia (N.L.) | AB. | R. | H. | O. | A. | E. | New York (A.L.) | AB. | R. | H. | O. | A. | E. |
|---|---|---|---|---|---|---|---|---|---|---|---|---|---|
| Waitkus, 1b | 3 | 0 | 1 | 9 | 1 | 0 | Woodling, lf | 4 | 1 | 2 | 4 | 0 | 1 |
| Ashburn, cf | 4 | 0 | 0 | 3 | 0 | 0 | Rizzuto, ss | 4 | 0 | 0 | 2 | 4 | 0 |
| Jones, 3b | 4 | 1 | 2 | 0 | 4 | 0 | Berra, c | 4 | 2 | 2 | 10 | 0 | 0 |
| Ennis, rf | 3 | 0 | 1 | 1 | 0 | 0 | DiMaggio, cf | 3 | 1 | 2 | 1 | 0 | 0 |
| Sisler, lf | 4 | 0 | 0 | 2 | 0 | 0 | Mize, 1b | 3 | 0 | 1 | 5 | 1 | 0 |
| †K. Johnson | 0 | 1 | 0 | 0 | 0 | 0 | Hopp, 1b | 1 | 0 | 0 | 1 | 1 | 0 |
| Hamner, ss | 4 | 0 | 1 | 2 | 2 | 0 | Brown, 3b | 3 | 1 | 1 | 0 | 1 | 1 |
| Seminick, c | 4 | 0 | 0 | 3 | 1 | 0 | W. Johnson, 3b | 1 | 0 | 0 | 0 | 0 | 0 |
| †Mayo | 0 | 0 | 0 | 0 | 0 | 0 | Bauer, rf | 3 | 0 | 0 | 1 | 0 | 0 |
| Goliat, 2b | 4 | 0 | 1 | 4 | 4 | 1 | Coleman, 2b | 3 | 0 | 0 | 2 | 3 | 0 |
| Miller, p | 0 | 0 | 0 | 0 | 0 | 0 | Ford, p | 3 | 0 | 0 | 1 | 0 | 0 |
| Konstanty, p | | 0 | 1 | 0 | 1 | 0 | Reynolds, p | 0 | 0 | 0 | 0 | 0 | 0 |
| *Caballero | 1 | 0 | 0 | 0 | 0 | 0 | | | | | | | |
| Roberts, p | 0 | 0 | 0 | 0 | 0 | 0 | | | | | | | |
| †††Lopata | 1 | 0 | 0 | 0 | 0 | 0 | | | | | | | |
| Totals | 34 | 2 | 7 | 24 | 13 | 1 | Totals | 32 | 5 | 8 | 27 | 10 | 2 |

| | | | | | | | | | | |
|---|---|---|---|---|---|---|---|---|---|---|
| Philadelphia | 0 | 0 | 0 | 0 | 0 | 0 | 0 | 0 | 2 — 2 |
| New York | 2 | 0 | 0 | 0 | 0 | 3 | 0 | 0 | x – 5 |

*Struck out for Konstanty in eighth. †Ran for Sisler in ninth. †Ran for Seminick in ninth. ††Struck out for Roberts in ninth. Two-base hits: Jones, DiMaggio. Three-base hit: Brown. Home run: Berra. Runs batted in: Berra 2, DiMaggio, Borwn, Bauer. Double plays: Mize and Berra; Coleman, Rizzuto and Mize. Base on balls: Off Ford 1. Struck out: By Ford 7, by Konstanty 3, by Reynolds 1. Pitching record: Miller 2 hits, 2 runs in 1/3 inning; Konstanty 5 hits 3 runs in 6 2/3 innings; Roberts 1 hit, 0 runs in 1 inning; ford 7 hits, 2 runs in 8 /3 innings; Reynolds 0 hits, 0 runs in 1/3 inning. Hit by pitcher: By Konstanty (DiMaggio), by Ford (Ennis). Wi'd pitch: Miller. Left on bases: Philadelphia 7, New York 4. Earned runs: Philcelphia 0, New York 4. Winning pitcher: Ford. Losing pitcher: Miller. Umpires: Berry (A.L.), Conlan (N.L.), McGowan (A.L.), Boggess (N.L.), McKinley (A.L.) and Barlick (N.L.) Time, 2:05. Attendance, 68,098.

---

## ROBIN ROBERTS WINS 28th
### Philadelphia at New York September 28, 1952

| PHILLIES | ab | r | h | rbi | NEW YORK | ab | r | h | rbi |
|---|---|---|---|---|---|---|---|---|---|
| Ryan, 2b | 0 | 0 | 0 | 0 | Mueller, rf | 5 | 1 | 3 | 0 |
| Young, 2b | 3 | 1 | 0 | 0 | D. Spencer, ss | 5 | 0 | 3 | 1 |
| Ashburn, cf | 4 | 0 | 1 | 0 | Lockman, lf | 1 | 0 | 0 | 0 |
| Nicholson, rf | 5 | 2 | 2 | 2 | Wilson, 1b | 4 | 0 | 0 | 0 |
| Ennis, lf | 3 | 2 | 2 | 0 | Thompson, 3b | 3 | 1 | 1 | 1 |
| Hamner, ss | 5 | 1 | 3 | 2 | Thomson, cf | 4 | 1 | 0 | 1 |
| Lopata, c | 5 | 0 | 2 | 1 | Rhodes, lf | 4 | 0 | 1 | 0 |
| Jones, 3b | 5 | 1 | 1 | 2 | Williams, 2b | 2 | 0 | 0 | 1 |
| Waitkus, 1b | 3 | 0 | 0 | 0 | Hofman, 2b | 1 | 0 | 0 | 0 |

## Philadelphia at New York September 28, 1952 (continued)

| | | | | | | | | |
|---|---|---|---|---|---|---|---|---|
| Roberts, p | 4 | 0 | 1 | 0 | Katt, c | 4 | 1 | 1 | 0 |
| | | | | | Harshman, p | 1 | 0 | 0 | 0 |
| | | | | | Corwin, p | 0 | 0 | 0 | 0 |
| | | | | | Hartung, ph | 1 | 0 | 0 | 0 |
| | | | | | Kennedy, p | 1 | 0 | 0 | 0 |
| | | | | | Irvin, ph | 1 | 0 | 0 | 0 |
| Totals | 37 | 7 | 12 | 7 | Totals | 37 | 4 | 9 | 4 |

| | | | | | | | | | | |
|---|---|---|---|---|---|---|---|---|---|---|
| PHILLIES | 0 | 0 | 0 | 3 | 3 | 0 | 0 | 0 | 1 — 7 |
| New York | 0 | 2 | 0 | 0 | 0 | 0 | 0 | 1 | 1 — 4 |

Errors: Young, Jones. Two-base hit: Lopata. Three-base hit: Hamner. Home run: Thompson, Jones, Nicholson. Stolen base: Young. Sacrifice: Ashburn. Double plays: Hamner and Waitkus. Left on base: Phillies 9, New York 8. Bases on balls: Harshman 2, Corwin 1, Roberts 1, Kennedy 2. Strikeouts: Harshman 6, Kennedy 2, Roberts 6. Hits: off Harshman 9 in 4 1/3 innings; Corwin 0 in 2/3 inning; Kennedy 3 in 4. Runs and Earned runs: Harshman 6-6, Kennedy 1-1, Roberts Hit by pitch: by Roberts (Hofman). Winning pitcher: Roberts (28-7). Losing pitcher: Harshman (0-2). Umpires: Boggess, Jackowski, Pinelli, and Engeln. Time, 2:31. Attendance, 5,933.

## ROBERTS' STREAK ENDS
### Brooklyn at Philadelphia  July 9, 1953

On August 28, 1952, Robin Roberts beat the Cardinals in St. Louis, 10-6, a complete game and the start of an unbelieveable streak. Following that victory, Roberts ran off twenty-seven consecutive complete games before being stopped by the Dodgers on July 9, 1953.

| BROOKLYN | ab | r | h | rbi | PHILLIES | ab | r | h | rbi |
|---|---|---|---|---|---|---|---|---|---|
| Cox, 3b | 5 | 1 | 3 | 0 | Waitkus, 1b | 5 | 0 | 2 | 2 |
| Reese, ss | 5 | 1 | 2 | 1 | Ashburn, cf | 3 | 1 | 0 | 0 |
| Snider, cf | 4 | 1 | 1 | 0 | Clark, rf | 4 | 1 | 2 | 1 |
| Robinson, 2b | 5 | 0 | 0 | 1 | Ennis, lf | 4 | 0 | 1 | 1 |
| Hodges, lf | 4 | 0 | 1 | 1 | Hamner, 2b-ss | 3 | 1 | 2 | 0 |
| Furillo, rf | 3 | 1 | 2 | 0 | Lopata, c | 3 | 2 | 1 | 0 |
| Campanella, c | 4 | 1 | 1 | 2 | Jones, 3b | 4 | 1 | 1 | 0 |
| Belardi, 1b | 3 | 0 | 0 | 0 | Kazanski, ss | 3 | 0 | 1 | 0 |
| Podres, p | 2 | 0 | 1 | 0 | c — Wyrostek | 1 | 0 | 0 | 0 |
| a - Walker | 1 | 0 | 1 | 0 | Ryan, 2b | 0 | 0 | 0 | 0 |
| b — Antonelli | 0 | 0 | 0 | 0 | Roberts, p | 2 | 0 | 0 | 0 |
| Hughes, p | 0 | 0 | 0 | 0 | Miller, p | 0 | 0 | 0 | 0 |
| e — Shuba | 1 | 0 | 0 | 0 | d — Burgess | 1 | 0 | 1 | 2 |
| | | | | | Konstanty, p | 0 | 0 | 0 | 0 |
| Totals | 37 | 5 | 12 | 5 | Totals | 33 | 6 | 11 | 6 |

a — Singled for Podres in seventh.
b — Ran for Walker in seventh.
c — Flied out for Kazanski in eighth.
d — Doubled for Miller in eighth.
e — Lined out for Hughes in ninth.

| | | | | | | | | | | |
|---|---|---|---|---|---|---|---|---|---|---|
| Brooklyn | 0 | 0 | 0 | 2 | 1 | 0 | 0 | 2 | 0 — 5 |
| PHILLIES | 0 | 2 | 0 | 2 | 0 | 0 | 0 | 2 | x — 6 |

Errors: Reese, Lopata. Second base: Cox, Snider. Third base: Clark, Hodges. Home Run: Campanella. Sacrifice: Roberts. Double Plays: Hamner, Kazanski and Waitkus; Roberts, Hamner and Waitkus; Robinson, Reese and Belardi. Left on base: Brooklyn 8, Phillies 7. Bases on balls: Roberts 1, Podres 1, Hughes 2, Miller 1, Konstanty 1. Strike outs: Roberts 3, Podres 2. Hits: off Podres, 9 in 6 innings; Hughes, 2 in 2; Roberts 11 in 7 1/3; Miller 0 in 2/3; Konstanty, 1 in 1.

Runs and Earned runs: Podres 4-2, Hughes 2-2, Roberts 5-5, Miller 0-0, Konstanty 0-0. Winning pitcher: Miller 1-3. Losing pitcher: Hughes (2-2). Umpires: Stewart, Pinelli, Boggess, Engeln. Time, 2:27. Attendance, 21,989.

## NEAR MISS FOR ROBERTS
### Cincinnati at Philadelphia May 13, 1954

One pitch deprived Robin Roberts of a perfect game. Cincinnati's lead-off batter, Bobby Adams, began the game with a home run and Roberts then retired the next twenty-seven Reds in order. Two weeks earlier, Roberts also one-hit the Milwaukee Braves, Del Crandall's third-inning double the lone hit off the great right-hander.

| Cincinnati | ab | r | h | rbi | | PHILLIES | ab | r | h | rbi |
|---|---|---|---|---|---|---|---|---|---|---|
| Adams, 3b | 4 | 1 | 1 | 1 | | Jones, 3b | 5 | 0 | 1 | 0 |
| McMillan, ss | 3 | 0 | 0 | 0 | | Ashburn, cf | 3 | 2 | 1 | 0 |
| Bell, cf | 3 | 0 | 0 | 0 | | Torgeson, lf | 5 | 1 | 2 | 1 |
| Kluszewski, 1b | 3 | 0 | 0 | 0 | | Ennis, lf | 4 | 1 | 1 | 1 |
| Greengrass, lf | 3 | 0 | 0 | 0 | | Hamner, 2b | 4 | 1 | 3 | 1 |
| Temple, 2b | 3 | 0 | 0 | 0 | | Wyrostek, rf | 2 | 2 | 0 | 0 |
| Post, rf | 3 | 0 | 0 | 0 | | Burgess, c | 4 | 1 | 1 | 0 |
| Bailey, c | 3 | 0 | 0 | 0 | | Morgan, ss | 4 | 0 | 1 | 1 |
| Valentine, p | 1 | 0 | 0 | 0 | | Roberts, p | 3 | 0 | 1 | 1 |
| Podbielan, p | 0 | 0 | 0 | 0 | | | | | | |
| Escalera, ph | 1 | 0 | 0 | 0 | | | | | | |
| Savransky, p | 0 | 0 | 0 | 0 | | | | | | |
| Merriman, ph | 1 | 0 | 0 | 0 | | | | | | |
| Totals | 28 | 1 | 1 | 1 | | Totals | 34 | 8 | 11 | 5 |

| | | | | | | | | | |
|---|---|---|---|---|---|---|---|---|---|
| Cincinnati | 1 | 0 | 0 | 0 | 0 | 0 | 0 | 0 | 0 — 1 |
| Phillies | 0 | 2 | 1 | 0 | 5 | 0 | 0 | 0 | x — 8 |

Errors: McMillan, Temple, Post. Three-base hits: Torgeson. Home Run: Adams. Stolen Base: Hamner. Sacrifices: Roberts. Double plays: McMillan, Temple, and Kluszewski; Adams, Temple, and Kluszewski. Left on base: Cincinnati 0, Phillies 7. Bases on balls: Valentine 3, Podbielan 1. Strike outs: Roberts 8. Hits: off Valentine 9 in 4 innings (faced 3 batters in 5th); Podbielan 1 in 1; Savransky 1 in 3. Runs and earned runs: Roberts 1-1, Valentine 6-6, Podbielan 2-0, Savransky 0-0. Winning pitcher: Roberts (4-3). Losing pitcher: Valentine (3-3). Umpires: Jackowski, Conlan, Gore and Secory. Time, 1:59. Attendance, 6,856.

## JONES' EIGHT-RBI GAME
### Philadelphia at St. Louis August 20, 1958

Four Phillies have collected eight-RBI games: Kitty Bransfield in 1910, Gavvy Cravath in 1915, Willie (Puddin-Head) Jones in 1958, and Mike Schmidt in 1976. Here's Jone's big game. Schmidt's is covered under his four home-run box score in this book.

| PHILLIES | ab | r | h | rbi | | ST. LOUIS | ab | r | h | rbi |
|---|---|---|---|---|---|---|---|---|---|---|
| Ashburn, cf | 5 | 2 | 3 | 0 | | Blasingame, 2b | 4 | 1 | 3 | 0 |
| Hemus, 2b | 4 | 2 | 2 | 2 | | Freese, ss | 4 | 0 | 0 | 0 |
| H. Anderson, lf | 5 | 3 | 3 | 1 | | Musial, 1b | 3 | 1 | 2 | 0 |
| Post, rf | 5 | 1 | 2 | 1 | | Cunningham, 1b | 1 | 0 | 1 | 0 |
| Bouchee, 1b | 4 | 2 | 1 | 0 | | Boyer, 3b | 3 | 0 | 2 | 2 |
| Jones, 3b | 5 | 2 | 4 | 8 | | Moon, rf | 4 | 0 | 1 | 0 |
| Fernandez, ss | 3 | 0 | 1 | 0 | | Ennis, lf | 4 | 0 | 0 | 0 |
| Kazanski, ss | 2 | 0 | 0 | 0 | | Flood, cf | 4 | 0 | 0 | 0 |
| Sawatski, c | 4 | 0 | 0 | 0 | | Landrith, c | 4 | 0 | 0 | 0 |
| Roberts, p | 4 | 0 | 1 | 0 | | Muffett, p | 0 | 0 | 0 | 0 |
| Totals | 41 | 12 | 17 | 12 | | Chittum, p | 0 | 0 | 0 | 0 |

## Jones' Eight-RBI Game (Continued)

| ST. LOUIS | ab | r | h | rbi |
|---|---|---|---|---|
| a — Green | 1 | 0 | 0 | 0 |
| Stobbs, p | 0 | 0 | 0 | 0 |
| b — Noren | 1 | 0 | 0 | 0 |
| Paine, p | 0 | 0 | 0 | 0 |
| Totals | 34 | 2 | 10 | 2 |

a — Popped out for Chittum in third.
b — Fanned for Stobbs in seventh.

| PHILLIES | 4 | 0 | 4 | 1 | 0 | 1 | 0 | 0 | 2 — 12 |
|---|---|---|---|---|---|---|---|---|---|
| St. Louis | 1 | 0 | 0 | 0 | 0 | 1 | 0 | 0 | 0 — 2 |

Error: Post. Two-base hit: Fernandez, Musial, Post, Jones. Home run: Jones 2, Anderson. Double plays: Bouchee, Fernandez and Bouchee; Kazanski, Hemus and Bouchee. Sacrifice fly: Boyer. Left on base: Phillies 6, St. Louis 6.

| | IP | H | R | ER | BB | SO |
|---|---|---|---|---|---|---|
| Roberts (13-11) W | 9 | 10 | 2 | 2 | 0 | 5 |
| Muffett (4-5) L | .2 | 3 | 4 | 4 | 1 | 1 |
| Chittum | 2.1 | 5 | 3 | 3 | 0 | 0 |
| Stobbs | 4 | 7 | 2 | 2 | 0 | 1 |
| Paine | 2 | 2 | 2 | 2 | 0 | 4 |

Hit by pitcher: By Paine (Hemus). Umpires: Dixon, Gorman, Delmore, Boggess. Time, 2:21. Attendance, 11, 928.

---

## ASHBURN WINS BATTING TITLE NUMBER TWO
### Philadelphia at Pittsburgh
### September 28, 1958

Centerfielder Richie Ashburn won his second batting title by beating out the New York Giants Willie Mays on the last day of the season. "Whitey" went 3-for-4 to finish at .350, three points ahead of Willie. From September 11 to the end of the season, Ashburn batted at an amazing .478 clip. His previous batting title came in 1955, .338.

| PHILLIES | ab | r | h | rb | o | a | e |
|---|---|---|---|---|---|---|---|
| Ashburn, cf | 4 | 2 | 3 | 0 | 3 | 1 | 0 |
| Young, 2b | 3 | 0 | 0 | 0 | 2 | 2 | 0 |
| d-Repulski | 1 | 0 | 0 | 0 | 0 | 0 | 0 |
| Kazanski, 2b | 0 | 0 | 0 | 0 | 0 | 1 | 0 |
| Bouchee, 1b | 5 | 0 | 1 | 1 | 7 | 0 | 0 |
| Post, rf | 4 | 1 | 1 | 0 | 5 | 0 | 1 |
| Anderson, lf | 5 | 1 | 3 | 1 | 1 | 0 | 0 |
| Herrara, 3b | 2 | 0 | 0 | 0 | 2 | 0 | 0 |
| a-Philley | 1 | 1 | 1 | 0 | 0 | 0 | 0 |
| Jones, 3b | 2 | 0 | 1 | 1 | 1 | 0 | 0 |
| Fernandez, ss | 4 | 1 | 1 | 0 | 2 | 5 | 0 |
| Lopata, o | 4 | 0 | 0 | 0 | 7 | 0 | 0 |
| Morehead, p | 3 | 0 | 1 | 1 | 0 | 0 | 0 |
| Farrell, p | 0 | 0 | 0 | 0 | 0 | 1 | 0 |
| e-Bowman | 1 | 0 | 0 | 0 | 0 | 0 | 0 |
| Meyer, p | 0 | 0 | 0 | 0 | 0 | 0 | 0 |
| Totals | 39 | 6 | 12 | x-4 | 30 | 10 | 1 |

## PITTSBURGH PIRATES

|  | ab | r | h | rbi | o | a | e |
|---|---|---|---|---|---|---|---|
| Virdon, cf | 5 | 0 | 2 | 0 | 1 | 0 | 0 |
| Mejias, rf | 5 | 0 | 1 | 0 | 5 | 0 | 0 |
| Thomas, 3b | 5 | 0 | 0 | 0 | 1 | 1 | 0 |
| Skinner, lf | 5 | 2 | 1 | 0 | 0 | 0 | 0 |
| Stevens, 1b | 4 | 1 | 2 | 0 | 15 | 1 | 0 |
| Mazeroski, 2b | 4 | 1 | 3 | 1 | 2 | 6 | 1 |
| Schofield, ss | 3 | 0 | 0 | 1 | 2 | 5 | 0 |
| Foiles, c | 4 | 0 | 1 | 0 | 3 | 0 | 0 |
| Daniels, p | 2 | 0 | 0 | 0 | 0 | 3 | 0 |
| b-Kluszewski | 1 | 0 | 1 | 1 | 0 | 0 | 0 |
| c-Powers | 0 | 0 | 0 | 0 | 0 | 0 | 0 |
| Smith, p | 0 | 0 | 0 | 0 | 0 | 1 | 1 |
| Porterfield, p | 0 | 0 | 0 | 0 | 1 | 0 | 0 |
| f-Kravitz | 1 | 0 | 0 | 0 | 0 | 0 | 0 |
| Gross, p | 0 | 0 | 0 | 0 | 0 | 1 | 0 |
| Totals | 39 | 4 | 11 | z-3 | 30 | 18 | 2 |

z-Stevens scored on Post's error in 7th.
x-Anderson scored on Mazeroski's error in 7th; Philley scored on DP in 7th.
a-Doubled for Herrera in 7th.
b-Singled for Daniels in 7th.
c-Ran for Kluszewski in 7th
d-Grounded out for Young in 8th.
e-Struck out for Ferrell in 9th
f-Grounded out for Porterfield in 9th.

| | | | | | | | | | | |
|---|---|---|---|---|---|---|---|---|---|---|
| PHILLIES | 0 | 0 | 1 | 0 | 0 | 0 | 2 | 1 | 0 | 2—6 |
| Pittsburgh | 0 | 0 | 0 | 0 | 0 | 0 | 3 | 1 | 0 | 0—4 |

Two-base hit: Mazeroski, Fernandez, Philley, Mejias. Sacrifice: Kazanski. Sacrifice fly: Schofield. Double Play: Schofield, Mazeroski and Stevens; Mazeroski, Stevens, Schofield and Stevens. Left on base: Phillies 7, Pittsburgh 6.

|  | IP | H | R | ER | BB | SO |
|---|---|---|---|---|---|---|
| Morehead | 7 | 8 | 3 | 3 | 0 | 4 |
| (faced one batter in 8th) | | | | | | |
| Farrell | 1 | 2 | 1 | 1 | 0 | 0 |
| Meyer (W.) | 2 | 1 | 0 | 0 | 0 | 1 |
| Daniels | 7 | 7 | 3 | 2 | 1 | 1 |
| Smith | 2/3 | 2 | 1 | 1 | 1 | 0 |
| Porterfield | 1 1/3 | 0 | 0 | 0 | 0 | 1 |
| Gross (L.) | 1 | 3 | 2 | 2 | 1 | 1 |

Passed ball: Foiles. Umpires: Jackowski, Delmore, Landes, Barlick. Time,

---

# MAHAFFEY STRIKES OUT 17 CUBS

### Chicago at Philadelphia
### April 23, 1961, 2nd game

Right-hander Art Mahaffey fanned seventeen Cubs to tie the National League record which has since been broken. St. Louis' Dizzy Dean held the record, also striking out seventeen Cubs in 1933.

## CHICAGO

| | ab. | r. | h. | rbi. | o | a. | e. |
|---|---|---|---|---|---|---|---|
| Heist, cf | 4 | 0 | 0 | 0 | 0 | 0 | 0 |
| Zimmer, 2b | 4 | 0 | 1 | 0 | 2 | 8 | 0 |
| Will, rf | 4 | 0 | 1 | 0 | 1 | 0 | 0 |
| Santo, 3b | 4 | 0 | 0 | 0 | 0 | 0 | 2 |
| Banks, ss | 4 | 0 | 0 | 0 | 4 | 4 | 0 |
| Thomas, 1b | 3 | 0 | 0 | 0 | 0 | 0 | 0 |
| Bouchee, 1b | 2 | 0 | 1 | 0 | 12 | 2 | 0 |
| S. Taylor, c | 2 | 0 | 0 | 0 | 2 | 0 | 0 |
| Thacker, o | 0 | 0 | 0 | 0 | 1 | 0 | 0 |
| a-Ashburn | 1 | 0 | 0 | 0 | 0 | 0 | 0 |
| Bartell, c | 0 | 0 | 0 | 0 | 1 | 1 | 0 |
| Anderson, p | 2 | 0 | 1 | 0 | 1 | 3 | 0 |
| b-Drake | 1 | 0 | 0 | 0 | 0 | 0 | 0 |
| Drott, p | 0 | 0 | 0 | 0 | 0 | 0 | 0 |
| Totals | 30 | 0 | 4 | 0 | 24 | 18 | 2 |

## PHILLIES

| | ab. | r. | h. | rbi. | o | a. | e. |
|---|---|---|---|---|---|---|---|
| Sadowski, 3b | 4 | 1 | 0 | 0 | 0 | 0 | 0 |
| T. Taylor, 2b | 2 | 2 | 1 | 0 | 2 | 1 | 0 |
| Callison, rf | 2 | 1 | 1 | 4 | 3 | 0 | 0 |
| Smith, lf | 4 | 0 | 0 | 0 | 1 | 0 | 0 |
| Gonzalez, cf | 4 | 0 | 2 | 2 | 1 | 0 | 0 |
| Herrera, 1b | 2 | 1 | 1 | 0 | 4 | 0 | 1 |
| Dairymple, c | 3 | 0 | 0 | 0 | 16 | 1 | 0 |
| Amaro, ss | 3 | 1 | 2 | 0 | 0 | 1 | 0 |
| Mahaffey, p | 2 | 0 | 0 | 0 | 0 | 1 | 0 |
| Totals | 26 | 6 | 7 | x5 | 27 | 4 | 1 |

x- Herrera scored on Santo's error in 2d.
a-Lined out for Thacker in 8th.
b-Struck out for Anderson in 8th.

| | | | | | | | | | |
|---|---|---|---|---|---|---|---|---|---|
| Chicago | 0 | 0 | 0 | 0 | 0 | 0 | 0 | 0 | 0 — 0 |
| PHILLIES | 1 | 1 | 0 | 0 | 3 | 0 | 0 | 1 | x — 6 |

Two-base hit: Herrera, Bouchee. Three-base hit: Amaro. Home Run: Callison. Sacrifice: T. Taylor, Mahaffey. Double Play: Zimmer, Banks and Bouchee; Banks, Zimmer and Bouchee; Zimmer and Banks. Left on Bases: Chicago, 5; Phillies, 2.

| | IP | H | R | ER | BB | SO |
|---|---|---|---|---|---|---|
| Mahaffey | 9 | 4 | 0 | 0 | 1 | 17 |
| Anderson (6) | 7 | 5 | 5 | 3 | 3 | 3 |
| Drott | 1 | 2 | 1 | 1 | 0 | 1 |

Umpires: Dascoli, Secory, Venzon, Sudol. Time, 2:16. Attendance, 16,027.

# TWO THREE-HOMER GAMES FOR CALLISON

In the long history of the Phillies, outfielder Johnny Callison is the lone player to hit three home runs in a single game twice.

| Milwaukee at Philadelphia<br>September 27, 1964 | | | | Philadelphia at Chicago<br>June 6, 1905, 2nd game | | | |
|---|---|---|---|---|---|---|---|

## MILWAUKEE

| | ab. | r. | h. | rbi. | po. | a. | o. |
|---|---|---|---|---|---|---|---|
| Alou, 1b | 6 | 3 | 3 | 3 | 7 | 1 | 0 |
| Maye, cf-lf | 6 | 2 | 5 | 2 | 4 | 0 | 0 |
| Aaron, rf | 4 | 0 | 2 | 2 | 3 | 0 | 0 |
| Kolb, rf | 2 | 0 | 1 | 0 | 1 | 0 | 0 |
| Mathews, 3b | 5 | 0 | 0 | 0 | 0 | 2 | 0 |
| Olivo, p | 1 | 0 | 0 | 0 | 1 | 0 | 0 |
| Torre, c | 5 | 2 | 3 | 1 | 6 | 0 | 0 |
| Carty, lf | 2 | 1 | 1 | 0 | 0 | 0 | 0 |
| Woodward, 2b | 3 | 0 | 1 | 0 | 0 | 3 | 0 |
| Menke, 2b-ss | 4 | 2 | 2 | 1 | 2 | 3 | 0 |
| Alomar, ss | 1 | 0 | 0 | 0 | 0 | 0 | 0 |
| a-Cline, cf | 3 | 2 | 2 | 1 | 2 | 0 | 0 |
| Cloninger, p | 4 | 2 | 2 | 2 | 1 | 0 | 0 |
| d-Klimchock | 1 | 0 | 0 | 0 | 0 | 0 | 0 |
| Totals | 47 | 14 | 22 | 12 | 27 | 9 | 0 |

## PHILLIES

| | ab. | r. | h. | rbi. | po. | a. | o. |
|---|---|---|---|---|---|---|---|
| Gonzalez, cf | 5 | 1 | 2 | 0 | 1 | 0 | 0 |
| Allen, 3b | 5 | 1 | 3 | 1 | 1 | 4 | 0 |
| Callison, rf | 5 | 3 | 3 | 4 | 3 | 0 | 0 |
| Covington, lf | 4 | 0 | 0 | 0 | 3 | 0 | 0 |
| Thomas, 1b | 4 | 1 | 1 | 0 | 10 | 0 | 1 |
| Dairymple, c | 4 | 1 | 1 | 0 | 3 | 0 | 0 |
| Taylor, 2b | 4 | 1 | 2 | 2 | 2 | 3 | 0 |
| Amaro, ss | 4 | 0 | 0 | 0 | 4 | 2 | 0 |
| Bunning, p | 0 | 0 | 0 | 1 | 0 | 0 | 0 |
| Green, p | 0 | 0 | 0 | 0 | 0 | 0 | 0 |
| Stevens, p | 0 | 0 | 0 | 0 | 0 | 0 | 0 |
| b-Shockley | 1 | 0 | 0 | 0 | 0 | 0 | 0 |
| Wise, p | 0 | 0 | 0 | 0 | 0 | 0 | 0 |
| c-Briggs | 0 | 0 | 0 | 0 | 0 | 0 | 0 |
| Baldschun, p | 0 | 0 | 0 | 0 | 0 | 0 | 0 |
| e-Rojas | 1 | 0 | 0 | 0 | 0 | 0 | 0 |
| Totals | 37 | 8 | 12 | 8 | 27 | 9 | 1 |

a-Doubled for Alomar in 4th.
b-Flied out for Stevens in 5th.
c-Walked for Wise in 7th.
d-Flied out for Cloninger in 8th.
e-Flied out for Baldschun in 9th.

| | | | | | | | | | |
|---|---|---|---|---|---|---|---|---|---|
| Milwaukee | 2 | 0 | 0 | 6 | 4 | 0 | 1 | 1 | 0 — 14 |
| PHILLIES | 1 | 2 | 0 | 0 | 0 | 1 | 0 | 2 | 2 — 8 |

Two-base hit: Maye, Aaron, Gonzalez, Dairymple, Cline, Alou 2, Thomas, Allen. Three-base hit: Taylor. Home Run: Callison 3, Torre. Sacrifice Fly: Bunning. Double Play: Amaro and Thomas; Matthews, Menke and Alou; Taylor and Thomas. Left on Base: Milwaukee, 8; Phillies, 5.

| | IP | H | R | ER | BB | SO |
|---|---|---|---|---|---|---|
| Cloninger (W) | 7 | 7 | 4 | 4 | 2 | 3 |
| Olivo | 2 | 5 | 4 | 4 | 0 | 3 |
| x-Bunning (L) | 3 | 10 | 7 | 7 | 0 | 0 |
| Green | 1 2/3 | 7 | 5 | 5 | 1 | 0 |
| Stevens | 1/3 | 0 | 0 | 0 | 0 | 0 |
| Wise | 2 | 3 | 1 | 1 | 0 | 1 |
| Baldschun | 2 | 2 | 1 | 1 | 1 | 2 |

x-Faced five men in fourth.

Wild pitch: Wise. Umpires: Jackowski, Crawford, Vargo, Forman. Time, 3:00. Attendance, 20,569.

## Second Game

### PHILADELPHIA                              CHICAGO

| | ab | r | h | bi | | ab | r | h | bi |
|---|---|---|---|---|---|---|---|---|---|
| Gonzalez cf | 5 | 0 | 0 | 0 | Landr'm, cf | 5 | 1 | 1 | 0 |
| Allen, 3b | 3 | 1 | 1 | 0 | Stewart, ss | 4 | 2 | 2 | 1 |
| Callison, rf | 5 | 3 | 4 | 4 | Williams, lf | 4 | 2 | 1 | 2 |
| Covin't'n, lf | 2 | 2 | 2 | 0 | Santo, 3b | 4 | 2 | 3 | 2 |
| Johnson, lf | 3 | 0 | 0 | 0 | Banks, 1b | 4 | 0 | 1 | 0 |
| Stuart, 1b | 4 | 2 | 2 | 1 | Clemens, rf | 4 | 1 | 2 | 3 |
| Wine, 1b | 0 | 0 | 0 | 0 | Bailey, c | 4 | 0 | 0 | 0 |
| Dal'mple c | 5 | 1 | 2 | 1 | Am'f'ano, 2b | 3 | 0 | 0 | 0 |
| Rojas, 2b | 4 | 1 | 2 | 4 | Jackson, p | 1 | 0 | 0 | 0 |
| Amaro, ss | 5 | 0 | 0 | 0 | Altman, ph | 1 | 0 | 0 | 0 |
| Mahaffey, p | 1 | 0 | 0 | 0 | Kuenn, ph | 1 | 0 | 0 | 0 |
| Belinsky, p | 1 | 0 | 1 | 0 | Bright, ph | 1 | 1 | 1 | 0 |
| Wagne, p | 2 | 0 | 0 | 0 | | | | | |
| Totals | 40 | 10 | 14 | 10 | Totals | 36 | 9 | 11 | 8 |

| | | | | | | | | | | |
|---|---|---|---|---|---|---|---|---|---|---|
| Philadelphia | 5 | 0 | 2 | 0 | 1 | 0 | 0 | 0 | 2— | 10 |
| Chicago | 2 | 0 | 3 | 0 | 1 | 0 | 0 | 0 | 3— | 9 |

Error: Amaro. Double play: Philadelphia 3. Left on Base: Philadelphia, 7, Chicago 5. Two-base hit: Stuart, Santo, Landrum. Home Run: Callison 3, (12), Rojas (1), Clemens (2), Stuart (6), Santo (11), Williams (6).

| | IP | H | R | ER | BB | SO |
|---|---|---|---|---|---|---|
| Mahaffey | 2 | 4 | 4 | 4 | 3 | 1 |
| Baldschun | 2/3 | 1 | 1 | 1 | 0 | 0 |
| Belinsky | 1/3 | 0 | 0 | 0 | 0 | 1 |
| Wagner W, 1-1 | 4 1/3 | 6 | 4 | 4 | 2 | 7 |
| Roebuck | 2/3 | 0 | 0 | 0 | 0 | 0 |
| Jackson, L. 3-7 | 2 1/3 | 8 | 7 | 7 | 0 | 2 |
| Humphreys | 1 | 1 | 0 | 0 | 1 | 0 |
| Hendley | 2/3 | 0 | 0 | 0 | 0 | 0 |
| McDaniel | 2 | 2 | 1 | 1 | 1 | 0 |
| Broglio | 3 | 3 | 2 | 2 | 1 | 2 |

Mahaffey faced three men in third.
Time, 3:17. Attendance, 16,845.

# CHRIS SHORT FANS 18
## Philadelphia at New York
### October 2, 1965

Left-hander Chris Short struck out eighteen New York Mets in fifteen innings of work as the Phils and Mets played the longest 0-0 night game in major league history. Short tied the National League record for most strikeouts in an extra inning game. The eighteen-inning game was the second game of a twi-nighter and halted by a 1 A.M. curfew.

| PHILLIES | AB | R | H | RBI | O | A |
|---|---|---|---|---|---|---|
| Phillips, cf | 6 | 0 | 1 | 0 | 5 | 0 |
| E. Callison, rf | 1 | 0 | 0 | 0 | 0 | 0 |
| Rojas, 2b | 6 | 0 | 1 | 0 | 2 | 3 |
| Allen, 3b | 7 | 0 | 2 | 0 | 2 | 2 |
| Stuart, 1b | 7 | 0 | 1 | 0 | 16 | 1 |
| Amaro, ss | 0 | 0 | 0 | 0 | 0 | 0 |
| Johnson, lf | 6 | 0 | 0 | 0 | 2 | 0 |
| G-Briggs, cf | 1 | 0 | 0 | 0 | 1 | 0 |
| Gonzalez, rf, cf, lf | 5 | 0 | 1 | 0 | 2 | 0 |
| Wine, ss | 5 | 0 | 0 | 0 | 1 | 8 |
| Hernnstein, 1b | 1 | 0 | 0 | 0 | 2 | 0 |
| Corrales, c | 6 | 0 | 0 | 0 | 19 | 1 |
| K-Dalrymple, c | 1 | 0 | 0 | 0 | 2 | 0 |
| Short, p | 5 | 0 | 0 | 0 | 0 | 1 |
| D-Covington | 1 | 0 | 0 | 0 | 0 | 0 |
| J-Sorrell | 1 | 0 | 0 | 0 | 0 | 0 |
| Baldschun, p | 0 | 0 | 0 | 0 | 0 | 1 |
| Wagner | 0 | 0 | 0 | 0 | 0 | 0 |
| Totals | 59 | 0 | 6 | 0 | 54 | 17 |

D-Flied out for Short in sixteenth.
E-Popped out for Phillips in sixteenth.
G-Grounded out for Johnson in seventeenth.
J-Popped out for Corrales in eighteenth.
K-Fouled out for Wagner in eighteenth.

| NEW YORK | AB | R | H | BI | O | A |
|---|---|---|---|---|---|---|
| Hunt, 2b | 8 | 0 | 2 | 0 | 6 | 5 |
| Christopher, rf, lf | 7 | 0 | 2 | 0 | 2 | 0 |
| Smith, 3b | 8 | 0 | 1 | 0 | 0 | 4 |
| Hickman, 1b | 6 | 0 | 2 | 0 | 20 | 1 |
| Swoboda, lf | 1 | 0 | 0 | 0 | 1 | 0 |
| Napoleon, lf | 5 | 0 | 0 | 0 | 6 | 0 |
| Gossen, c | 4 | 0 | 1 | 0 | 8 | 0 |
| Klaus, ss | 1 | 0 | 0 | 0 | 2 | 5 |
| Jones, cf | 7 | 0 | 1 | 0 | 5 | 0 |
| Harrelson, ss | 3 | 0 | 0 | 0 | 1 | 3 |
| Cannizzaro, c | 2 | 0 | 0 | 0 | 2 | 1 |
| Gardner, p | 5 | 0 | 0 | 0 | 0 | 3 |
| a-Selma | 0 | 0 | 0 | 0 | 0 | 0 |
| b-McMillan | 1 | 0 | 0 | 0 | 0 | 0 |
| c-Shaffer | 1 | 0 | 0 | 0 | 0 | 0 |
| f-Lewis, rf | 0 | 0 | 0 | 0 | 0 | 0 |
| h-Stephenson, c | 1 | 0 | 0 | 0 | 1 | 0 |
| i-Kranepool | 1 | 0 | 0 | 0 | 0 | 0 |
| Sutherland, p | 0 | 0 | 0 | 0 | 0 | 0 |
| Rabant, p | 0 | 0 | 0 | 0 | 0 | 0 |
| Totals | 61 | 0 | 9 | 0 | 54 | 22 |

## Chris Short Fans 18 (continued)

a-Ran for Goosen in ninth.
b-Struck out for Harrelson in ninth.
c-Struck out for Gardner in fifteenth.
f-Hit by pitch for Napoleon in sixteenth.
h-Flied out for Canizzaro in seventeenth.
i-Struck out for Sutherland in seventeenth.

```
PHILLIES  0 0 0 0 0 0 0 0 0 0 0 0 0 0 0 0 0 0
New York  0 0 0 0 0 0 0 0 0 0 0 0 0 0 0 0 0 0
```

Errors: Harrelson, Goosen. Double play: Rojas, Wine, Stuart. Left on Bases: Phillies 9, New York 12. Two-base hits: Hunt, Christopher, Hickman, Gonzalez. Stolen Base: Rojas, Hickman, Hunt. Sacrifice: Wine.

|            | IP | H | R | ER | B | SO |
|------------|----|---|---|----|---|----|
| Short      | 15 | 9 | 0 | 0  | 3 | 18 |
| Wagner     | 2  | 0 | 0 | 0  | 1 | 1  |
| Baldschun  | 1  | 0 | 0 | 0  | 0 | 2  |
| Gardner    | 15 | 5 | 0 | 0  | 2 | 7  |
| Sutherland | 2  | 1 | 0 | 0  | 1 | 0  |
| Ribant     | 1  | 0 | 0 | 0  | 0 | 0  |

Hit by Pitcher: By Wagner, Lewis. Umpires: Weyer, Kibler, Secory, Burkhart. Time, 4:29. Attendance, 10,371.

---

## LAST GAME IN CONNIE MACK STADIUM
### October 1, 1970

| Montreal       | ab | r | h | bi | Philadelphia | ab | r | h | bi |
|----------------|----|---|---|----|--------------|----|---|---|----|
| Gosger, lf     | 5  | 0 | 0 | 0  | Taylor, 2b   | 5  | 1 | 0 | 0  |
| Sutherland 2b  | 4  | 0 | 0 | 0  | McCarver, c  | 5  | 1 | 3 | 1  |
| Staub, rf      | 3  | 0 | 0 | 0  | Gamble, rf   | 4  | 0 | 2 | 1  |
| Fairly, 1b     | 5  | 0 | 1 | 0  | Johnson, 1b  | 3  | 0 | 0 | 0  |
| Bailey, 3b     | 4  | 0 | 0 | 0  | Stone, lf    | 4  | 0 | 1 | 0  |
| Day, cf        | 4  | 0 | 1 | 0  | Money, 3b    | 4  | 0 | 1 | 0  |
| Bateman, c     | 4  | 0 | 1 | 0  | Browne, cf   | 4  | 0 | 1 | 0  |
| Philips, pr.   | 0  | 1 | 0 | 0  | Bowa, ss     | 4  | 0 | 0 | 0  |
| Brand, c       | 0  | 0 | 0 | 0  | Lersch, p    | 3  | 0 | 1 | 0  |
| Wine, ss       | 4  | 0 | 2 | 1  | Selma, p     | 1  | 0 | 0 | 0  |
| Morton, p      | 2  | 0 | 0 | 0  |              |    |   |   |    |
| Jones, ph      | 0  | 0 | 0 | 0  |              |    |   |   |    |
| Marshall, p    | 0  | 0 | 0 | 0  |              |    |   |   |    |
| Fairey, ph     | 1  | 0 | 0 | 0  |              |    |   |   |    |
| Reed, p        | 0  | 0 | 0 | 0  |              |    |   |   |    |
| Totals         | 36 | 1 | 5 | 1  | Totals       | 37 | 2 | 9 | 2  |

```
Montreal      0  0  0  0  0  0  0  0  1   0 — 1
Philadelphia  0  0  1  0  0  0  0  0  0   1 — 2
```

Errors: Money, Bailey, Taylor. Left on Bases: Montreal 9, Philadelphia, 8. Two-base hit: Wine. Three-Base hit: McCarver. Stolen Bases: Bateman, McCarver. Sacrifice: Sutherland.

|                | IP     | H | R | ER | BB | SO |
|----------------|--------|---|---|----|----|----|
| Morton         | 7      | 7 | 1 | 1  | 1  | 3  |
| Marshall       | 1      | 0 | 0 | 0  | 1  | 0  |
| Reed (L, 6-5)  | 1 2/3  | 2 | 1 | 1  | 0  | 1  |
| Lersch         | 8 1/3  | 5 | 1 | 1  | 3  | 7  |
| Selma (W, 8-9) | 1 2/3  | 0 | 0 | 0  | 0  | 1  |

Time, 2:46. Attendance, 31,822.

# FIRST GAME IN VETERANS STADIUM
## Montreal at Philadelphia  April 10, 1971

| Montreal | ab | r | h | rbi | PHILLIES | ab | r | h | rbi |
|---|---|---|---|---|---|---|---|---|---|
| Day, cf | 4 | 0 | 0 | 0 | Bowa, ss | 4 | 1 | 2 | 0 |
| Raymond, p | 0 | 0 | 0 | 0 | Money, 3b | 3 | 1 | 1 | 2 |
| Reed, p | 0 | 0 | 0 | 0 | Montanez, cf | 2 | 1 | 1 | 0 |
| Brand, ph | 1 | 0 | 0 | 0 | Johnson, 1b | 3 | 1 | 1 | 0 |
| Hunt, 2b | 3 | 1 | 1 | 0 | Briggs, lf | 3 | 0 | 0 | 0 |
| Staub, rf | 4 | 0 | 1 | 0 | Freed, rf | 3 | 0 | 2 | 1 |
| Bailey, 3b | 4 | 0 | 1 | 1 | McCarver, c | 3 | 0 | 1 | 1 |
| Fairly, lf | 2 | 0 | 1 | 0 | Doyle, 2b | 2 | 0 | 0 | 0 |
| Jones, lf | 4 | 0 | 0 | 0 | Taylor, ph, 2b | 2 | 0 | 0 | 0 |
| Bateman, c | 4 | 0 | 2 | 0 | Bunning, p | 2 | 0 | 0 | 0 |
| Wine, ss | 1 | 0 | 0 | 0 | Hoerner, p | 0 | 0 | 0 | 0 |
| Fairey, ph | 1 | 0 | 0 | 0 | | | | | |
| Laboy, ph | 1 | 0 | 0 | 0 | | | | | |
| Stoneman, p | 2 | 0 | 0 | 0 | | | | | |
| O'Donoghue, p | 0 | 0 | 0 | 0 | | | | | |
| Marshall, p | 0 | 0 | 0 | 0 | | | | | |
| Sutherland, ph | 0 | 0 | 0 | 0 | | | | | |
| Totals | 31 | 1 | 6 | 1 | Totals | 27 | 4 | 8 | 4 |

| | | | | | | | | | |
|---|---|---|---|---|---|---|---|---|---|
| Montreal | 0 | 0 | 0 | 0 | 0 | 1 | 0 | 0 | 0 — 1 |
| PHILLIES | 0 | 0 | 0 | 0 | 0 | 3 | 1 | 0 | x — 6 |

Errors: Jones, Money. Double play: Bunning, Bowa and Johnson. Wine and Fairly. Left on Base: Montreal 10, Phillies 7. Two base hits: Hunt, Bailey. Three base hits: Bowa. Home Run: Money. Stolen Base: Hunt, Bowa. Sacrifice: Bunning. Sacrifice Fly: McCarver, Money.

| | IP | H | R | ER | BB | SO |
|---|---|---|---|---|---|---|
| Stoneman (L 0-1) | 5 | 7 | 3 | 3 | 3 | 1 |
| O'Donoghue | .1 | 0 | 0 | 0 | 0 | 0 |
| Marshall | .1 | 0 | 0 | 0 | 0 | 0 |
| Raymond | .2 | 1 | 1 | 1 | 2 | 1 |
| Reed | 1.1 | 0 | 0 | 0 | 0 | 1 |
| Bunning (W 1-0) | 7.1 | 6 | 1 | 1 | 3 | 4 |
| Hoerner | 1.2 | 0 | 0 | 0 | 1 | 2 |

Save: Hoerner (1). Hit By Pitcher: by Bunning (Hunt). Time, 2:43, Attendance, 55,352.

# CARLTON'S 15TH CONSECUTIVE VICTORY
## Cincinnati at Philadelphia  August 17, 1972

| CINCINNATI | AB | R | H | BI | O | A | E |
|---|---|---|---|---|---|---|---|
| Rose, lf | 5 | 1 | 1 | 1 | 4 | 0 | 0 |
| Morgan, 2b | 3 | 0 | 1 | 1 | 2 | 4 | 0 |
| Tolan, cf | 3 | 1 | 0 | 0 | 3 | 0 | 0 |
| Bench, 1b | 3 | 0 | 1 | 1 | 9 | 0 | 1 |
| Menke, 3b | 4 | 0 | 0 | 0 | 2 | 2 | 0 |
| Foster, rf | 4 | 0 | 0 | 0 | 1 | 0 | 0 |
| Concepcion, ss | 3 | 1 | 2 | 0 | 4 | 4 | 0 |
| Plummer, c | 4 | 1 | 2 | 1 | 2 | 3 | 0 |
| Grimsley, p | 0 | 0 | 0 | 0 | 0 | 0 | 0 |
| a-Sprague, p | 0 | 0 | 0 | 0 | 0 | 0 | 0 |
| b-Javier | 1 | 0 | 0 | 0 | 0 | 0 | 0 |
| c-Carroll | 0 | 0 | 0 | 0 | 0 | 0 | 0 |
| I. McCrae | 1 | 0 | 0 | 0 | 0 | 0 | 0 |
| Totals | 31 | 4 | 7 | 4 | 27 | 13 | 1 |

## Carlton's 15th Consecutive Victory (continued)

| PHILLIES | AB | R | H | BI | O | A | E |
|---|---|---|---|---|---|---|---|
| Harmon, 2b | 3 | 2 | 2 | 0 | 2 | 2 | 0 |
| Bowa, ss | 4 | 1 | 2 | 1 | 1 | 3 | 0 |
| Money, 3b | 4 | 0 | 0 | 1 | 1 | 2 | 0 |
| Montanez, cf | 4 | 2 | 2 | 2 | 4 | 0 | 0 |
| Luzinski, lf | 4 | 2 | 3 | 1 | 2 | 0 | 0 |
| Johnson, 1b | 4 | 1 | 2 | 2 | 10 | 0 | 0 |
| Hutton | 0 | 0 | 0 | 0 | 1 | 0 | 0 |
| Robinson, rf | 3 | 0 | 3 | 1 | 3 | 0 | 0 |
| Bateman, c | 3 | 1 | 2 | 0 | 3 | 1 | 0 |
| Carlton, p | 4 | 0 | 0 | 0 | 0 | 4 | 0 |
| Totals | 33 | 9 | 16 | 8 | 27 | 12 | 8 |

b-Flied to Robinson for Sprague in 7th.
d-Flied to Luzinski for Carroll in 9th.

| | | | | | | | | | | | |
|---|---|---|---|---|---|---|---|---|---|---|---|
| Cincinnati | 0 | 0 | 3 | 0 | 0 | 0 | 1 | 0 | 0 — | 4 |
| Phillies | 0 | 2 | 0 | 0 | 3 | 2 | 2 | 0 | x — | 9 |

Double play: 1 Cincinnati, Concepcion to Bench. Left on Base: Phillies 4, Cincinnati 5. Two base hits: Robinson, 2, Plummer, Morgan. Three base hits: Montanez. Home Run: Johnson (7), Montanez (12), Rose. Stolen Base: Harmon, Tolan (2), Rose. Sacrifice: Bowa, Grimsley (2). Sacrifice Fly: Money, Robinson.

| | IP | H | R | ER | BB | SO |
|---|---|---|---|---|---|---|
| Carlton | 9 | 7 | 4 | 4 | 4 | 2 |
| Grimsley | 4 1/3 | 9 | 5 | 5 | 1 | 2 |
| Sprague | 1 2/3 | 4 | 2 | 1 | 1 | 0 |
| Carroll | 2 | 3 | 2 | 2 | 1 | 1 |

Winning pitcher: Carroll 7th. Umpires: Froemming, Landes, Davidson, Donatelli. Time, 2:04, Attendance, 42,635.

---

## LONGEST HOME GAME
### Atlanta at Philadelphia    May 4, 1973

The longest Phillies game is twenty-one innings in 1918 but the longest home game is twenty innings, three times. The first one was 1905, Cubs beating the Phillies, 2-1. In 1919, the Phillies and Dodgers battled to a 9-9 tie and the most recent twenty inning home game came at Veterans Stadium in 1973.

| ATLANTA | ab | r | h | bi | PHILADELPHIA | ab | r | h | bi |
|---|---|---|---|---|---|---|---|---|---|
| Brown, lf | 4 | 1 | 2 | 0 | Lonborg, p | 0 | 0 | 0 | 0 |
| Evans, 3b | 9 | 1 | 3 | 4 | Pagan, ph | 0 | 0 | 0 | 1 |
| Lum, | 8 | 0 | 3 | 0 | Unser, cf | 7 | 0 | 0 | 1 |
| Baker, cf | 8 | 0 | 1 | 0 | Montanez | 6 | 0 | 0 | 0 |
| Da. Johnson 2b | 8 | 0 | 2 | 0 | Boone, c | 8 | 0 | 2 | 0 |
| Oates, c | 8 | 0 | 1 | 0 | Schmidt, 3b | 7 | 0 | 0 | 0 |
| Reed, p | 4 | 1 | 0 | 0 | Anderson, rf | 8 | 2 | 2 | 0 |
| Frisella, p | 0 | 0 | 0 | 0 | Doyle, 2b | 7 | 2 | 2 | 1 |
| Gilbreath, ph | 1 | 0 | 0 | 0 | Ruthven, p | 2 | 0 | 0 | 0 |
| P. Niekro, p | 0 | 0 | 0 | 0 | Rgdznski, ph | 0 | 0 | 0 | 0 |
| Dietz, ph | 0 | 0 | 0 | 0 | Scarce, p | 1 | 0 | 0 | 0 |
| Pierce, ph | 1 | 0 | 0 | 0 | B. Wilson, p | 0 | 0 | 0 | 0 |
| House, p | 0 | 0 | 0 | 0 | Hutton, ph | 1 | 0 | 1 | 0 |
| Schueler, p | 2 | 0 | 1 | 0 | Harmon, pr | 0 | 1 | 0 | 0 |
| Blanks, ph | 1 | 0 | 1 | 0 | Twitchell, p | 0 | 0 | 0 | 0 |
| T. Kelley, p | 1 | 0 | 0 | 0 | Luzinski, lf | 2 | 0 | 0 | 0 |
| Total | 76 | 4 | 17 | 4 | Total | 64 | 5 | 9 | 3 |

One out when winning run scored.

| | | | | | | | | | | | | | | | | | | | | | |
|---|---|---|---|---|---|---|---|---|---|---|---|---|---|---|---|---|---|---|---|---|---|
| Braves | 0 | 0 | 2 | 0 | 0 | 0 | 0 | 0 | 0 | 0 | 0 | 0 | 2 | 0 | 0 | 0 | 0 | 0 | 00 — | 4 |
| Phillies | 0 | 0 | 0 | 0 | 0 | 0 | 0 | 2 | 0 | 0 | 0 | 0 | 2 | 0 | 0 | 0 | 0 | 0 | 01 — | 5 |

Errors: Schmidt, Doyle 2, Baker, Lonborg. Double Play: Atlanta 1. Left on Base: Atlanta 27, Philadelphia 11. Two-base hit: Evans, Tovar, DaJohnson, Anderson, Lum, Boone. Three-base hits: Doyle. Home Run: Evans (7). Sacrifice: Rogodzinski, Lum, OsBrown. Sacrifice Fly: Unser, Pagan.

| | IP | H | R | ER | BB | SO |
|---|---|---|---|---|---|---|
| Reed | 7 | 3 | 2 | 1 | 2 | 2 |
| Frisella | 3 | 0 | 0 | 0 | 0 | 3 |
| P. Niekro | 1 | 0 | 0 | 0 | 0 | 0 |
| House | 1 | 1 | 1 | 1 | 0 | 1 |
| Schueler | 5 | 3 | 1 | 1 | 3 | 4 |
| T. Kelley (L,0-1) | 2 1/3 | 2 | 1 | 1 | 2 | 2 |
| Ruthven | 8 | 6 | 2 | 0 | 3 | 6 |
| Scarce | 3 2/3 | 2 | 0 | 0 | 3 | 4 |
| B. Wilson | 1 1/3 | 3 | 2 | 2 | 0 | 2 |
| Twitchell | 2 | 1 | 0 | 0 | 2 | 3 |
| Lersch | 3 | 4 | 0 | 0 | 1 | 0 |
| Lonborg (W, 2-4) | 2 | 1 | 0 | 0 | 1 | 0 |

Hit by Pitcher: by Ruthven (S. Jackson), by Scarce (Lum), by Twitchell (DaJohnson). Winning Pitcher: Schueler. Balk: Ruthven. Passed Ball: Oates. Time, 5:16. Attendance, 10,158.

# MIKE SCHMIDT'S FOUR HOMERS
## April 17, 1976
### At Chicago

| PHILLIES | ab | r | bh | rbi | po | a | e |
|---|---|---|---|---|---|---|---|
| Cash, 2b | 6 | 1 | 2 | 2 | 4 | 3 | 0 |
| Bowa, ss | 6 | 3 | 3 | 1 | 2 | 0 | 0 |
| Johnstone, rf | 5 | 2 | 4 | 2 | 5 | 0 | 0 |
| Luzinski, lf | 5 | 0 | 1 | 1 | 0 | 0 | 0 |
| Brown, lf | 0 | 0 | 0 | 0 | 0 | 0 | 0 |
| Allen, 1b | 5 | 2 | 1 | 2 | 5 | 0 | 0 |
| Schmidt, 3b | 6 | 4 | 5 | 3 | 2 | 3 | 0 |
| Maddox, cf | 5 | 2 | 2 | 1 | 4 | 0 | 0 |
| McGraw, p | 0 | 0 | 0 | 0 | 0 | 0 | 0 |
| e-McCarver, ph | 1 | 1 | 1 | 0 | 0 | 0 | 0 |
| Underwood, p | 0 | 0 | 0 | 0 | 0 | 0 | 0 |
| Lonborg, p | 0 | 0 | 0 | 0 | 0 | 0 | 0 |
| Boone, c | 6 | 1 | 3 | 1 | 8 | 0 | 0 |
| Carlton, p | 1 | 0 | 0 | 0 | 0 | 0 | 0 |
| Schueler, p | 0 | 0 | 0 | 0 | 0 | 0 | 0 |
| Garber, p | 0 | 0 | 0 | 0 | 0 | 0 | 0 |
| a-Hutton, ph | 0 | 0 | 0 | 0 | 0 | 0 | 0 |
| Reed, p | 0 | 0 | 0 | 0 | 0 | 0 | 0 |
| b-Martin, ph | 1 | 0 | 0 | 0 | 0 | 0 | 0 |
| Twitchell, p | 0 | 0 | 0 | 0 | 0 | 0 | 0 |
| c-Tolan, ph, cf | 3 | 2 | 2 | 0 | 0 | 0 | 0 |
| Totals | 50 | 18 | 24 | 18 | 30 | 6 | 0 |

## Mike Schmidt's Four Homers (continued)

| CHICAGO | ab | r | bh | rbi | po | a | e |
|---|---|---|---|---|---|---|---|
| Monday, cf | 6 | 3 | 4 | 4 | 4 | 0 | 0 |
| Cardenal, lf | 5 | 1 | 1 | 0 | 0 | 0 | 0 |
| Summers, lf | 0 | 0 | 0 | 0 | 3 | 0 | 0 |
| d-Mitterwald, ph | 1 | 0 | 0 | 0 | 0 | 0 | 0 |
| Wallis, lf | 1 | 0 | 0 | 0 | 0 | 0 | 0 |
| Madlock, 3b | 7 | 2 | 3 | 3 | 0 | 0 | 0 |
| Morales, rf | 5 | 2 | 1 | 0 | 1 | 0 | 0 |
| Thorton, 1b | 4 | 3 | 1 | 1 | 9 | 2 | 0 |
| Trillo, 2b | 5 | 0 | 2 | 3 | 3 | 4 | 0 |
| Swisher, c | 6 | 1 | 3 | 4 | 5 | 0 | 0 |
| Rosello, ss | 4 | 1 | 2 | 1 | 2 | 3 | 0 |
| Kelleher, ss | 2 | 0 | 1 | 0 | 2 | 1 | 0 |
| R. Reuschel, p | 1 | 2 | 0 | 0 | 1 | 3 | 0 |
| Garman, p | 0 | 0 | 0 | 0 | 0 | 0 | 0 |
| Knowles, p | 0 | 0 | 0 | 0 | 0 | 0 | 0 |
| P. Reuschel, p | 0 | 0 | 0 | 0 | 0 | 0 | 0 |
| Schultz, p | 0 | 0 | 0 | 0 | 0 | 1 | 0 |
| f-Adams, ph | 1 | 1 | 1 | 0 | 0 | 0 | 0 |
| Totals | 48 | 16 | 19 | 16 | 30 | 14 | 0 |

a-Walked for Garber in 4th.
b-Grounded out for Reed in 6th.
c-Singled for Twitchell in 8th.
d-Struck out for Summers in 8th.
e-Singled for McGraw in 10th.
f-Doubled for Schultz in 10th.

| | | | | | | | | | | |
|---|---|---|---|---|---|---|---|---|---|---|
| PHILLIES | 0 | 1 | 0 | 1 | 2 | 0 | 3 | 5 | 3 | 3—18 |
| Chicago | 0 | 7 | 5 | 1 | 0 | 0 | 0 | 0 | 2 | 1—16 |

Double Play: Trillo, Rosello and Thorton; Schmidt, Cash and Allen. Left on Base: Phillies 8, Chicago 12. Twbase hits: Cardenal, Madlock 2, Thorton, Boone, Adams. Three-base hits: Johnstone, Bowa. Home Run: Maddox (1), Swisher (1), Monday 2 (3), Schmidt 4 (5), Boone (1). Sacrifice: R. Reuschel, Johnstone. Sacrifice Fly: Luzinski, Cash.

| | IP | H | R | ER | BB | SO |
|---|---|---|---|---|---|---|
| Carlton | 1 2/3 | 7 | 7 | 7 | 2 | 1 |
| Schueler | 2/3 | 3 | 3 | 3 | 0 | 0 |
| Garber | 2/3 | 2 | 2 | 2 | 1 | 1 |
| Reed | 2 | 1 | 1 | 1 | 1 | 1 |
| Twitchell | 2 | 0 | 0 | 0 | 1 | 1 |
| McG'w (W, 1-1) | 2 | 4 | 2 | 2 | 1 | 2 |
| Underwood | 2/3 | 2 | 1 | 1 | 0 | 1 |
| Lonborg | 1/3 | 0 | 0 | 0 | 0 | 0 |
| R. Reuschel | 7 | 14 | 7 | 7 | 1 | 4 |
| Garman | 2/3 | 4 | 5 | 5 | 1 | 1 |
| Kno'les (L, 1-1) | 1 1/3 | 3 | 4 | 4 | 1 | 0 |
| P. Reuschel | 0 | 3 | 2 | 2 | 1 | 0 |
| Schultz | 1 | 0 | 0 | 0 | 0 | 0 |

Save: Longborg (1), Hit by Pitcher: By Schueler (R. Reuschel), by Garber (Thorton), by Twitchell (Monday). B: Schultz. Umpires: Olsen, Davidson, Rennert, Vargo. Time, 3:42. Attendance, 28,287.

# PHILLIES WIN DIVISION
## Philadelphia at Montreal
### September 26, 1976 First Game

| PHILLIES | ab | r | h | rbi | | MONTREAL | ab | r | h | rbi |
|---|---|---|---|---|---|---|---|---|---|---|
| Cash, 2b | 3 | 1 | 2 | 0 | | Unser, lf | 4 | 0 | 1 | 0 |
| Martin, rf, lf | 4 | 1 | 1 | 0 | | Garrett, 2b | 3 | 1 | 0 | 0 |
| Schmidt, 3b | 4 | 0 | 2 | 0 | | Dawson, cf | 4 | 0 | 1 | 1 |
| Luzinski, lf | 3 | 1 | 1 | 3 | | Valentine, rf | 4 | 0 | 0 | 0 |
| b-Tolan, 1b | 0 | 0 | 0 | 0 | | Williams, 1b | 4 | 0 | 0 | 0 |
| Allen, 1b | 4 | 0 | 0 | 0 | | Parrish, 3b | 3 | 0 | 0 | 0 |
| Brown, rf | 0 | 0 | 0 | 0 | | Foli, ss | 3 | 0 | 2 | 0 |
| Maddox, cf | 4 | 1 | 2 | 0 | | Foote, c | 3 | 0 | 0 | 0 |
| Boone, c | 4 | 0 | 0 | 0 | | Warthen, p | 1 | 0 | 0 | 0 |
| Bowa, ss | 4 | 0 | 1 | 0 | | a-Cromartie | 1 | 0 | 0 | 0 |
| Lonborg, p | 4 | 0 | 1 | 1 | | Kerrigan, p | 0 | 0 | 0 | 0 |
| | | | | | | c-Jorgenson | 1 | 0 | 0 | 0 |
| | | | | | | Murray, p | 0 | 0 | 0 | 0 |
| Totals | 34 | 4 | 10 | 4 | | Totals | 31 | 1 | 4 | 1 |

a-Grounded out for Warthen in sixth.
b-Ran for Luzinski in eighth.
c-Grounded out for Kerrigan in eighth.

| | | | | | | | | | | |
|---|---|---|---|---|---|---|---|---|---|---|
| Phillies | 0 | 0 | 0 | 0 | 0 | 3 | 1 | 0 | 0— | 4 |
| Montreal | 0 | 0 | 0 | 0 | 0 | 1 | 0 | 0 | 0— | 1 |

Errors: Dawson. Left on Base: Phillies 5, Montreal 4. Two-base Hit: Dawson. Three-base hit: Bowa. Home Run: Luzinski (21). Stolen Base: Cash, Maddox.

| | IP | H | R | ER | BB | SO |
|---|---|---|---|---|---|---|
| Lonborg (W, 17-10) | 9 | 4 | 1 | 1 | 1 | 5 |
| Warthen (L, 2-9) | 6 | 4 | 3 | 3 | 1 | 6 |
| Kerrigan | 2 | 5 | 1 | 1 | 0 | 0 |
| Murray | 1 | 1 | 0 | 0 | 0 | 0 |

Hit by Pitcher: by Kerrigan (Luzinski). Winning Pitcher: Warthen. Umpires: Tata, Gorman, B. Williams, McSherry. Time, 2:00.

---

# 1976
## LEAGUE CHAMPIONSHIP SERIES

### Game of Saturday, October 9, at Philadelphia

| Cincinnati | AB. | R. | H. | RBI. | PO. | A. |
|---|---|---|---|---|---|---|
| Rose, 3b | 5 | 1 | 3 | 1 | 1 | 2 |
| Griffey, rf | 4 | 0 | 1 | 0 | 5 | 0 |
| Morgan, 2b | 2 | 0 | 0 | 0 | 1 | 1 |
| Eastwick, p | 0 | 0 | 0 | 0 | 0 | 1 |
| Perez, 1b | 3 | 0 | 0 | 1 | 8 | 0 |
| Foster, lf | 5 | 1 | 1 | 1 | 4 | 0 |
| Bench, c | 5 | 1 | 2 | 0 | 4 | 2 |
| Concepcion, ss | 3 | 2 | 1 | 0 | 0 | 2 |
| Geronimo, cf | 4 | 0 | 0 | 0 | 4 | 0 |
| Gullett, p | 4 | 1 | 2 | 3 | 0 | 0 |
| Flynn, 2b | 0 | 0 | 0 | 0 | 0 | 0 |
| Totals | 35 | 6 | 10 | 6 | 27 | 8 |

| Philadelphia | AB. | R. | H. | RBI. | PO. | A. |
|---|---|---|---|---|---|---|
| Cash, 2b | 4 | 1 | 1 | 0 | 2 | 0 |
| Maddox, cf | 4 | 1 | 2 | 0 | 2 | 0 |
| Schmidt, 3b | 3 | 0 | 0 | 1 | 3 | 3 |
| Luzinski, lf | 3 | 1 | 1 | 1 | 2 | 0 |
| Allen, 1b | 3 | 0 | 1 | 0 | 5 | 0 |
| Brown, rf | 2 | 0 | 0 | 0 | 2 | 0 |
| Johnstone, ph | 1 | 0 | 1 | 1 | 0 | 0 |
| McCarver, c | 3 | 0 | 0 | 0 | 6 | 0 |
| McGraw, p | 0 | 0 | 0 | 0 | 0 | 0 |
| Tolan, ph | 1 | 0 | 0 | 0 | 0 | 0 |
| Bowa, ss | 3 | 0 | 0 | 0 | 1 | 4 |
| Hutton, ph | 1 | 0 | 0 | 0 | 0 | 0 |
| Carlton, p | 2 | 0 | 0 | 0 | 0 | 0 |
| Boone, c | 1 | 0 | 0 | 0 | 4 | 0 |
| Totals | 31 | 3 | 6 | 3 | 27 | 7 |

| | | | | | | | | | |
|---|---|---|---|---|---|---|---|---|---|
| Cincinnati | 0 | 0 | 1 | 0 | 0 | 2 | 0 | 3 | 0—6 |
| Philadelphia | 1 | 0 | 0 | 0 | 0 | 0 | 0 | 0 | 2—3 |

| Cincinnati | IP. | H. | R. | ER. | BB. | SO. |
|---|---|---|---|---|---|---|
| Gullett (Winner) | 8 | 2 | 1 | 1 | 3 | 4 |
| Eastwick | 1 | 4 | 2 | 2 | 0 | 0 |
| Philadelphia | IP. | H. | R. | ER. | BB. | SO. |
| Carlton (Loser) | 7* | 8 | 5 | 4 | 5 | 6 |
| McGraw | 2 | 2 | 1 | 1 | 1 | 4 |

*Pitched to two batters in eighth.

Error: Schmidt. Double plays: Philadelphia 2. Left on bases: Cincinnati 9, Philadelphia 5. Two-base hits: Rose 2, Concepcion, Bench, Gullett, Cash, Luzinski. Three-base hits: Rose, Griffey. Home run: Foster. Stolen bases: Griffey, Bench, Morgan 2. Sacrifice flies: Schmidt, Perez. Wild Pitches: McGraw, Eastwick. Umpires: Sudol, Dale, Stello, Vargo, Harvey and Tata. Time, 2:39. Attendance, 62,640.

### Game of Sunday, October 10, at Philadelphia

| Cincinnati | AB. | R. | H. | RBI. | PO. | A. |
|---|---|---|---|---|---|---|
| Rose, 3b | 5 | 2 | 2 | 1 | 1 | 2 |
| Griffey, rf | 4 | 1 | 2 | 1 | 4 | 0 |
| Morgan, 2b | 2 | 1 | 0 | 0 | 5 | 1 |
| Perez, 1b | 3 | 0 | 0 | 1 | 10 | 1 |
| Foster, lf | 4 | 0 | 0 | 1 | 0 | 0 |
| Bench, c | 4 | 0 | 1 | 0 | 4 | 1 |
| Geronimo, cf | 4 | 0 | 1 | 0 | 1 | 0 |
| Concepcion, ss | 3 | 1 | 0 | 0 | 1 | 5 |
| Zachry, p | 1 | 0 | 0 | 0 | 1 | 3 |
| Driessen, ph | 1 | 0 | 0 | 0 | 0 | 0 |
| Borbon, p | 2 | 1 | 0 | 0 | 0 | 0 |
| Totals | 33 | 6 | 6 | 4 | 27 | 13 |

## Game of Sunday, October 10, at Philadelphia (continued)

| Philadelphia | AB. | R. | H. | RBI. | PO. | A. |
|---|---|---|---|---|---|---|
| Cash, 2b | 5 | 0 | 2 | 0 | 0 | 3 |
| Maddox, cf | 4 | 0 | 0 | 0 | 6 | 0 |
| Schmidt, 3b | 5 | 0 | 1 | 0 | 0 | 2 |
| Luzinski, lf | 4 | 1 | 1 | 1 | 4 | 0 |
| Allen, 1b | 3 | 1 | 1 | 0 | 12 | 0 |
| Johnstone, rf | 4 | 0 | 3 | 0 | 1 | 0 |
| Boone, c | 3 | 0 | 2 | 1 | 3 | 2 |
| Bowa, ss | 2 | 0 | 0 | 0 | 1 | 4 |
| Lonborg, p | 1 | 0 | 0 | 0 | 0 | 2 |
| Garber, p | 0 | 0 | 0 | 0 | 0 | 0 |
| Tolan, ph | 1 | 0 | 0 | 0 | 0 | 0 |
| McGraw, p | 0 | 0 | 0 | 0 | 0 | 1 |
| Reed, p | 0 | 0 | 0 | 0 | 0 | 0 |
| McCarver, ph | 1 | 0 | 0 | 0 | 0 | 0 |
| Totals | 33 | 2 | 10 | 2 | 27 | 14 |

| | | | | | | | | | |
|---|---|---|---|---|---|---|---|---|---|
| Cincinnati | 0 | 0 | 0 | 0 | 0 | 4 | 2 | 0 | 0—6 |
| Philadelphia | 0 | 1 | 0 | 0 | 1 | 0 | 0 | 0 | 0—2 |

| Cincinnati | IP. | H. | R. | ER. | BB. | SO. |
|---|---|---|---|---|---|---|
| Zachry (Winner) | 5 | 6 | 2 | 2 | 3 | 3 |
| Borbon (Save) | 4 | 4 | 0 | 0 | 1 | 0 |

| Philadelphia | IP. | H. | R. | ER. | BB. | SO. |
|---|---|---|---|---|---|---|
| Lonborg (Loser) | 5 1/3 | 2 | 3 | 1 | 2 | 2 |
| Garber | 2/3 | 1 | 1 | 0 | 1 | 0 |
| McGraw | 1/3 | 2 | 2 | 2 | 0 | 1 |
| Reed | 2 2/3 | 1 | 0 | 0 | 1 | 1 |

Error: Allen. Double plays: Cincinnati 2. Left on bases: Cincinnati 5, Philadelphia 10. Home run: Luzinski. Stolen base: Griffey. Sacrifice hits: Boone, Lonborg. Sacrifice fly: Perez. Wild pitch: McGraw. Umpires: Dale, Stello, Vargo, Harvey, Tata and Sudol. Time, 2:24. Attendance, 62,651.

## Game of Tuesday, October 12, at Cincinnati

| Philadelphia | AB. | R. | H. | RBI. | PO. | A. |
|---|---|---|---|---|---|---|
| Cash, 2b | 4 | 0 | 1 | 1 | 6 | 5 |
| Maddox, cf | 5 | 1 | 1 | 1 | 1 | 0 |
| Schmidt, 3b | 5 | 1 | 3 | 1 | 1 | 4 |
| Luzinski, lf | 4 | 0 | 1 | 1 | 0 | 0 |
| Reed, p | 1 | 0 | 0 | 0 | 0 | 0 |
| Garber, p | 0 | 0 | 0 | 0 | 0 | 0 |
| Underwood, p | 0 | 0 | 0 | 0 | 0 | 0 |
| Allen, 1b | 3 | 0 | 0 | 0 | 11 | 0 |
| Martin, lf | 1 | 1 | 0 | 0 | 1 | 0 |
| Johnstone, rf | 4 | 1 | 4 | 1 | 2 | 0 |
| Boone, c | 3 | 0 | 0 | 0 | 1 | 0 |
| Harmon, pr | 0 | 1 | 0 | 0 | 0 | 0 |
| Oates, c | 1 | 0 | 0 | 0 | 1 | 0 |
| Bowa, ss | 3 | 1 | 1 | 1 | 0 | 3 |
| Kaat, p | 2 | 0 | 1 | 0 | 0 | 1 |
| Tolan, lf-1b | 0 | 0 | 0 | 0 | 1 | 0 |
| Totals | 36 | 6 | 11 | 6 | 25 | 13 |

241

## Game of Tuesday, October 12, at Cincinnati (continued)

| Cincinnati | AB. | R. | H. | RBI. | PO. | A. |
|---|---|---|---|---|---|---|
| Rose, 3b | 4 | 0 | 1 | 0 | 0 | 1 |
| Griffey, rf | 5 | 1 | 2 | 1 | 2 | 0 |
| Morgan, 2b | 3 | 1 | 0 | 0 | 3 | 3 |
| Perez, 1b | 4 | 1 | 2 | 1 | 9 | 1 |
| Foster, lf | 3 | 1 | 1 | 2 | 3 | 0 |
| Bench, c | 3 | 2 | 1 | 1 | 3 | 1 |
| Concepcion, ss | 4 | 1 | 1 | 0 | 1 | 5 |
| Geronimo, cf | 3 | 0 | 1 | 2 | 5 | 0 |
| Nolan, p | 0 | 0 | 0 | 0 | 1 | 0 |
| Sarmiento, p | 1 | 0 | 0 | 0 | 0 | 0 |
| Borbon, p | 0 | 0 | 0 | 0 | 0 | 0 |
| Lum, ph | 1 | 0 | 0 | 0 | 0 | 0 |
| Eastwick, p | 0 | 0 | 0 | 0 | 0 | 0 |
| Armbrister, ph | 0 | 0 | 0 | 0 | 0 | 0 |
| Totals | 31 | 7 | 9 | 7 | 27 | 11 |

| | | | | | | | | | |
|---|---|---|---|---|---|---|---|---|---|
| Philadelphia | 0 | 0 | 0 | 1 | 0 | 0 | 2 | 2 | 1 — 6 |
| Cincinnati | 0 | 0 | 0 | 0 | 0 | 0 | 4 | 0 | 3 — 7 |

One out when winning run scored.

| Philadelphia | IP. | H. | R. | ER. | BB. | SO. |
|---|---|---|---|---|---|---|
| Kaat | 6* | 2 | 2 | 2 | 2 | 1 |
| Reed | 2† | 5 | 4 | 4 | 1 | 1 |
| Garber (Loser) | 0† | 1 | 1 | 1 | 0 | 0 |
| Underwood | 1/3 | 1 | 0 | 0 | 2 | 0 |
| Cincinnati | IP. | H. | R. | ER. | BB. | SO. |
| Nolan | 5 2/3 | 6 | 1 | 1 | 2 | 1 |
| Sarmiento | 1 | 2 | 2 | 2 | 1 | 0 |
| Borbon | 1/3 | 0 | 0 | 0 | 0 | 0 |
| Eastwick (Winner) | 2 | 3 | 3 | 2 | 2 | 1 |

*Pitched to two batters in seventh.
†Pitched to two batters in ninth.
†Pitched to one batter in ninth.

Errors: Rose, Perez. Double plays: Philadelphia 1, Cincinnati 1. Left on bases: Philadelphia 10. Cincinnati 6. Two-base hits: Maddox, Schmidt 2, Luzinski, Johnstone, Bowa. Three-base hits: Johnstone, Geronimo. Home runs: Foster, Bench. Sacrifice hits: Kaat, Armbrister. Sacrifice flies: Cash, Foster. Wild pitch: Eastwick. Umpires: Stello, Vargo, Harvey, Tata, Sudol and Dale. Time, 2:43. Attendance, 55,047.

---

## PHILLIES WIN DIVISION
### September 27, 1977, at Chicago

| PHILLIES | ab | r | h | rbi | o | a | e |
|---|---|---|---|---|---|---|---|
| McBride, rf | 6 | 1 | 2 | 0 | 5 | 0 | 1 |
| Bowa, ss | 6 | 3 | 4 | 0 | 1 | 3 | 0 |
| Schmidt, 3b | 5 | 3 | 2 | 2 | 1 | 1 | 0 |
| Luzinski, lf | 4 | 1 | 1 | 1 | 3 | 0 | 1 |
| Martin, 1b | 1 | 0 | 1 | 2 | 0 | 0 | 0 |
| Hebner, 1b | 1 | 1 | 0 | 0 | 7 | 0 | 0 |
| b-Brown | 1 | 0 | 0 | 0 | 0 | 0 | 0 |
| Hutton, 1b | 2 | 0 | 1 | 0 | 2 | 0 | 0 |
| Maddox, cf | 4 | 1 | 1 | 2 | 3 | 0 | 0 |
| Boone, c | 5 | 2 | 2 | 3 | 5 | 0 | 0 |
| Sizemore, 2b | 3 | 1 | 1 | 0 | 0 | 1 | 0 |
| Christenson, p | 3 | 1 | 1 | 5 | 0 | 1 | 0 |
| McGraw, p | 0 | 1 | 0 | 0 | 0 | 1 | 0 |
| Totals | 41 | 15 | 16 | 15 | 27 | 7 | 2 |

| CHICAGO | ab | r | h | rbi | o | a | e |
|---|---|---|---|---|---|---|---|
| DeJesus, ss | 5 | 2 | 4 | 1 | 3 | 4 | 0 |
| Gross, cf | 5 | 2 | 2 | 2 | 1 | 0 | 0 |
| Blittner, 1b | 4 | 1 | 1 | 1 | 14 | 0 | 0 |
| Murcer, rf | 4 | 0 | 1 | 1 | 2 | 0 | 0 |
| Ontiveros, 3b | 5 | 1 | 3 | 2 | 1 | 5 | 0 |
| Clines, lf | 5 | 1 | 2 | 1 | 1 | 0 | 0 |
| Trillo, 2b | 4 | 1 | 2 | 0 | 1 | 3 | 1 |
| Gordon, c | 5 | 0 | 0 | 0 | 4 | 1 | 0 |
| Bonham, p | 2 | 1 | 1 | 0 | 0 | 0 | 0 |
| a-Cardenal | 1 | 0 | 0 | 0 | 0 | 0 | 0 |
| P. Reuschel, p | 0 | 0 | 0 | 0 | 0 | 1 | 0 |
| Roberts, p | 0 | 0 | 0 | 0 | 0 | 0 | 0 |
| Lamp, p | 0 | 0 | 0 | 0 | 0 | 0 | 0 |
| c-Wallis | 1 | 0 | 0 | 0 | 0 | 0 | 0 |
| Giusti, p | 0 | 0 | 0 | 0 | 0 | 0 | 0 |
| Moore, p | 0 | 0 | 0 | 0 | 0 | 1 | 0 |
| d-Rosello | 1 | 0 | 0 | 0 | 0 | 0 | 0 |
| Totals | 42 | 9 | 16 | 8 | 27 | 15 | 1 |

a-Fouled out for Bonham in sixth.
b-Struck out for Hebner in seventh.
c-Struck out for Lamp in eighth.
d-Hit into doubleplay for Moore in ninth.

| | | | | | | | | | |
|---|---|---|---|---|---|---|---|---|---|
| PHILLIES | 0 | 2 | 0 | 0 | 0 | 2 | 7 | 1 | 3 — 15 |
| Chicago | 0 | 0 | 1 | 0 | 0 | 1 | 2 | 5 | 0 — 9 |

Double play: Moore, DeJesus and Blittner, McGraw, Bowa and Hutton. Left on bases: Phillies, 8, Chicago 9. Two-base hit: Bonham, Ontiveros, Clines, Trillo. Three-base hits: Gross. Home Run: Christenson (3), Schmidt (38). Stolen Base: DeJesus 2. Sacrifice: Christenson, Hebner. Sacrifice flies: Murcer. Errors: Luzinski, McBride, Trillo.

| | IP | H | R | ER | BB | SO |
|---|---|---|---|---|---|---|
| Chr'n (W, 18-6) | 7 | 10 | 6 | 5 | 2 | 3 |
| McGraw | 2 | 6 | 3 | 3 | 0 | 2 |
| B'am (L, 10-13) | 6 | 5 | 4 | 4 | 3 | 3 |
| P. Reuschel | 1/3 | 2 | 2 | 2 | 0 | 0 |
| Roberts | 1/3 | 0 | 1 | 1 | 1 | 1 |
| Lamp | 1 1/3 | 5 | 5 | 5 | 1 | 0 |
| Giusti | 1/3 | 4 | 3 | 3 | 1 | 0 |
| Moore | 2/3 | 0 | 0 | 0 | 0 | 0 |

Hit by pitcher: By Bonham (Schmidt). Wild Pitch: P. Reuschel. Umpires: Olsen, Harvey, Rennert, Colosi. Time, 2:42. Attendance, 4,606.

# 1977 LEAGUE CHAMPIONSHIP SERIES
## Game of Tuesday, October 4, at Los Angeles

| Philadelphia | AB. | R. | H. | RBI. | PO. | A. |
|---|---|---|---|---|---|---|
| McBride, cf | 5 | 1 | 2 | 0 | 3 | 0 |
| Bowa, ss | 5 | 2 | 1 | 0 | 0 | 5 |
| Schmidt, 3b | 5 | 2 | 1 | 1 | 1 | 5 |
| Luzinski, lf | 3 | 1 | 1 | 2 | 1 | 0 |
| Johnson, 1b | 4 | 0 | 1 | 2 | 8 | 0 |
| Hutton, 1b | 1 | 0 | 0 | 0 | 5 | 0 |
| Martin, rf | 3 | 0 | 0 | 0 | 1 | 0 |
| Johnstone, ph-rf | 1 | 0 | 0 | 0 | 0 | 0 |
| McCarver, c | 3 | 1 | 1 | 0 | 4 | 0 |
| Boone, c | 0 | 0 | 0 | 0 | 1 | 0 |
| Sizemore, 2b | 3 | 0 | 0 | 0 | 3 | 2 |
| Carlton, p | 2 | 0 | 2 | 1 | 0 | 0 |
| Garber, p | 0 | 0 | 0 | 0 | 0 | 1 |
| Hebner, ph | 1 | 0 | 0 | 0 | 0 | 0 |
| McGraw, p | 0 | 0 | 0 | 0 | 0 | 0 |
| Totals | 36 | 7 | 9 | 6 | 27 | 13 |

| Los Angeles | AB. | R. | H. | RBI. | PO. | A. |
|---|---|---|---|---|---|---|
| Lopes, 2b | 5 | 1 | 2 | 1 | 3 | 3 |
| Russell, ss | 5 | 1 | 0 | 0 | 2 | 3 |
| Smith, rf | 4 | 1 | 0 | 0 | 1 | 0 |
| Cey, 3b | 4 | 1 | 2 | 4 | 2 | 4 |
| Garvey, 1b | 4 | 0 | 3 | 0 | 12 | 0 |
| Baker, lf | 3 | 0 | 1 | 0 | 0 | 0 |
| Burke, cf | 3 | 0 | 0 | 0 | 1 | 0 |
| Monday, ph-cf | 1 | 0 | 0 | 0 | 0 | 0 |
| Yeager, c | 4 | 0 | 0 | 0 | 6 | 1 |
| John, p | 1 | 0 | 0 | 0 | 0 | 1 |
| Garman, p | 0 | 0 | 0 | 0 | 0 | 0 |
| Lacy, ph | 1 | 1 | 1 | 0 | 0 | 0 |
| Hough, p | 0 | 0 | 0 | 0 | 0 | 1 |
| Grote, ph | 0 | 0 | 0 | 0 | 0 | 0 |
| Sosa, p | 1 | 0 | 0 | 0 | 0 | 0 |
| Totals | 36 | 5 | 9 | 5 | 27 | 13 |

| | | | | | | | | | |
|---|---|---|---|---|---|---|---|---|---|
| Philadelphia | 2 | 0 | 0 | 0 | 2 | 1 | 0 | 0 | 2—7 |
| Los Angeles | 0 | 0 | 0 | 0 | 1 | 0 | 4 | 0 | 0—5 |

| Philadelphia | IP. | H. | R. | ER. | BB. | SO. |
|---|---|---|---|---|---|---|
| Carlton | 6 2/3 | 9 | 5 | 5 | 3 | 3 |
| Garber (Winner) | 1 1/3 | 0 | 0 | 0 | 0 | 2 |
| McGraw (Save) | 1 | 0 | 0 | 0 | 0 | 0 |

| Los Angeles | IP. | H. | R. | ER. | BB. | SO. |
|---|---|---|---|---|---|---|
| John | 4 2/3 | 4 | 4 | 0 | 3 | 3 |
| Garman | 1/3 | 0 | 0 | 0 | 0 | 1 |
| Hough | 2 | 2 | 1 | 1 | 0 | 3 |
| Sosa (Loser) | 2 | 3 | 2 | 2 | 0 | 0 |

Errors: Russell 2. Double play: Los Angeles 1. Left on bases: Philadelphia 7, Los Angeles 7. Home runs: Luzinski, Cey. Stolen bases: Luzinski, Garvey. Sacrifice hit: Sizemore. Hit by pitcher: By John (Carlton). Balks: Carlton, Sosa. Umpires: Pryor, Engel, Wendelstedt, Froemming, Rennert and Runge. Time, 2:35. Attendance, 55,968.

### Game of Wednesday, October 5, at Los Angeles

| Philadelphia | AB. | R. | H. | RBI. | PO. | A. |
|---|---|---|---|---|---|---|
| McBride, cf | 4 | 1 | 2 | 1 | 0 | 1 |
| Bowa, ss | 4 | 0 | 1 | 0 | 0 | 5 |
| Schmidt, 3b | 4 | 0 | 0 | 0 | 1 | 1 |
| Luzinski, lf | 4 | 0 | 1 | 0 | 0 | 0 |
| Hebner, 1b | 4 | 0 | 2 | 0 | 11 | 0 |
| Johnstone, rf | 4 | 0 | 1 | 0 | 4 | 0 |
| Boone, c | 4 | 0 | 1 | 0 | 6 | 1 |
| Sizemore, 2b | 4 | 0 | 1 | 0 | 2 | 1 |
| Lonborg, p | 1 | 0 | 0 | 0 | 0 | 2 |
| Hutton, ph | 1 | 0 | 0 | 0 | 0 | 0 |
| Reed, p | 0 | 0 | 0 | 0 | 0 | 0 |
| Brown, ph | 1 | 0 | 0 | 0 | 0 | 0 |
| Brusstar, p | 0 | 0 | 0 | 0 | 0 | 0 |
| Totals | 35 | 1 | 9 | 1 | 24 | 11 |

| Los Angeles | AB. | R. | H. | RBI. | PO. | A. |
|---|---|---|---|---|---|---|
| Lopes, 2b | 4 | 0 | 1 | 1 | 2 | 1 |
| Russell, ss | 4 | 2 | 2 | 0 | 3 | 2 |
| Smith, rf | 4 | 1 | 2 | 1 | 2 | 0 |
| Cey, 3b | 3 | 1 | 1 | 0 | 2 | 1 |
| Garvey, 1b | 3 | 1 | 0 | 0 | 7 | 1 |
| Baker, lf | 4 | 1 | 1 | 4 | 3 | 0 |
| Monday, cf | 3 | 1 | 1 | 0 | 3 | 0 |
| Burke, cf | 0 | 0 | 0 | 0 | 0 | 0 |
| Yeager, c | 3 | 0 | 1 | 1 | 5 | 0 |
| Sutton, p | 3 | 0 | 0 | 0 | 0 | 2 |
| Totals | 31 | 7 | 9 | 7 | 27 | 7 |

| | | | | | | | | | |
|---|---|---|---|---|---|---|---|---|---|
| Philadelphia | 0 | 0 | 1 | 0 | 0 | 0 | 0 | 0 | 0 — 1 |
| Los Angeles | 0 | 0 | 1 | 4 | 0 | 1 | 1 | 0 | x — 7 |

| Philadelphia | IP. | H. | R. | ER. | BB. | SO. |
|---|---|---|---|---|---|---|
| Lonborg (Loser) | 4 | 5 | 5 | 5 | 1 | 1 |
| Reed | 2 | 2 | 1 | 1 | 1 | 2 |
| Brusstar | 2 | 2 | 1 | 1 | 0 | 2 |

| Los Angeles | IP. | H. | R. | ER. | BB. | SO. |
|---|---|---|---|---|---|---|
| Sutton (Winner) | 9 | 9 | 1 | 1 | 0 | 4 |

Errors: Sizemore, Lopes. Double play: Los Angeles 2. Left on bases: Philadelphia 7, Los Angeles 3. Two-base hits: Luzinski, Monday. Three-base hits: Smith. Home runs: McBride, Baker. Stolen base: Cey. Sacrifice hit: Cey. Umpires: Engel, Wendelstedt, Froemming, Rennert, Runge and Pryor. Time, 2:14. Attendance, 55,973.

## 1977 League Championship Series (continued)
### Game of Friday, October 7, at Philadelphia

| Los Angeles | AB. | R. | H. | RBI. | PO. | A. |
|---|---|---|---|---|---|---|
| Lopes, 2b | 5 | 1 | 1 | 1 | 3 | 3 |
| Russell, ss | 5 | 0 | 2 | 1 | 5 | 2 |
| Smith, rf | 5 | 0 | 0 | 0 | 2 | 0 |
| Cey, 3b | 4 | 1 | 1 | 0 | 1 | 4 |
| Garvey, 1b | 4 | 1 | 1 | 0 | 9 | 0 |
| Baker, lf | 4 | 1 | 2 | 2 | 0 | 0 |
| Monday, cf | 3 | 0 | 1 | 0 | 3 | 0 |
| Grote, c | 0 | 0 | 0 | 0 | 0 | 0 |
| Yeager, c | 2 | 0 | 1 | 1 | 3 | 0 |
| Davalillo, ph | 1 | 1 | 1 | 0 | 0 | 0 |
| Burke, cf | 0 | 0 | 0 | 0 | 1 | 0 |
| Hooton, p | 1 | 0 | 1 | 0 | 0 | 1 |
| Rhoden, p | 1 | 0 | 0 | 0 | 0 | 0 |
| Goodson, ph | 1 | 0 | 0 | 0 | 0 | 0 |
| Rau, p | 0 | 0 | 0 | 0 | 0 | 0 |
| Sosa, p | 0 | 0 | 0 | 0 | 0 | 1 |
| Rautzhan, p | 0 | 0 | 0 | 0 | 0 | 0 |
| Mota, ph | 1 | 1 | 1 | 0 | 0 | 0 |
| Garman, p | 0 | 0 | 0 | 0 | 0 | 0 |
| Totals | 37 | 6 | 12 | 5 | 27 | 11 |

| Philadelphia | AB. | R. | H. | RBI. | PO. | A. |
|---|---|---|---|---|---|---|
| McBride, rf | 4 | 0 | 0 | 1 | 1 | 1 |
| Bowa, ss | 4 | 0 | 0 | 1 | 0 | 5 |
| Schmidt, 3b | 4 | 0 | 0 | 0 | 1 | 6 |
| Luzinski, lf | 3 | 0 | 1 | 0 | 0 | 1 |
| Martin, pr | 0 | 0 | 0 | 0 | 0 | 0 |
| Hebner, 1b | 5 | 2 | 1 | 0 | 14 | 0 |
| Maddox, cf | 4 | 1 | 1 | 1 | 3 | 0 |
| Boone, c | 4 | 1 | 2 | 0 | 6 | 0 |
| Sizemore, 2b | 3 | 1 | 1 | 0 | 2 | 3 |
| Christenson, p | 0 | 0 | 0 | 1 | 0 | 0 |
| Brusstar, p | 0 | 0 | 0 | 0 | 0 | 0 |
| Hutton, ph | 1 | 0 | 0 | 0 | 0 | 0 |
| Reed, p | 0 | 0 | 0 | 0 | 0 | 0 |
| McCarver, ph | 1 | 0 | 0 | 0 | 0 | 0 |
| Garber, p | 0 | 0 | 0 | 0 | 0 | 1 |
| Totals | 33 | 5 | 6 | 4 | 27 | 17 |

| | | | | | | | | | |
|---|---|---|---|---|---|---|---|---|---|
| Los Angeles | 0 | 2 | 0 | 1 | 0 | 0 | 0 | 0 | 3—6 |
| Philadelphia | 0 | 3 | 0 | 0 | 0 | 0 | 0 | 2 | 0—5 |

| Los Angeles | IP. | H. | R. | ER. | BB. | SO. |
|---|---|---|---|---|---|---|
| Hooton | 1 2/3 | 2 | 3 | 3 | 4 | 1 |
| Rhoden | 4 1/3 | 2 | 0 | 0 | 2 | 0 |
| Rau | 1 | 0 | 0 | 0 | 0 | 1 |
| Sosa | 2/3 | 2 | 2 | 1 | 0 | 0 |
| Rautzhan (Winner | 1/3 | 0 | 0 | 0 | 0 | 0 |
| Garman (Save) | 1 | 0 | 0 | 0 | 0 | 0 |

| Philadelphia | IP. | H. | R. | ER. | BB. | SO. |
|---|---|---|---|---|---|---|
| Christenson | 3 1/3 | 7 | 3 | 3 | 0 | 2 |
| Brusstar | 2/3 | 0 | 0 | 0 | 1 | 0 |
| Reed | 2 | 1 | 0 | 0 | 1 | 2 |
| Garber (Loser) | 3 | 4 | 3 | 2 | 0 | 0 |

246

## Game of Friday, October 7, at Philadelphia (continued)

Errors: Cey, Sizemore, Garber, Smith. Double play: Philadelphia 1. Left on bases: Los Angeles 6, Philadelphia 9. Two-base hits: Baker, Hooton, Cey, Russell, Hebner, Mota. Sacrifice hit: Garber. Hit by pitcher: By Garman (Luzinski) Passed ball: Boone. Umpires: Wendelstedt, Froemming, Rennert, Runge, Pryor and Engel. Time, 2:51. Attendance, 63,719.

## Game of Saturday, October 8, at Philadelphia

| Los Angeles | AB. | R. | H. | RBI. | PO. | A. |
|---|---|---|---|---|---|---|
| Lopes, 2b | 3 | 0 | 0 | 0 | 1 | 3 |
| Russell, ss | 4 | 0 | 1 | 1 | 1 | 5 |
| Smith, rf | 3 | 0 | 1 | 0 | 2 | 0 |
| Cey, 3b | 2 | 1 | 0 | 0 | 2 | 5 |
| Garvey, 1b | 2 | 0 | 0 | 0 | 12 | 0 |
| Baker, lf | 3 | 2 | 1 | 2 | 0 | 0 |
| Burke, cf | 4 | 0 | 0 | 0 | 1 | 0 |
| Yeager, c | 4 | 1 | 1 | 0 | 8 | 0 |
| John, p | 4 | 0 | 1 | 0 | 0 | 0 |
| Totals | 29 | 4 | 5 | 3 | 27 | 13 |

| Philadelphia | AB. | R. | H. | RBI. | PO. | A. |
|---|---|---|---|---|---|---|
| McBride, rf | 5 | 0 | 0 | 0 | 2 | 0 |
| Bowa, ss | 4 | 0 | 0 | 0 | 0 | 2 |
| Schmidt, 3b | 3 | 0 | 0 | 0 | 1 | 3 |
| Luzinski, lf | 4 | 1 | 1 | 0 | 3 | 0 |
| Hebner, 1b | 4 | 0 | 2 | 0 | 7 | 0 |
| Maddox, cf | 3 | 0 | 2 | 1 | 3 | 0 |
| McCarver, c | 2 | 0 | 0 | 0 | 3 | 0 |
| Reed, p | 0 | 0 | 0 | 0 | 0 | 0 |
| Brown, ph | 1 | 0 | 0 | 0 | 0 | 0 |
| McGraw, p | 0 | 0 | 0 | 0 | 0 | 0 |
| Martin, ph | 1 | 0 | 0 | 0 | 0 | 0 |
| Garber, p | 0 | 0 | 0 | 0 | 0 | 0 |
| Sizemore, 2b | 3 | 0 | 1 | 0 | 3 | 2 |
| Carlton, p | 2 | 0 | 0 | 0 | 0 | 0 |
| Boone, c | 2 | 0 | 1 | 0 | 5 | 1 |
| Totals | 34 | 1 | 7 | 1 | 27 | 8 |

| | | | | | | | | | |
|---|---|---|---|---|---|---|---|---|---|
| Los Angeles | 0 | 2 | 0 | 0 | 2 | 0 | 0 | 0 | 0 – 4 |
| Philadelphia | 0 | 0 | 0 | 1 | 0 | 0 | 0 | 0 | 0 – 1 |

| Los Angeles | IP. | H. | R. | ER. | BB. | SO. |
|---|---|---|---|---|---|---|
| John (Winner) | 9 | 7 | 1 | 1 | 2 | 8 |

| Philadelphia | IP. | H. | R. | ER. | BB. | SO. |
|---|---|---|---|---|---|---|
| Carlton (Loser) | 5* | 4 | 4 | 4 | 5 | 3 |
| Reed | 1 | 0 | 0 | 0 | 0 | 1 |
| McGraw | 2 | 1 | 0 | 0 | 2 | 3 |
| Garber | 1 | 0 | 0 | 0 | 0 | 1 |

*Pitched to one batter in sixth.

Errors: None. Double plays: Philadelphia 2. Left on bases: Los Angeles 6, Philadelphia 9. Two-base hit: Hebner. Home run: Baker. Stolen base: Smith. Sacrifice hit: Garvey. Hit by pitcher: By John (Maddox). Wild pitch: Carlton. Umpires: Froemming, Rennert, Runge, Pryor, Engel and Wendelstedt. Time, 2:39. Attendance, 64,924.

# PHILLIES WIN DIVISION
## September 30, 1978    At Pittsburgh

| PHILADELPHIA | ab | r | h | bi | PITTSBURGH | ab | r | h | bi |
|---|---|---|---|---|---|---|---|---|---|
| McBride, rf | 6 | 2 | 3 | 0 | Taveras, ss | 5 | 0 | 1 | 0 |
| Bowa, ss | 6 | 1 | 1 | 0 | Moreno, cf | 4 | 2 | 0 | 1 |
| G Mddx, cf | 4 | 2 | 3 | 0 | Parker, rf | 5 | 2 | 2 | 2 |
| Luzinski, lf | 4 | 1 | 3 | 3 | B Rbnsn, 3b | 5 | 1 | 3 | 1 |
| J Martin, lf | 0 | 1 | 0 | 0 | Stargell, 1b | 5 | 1 | 1 | 4 |
| Hebner, 1b | 4 | 1 | 2 | 4 | Garner, 2b | 4 | 0 | 1 | 0 |
| Schmdt, 3b | 3 | 0 | 0 | 1 | Berra, 3b | 2 | 0 | 1 | 0 |
| Boone, c | 5 | 0 | 2 | 0 | Milner, lf | 2 | 0 | 0 | 0 |
| Sizemor, 2b | 2 | 0 | 0 | 0 | Ott, c | 3 | 1 | 2 | 0 |
| Morrsn, ph | 1 | 0 | 0 | 0 | D Robnsn, p | 2 | 0 | 1 | 0 |
| Harrisn, 2b | 0 | 0 | 0 | 0 | G Jacksn, p | 0 | 0 | 0 | 0 |
| Lerch, p | 2 | 2 | 2 | 2 | D May ph | 1 | 0 | 0 | 0 |
| Cardenl, ph | 1 | 0 | 0 | 0 | Whitson, p | 0 | 0 | 0 | 0 |
| Brusstar, p | 0 | 0 | 0 | 0 | Tekulve, p | 0 | 0 | 0 | 0 |
| McCrvr, ph | 1 | 0 | 0 | 0 | Bibby, p | 0 | 0 | 0 | 0 |
| McGraw, p | 0 | 0 | 0 | 0 | Gaston, ph | 1 | 1 | 1 | 0 |
| Reed, p | 0 | 0 | 0 | 0 | | | | | |
| Totals | 39 | 10 | 16 | 10 | Totals | 39 | 8 | 13 | 8 |

| | | | | | | | | | |
|---|---|---|---|---|---|---|---|---|---|
| Philadelphia | 1 | 1 | 0 | 1 | 0 | 3 | 0 | 4 | 0 — 10 |
| Pittsburgh | 4 | 0 | 0 | 0 | 0 | 0 | 0 | 0 | 4 — 8 |

Error: Taveras, G Jackson, Bowa. Double play: Pittsburgh 1. Left on base: Philadelphia 10, Pittsburgh 7. Two-base hit: Hebner 2, Luzinski, B Robinson. Home run: Lerch 2 (3), Stargel (28), Luzinski (35). Stolen base: Garner. Sacrifice: Harrelson, G. Maddox, McGraw. Sacrifice fly: Schmidt.

| Philadelphia | IP | H | R | ER | BB | SO |
|---|---|---|---|---|---|---|
| Lerch W, 11-8 | 5 | 5 | 4 | 4 | 3 | 4 |
| Brusstar | 1 | 2 | 0 | 0 | 0 | 1 |
| McGraw | 2 1/3 | 5 | 4 | 3 | 0 | 2 |
| Reed | 2/3 | 1 | 0 | 0 | 0 | 1 |
| Pittsburgh | | | | | | |
| D Robinson | 4 | 9 | 3 | 3 | 0 | 1 |
| G Jackson, L, 7-5 | 2 | 3 | 3 | 3 | 1 | 2 |
| Whitson | 1 | 3 | 2 | 2 | 0 | 1 |
| Tekulve | 1 | 1 | 2 | 2 | 0 | 0 |
| Bibby | 1 | 0 | 0 | 0 | 1 | 0 |

Hit by pitcher: Hebner (by D Robinson) Luzinski (by Tekulve). Time, 3:00. Attendance, 28,905.

# 1978 LEAGUE CHAMPIONSHIP SERIES
## Game of Wednesday, October 4, at Philadelphia

| LOS ANGELES | Ab | R | H | BI | O | A |
|---|---|---|---|---|---|---|
| Lopes, 2b | 5 | 2 | 3 | 2 | 2 | 3 |
| Russell, ss | 5 | 1 | 1 | 0 | 2 | 2 |
| Smith, rf | 3 | 1 | 1 | 1 | 1 | 0 |
| North, cf | 1 | 0 | 0 | 0 | 0 | 0 |
| Garvey, 1b | 5 | 3 | 3 | 4 | 6 | 1 |
| Cey, 3b | 5 | 0 | 2 | 1 | 0 | 1 |
| Baker, lf | 3 | 0 | 1 | 0 | 1 | 0 |
| Monday, cf, rf | 4 | 1 | 1 | 0 | 4 | 0 |
| Yeager, c | 4 | 1 | 1 | 1 | 10 | 0 |
| Hooton, p | 2 | 0 | 0 | 0 | 1 | 0 |
| Welch, p | 2 | 0 | 0 | 0 | 0 | 1 |
| Totals | 39 | 9 | 13 | 9 | 27 | 8 |

| PHILLIES | Ab | R | H | BI | O | A |
|---|---|---|---|---|---|---|
| McBride, rf | 5 | 1 | 1 | 0 | 1 | 0 |
| Bowa, ss | 5 | 1 | 3 | 0 | 0 | 4 |
| Maddox, cf | 5 | 0 | 2 | 2 | 4 | 0 |
| Luzinski, lf | 4 | 1 | 1 | 0 | 1 | 1 |
| Hebner, 1b | 4 | 0 | 1 | 1 | 11 | 0 |
| Schmidt, 3b | 3 | 0 | 0 | 1 | 2 | 4 |
| Boone, c | 4 | 0 | 1 | 0 | 6 | 1 |
| Sizemore, 2b | 4 | 1 | 2 | 0 | 2 | 3 |
| Christenson, p | 1 | 1 | 0 | 0 | 0 | 0 |
| Brusstar, p | 0 | 0 | 0 | 0 | 0 | 0 |
| a-Gonzalez | 1 | 0 | 0 | 0 | 0 | 0 |
| Eastwick, p | 0 | 0 | 0 | 0 | 0 | 0 |
| b-McCarver | 1 | 0 | 0 | 0 | 0 | 0 |
| McGraw, p | 0 | 0 | 0 | 0 | 0 | 0 |
| c-Martin | 1 | 1 | 1 | 1 | 0 | 0 |
| Totals | 39 | 5 | 12 | 5 | 27 | 13 |

a-struck out for Brusstar in fifth.
b-flied out for Eastwick in sixth.
c-hit home run for McGraw in ninth.

| | | | | | | | | | | |
|---|---|---|---|---|---|---|---|---|---|---|
| Los Angeles | 0 | 0 | 4 | 2 | 1 | 1 | 0 | 0 | 1 | 9 |
| Phillies | 0 | 1 | 0 | 0 | 0 | 3 | 0 | 0 | 1 | 5 |

Errors: Lopes, Schmidt. Double play: Russell and Garvey, Bowa, Sizemore and Hebner. Left on base: Los Angeles 8, Phillies 7. Two-base hit: Lopes. Three-base hit: Luzinski, Monday, Garvey. Home Run: Garvey 2 (2), Lopes (1), Yeager (1), Martin (1). Sacrifice fly: Schmidt.

| | IP | H | R | Er | Bb | So |
|---|---|---|---|---|---|---|
| Hooton | 4 2/3 | 10 | 4 | 4 | 0 | 5 |
| Welch (W 1-0) | 4 1/3 | 2 | 1 | 1 | 0 | 5 |
| Christnson (L, 0-1) | 4 1/3 | 7 | 7 | 7 | 1 | 3 |
| Brusstar | 2/3 | 1 | 0 | 0 | 0 | 0 |
| Eastwick | 1 | 3 | 1 | 1 | 0 | 1 |
| McGraw | 3 | 2 | 1 | 1 | 3 | 2 |

Hit by pitcher: Smith (by Eastwick). Umpires: Lee, Weyer, hp, Nick Colosi, 1b, Andy Olsen, 2b, Satch Davidson, 3b, Billy Williams, lf, Lee McSherry, rf. Time, 27. Attendance, 63,460.

---

## Game of Thursday, October 5, at Philadelphia

| LOS ANGELES | AB | R | H | BI | O | A |
|---|---|---|---|---|---|---|
| Lopes, 2b | 4 | 1 | 3 | 3 | 4 | 4 |
| Russell, ss | 4 | 0 | 1 | 0 | 1 | 9 |
| Smith, rf | 4 | 0 | 1 | 0 | 0 | 0 |
| north, cf | 0 | 0 | 0 | 0 | 0 | 0 |
| Garvey, 1b | 4 | 0 | 0 | 0 | 16 | 0 |
| Cey, 3b | 4 | 0 | 0 | 0 | 0 | 7 |
| Baker, lf | 4 | 1 | 1 | 0 | 0 | 0 |
| Monday, cf, rf | 4 | 1 | 1 | 0 | 2 | 0 |
| Yeager, c | 3 | 1 | 1 | 1 | 4 | 1 |
| John, p | 3 | 0 | 0 | 0 | 0 | 0 |
| Totals | 34 | 4 | 8 | 4 | 27 | 21 |

| PHILLIES | AB | R | H | BI | O | A |
|---|---|---|---|---|---|---|
| Schmidt, 3b | 4 | 0 | 1 | 0 | 0 | 4 |
| Bowa, ss | 4 | 0 | 0 | 0 | 1 | 4 |
| Maddox, cf | 4 | 0 | 1 | 0 | 5 | 0 |
| Luzinski, lf | 3 | 0 | 1 | 0 | 2 | 0 |
| Cardenal, 1b | 2 | 0 | 0 | 0 | 10 | 0 |
| Boone, c | 3 | 0 | 1 | 0 | 5 | 0 |
| Martin, rf | 2 | 0 | 0 | 0 | 1 | 0 |
| Sizemore, 2b | 3 | 0 | 0 | 0 | 3 | 1 |
| Ruthven, p | 1 | 0 | 0 | 0 | 0 | 0 |
| Brusstar, p | 0 | 0 | 0 | 0 | 0 | 0 |
| a-Morrison | 1 | 0 | 0 | 0 | 0 | 0 |
| Reed, p | 0 | 0 | 0 | 0 | 0 | 0 |
| b-Foote | 1 | 0 | 0 | 0 | 0 | 0 |
| McGraw, p | 0 | 0 | 0 | 0 | 0 | 0 |
| Totals | 28 | 0 | 4 | 0 | 27 | 9 |

a-Struck out for Brusstar in sixth.
b-Struck out for Reed in eighth.

| | | | | | | | | | |
|---|---|---|---|---|---|---|---|---|---|
| Los Angeles | 0 | 0 | 0 | 1 | 2 | 0 | 1 | 0 | 0—4 |
| PHILLIES | 0 | 0 | 0 | 0 | 0 | 0 | 0 | 0 | 0—0 |

Double play: Russell-Lopes-Garvey; Lopes-Russell-Garvey; Cey-Lopes-Garvey. Left on base: Los Angeles 5, Phillies 3. Two-base hit: Smith, Baker. Three-base hit: Lopes. Home run: Lopes (2). Stolen base: Yeager. Sacrifice: John.

| | IP | H | R | ER | BB | SO |
|---|---|---|---|---|---|---|
| John (W,1-0) | 9 | 4 | 0 | 0 | 2 | 4 |
| Ruthven (L,0-1) | 4 2/3 | 6 | 3 | 3 | 0 | 3 |
| Brusstar | 1 1/3 | 0 | 0 | 0 | 0 | 0 |
| Reed | 2 | 2 | 1 | 1 | 0 | 0 |
| McGraw | 1 | 0 | 0 | 0 | 1 | 0 |

Umpires: Nick Colosi, Andy Olsen, Satch Davidson, Billy Williams, John McSherry, Lee Weyer. Time, 2:06. Attendance, 60,643.

---

Game of Friday, October 5, at Los Angeles

| PHILLIES | Ab | R | H | BI | O | A |
|---|---|---|---|---|---|---|
| McBride, rf | 3 | 0 | 0 | 0 | 0 | 0 |
| a-Martin, rf | 2 | 0 | 1 | 1 | 1 | 0 |
| Bowa, ss | 5 | 0 | 1 | 0 | 2 | 4 |
| Maddox, cf | 5 | 1 | 1 | 0 | 3 | 0 |
| Luzinski, lf | 5 | 1 | 3 | 1 | 1 | 0 |
| Hebner, 1b | 4 | 0 | 0 | 0 | 10 | 0 |
| Schmidt, 3b | 4 | 1 | 1 | 0 | 1 | 5 |
| McCarver, c | 3 | 2 | 0 | 1 | 8 | 0 |
| Sizemore, 2b | 2 | 2 | 2 | 1 | 1 | 1 |
| Carlton, p | 4 | 2 | 2 | 4 | 0 | 0 |
| Totals | 37 | 9 | 11 | 8 | 27 | 10 |

## Game of Friday, October 5, at Los Angeles (continued)

| Los Angeles | Ab | R | H | BI | O | A |
|---|---|---|---|---|---|---|
| Lopes, 2b | 4 | 0 | 0 | 0 | 2 | 2 |
| North, cf | 4 | 0 | 0 | 0 | 2 | 0 |
| Smith, rf | 4 | 1 | 1 | 0 | 2 | 0 |
| Garvey, 1b | 4 | 2 | 2 | 2 | 16 | 2 |
| Cey, 3b | 3 | 1 | 1 | 1 | 2 | 3 |
| Baker, lf | 3 | 0 | 1 | 0 | 0 | 0 |
| Russell, s | 4 | 0 | 2 | 1 | 0 | 2 |
| Yeager, c | 3 | 0 | 0 | 0 | 2 | 0 |
| c-Lacy | 1 | 0 | 0 | 0 | 0 | 0 |
| Sutton, p | 2 | 0 | 0 | 0 | 0 | 1 |
| Rautzhan, p | 0 | 0 | 0 | 0 | 0 | 1 |
| b-Mota | 1 | 0 | 1 | 0 | 0 | 0 |
| Hough, p | 0 | 0 | 0 | 0 | 1 | 1 |
| d-Ferguson | 1 | 0 | 0 | 0 | 0 | 0 |
| Totals | 34 | 4 | 8 | 4 | 27 | 12 |

a-doubled for McBride in sixth.
b-doubled for Rautzhan in seventh.
c-flied out for Yeager in ninth.
d-grounded into double play for Hough in ninth.

| | | | | | | | | | |
|---|---|---|---|---|---|---|---|---|---|
| PHILLIES | 0 | 4 | 0 | 0 | 0 | 3 | 1 | 0 | 1 — 9 |
| Los Angeles | 0 | 1 | 2 | 0 | 0 | 0 | 0 | 1 | 0 — 4 |

Errors: Schmidt, Lopes, Smith. Double play: Sizemore-Bowa-Hebner (2). Left on base: Phillies 7, Los Angeles 5. Two-base hit: Schmidt, Russell, Garvey, Martin, Mota. Home run: Carlton (1), Garvey (3), Luzinski (1). Sacrifice: Sizemore, Hebner.

| | IP | H | R | Er | Bb | So |
|---|---|---|---|---|---|---|
| Carlton (w, 1-0) | 9 | 8 | 4 | 4 | 2 | 3 |
| Sutton (L, 0-1) | 5 2/3 | 7 | 7 | 4 | 2 | 0 |
| Rautzhan | 1 1/3 | 3 | 1 | 1 | 2 | 0 |
| Hough | 1 | 1 | 1 | 0 | 1 | |

Umpires: Olsen, Davidson, Williams, McSherry, Colosi, Wever. Time, 2:18. Attendance, 55,043.

---

## Game of Saturday, October 6, at Los Angeles

| PHILLIES | Ab | R | H | BI | O | A |
|---|---|---|---|---|---|---|
| Schmidt, 3b | 4 | 0 | 1 | 0 | 0 | 5 |
| Bowa, ss | 4 | 1 | 2 | 0 | 2 | 3 |
| Maddox, cf | 5 | 0 | 1 | 0 | 4 | 0 |
| Luzinski, lf | 4 | 1 | 1 | 2 | 1 | 0 |
| Cardenal, 1b | 4 | 0 | 1 | 0 | 11 | 0 |
| Martin, rf | 4 | 0 | 0 | 0 | 5 | 0 |
| Boone, c | 4 | 0 | 0 | 0 | 5 | 1 |
| Sizemore, 2b | 4 | 0 | 1 | 0 | 1 | 2 |
| Lerch, p | 2 | 0 | 0 | 0 | 0 | 1 |
| Brusstar, p | 0 | 0 | 0 | 0 | 0 | 0 |
| b-McBride | 1 | 1 | 1 | 1 | 0 | 0 |
| Reed, p | 0 | 0 | 0 | 0 | 0 | 0 |
| e-Hebner | 1 | 0 | 0 | 0 | 0 | 0 |
| McGraw, p | 0 | 0 | 0 | 0 | 0 | 0 |
| Totals | 37 | 3 | 8 | 3 | 29 | 12 |

251

| LOS ANGELES | Ab | R | H | BI | O | A |
|---|---|---|---|---|---|---|
| Lopes, 2b | 5 | 0 | 1 | 0 | 0 | 2 |
| North, cf | 3 | 0 | 0 | 0 | 7 | 0 |
| c-Monday, cf | 2 | 0 | 0 | 0 | 0 | 0 |
| Smith, rf | 5 | 0 | 0 | 0 | 2 | 0 |
| Garvey, 1b | 5 | 1 | 2 | 1 | 6 | 2 |
| Cey, 3b | 4 | 3 | 2 | 1 | 0 | 2 |
| Baker, lf | 5 | 0 | 4 | 1 | 4 | 0 |
| Russell, ss | 4 | 0 | 3 | 1 | 3 | 0 |
| Yeager, c | 3 | 0 | 1 | 0 | 5 | 1 |
| d-Lacy | 1 | 0 | 0 | 0 | 0 | 0 |
| Grote, c | 0 | 0 | 0 | 0 | 2 | 0 |
| Rau, p | 1 | 0 | 0 | 0 | 1 | 0 |
| a-Mota | 0 | 0 | 0 | 0 | 0 | 0 |
| Rhoden, p | 1 | 0 | 0 | 0 | 0 | 2 |
| f-Ferguson | 1 | 0 | 0 | 0 | 0 | 0 |
| Forster, p | 0 | 0 | 0 | 0 | 0 | 0 |
| Totals | 40 | 4 | 13 | 4 | 20 | 9 |

a-hit sacrifice bunt for Rau in fifth.
b-hit home run for Brusstar in seventh.
c-struck out for North in seventh
d-fouled out for Yeager in eighth.
e-fouled out for Reed in ninth.
f-struck out for Rhoden in ninth.
(Two out when winning run scored)

| | | | | | | | | | | |
|---|---|---|---|---|---|---|---|---|---|---|
| PHILLIES | 0 | 0 | 2 | 1 | 0 | 0 | 0 | 0 | 0 | 0 − 3 |
| Los Angeles | 0 | 1 | 0 | 1 | 0 | 1 | 0 | 0 | 0 | 1 − 4 |

Errors: Boone, Maddox. Double play: Sizemore, Bowa and Cardenal. Left on base: Philadelphia 7, Los Angeles 10. Two-base hit: Smith, Cey, Baker. Three-base hit: Sizemore. Home run: Luzinski, Cey, Garvey, McBride. Stolen base: Lopes. Sacrifice hit: Mota.

| | IP | H | R | Er | Bb | So |
|---|---|---|---|---|---|---|
| Lerch | 5 1/3 | 7 | 3 | 3 | 0 | 0 |
| Brusstar | 2/3 | 1 | 0 | 0 | 1 | 0 |
| Reed | 2 | 4 | 0 | 0 | 0 | 1 |
| McGraw (L, 0-1) | 1 2/3 | 1 | 1 | 0 | 1 | 2 |
| Rau | 5 | 5 | 2 | 2 | 2 | 1 |
| Rhoden | 4 | 2 | 1 | 1 | 1 | 3 |
| Forster (W, 1-0) | 1 | 1 | 0 | 0 | 0 | 2 |

Umpires: Davidson, hp, Williams, 1b, McSherry, 2b Weyer, 3b, Colosi, lf, Olsen, rf. Time, 2:53. Attendance, 55,124.

# NO-HIT GAMES BY PHILLIES

(From 1893, when mound was moved to its present distance of sixty feet, six inches, through 1978)

## Red Donahue, July 8, 1898, Boston at Philadelphia

| Boston | ab | r | h | o | a | Philadelphia | ab | r | h | o | a |
|---|---|---|---|---|---|---|---|---|---|---|---|
| Long, ss | 3 | 0 | 0 | 3 | 2 | Cooley, cf | 4 | 0 | 0 | 5 | 0 |
| Tenney, 1b | 4 | 0 | 0 | 6 | 0 | Douglas, 1b | 3 | 2 | 2 | 8 | 0 |
| Duffy, cf | 4 | 0 | 0 | 2 | 0 | Delahanty, lf | 4 | 1 | 3 | 5 | 0 |
| Collins, 3b | 4 | 0 | 0 | 2 | 0 | Lajoie, 2b | 4 | 0 | 0 | 2 | 4 |
| Stahl, lf | 3 | 0 | 0 | 1 | 0 | Flick, rf | 2 | 1 | 0 | 4 | 0 |
| Stivetts, rf | 3 | 0 | 0 | 0 | 0 | McFarland, c | 2 | 0 | 1 | 1 | 0 |
| Lowe, 2b | 3 | 0 | 0 | 3 | 1 | Lauder, 3b | 4 | 0 | 0 | 0 | 1 |
| Bergen, c | 3 | 0 | 0 | 7 | 2 | Cross, ss | 2 | 1 | 1 | 2 | 3 |
| Willis, p | 2 | 0 | 0 | 0 | 2 | Donahue, p | 2 | 0 | 1 | 0 | 0 |
| Totals | 29 | 0 | 0 | 24 | 7 | Totals | 27 | 5 | 7 | 27 | 8 |

| | | | | | | | | | | |
|---|---|---|---|---|---|---|---|---|---|---|
| Boston | 0 | 0 | 0 | 0 | 0 | 0 | 0 | 0 | 0 — 0 |
| Philadelphia | 1 | 1 | 0 | 0 | 3 | 0 | 0 | 0 | x — 5 |

Errors: Cross, Stahl, Lauder. Two-base hit: McFarland. Stolen bases: Long, Douglas, Delahanty 2. Sacrifices: Donahue, Cooley. Left on base: Boston 4, Philadelphia 10. Bases on balls: Donahue 2, Willis 8, Strikeouts: Donahue 1, Willis 7. Hit by pitcher: By Willis (Douglas, Cross) Passed ball: Bergen. Umpires: Gaffney and Brown. Time, 1:50;

---

## Chick Fraser, September 18, 1903 Philadelphia at Chicago

| PHILADELPHIA | ab | r | h | p | a | e |
|---|---|---|---|---|---|---|
| Thomas, cf | 3 | 0 | 1 | 4 | 0 | 0 |
| Hallman, 2b | 5 | 2 | 1 | 2 | 3 | 1 |
| Wolverton, 3b | 4 | 2 | 2 | 1 | 2 | 0 |
| Barry, lf | 5 | 3 | 3 | 1 | 0 | 0 |
| Titus, lf | 4 | 2 | 2 | 1 | 0 | 0 |
| Douglas, 1b | 5 | 1 | 3 | 13 | 0 | 0 |
| Hulswitt, ss | 4 | 0 | 1 | 1 | 5 | 3 |
| Zimmer, c | 4 | 0 | 1 | 4 | 1 | 0 |
| Fraser, p | 3 | 0 | 0 | 0 | 2 | 0 |
| Totals | 37 | 10 | 14 | 27 | 13 | 4 |

| Chicago | ab | r | h | p | a | e |
|---|---|---|---|---|---|---|
| Slagle, cf | 3 | 0 | 0 | 0 | 0 | 1 |
| McCarthy, lf | 4 | 0 | 0 | 1 | 0 | 1 |
| Chance, 1b | 2 | 0 | 0 | 12 | 0 | 0 |
| Jones, rf | 4 | 0 | 0 | 0 | 0 | 0 |
| Tinker, ss | 4 | 0 | 0 | 2 | 5 | 0 |
| Kling, c | 4 | 0 | 0 | 5 | 5 | 1 |
| Evers, 2b | 3 | 0 | 0 | 5 | 5 | 0 |
| Casey, 3b | 2 | 0 | 0 | 2 | 3 | 0 |
| Graham, p | 2 | 0 | 0 | 0 | 3 | 0 |
| Currie, p | 1 | 0 | 0 | 0 | 1 | 0 |
| Totals | 29 | 0 | 0 | 27 | 22 | 3 |

| | | | | | | | | | | |
|---|---|---|---|---|---|---|---|---|---|---|
| Philadelphia | 4 | 0 | 0 | 0 | 2 | 0 | 1 | 0 | 3 — 10 |
| Chicago | 0 | 0 | 0 | 0 | 0 | 0 | 0 | 0 | 0 — 0 |

Left on bases: Chicago 7, Philadelphia 7. Two-base hits: Zimmer, Barry. Double plays: Kling, Casey; Zimmer, Wolverton; Fraser, Hulswitt, Douglas. Sacrifice hit: Titus. Stolen bases: Chance 2. Struck out: By Graham 4, Fraser 4. First base on balls: Off Graham 3, Fraser 5. Hit by pitcher: Wolverton. Umpires: Emslie, and Moran. Time, 1:40. Attendance, 2,000.

## John Lush, May 1, 1906 Philadelphia at Brooklyn

| Philadelphia | ab | r | bh | tb | po | a | e |
|---|---|---|---|---|---|---|---|
| Thomas, cf | 4 | 2 | 2 | 2 | 1 | 0 | 0 |
| Ward, 3b | 5 | 2 | 4 | 6 | 0 | 2 | 0 |
| Magee. rf | 4 | 1 | 1 | 1 | 0 | 0 | 0 |
| Titus, lf | 4 | 1 | 2 | 2 | 2 | 0 | 0 |
| Bransfield, 1b | 4 | 0 | 1 | 1 | 7 | 1 | 0 |
| Doolin, ss | 2 | 0 | 0 | 0 | 1 | 3 | 1 |
| Gleason, 2b | 4 | 0 | 1 | 1 | 2 | 2 | 0 |
| Dooin, c | 4 | 0 | 0 | 0 | 11 | 0 | 0 |
| Lush, p | 4 | 0 | 0 | 0 | 3 | 1 | 0 |
| Totals | 35 | 6 | 11 | 13 | 27 | 9 | 1 |

| Brooklyn | ab | r | bh | tb | po | a | e |
|---|---|---|---|---|---|---|---|
| Lumley, rf | 4 | 0 | 0 | 0 | 3 | 0 | 0 |
| Maloney, cf | 3 | 0 | 0 | 0 | 3 | 0 | 0 |
| Casey, 3b | 4 | 0 | 0 | 0 | 2 | 3 | 2 |
| Jordan, 1b | 4 | 0 | 0 | 0 | 6 | 1 | 0 |
| Batch, lf | 2 | 0 | 0 | 0 | 1 | 0 | 0 |
| Lewis, ss | 2 | 0 | 0 | 0 | 1 | 0 | 0 |
| Hummel, 2b | 3 | 0 | 0 | 0 | 4 | 2 | 0 |
| Bergen, c | 3 | 0 | 0 | 0 | 6 | 3 | 1 |
| Eason, p | 2 | 0 | 0 | 0 | 1 | 2 | 1 |
| *McIntyre | 1 | 0 | 0 | 0 | 0 | 0 | 0 |
| Knolls, p | 0 | 0 | 0 | 0 | 0 | 0 | 1 |
| Totals | 28 | 0 | 0 | 0 | 27 | 11 | 5 |

*Batted for Eason in eighth inning.

| | | | | | | | | | |
|---|---|---|---|---|---|---|---|---|---|
| Philadelphia | 2 | 0 | 0 | 1 | 0 | 0 | 0 | 2 | 1 — 6 |
| Brooklyn | 0 | 0 | 0 | 0 | 0 | 0 | 0 | 0 | 0 — 0 |

Three-base hit: Ward. Hits: Off Eason 9, in eighth innings; off Knolls 2, in one inning. Sacrifice hits: Doolin. Casey, Stolen base: Titus. Left on bases: Philadelphia 6, Brooklyn 4. First base on balls: Off Eason 3, off Knolls 1, off Lush 3. First base on errors: Philadelphia 2, Brooklyn 1. Struck out: By Eason 1, by Knolls 1, by Lush 11. Umpire: O'Day. Time, 1:45

---

## Jim Bunning, June 21, 1964 Philadelphia at New York

| PHILADELPHIA | ab | r | h | tb | po | a | e |
|---|---|---|---|---|---|---|---|
| Briggs, cf | 4 | 1 | 0 | 0 | 2 | 0 | 0 |
| Herrnstein, 1b | 4 | 0 | 0 | 0 | 7 | 0 | 0 |
| Callison, rf | 4 | 1 | 2 | 5 | 1 | 0 | 0 |
| Allen, 3b | 3 | 0 | 1 | 1 | 0 | 2 | 0 |
| Covington, lf | 2 | 0 | 0 | 0 | 1 | 0 | 0 |
| *Wine, ss | 1 | 1 | 0 | 0 | 2 | 1 | 0 |
| T. Taylor, 2b | 3 | 2 | 1 | 1 | 0 | 3 | 0 |
| Rojas, ss-lf | 3 | 0 | 1 | 1 | 3 | 0 | 0 |
| Triandos, c | 4 | 1 | 2 | 3 | 11 | 1 | 0 |
| Bunning, p | 4 | 0 | 1 | 2 | 0 | 0 | 0 |
| Totals | 32 | 6 | 8 | 13 | 27 | 7 | 0 |

254

## Jim Bunning, June 21, 1964 Philadelphia at New York (continued)

| NEW YORK | ab | r | h | tb | po | a | e |
|---|---|---|---|---|---|---|---|
| Hickman, cf | 3 | 0 | 0 | 0 | 2 | 0 | 0 |
| Hunt, 2b | 3 | 0 | 0 | 0 | 3 | 2 | 0 |
| Kranepool, 1b | 3 | 0 | 0 | 0 | 8 | 1 | 0 |
| Christopher, rf | 3 | 0 | 0 | 0 | 4 | 0 | 0 |
| Gonder, c | 3 | 0 | 0 | 0 | 6 | 2 | 0 |
| R. Taylor, lf | 3 | 0 | 0 | 0 | 1 | 0 | 0 |
| C. Smith, ss | 3 | 0 | 0 | 0 | 2 | 1 | 0 |
| Samuel, 3b | 2 | 0 | 0 | 0 | 0 | 1 | 0 |
| ††Altman | 1 | 0 | 0 | 0 | 0 | 0 | 0 |
| Stallard, p | 1 | 0 | 0 | 0 | 0 | 2 | 0 |
| Wakefield, p | 0 | 0 | 0 | 0 | 0 | 0 | 0 |
| †Kanehl | 1 | 0 | 0 | 0 | 0 | 0 | 0 |
| Sturdivant, p | 0 | 0 | 0 | 0 | 1 | 0 | 0 |
| =Stephenson | 1 | 0 | 0 | 0 | 0 | 0 | 0 |
| Totals | 27 | 0 | 0 | 0 | 27 | 9 | 0 |

*Ran for Covington in sixth.
†Grounded out for Wakefield in sixth.
††Struck out for Sameul in ninth.
=Struck out for Sturdivant in ninth.

| | | | | | | | | | |
|---|---|---|---|---|---|---|---|---|---|
| Philadelphia | 1 | 1 | 0 | 0 | 0 | 4 | 0 | 0 | 0 − 6 |
| New York | 0 | 0 | 0 | 0 | 0 | 0 | 0 | 0 | 0 − 0 |

Runs batted in: Callison, Allen, Triandos 2, Bunning 2. Two-base hits: Triandos, Bunning. Home run: Callison. Sacrifices: Herrnstein, Rojas. Left on bases: Philadelphia 5, New York 0. Bases on balls: Off Stallard 4 (Briggs, T. Taylor, Allen, Covington). Strikeouts: By Bunning 10 (Hickman 3, C. Smith, Hunt, Kranepool, Christopher, R. Taylor, Altman, Stephenson), by Stallard 3 (Callison, Herrnstein, Allen), by Sturdivant 3 (Rojas, Triandos, Briggs). Runs and earned runs: Stallard 6-6. Hits: Off Stallard 7 in 5 2/3 innings, off Wakefield 0 in 1/3 inning, off Sturdivant 1 in 3 innings. Wild pitch: Stallard. Winning pitcher: Bunning (7-2). Losing pitcher: Stallard (4-3). Umpires: Sudol, Pryor, Secory and Burkhart. Time, 2:19. Attendance, 32,036.

---

## Rick Wise, June 23, 1971 Philadelphia at Cincinnati

| PHILADELPHIA | ab | r | h | rbi | e | CINCINNATI | ab | r | h | rbi | e |
|---|---|---|---|---|---|---|---|---|---|---|---|
| Harmon, 2b | 4 | 0 | 0 | 0 | 0 | Rose, rf | 4 | 0 | 0 | 0 | 0 |
| Bowa, ss | 4 | 0 | 0 | 0 | 0 | Foster, cf | 3 | 0 | 0 | 0 | 0 |
| McCarver, c | 3 | 0 | 2 | 0 | 0 | May, 1b | 3 | 0 | 0 | 0 | 0 |
| Johnson, 1b | 2 | 0 | 0 | 0 | 0 | Bench, c | 3 | 0 | 0 | 0 | 0 |
| Lis, lf | 2 | 1 | 0 | 0 | 0 | Perez, 3b | 3 | 0 | 0 | 0 | 0 |
| Stone, lf | 1 | 0 | 0 | 0 | 0 | McRae, lf | 3 | 0 | 0 | 0 | 0 |
| Montanez, cf | 4 | 0 | 1 | 0 | 0 | Granger, p | 0 | 0 | 0 | 0 | 0 |
| Freed, rf | 4 | 1 | 1 | 1 | 0 | Helms, 2b | 3 | 0 | 0 | 0 | 0 |
| Vukovich, 3b | 4 | 0 | 1 | 0 | 0 | Concepcion, ss | 1 | 0 | 0 | 0 | 0 |
| Wise, p | 4 | 2 | 2 | 3 | 0 | Stewart, ph | 1 | 0 | 0 | 0 | 0 |
| Totals | 32 | 4 | 7 | 4 | 0 | Grimsley, p | 1 | 0 | 0 | 0 | 0 |
| | | | | | | Carbo, ph | 1 | 0 | 0 | 0 | 0 |
| | | | | | | Carroll, p | 0 | 0 | 0 | 0 | 0 |
| | | | | | | Cline, lf | 1 | 0 | 0 | 0 | 0 |
| | | | | | | Totals | 27 | 0 | 0 | 0 | 0 |

| | | | | | | | | | |
|---|---|---|---|---|---|---|---|---|---|
| Philadelphia | 0 | 1 | 0 | 0 | 2 | 0 | 0 | 1 | 0 − 4 |
| Cincinnati | 0 | 0 | 0 | 0 | 0 | 0 | 0 | 0 | 0 − 0 |

Rick Wise, June 23, 1971 (continued)

| Philadelphia | ip | h | r | er | bb | so |
|---|---|---|---|---|---|---|
| Wise (W, 8-4) | 9 | 0 | 0 | 0 | 1 | 3 |

| Cincinnati | ip | h | r | er | bb | so |
|---|---|---|---|---|---|---|
| Grimsley (L, 4-3) | 6 | 4 | 3 | 3 | 2 | 1 |
| Carroll | 2 | 2 | 1 | 1 | 1 | 1 |
| Granger | 1 | 1 | 0 | 0 | 0 | 1 |

Double plays: Cincinnati 2. Left on bases: Philadelphia 5, Cincinnati 1. Two-base hits: Montanez, Freed. Home runs: Wise 2 (4). Hit by pitcher: By Grimsley (Lis). Umpires: Dale, Gorman, Pelekoudas and Harvey. Time, 1:53. Attendance, 13,329.

# NO-HIT GAMES AGAINST PHILLIES
## Noodles Hahn, July 12, 1900, Philadelphia at Cincinnati

| Philadelphia | ab | r | h | o | a | | Cincinnati | ab | r | h | o | a |
|---|---|---|---|---|---|---|---|---|---|---|---|---|
| Thomas | 4 | 0 | 0 | 0 | 0 | | Barrett, cf | 2 | 1 | 1 | 2 | 0 |
| Slagle, lf | 3 | 0 | 0 | 1 | 0 | | Corcoran, ss | 4 | 1 | 1 | 1 | 5 |
| Delahanty, 1b | 2 | 0 | 0 | 15 | 0 | | Beckley, 1b | 3 | 1 | 1 | 8 | 1 |
| Flick, rf | 2 | 0 | 0 | 1 | 0 | | Crawford, lf | 2 | 1 | 1 | 3 | 0 |
| McFarland, c | 2 | 0 | 0 | 4 | 0 | | McBride, rf | 3 | 0 | 0 | 1 | 0 |
| Wolverton, 3b | 3 | 0 | 0 | 1 | 2 | | Quinn, 2b | 4 | 0 | 0 | 2 | 1 |
| Dolan, 2b | 3 | 0 | 0 | 0 | 4 | | Wood, 3b | 4 | 0 | 1 | 0 | 2 |
| Cross, ss | 3 | 0 | 0 | 2 | 7 | | Peitz, c | 4 | 0 | 0 | 10 | 2 |
| Bernhard, p | 2 | 0 | 0 | 0 | 1 | | Hahn, p | 4 | 0 | 2 | 0 | 1 |
| a-Chiles | 1 | 0 | 0 | 0 | 0 | | Totals | 30 | 4 | 7 | 27 | 12 |
| Totals | 25 | 0 | 0 | 24 | 14 | | | | | | | |

a-Batted for Bernhard in ninth.

| | | | | | | | | | |
|---|---|---|---|---|---|---|---|---|---|
| Philadelphia | 0 | 0 | 0 | 0 | 0 | 0 | 0 | 0 | 0 – 0 |
| Cincinnati | 1 | 0 | 2 | 0 | 0 | 0 | 1 | 0 | x – 4 |

Errors: Wood, Wolverton. Three-base hit: Beckley. Home run: Crawford. Stolen bases: Delahanty, Barrett, Corcoran. Sacrifice: Barrett. Double plays: Bernhard, Cross and Delahanty; Wood, Corcoran and Beckley. Left on base: Philadelphia 1, Cincinnati 8. Bases on balls: Hahn 2, Bernhard 5. Strikeouts: Hahn 8, Bernhard 2. Hit by pitcher: By Hahn (Flick). Wild pitch: Bernhard. Passed ball: McFarland. Umpire: Terry. Time, 1:50.

## Hooks Wiltse, July 4, 1908 Philadelphia at New York

| PHILLIES | ab | h | o | a | e | | NEW YORK | ab | h | o | a | e |
|---|---|---|---|---|---|---|---|---|---|---|---|---|
| Grant, 3b | 4 | 0 | 3 | 4 | 1 | | Tenney, 1b | 4 | 2 | 14 | 1 | 0 |
| Knabe, 2b | 4 | 0 | 1 | 4 | 0 | | Doyle, 2b | 3 | 0 | 0 | 1 | 0 |
| Titus, rf | 4 | 0 | 1 | 0 | 0 | | Bresnahan, c | 4 | 0 | 5 | 1 | 0 |
| Magee, lf | 4 | 0 | 2 | 0 | 0 | | Donlin, rf | 3 | 1 | 4 | 0 | 0 |
| Bransfield, 1b | 3 | 0 | 14 | 0 | 0 | | Seymour, cf | 4 | 1 | 0 | 0 | 0 |
| Osborne, cf | 3 | 0 | 2 | 0 | 0 | | Devlin, 3b | 4 | 2 | 0 | 0 | 0 |
| Doolin, ss | 1 | 0 | 2 | 2 | 0 | | Shannon, lf | 2 | 0 | 3 | 0 | 0 |
| Dooin, c | 3 | 0 | 1 | 1 | 1 | | Bridwell, ss | 4 | 2 | 3 | 7 | 0 |
| McQuillen, p | 2 | 0 | 0 | 3 | 0 | | Wiltse, p | 1 | 0 | 1 | 4 | 0 |
| Courtney, ss | 2 | 0 | 1 | 3 | 1 | | Totals | 29 | 8 | 30 | 14 | 0 |
| Totals | 30 | 0* | 27 | 17 | 3 | | | | | | | |

## Hooks Wiltse, July 4, 1908 (continued)

*None out when winning run was made.

| | | | | | | | | | |
|---|---|---|---|---|---|---|---|---|---|
| Philadelphia | 0 | 0 | 0 | 0 | 0 | 0 | 0 | 0 | 0—0 |
| New York | 0 | 0 | 0 | 0 | 0 | 0 | 0 | 0 | 1—1 |

Stolen base: Donlin. Double plays: Knabe and Bransfield; Grant and Bransfield. Hit by pitcher: By Wiltse 1. Struck out: By Wiltse 5, by McQuillen 1.

---

## Jeff Tesreau, September 6, 1912 New York at Philadelphia

| NEW YORK | ab | r | b | p | a | e |
|---|---|---|---|---|---|---|
| Devore, lf | 1 | 0 | 0 | 2 | 0 | 0 |
| Becker, lf, rf | 2 | 0 | 1 | 2 | 0 | 0 |
| Doyle, 2b | 5 | 0 | 2 | 0 | 2 | 0 |
| Snodgr's, cf | 3 | 0 | 0 | 2 | 0 | 0 |
| Murray, rf, lf | 4 | 0 | 2 | 4 | 0 | 0 |
| Merkle, 1b | 4 | 0 | 2 | 7 | 0 | 1 |
| Herzog, 3b | 3 | 1 | 0 | 1 | 1 | 0 |
| Wilson, c | 1 | 1 | 1 | 3 | 1 | 0 |
| Fletcher, ss | 4 | 1 | 2 | 5 | 1 | 1 |
| Tesreau, p | 3 | 0 | 1 | 1 | 1 | 0 |
| Totals | 30 | 3 | 11 | 27 | 6 | 2 |

| PHILADELPHIA | ab | r | b | p | a | e |
|---|---|---|---|---|---|---|
| Paskert, cf | 3 | 0 | 0 | 3 | 0 | 0 |
| Mangus, lf | 4 | 0 | 0 | 2 | 0 | 0 |
| Miller, rf | 4 | 0 | 0 | 0 | 0 | 0 |
| Luderus, 1b | 3 | 0 | 0 | 4 | 2 | 0 |
| Walsh, 2b | 3 | 0 | 0 | 4 | 3 | 2 |
| Doolan, ss | 3 | 0 | 0 | 5 | 4 | 0 |
| Dodge, 3b | 2 | 0 | 0 | 0 | 2 | 0 |
| Killifer, c | 3 | 0 | 0 | 8 | 3 | 2 |
| Rixey, p | 1 | 0 | 0 | 0 | 2 | 0 |
| Nicholson, p | 0 | 0 | 0 | 0 | 0 | 0 |
| Nelson, p | 0 | 0 | 0 | 0 | 1 | 0 |
| *Magee | 1 | 0 | 0 | 0 | 0 | 0 |
| †Cravath | 1 | 0 | 0 | 0 | 0 | 0 |
| Totals | 28 | 0 | 0 | ††26 | 17 | 4 |

*Batted for Rixey in sixth inning.
†Batted for Nicholson in eighth inning.
††Merkle out, hit by batted ball.

| | | | | | | | | | |
|---|---|---|---|---|---|---|---|---|---|
| New York | 0 | 0 | 2 | 1 | 0 | 0 | 0 | 0 | 0—3 |
| Philadelphia | 0 | 0 | 0 | 0 | 0 | 0 | 0 | 0 | 0—0 |

Left on bases: New York 11, Philadelphia 3. Struck out: By Rixey 4, Nelson 1, Tesreau 2. Double play: Paskert, Killifer. First on errors: Philadelphia 2, New York 1. First on balls: Off Rixey 4, Nicholson 2, Nelson 1, Tesreau 2. Hits: Off Rixey 8 in 6 innings, Nicholson 2 in 2 innings, Nelson 1 in 1 inning. Wild pitch: Tesreau. Passed balls: Killifer 2. Sacrifice hits: Wilson, Tesreau. Stolen bases: Merkle, Herzog. Umpires: Klem and Orth. Time, 1:55.

## George Davis, September 9, 1914 Philadelphia at Boston

| Philadelphia | ab | r | b | p | a | e |
|---|---|---|---|---|---|---|
| Lobert, 3b | 4 | 0 | 0 | 3 | 2 | 0 |
| Becker, lf | 3 | 0 | 0 | 0 | 0 | 0 |
| Magee, 1b | 4 | 0 | 0 | 4 | 1 | 0 |
| Hilley, rf | 4 | 0 | 0 | 2 | 0 | 0 |
| Byrne, 2b | 3 | 0 | 0 | 3 | 0 | 0 |
| Paskert, cf | 1 | 0 | 0 | 5 | 0 | 1 |
| Martin, ss | 2 | 0 | 0 | 3 | 3 | 0 |
| Burns, c | 3 | 0 | 0 | 4 | 0 | 0 |
| Tineup, p | 1 | 0 | 0 | 0 | 0 | 0 |
| Rixey, p | 0 | 0 | 0 | 0 | 1 | 0 |
| Oeschger, p | 0 | 0 | 0 | 0 | 0 | 0 |
| *Cravath | 1 | 0 | 0 | 0 | 0 | 0 |
| †Killifer | 1 | 0 | 0 | 0 | 0 | 0 |
| Totals | 27 | 0 | 0 | 24 | 7 | 1 |

| Boston | ab | r | b | p | a | e |
|---|---|---|---|---|---|---|
| Moran, cf | 2 | 0 | 0 | 0 | 0 | 0 |
| Mann, cf | 2 | 1 | 2 | 1 | 0 | 0 |
| Evers, 2b | 4 | 0 | 0 | 2 | 2 | 0 |
| Connolly, lf | 2 | 0 | 0 | 0 | 0 | 0 |
| Cather, lf | 2 | 0 | 0 | 0 | 0 | 0 |
| Whitted, rf | 4 | 1 | 2 | 1 | 0 | 0 |
| Schmidt, 1b | 4 | 0 | 1 | 14 | 0 | 0 |
| Smith, 3b | 4 | 2 | 2 | 2 | 3 | 2 |
| Maranv'e, ss | 3 | 1 | 1 | 3 | 2 | 0 |
| Gowdy, c | 4 | 1 | 1 | 4 | 1 | 0 |
| Davis, p | 4 | 1 | 3 | 0 | 3 | 0 |
| Totals | 35 | 7 | 12 | 27 | 11 | 2 |

*Batted for Tineup in fifth inning.
†Batted for Rixey in eighth inning.

| | | | | | | | | | |
|---|---|---|---|---|---|---|---|---|---|
| Philadelphia | 0 | 0 | 0 | 0 | 0 | 0 | 0 | 0 | 0 – 0 |
| Boston | 0 | 2 | 0 | 2 | 0 | 0 | 1 | 2 | x – 7 |

Hits: Off Tineup 5 in 4 innings, Rixey 4 in 3 innings, Oeschger 3 in 1 inning. Three-base hit: Mann. Sacrifice hit: Evers. Stolen base: Whitted. Double plays: Maranville, Evers, Schmidt 2. Left on bases: Boston 7, Philadelphia 5. First on balls: Off Tineup 2, Davis 5. First on errors: Philadelphia 2. Struck out: By Rixey 3, Davis 4. Umpires: Eason and Quigley. Time, 2:00.

---

## Jesse Barnes, May 7, 1922 Philadelphia at New York

| Philadelphia | a | r | h | o | a | New York | a | r | h | o | a |
|---|---|---|---|---|---|---|---|---|---|---|---|
| Lebourv'u, lf | 3 | 0 | 0 | 2 | 0 | Bancroft, s | 2 | 1 | 1 | 1 | 5 |
| Rapp, 3b | 3 | 0 | 0 | 0 | 1 | Rawlings, 2 | 4 | 0 | 0 | 0 | 7 |
| Walker, rf | 3 | 0 | 0 | 1 | 0 | Groh, 3 | 4 | 1 | 2 | 1 | 0 |
| Williams, cf | 2 | 0 | 0 | 3 | 0 | Young, rf | 4 | 2 | 2 | 0 | 0 |
| Parkinson, 2b | 3 | 0 | 0 | 1 | 6 | Meusel, lf | 4 | 0 | 1 | 1 | 0 |
| Fletcher, s | 3 | 0 | 0 | 4 | 3 | Kelly, 1 | 4 | 1 | 3 | 16 | 0 |
| Leslie, 1b | 2 | 0 | 0 | 12 | 0 | Shinners, cf | 3 | 0 | 0 | 3 | 0 |
| *King | 1 | 0 | 0 | 0 | 0 | E. Smith, c | 3 | 0 | 0 | 5 | 1 |
| Henline, c | 2 | 0 | 0 | 1 | 2 | J. Barnes, p | 2 | 1 | 0 | 0 | 2 |
| †Lee | 1 | 0 | 0 | 0 | 0 | | | | | | |
| Meadows, p | 0 | 0 | 0 | 0 | 0 | | | | | | |
| G. Smith, p | 2 | 2 | 0 | 0 | 0 | | | | | | |
| ††Wrightst'ne | 1 | 0 | 0 | 0 | 0 | | | | | | |
| Totals | 26 | 0 | 0 | 24 | 14 | Totals | 30 | 6 | 9 | 27 | 15 |

## Jesse Barnes, May 7, 1922 (continued)

*Batted for Leslie in the ninth inning.
†Batted for Henline in the ninth inning.
††Batted for G. Smith in the ninth inning.

| Philadelphia | 0 | 0 | 0 | 0 | 0 | 0 | 0 | 0 | 0 — 0 |
|---|---|---|---|---|---|---|---|---|---|
| New York | 2 | 3 | 0 | 0 | 1 | 0 | 0 | 0 | x -- 6 |

Two-base hits: Kelly 2. Stolen bases: Young 2. Double plays: Rawlings, Bancroft and Kelly, Fletcher, Parkinson and Leslie. Left on bases: New York 4. Bases on balls: Off Meadows 2, off Barnes 1. Struck out: By Barnes 5. Hits: Off Meadows, 4 in 1 1/3 innings; off G. Smith, 5 in 6 2/3 innings. Hit by pitcher: By Meadows (Shinners); by G. Smith (Bancroft). Losing pitcher: Meadows. Umpires: Hart. O'Day and Emslie. Time, 1:37.

---

## Dazzy Vance, September 13, 1925 Philadelphia at Brooklyn

| Philadelphia | a | r | h | o | a | Brooklyn | a | r | h | o | a |
|---|---|---|---|---|---|---|---|---|---|---|---|
| Sand, s | 1 | 0 | 0 | 2 | 1 | J. Mitchell, s | 5 | 2 | 3 | 1 | 2 |
| *Wright'e | 1 | 0 | 0 | 0 | 0 | Stock, 2 | 4 | 3 | 2 | 1 | 2 |
| Metz, s | 0 | 0 | 0 | 1 | 1 | Johnston, lf | 4 | 2 | 3 | 3 | 0 |
| †Kimmick | 1 | 0 | 0 | 0 | 0 | Cox, | 5 | 1 | 4 | 2 | 0 |
| Leach, cf | 4 | 0 | 0 | 3 | 0 | Brown, cf | 4 | 0 | 0 | 3 | 0 |
| Williams, rf | 3 | 0 | 0 | 2 | 0 | Hargreaves, 1 | 4 | 1 | 1 | 6 | 2 |
| Harper, lf | 3 | 0 | 0 | 3 | 0 | Tierney, 3 | 3 | 0 | 1 | 0 | 0 |
| Hawks, l | 3 | 1 | 0 | 3 | 0 | Deberry, c | 3 | 1 | 1 | 9 | 0 |
| Huber, 3 | 3 | 0 | 0 | 1 | 2 | Vance, p | 4 | 0 | 0 | 2 | 1 |
| Friberg, 2 | 2 | 0 | 0 | 4 | 0 | | | | | | |
| Wilson, c | 2 | 0 | 0 | 0 | 0 | | | | | | |
| Wendell, c | 1 | 0 | 0 | 5 | 2 | | | | | | |
| C. Mitchell, p | 0 | 0 | 0 | 0 | 0 | | | | | | |
| Decatur, p | 1 | 0 | 0 | 0 | 0 | | | | | | |
| Betts, p | 1 | 0 | 0 | 0 | 1 | | | | | | |
| ††Fonseca | 1 | 0 | 0 | 0 | 0 | | | | | | |
| Totals | 27 | 1 | 0 | 24 | 7 | Totals | 36 | 10 | 15 | 27 | 7 |

*Batted for Sand in sixth.
†Batted for Metz in ninth.
††Batted for Betts in ninth.

| Philadelphia | 0 | 1 | 0 | 0 | 0 | 0 | 0 | 0 | 0 — 1 |
|---|---|---|---|---|---|---|---|---|---|
| Brooklyn | 4 | 0 | 0 | 4 | 0 | 1 | 1 | 0 | x — 10 |

Errors: Friberg, Sand, Johnston 2, Hargreaves. Two-base hits: J. Mitchell, Cox. Three-base hit: Johnson. Stolen bases: J. Mitchell, Stock, Johnston, Cox, Hargreaves. Sacrifices: Friberg, Deberry. Double plays: Huber and Sand; Wendell and Friberg. Left on bases: Philadelphia 1, Brooklyn 6. Bases on balls: Off Decatur 2, off Betts 1, off Vance 1. Struck out: By Betts 4, by Vance 9. Passed balls: Deberry, Wilson. Hits: Off C. Mitchell 3 (none out in first) off Decatur 7 in 4 innings; off Betts 5 in 4 innings. Losing pitcher: C. Mitchell. Umpires: Pfirman, Wilson and O'Day. Time, 1:45.

## Jim Wilson, June 12, 1954 Philadelphia at Milwaukee

| Philadelphia | ab | r | h | tb | po | a | e |
|---|---|---|---|---|---|---|---|
| Jones, 3b | 4 | 0 | 0 | 0 | 3 | 2 | 0 |
| Ashburn, cf | 1 | 0 | 0 | 0 | 0 | 0 | 0 |
| Schell, cf | 2 | 0 | 0 | 0 | 1 | 0 | 0 |
| Torgeson, 1b | 3 | 0 | 0 | 0 | 7 | 2 | 0 |
| Ennis, lf | 3 | 0 | 0 | 0 | 2 | 0 | 0 |
| Hamner, 2b | 3 | 0 | 0 | 0 | 3 | 1 | 0 |
| Burgess, c | 1 | 0 | 0 | 0 | 4 | 1 | 0 |
| Wyrostek, rf | 3 | 0 | 0 | 0 | 3 | 0 | 0 |
| Morgan, ss | 3 | 0 | 0 | 0 | 0 | 3 | 0 |
| Roberts, p | 2 | 0 | 0 | 0 | 1 | 2 | 0 |
| *Clark | 1 | 0 | 0 | 0 | 0 | 0 | 0 |
| Totals | 26 | 0 | 0 | 0 | 24 | 11 | 0 |

| Milwaukee | ab | r | h | tb | po | a | e |
|---|---|---|---|---|---|---|---|
| Bruton, cf | 4 | 0 | 2 | 2 | 2 | 0 | 0 |
| Logan, ss | 3 | 1 | 1 | 4 | 2 | 2 | 0 |
| Aaron, lf | 4 | 0 | 1 | 1 | 4 | 0 | 0 |
| Mathews, 3b | 3 | 0 | 0 | 0 | 0 | 2 | 0 |
| Adcock, 1b | 3 | 0 | 0 | 0 | 9 | 0 | 0 |
| Pafko, rf | 3 | 0 | 0 | 0 | 2 | 0 | 0 |
| O'Connell, 2b | 3 | 0 | 1 | 1 | 2 | 1 | 0 |
| Crandall, c | 3 | 1 | 1 | 4 | 6 | 1 | 0 |
| Wilson, p | 3 | 0 | 1 | 2 | 0 | 2 | 0 |
| Totals | 29 | 2 | 7 | 14 | 27 | 8 | 0 |

*Struck out for Roberts in ninth.

| Philadelphia | 0 | 0 | 0 | 0 | 0 | 0 | 0 | 0 | 0 — 0 |
|---|---|---|---|---|---|---|---|---|---|
| Milwaukee | 1 | 0 | 0 | 0 | 1 | 0 | 0 | 0 | x — 2 |

Runs batted in: Logan, Crandall. Two-base hit: Wilson. Home runs: Logan, Crandall. Sacrifice hit: Logan. Stolen base: Bruton. Bases on balls: Off Wilson 2 (Burgess 2). Struck out: By Wilson 6 (Wyrostek 2, Roberts 2, Morgan, Clark) by Roberts 3 (Aaron 2, Adcock). Caught stealing: By Crandall (Burgess), by Burgess (Aaron). Double play: Crandall and Logan. Earned runs: Off Roberts 2. Winning pitcher: Wilson (2-0). Losing pitcher: Roberts (7-7). Umpires: Pinelli, Boggess and Engeln. Time, 1:40. Attendance, 28,218. Official scorer: Sam Levy.

## Sal Maglie, September 25, 1956 Philadelphia at Brooklyn

| Philadelphia | ab | r | h | tb | o | a | e |
|---|---|---|---|---|---|---|---|
| Ashburn, cf | 3 | 0 | 0 | 0 | 2 | 0 | 0 |
| Blaylock, 1b | 4 | 0 | 0 | 0 | 7 | 3 | 0 |
| Lopata, c | 3 | 0 | 0 | 0 | 6 | 2 | 1 |
| Ennis, lf | 3 | 0 | 0 | 0 | 0 | 0 | 0 |
| Jones, 3b | 2 | 0 | 0 | 0 | 1 | 0 | 0 |
| Valo, rf | 3 | 0 | 0 | 0 | 2 | 0 | 0 |
| Hemus, 2b | 3 | 0 | 0 | 0 | 3 | 1 | 0 |
| Kazanski, 2b | 0 | 0 | 0 | 0 | 1 | 0 | 0 |
| Smalley, ss | 2 | 0 | 0 | 0 | 2 | 4 | 0 |
| †Baumholtz | 1 | 0 | 0 | 0 | 0 | 0 | 0 |
| Meyer, p | 0 | 0 | 0 | 0 | 0 | 0 | 1 |
| R. Miller, p | 0 | 0 | 0 | 0 | 0 | 2 | 0 |
| *Bouchee | 1 | 0 | 0 | 0 | 0 | 0 | 0 |
| Sanford, p | 0 | 0 | 0 | 0 | 0 | 0 | 0 |
| ††Haddix | 1 | 0 | 0 | 0 | 0 | 0 | 0 |
| Totals | 26 | 0 | 0 | 0 | 24 | 12 | 2 |

| Brooklyn | ab | r | h | tb | o | a | e |
|---|---|---|---|---|---|---|---|
| Gilliam, 2b | 3 | 1 | 1 | 1 | 2 | 4 | 0 |
| Reese, ss | 3 | 0 | 0 | 0 | 2 | 3 | 0 |
| Snider, cf | 2 | 1 | 0 | 0 | 1 | 0 | 0 |
| Robinson, 3b | 2 | 1 | 1 | 2 | 0 | 3 | 0 |
| Amoros, lf | 4 | 0 | 0 | 0 | 4 | 0 | 0 |
| Hodges, 1b | 2 | 1 | 1 | 1 | 14 | 1 | 0 |
| Furillo, rf | 3 | 0 | 0 | 0 | 0 | 0 | 0 |
| Campanella, c | 2 | 1 | 1 | 4 | 4 | 0 | 0 |
| Maglie, p | 3 | 0 | 0 | 0 | 0 | 1 | 0 |
| Totals | 24 | 5 | 4 | 8 | 27 | 12 | 0 |

*Struck out for R. Miller in sixth.
†Fouled out for Smalley in ninth.
††Struck out for Sanford in ninth.

| | | | | | | | | | |
|---|---|---|---|---|---|---|---|---|---|
| Philadelphia | 0 | 0 | 0 | 0 | 0 | 0 | 0 | 0 | 0 — 0 |
| Brooklyn | 0 | 3 | 2 | 0 | 0 | 0 | 0 | 0 | x — 5 |

Runs batted in: Furillo, Campanella 2. Two-base hit: Robinson. Home run: Campanella. Sacrifice hits: Reese, Robinson. Double plays: R. Miller, Lopata and Blaylock; Lopata and Hemus; Blaylock and Hemus; Hodges, Reese and Hodges. Left on base: Philadelphia 2, Brooklyn 4. Bases on balls: Maglie 2, Meyer 3, R. Miller 1, Sanford 3. Strikeouts: Maglie 3, R. Miller 2, Sanford 2. Hits: Meyer 3 in 2 1/3, R. Miller 0 in 2 2/3, Sanford 1 in 3. Runs and earned runs: Meyer 5-3. Hit by pitcher: Maglie (Ashburn). Winning pitcher: Maglie (12-5). Losing pitcher: Meyer (7-11). Umpires: Dixon, Donatelli, Gorman and Pinelli. Time, 2:07. Attendance, 15,204.

## Lew Burdette, August 18, 1960 Philadelphia at Milwaukee

| Philadelphia | ab | r | h | tb | po | a | e |
|---|---|---|---|---|---|---|---|
| Callison, rf | 3 | 0 | 0 | 0 | 4 | 0 | 0 |
| Taylor, 2b | 3 | 0 | 0 | 0 | 2 | 5 | 0 |
| Curry, lf | 3 | 0 | 0 | 0 | 1 | 0 | 0 |
| Herrera, 1b | 3 | 0 | 0 | 0 | 9 | 0 | 2 |
| Gonzalez, cf | 2 | 0 | 0 | 0 | 1 | 0 | 0 |
| Walls, 3b | 3 | 0 | 0 | 0 | 0 | 3 | 0 |
| Malkmus, 3b | 0 | 0 | 0 | 0 | 0 | 0 | 0 |
| Coker, c | 3 | 0 | 0 | 0 | 6 | 0 | 0 |
| Amaro, ss | 2 | 0 | 0 | 0 | 1 | 2 | 0 |
| *Walters | 1 | 0 | 0 | 0 | 0 | 0 | 0 |
| Conley, p | 2 | 0 | 0 | 0 | 0 | 3 | 0 |
| †Smith | 1 | 0 | 0 | 0 | 0 | 0 | 0 |
| Totals | 26 | 0 | 0 | 0 | 24 | 13 | 2 |

| Milwaukee | ab | r | h | tb | po | a | e |
|---|---|---|---|---|---|---|---|
| Bruton, cf | 4 | 0 | 2 | 3 | 4 | 0 | 0 |
| Crandall, c | 4 | 0 | 2 | 2 | 3 | 0 | 0 |
| Mathews, 3b | 4 | 0 | 1 | 1 | 0 | 4 | 0 |
| Aaron, rf | 4 | 0 | 1 | 1 | 0 | 0 | 0 |
| Covington, lf | 3 | 0 | 1 | 1 | 0 | 0 | 0 |
| Spangler, lf | 0 | 0 | 0 | 0 | 0 | 0 | 0 |
| Roach, 2b | 3 | 0 | 1 | 1 | 0 | 3 | 0 |
| Cottier, 2b | 0 | 0 | 0 | 0 | 0 | 0 | 0 |
| Adcock, 1b | 3 | 0 | 0 | 0 | 18 | 2 | 0 |
| Logan, ss | 3 | 0 | 0 | 0 | 1 | 7 | 0 |
| Burdette, p | 3 | 1 | 2 | 3 | 1 | 3 | 0 |
| Totals | 31 | 1 | 10 | 12 | 27 | 19 | 0 |

*Grounded out for Amaro in ninth.
†Flied out for Conley in ninth.

| | | | | | | | | | |
|---|---|---|---|---|---|---|---|---|---|
| Philadelphia | 0 | 0 | 0 | 0 | 0 | 0 | 0 | 0 | 0 − 0 |
| Milwaukee | 0 | 0 | 0 | 0 | 0 | 0 | 0 | 1 | x − 1 |

Run batted in: Bruton. Two-base hits: Burdette, Bruton. Double plays: Conley, Taylor and Herrera; Mathews, Adcock and Logan. Left on bases: Milwaukee 6, Philadelphia 0. Bases on balls: none. Struck out: By Conley 6 (Bruton, Mathews, Aaron, Covington, Roach, Burdette), by Burdette 3 (Taylor, Gonzalez, Conley). Runs and earned runs: Off Conley 1-1. Hit by pitcher: By Burdette (Gonzalez) Winning pitcher: Burdette (14-7). Losing pitcher: Conley (7-10). Umpires: Jackowski, Landes, Pelekoudas and Barlick. Time, 2:10. Attendance, 16,338.

---

Warren Spahn, September 16, 1960 Philadelphia at Milwaukee

| PHILADELPHIA | ab | r | h | tb | po | a | e |
|---|---|---|---|---|---|---|---|
| Callison, lf | 3 | 0 | 0 | 0 | 1 | 0 | 0 |
| †††Del Greco | 1 | 0 | 0 | 0 | 0 | 0 | 0 |
| Malkmus, 2b | 4 | 0 | 0 | 0 | 4 | 6 | 0 |
| Walters, rf | 2 | 0 | 0 | 0 | 4 | 0 | 0 |
| Herrera, 1b | 3 | 0 | 0 | 0 | 9 | 1 | 0 |
| Gonzalez, cf | 3 | 0 | 0 | 0 | 4 | 0 | 0 |
| Neeman, c | 2 | 0 | 0 | 0 | 2 | 1 | 0 |
| Woods, 3b | 2 | 0 | 0 | 0 | 0 | 0 | 0 |
| *Taylor | 1 | 0 | 0 | 0 | 0 | 0 | 0 |
| Lepcio, 3b | 0 | 0 | 0 | 0 | 0 | 0 | 0 |
| Amaro, ss | 2 | 0 | 0 | 0 | 0 | 2 | 0 |
| †Walls | 1 | 0 | 0 | 0 | 0 | 0 | 0 |
| Koppe, ss | 0 | 0 | 0 | 0 | 0 | 0 | 0 |
| Buzhardt, p | 2 | 0 | 0 | 0 | 0 | 2 | 0 |
| ††Smith | 1 | 0 | 0 | 0 | 0 | 0 | 0 |
| Totals | 27 | 0 | 0 | 0 | 24 | 12 | 0 |

| MILWAUKEE | ab | r | h | tb | po | a | e |
|---|---|---|---|---|---|---|---|
| Bruton, cf | 3 | 1 | 2 | 2 | 4 | 0 | 0 |
| Crandall, c | 4 | 0 | 2 | 2 | 15 | 0 | 0 |
| Mathews, 3b | 4 | 0 | 2 | 2 | 0 | 1 | 0 |
| Aaron, rf | 3 | 1 | 1 | 1 | 1 | 0 | 0 |
| Dark, lf | 4 | 1 | 1 | 3 | 1 | 0 | 0 |
| Adcock, 1b | 2 | 0 | 1 | 1 | 4 | 1 | 0 |
| Logan, ss | 3 | 0 | 0 | 0 | 1 | 2 | 0 |
| Cottier, 2b | 3 | 0 | 0 | 0 | 0 | 0 | 0 |
| Spahn, p | 3 | 1 | 1 | 1 | 1 | 2 | 0 |
| Totals | 29 | 4 | 10 | 12 | 27 | 6 | 0 |

*Struck out for Woods in eighth.
†Struck out for Amaro in eighth.
†Struck out for Buzhardt in ninth.
†††Struck out for Callison in ninth.

| | | | | | | | | | |
|---|---|---|---|---|---|---|---|---|---|
| Philadelphia | 0 | 0 | 0 | 0 | 0 | 0 | 0 | 0 | 0 − 0 |
| Milwaukee | 0 | 0 | 0 | 2 | 1 | 0 | 1 | 0 | x − 4 |

Runs batted in: Crandall, Mathews, Dark, Adcock. Three-base hit: Dark. Stolen base: Bruton. Sacrifice hit: Logan. Sacrifice fly: Adcock. Dougle plays: Amaro Malkmus and Herrera 2. Left on bases: Philadelphia 2, Milwaukee 6. Bases on balls: Off Buzhardt 3 (Bruton, Aaron, Adcock), off Spahn 2 (Walters, Neeman). Struck out: By Buzhardt 1 (Logan), by Spahn 15 (Callison, Del Greco, Walters, Herrera 2, Gonzalez 3, Neeman, Woods 2, Taylor, Walls Buzhardt, Smith). Runs and earned runs: off Buzhardt 4-4. Winning pitcher: Spahn (20-9). Losing pitcher: Buzhardt (4-16). Umpires: Gorman, Smith, Sudol and Boggess. Time, 2:02. Attendance, 6,117.

---

## Don Nottebart, May 17, 1963 Philadelphia at Houston

| Philadelphia | ab | r | h | tb | po | a | e |
|---|---|---|---|---|---|---|---|
| Taylor, 2b | 3 | 0 | 0 | 0 | 1 | 0 | 0 |
| Callison, rf | 4 | 0 | 0 | 0 | 2 | 0 | 0 |
| Gonzalez, cf | 4 | 0 | 0 | 0 | 4 | 0 | 0 |
| Covington, lf | 4 | 0 | 0 | 0 | 0 | 0 | 0 |
| Demeter, 1b-3b | 3 | 1 | 0 | 0 | 5 | 6 | 0 |
| Dalrymple, c | 1 | 0 | 0 | 0 | 7 | 0 | 0 |
| Hoak, 3b | 1 | 0 | 0 | 0 | 0 | 0 | 0 |
| †Sievers, 1b | 1 | 0 | 0 | 0 | 2 | 0 | 0 |
| Wine, ss | 2 | 0 | 0 | 0 | 2 | 3 | 0 |
| Hamilton, p | 2 | 0 | 0 | 0 | 1 | 1 | 0 |
| †Klaus | 1 | 0 | 0 | 0 | 0 | 0 | 0 |
| Duren, p | 0 | 0 | 0 | 0 | 0 | 0 | 0 |
| Totals | 26 | 1 | 0 | 0 | 24 | 10 | 0 |

| Houston | ab | r | h | tb | po | a | e |
|---|---|---|---|---|---|---|---|
| Temple, 3b | 4 | 0 | 1 | 1 | 0 | 2 | 0 |
| Aspromonte, 3b | 0 | 0 | 0 | 0 | 0 | 0 | 0 |
| Spangler, lf | 4 | 1 | 0 | 0 | 3 | 0 | 0 |
| Warwick, rf | 4 | 1 | 4 | 9 | 1 | 0 | 0 |
| Staub, 1b | 2 | 0 | 1 | 1 | 4 | 0 | 0 |
| *Runnels, 1b | 1 | 1 | 0 | 0 | 4 | 0 | 0 |
| Goss, cf | 4 | 1 | 1 | 4 | 6 | 0 | 0 |
| Bateman, c | 3 | 0 | 0 | 0 | 8 | 0 | 0 |
| Lillis, 2b | 3 | 0 | 0 | 0 | 0 | 1 | 0 |
| Hartman, ss | 3 | 0 | 0 | 0 | 1 | 2 | 1 |
| Nottebart, p | 3 | 0 | 0 | 0 | 0 | 1 | 0 |
| Totals | 31 | 4 | 7 | 15 | 27 | 6 | 1 |

*Ran for Staub in sixth.
†Flied out for Hoak in seventh.
††Grounded out for Hamilton in eighth.

| Philadelphia | 0 | 0 | 0 | 0 | 1 | 0 | 0 | 0 | 0 — 1 |
|---|---|---|---|---|---|---|---|---|---|
| Houston | 1 | 0 | 0 | 0 | 0 | 3 | 0 | 0 | x — 4 |

Runs batted in: Hoak, Warwick, Goss 3. Three-base hit: Warwick. Home runs: Warwick, Goss. Sacrifice hit: Dalrymple. Sacrifice fly: Hoak. Left on bases: Philadelphia 3, Houston 4. Bases on balls: Off Duren 1 (Runnels), off Nottebart 3 (Taylor, Dalrymple, Wine). Strikeouts: By Hamilton 5 (Temple 2, Nottebart 2, Staub), by Duren 2 (Spangler, Goss), by Nottebart 8 (Hamilton 2, Taylor, Callison, Gonzalez, Covington, Demeter, Hoak). Runs and earned runs: Hamilton 4-4, Nottebart 1-0. Hits: Off Hamilton 6 in 7 innings, off Duren 1 in 1 inning. Winning pitcher: Nottebart (5-1). Losing pitcher: Hamilton (2-1). Umpires — Vargo, Harvey, Weyer and Barlick. Time, 2:12. Attendance, 8,223.

## Sandy Koufax, June 4, 1964 Los Angeles at Philadelphia

| LOS ANGELES | ab | r | h | tb | po | a | e |
|---|---|---|---|---|---|---|---|
| W. Davis, cf | 4 | 0 | 0 | 0 | 1 | 0 | 0 |
| Wills, ss | 4 | 0 | 1 | 1 | 0 | 2 | 0 |
| Gilliam, 3b | 4 | 1 | 1 | 1 | 0 | 3 | 0 |
| T. Davis, lf | 4 | 1 | 2 | 2 | 1 | 0 | 0 |
| Howard, rf | 3 | 1 | 1 | 4 | 1 | 0 | 0 |
| Fairly, 1b | 1 | 0 | 0 | 0 | 3 | 0 | 0 |
| McMullen, 1b | 3 | 0 | 1 | 1 | 7 | 0 | 0 |
| Parker, rf | 1 | 0 | 1 | 2 | 1 | 0 | 0 |
| Camilli, c | 4 | 0 | 0 | 0 | 12 | 1 | 0 |
| Tracewski, 2b | 3 | 0 | 1 | 2 | 1 | 0 | 0 |
| Koufax, p | 3 | 0 | 1 | 1 | 0 | 2 | 0 |
| Totals | 34 | 3 | 9 | 14 | 27 | 8 | 0 |

| PHILADELPHIA | ab | r | h | tb | po | a | e |
|---|---|---|---|---|---|---|---|
| Rojas, cf | 3 | 0 | 0 | 0 | 1 | 0 | 0 |
| Callison, rf | 3 | 0 | 0 | 0 | 2 | 0 | 0 |
| Allen, 3b | 2 | 0 | 0 | 0 | 1 | 0 | 1 |
| Cater, lf | 3 | 0 | 0 | 0 | 1 | 1 | 0 |
| Triandos, c | 3 | 0 | 0 | 0 | 6 | 0 | 0 |
| Sievers, 1b | 3 | 0 | 0 | 0 | 12 | 0 | 0 |
| Taylor, 2b | 3 | 0 | 0 | 0 | 2 | 2 | 0 |
| Amaro, ss | 3 | 0 | 0 | 0 | 2 | 8 | 0 |
| Short, p | 2 | 0 | 0 | 0 | 0 | 2 | 0 |
| Roebuck, p | 0 | 0 | 0 | 0 | 0 | 0 | 0 |
| Culp, p | 0 | 0 | 0 | 0 | 0 | 0 | 0 |
| *Wine | 1 | 0 | 0 | 0 | 0 | 0 | 0 |
| Totals | 26 | 0 | 0 | 0 | 27 | 13 | 1 |

*Struck out for Culp in ninth.

```
Los Angeles    0  0  0  0  0  0  3  0  0 — 3
Philadelphia   0  0  0  0  0  0  0  0  0 — 0
```

Runs batted in: Howard 3. Two-base hits: Tracewski, Parker. Home run: Howard. Double play: Taylor, Amaro and Sievers. Left on bases: Los Angeles 4, Philadelphia 0. Bases on balls: Off Koufax 1 (Allen). Strikeouts: By Koufax 12 (Callison, Allen, Carter, Triandos 2, Sievers, Taylor 2, Amaro, Short 2, Wine) by Short 4 (Howard, Camilli, Koufax, Wills), by Culp 2 (Gilliam, T. Davis). Runs and earned runs: Short 3-3. Hits: Off Short 8 in 6 2/3 innings, off Roebuck 0 in 1/3 inning, off Culp 1 in 2 innings. Winning pitcher: Koufax (6-4). Losing pitcher: Short (3-3). Umpires: Vargo, Forman, Jackowski and Crawford. Time, 1:55. Attendance, 29,709.

---

## George Culver, July 29, 1968 Cincinnati at Philadelphia

| Cincinnati | ab | r | h | rbi | Philadelphia | ab | r | h | rbi |
|---|---|---|---|---|---|---|---|---|---|
| Rose, cf | 5 | 2 | 2 | 0 | Taylor, 3b | 3 | 0 | 0 | 0 |
| Helms, 2b | 5 | 1 | 2 | 0 | Pena, ss | 4 | 0 | 0 | 0 |
| Johnson, lf | 4 | 2 | 3 | 2 | Callison, rf | 3 | 0 | 0 | 0 |
| May, rf | 4 | 0 | 1 | 0 | Allen, lf | 3 | 1 | 0 | 0 |
| Perez, 3b | 4 | 1 | 0 | 0 | White, 1b | 4 | 0 | 0 | 0 |
| Pay'tich, 1b | 4 | 0 | 2 | 2 | Lock, cf | 3 | 0 | 0 | 0 |
| Corrales, c | 5 | 0 | 2 | 2 | Rojas, 2b | 3 | 0 | 0 | 1 |
| W'dward, ss | 5 | 0 | 0 | 0 | Dalrymple, c | 3 | 0 | 0 | 0 |
| Culver, p | 4 | 0 | 0 | 0 | Short, p | 0 | 0 | 0 | 0 |
| | | | | | Wagner, p | 1 | 0 | 0 | 0 |
| | | | | | Gonzalez, ph | 0 | 0 | 0 | 0 |
| | | | | | Farrell, p | 0 | 0 | 0 | 0 |
| Totals | 40 | 6 | 12 | 6 | Totals | 27 | 1 | 0 | 1 |

| Cincinnati | 0 | 0 | 3 | 3 | 0 | 0 | 0 | 0 | 0 − 6 |
| Philadelphia | 0 | 1 | 0 | 0 | 0 | 0 | 0 | 0 | 0 − 1 |

| Cincinnati | ip | h | r | er | bb | so |
|---|---|---|---|---|---|---|
| Culver (W. 9-9) | 9 | 0 | 1 | 0 | 5 | 4 |

| Philadelphia | ip | h | r | er | bb | so |
|---|---|---|---|---|---|---|
| Short (L. 9-11) | 3 2/3 | 9 | 6 | 6 | 3 | 4 |
| Wagner | 4 1/3 | 2 | 0 | 0 | 0 | 3 |
| Farrell | 1 | 1 | 0 | 0 | 0 | 1 |

Errors: Perez, Corrales, Woodward, Taylor. Left on base: Cincinnati 11, Philadelphia 6. Two-base hit: Johnson 2. Stolen base: Johnson. Sacrifice fly: Rojas. Hit By Pitcher: Wagner (Johnson). Umpires: Jackowski, Secory, Burkhart and Wendelstedt. Time, 2:43. Attendance, 14,083.

---

### Bill Stoneman, April 17, 1969 Montreal at Philadelphia

| Montreal | ab | r | h | rbi | e |
|---|---|---|---|---|---|
| Bosch, cf | 4 | 1 | 0 | 0 | 0 |
| Wills, ss | 5 | 1 | 1 | 0 | 0 |
| Staub, rf | 5 | 2 | 4 | 3 | 0 |
| Jones, lf | 4 | 0 | 0 | 0 | 0 |
| Bailey, 1b | 1 | 0 | 1 | 0 | 0 |
| Cline, 1b | 3 | 0 | 2 | 1 | 0 |
| Bateman, c | 4 | 0 | 1 | 0 | 0 |
| Laboy, 3b | 5 | 2 | 4 | 1 | 0 |
| Sutherland, 2b | 3 | 0 | 0 | 0 | 0 |
| Stoneman, p | 3 | 1 | 0 | 0 | 0 |
| Totals | 37 | 7 | 13 | 5 | 0 |
| Philadelphia | ab | r | h | rbi | e |
| Taylor, 2b | 3 | 0 | 0 | 0 | 1 |
| Stone, lf | 4 | 0 | 0 | 0 | 0 |
| Briggs, 1b | 3 | 0 | 0 | 0 | 0 |
| D. Johnson, 3b | 4 | 0 | 0 | 0 | 1 |
| Callison, rf | 2 | 0 | 0 | 0 | 0 |
| Money, ss | 3 | 0 | 0 | 0 | 0 |
| Hisle, cf | 2 | 0 | 0 | 0 | 1 |
| Ryan, c | 3 | 0 | 0 | 0 | 0 |
| Wilson, p | 0 | 0 | 0 | 0 | 0 |
| Farrell, p | 0 | 0 | 0 | 0 | 0 |
| J. Johnson, p | 2 | 0 | 0 | 0 | 0 |
| Roznovsky, ph-c | 0 | 0 | 0 | 0 | 0 |
| Totals | 26 | 0 | 0 | 0 | 3 |

| Montreal | 0 | 0 | 1 | 1 | 0 | 2 | 0 | 0 | 3 − 7 |
| Philadelphia | 0 | 0 | 0 | 0 | 0 | 0 | 0 | 0 | 0 − 0 |

| Montreal | ip | h | r | er | bb | so |
|---|---|---|---|---|---|---|
| Stoneman (W. 1-2). | 9 | 0 | 0 | 0 | 5 | 8 |

| Philadelphia | ip | h | r | er | bb | so |
|---|---|---|---|---|---|---|
| J. Johnson (L. 0-2) | 8 | 11 | 4 | 3 | 3 | 7 |
| Wilson | 0* | 2 | 3 | 3 | 1 | 0 |
| Farrell | 1 | 0 | 0 | 0 | 1 | 3 |

*Pitched for four batters in ninth.

Double plays: Montreal 1, Philadelphia 2. Left on bases: Montreal 9, Philadelphia 4. Two-base hits: Bailey, Staub 3. Home run: Staub. Stolen base: D. Johnson. Sacrifice hit: Bosch. Wild pitch: J. Johnson. Balk: Farrell. Umpires: Gorman, Landes, Williams and Colosi. Time, 2:24. Attendance, 6,494.

## Bill Singer, July 20, 1970 Philadelphia at Los Angeles

| Philadelphia | ab | r | h | rbi | e | | Los Angeles | ab | r | h | rbi | e |
|---|---|---|---|---|---|---|---|---|---|---|---|---|
| Doyle, 2b | 4 | 0 | 0 | 0 | 0 | | Grabarkewitz, ss | 4 | 1 | 1 | 0 | 0 |
| Gamble, rf | 1 | 0 | 0 | 0 | 0 | | Sizemore, lf | 4 | 1 | 1 | 0 | 0 |
| Browne, rf | 2 | 0 | 0 | 0 | 0 | | Willis, 3b | 0 | 0 | 0 | 0 | 0 |
| Money, 3b | 3 | 0 | 0 | 0 | 1 | | Davis, cf | 3 | 1 | 1 | 1 | 0 |
| Johnson, 1b | 3 | 0 | 0 | 0 | 0 | | Parker, 1b | 4 | 1 | 2 | 1 | 0 |
| Briggs, lf | 3 | 0 | 0 | 0 | 0 | | Lefebvre, 2b | 4 | 0 | 3 | 1 | 0 |
| Hisle, cf | 3 | 0 | 0 | 0 | 0 | | Garvey, 3b | 4 | 1 | 0 | 0 | 0 |
| Bowa, ss | 3 | 0 | 0 | 0 | 1 | | Joshua, lf | 0 | 0 | 0 | 0 | 0 |
| Ryan, c | 3 | 0 | 0 | 0 | 0 | | Russell, rf | 4 | 0 | 2 | 2 | 0 |
| Fryman, p | 1 | 0 | 0 | 0 | 0 | | Torborg, c | 4 | 0 | 1 | 0 | 0 |
| Plamer, p | 1 | 0 | 0 | 0 | 0 | | Singer, p | 4 | 0 | 0 | 0 | 2 |
| Harmon, ph | 1 | 0 | 0 | 0 | 0 | | Totals | 35 | 5 | 11 | 5 | 2 |
| Totals | 28 | 0 | 0 | 0 | 2 | | | | | | | |

| | | | | | | | | | | | |
|---|---|---|---|---|---|---|---|---|---|---|---|
| Philadelphia | 0 | 0 | 0 | 0 | 0 | 0 | 0 | 0 | 0 — 0 | | |
| Los Angeles | 2 | 0 | 1 | 0 | 2 | 0 | 0 | 0 | x — 5 | | |

| Philadelphia | ip | h | r | er | bb | so |
|---|---|---|---|---|---|---|
| Fryman (L. 6-6) | 4 2/3 | 10 | 5 | 5 | 0 | 3 |
| Plamer | 3 1/3 | 1 | 0 | 0 | 0 | 5 |

| Los Angeles | ip | h | r | er | bb | so |
|---|---|---|---|---|---|---|
| Singer (W. 7-3) | 9 | 0 | 0 | 0 | 0 | 10 |

Left on bases: Philadelphia 2, Los Angeles 7. Two-base hits: Parker, Russell. Stolen bases: Davis, Parker. Sacrifice fly: Davis. Hit by pitcher: By Singer (Gamble). Umpires: Sudol, Steiner, Williams and Colosi. Time, 2:10. Attendance, 12,454.

---

## Burt Hooton, April 16, 1972 Philadelphia at Chicago

| Philadelphia | ab | r | h | rbi | e | | Chicago | ab | r | h | rbi | e |
|---|---|---|---|---|---|---|---|---|---|---|---|---|
| Bowa, ss | 3 | 0 | 0 | 0 | 0 | | Cardenal, rf | 5 | 1 | 2 | 0 | 0 |
| McCarver, c | 4 | 0 | 0 | 0 | 1 | | Beckert, 2b | 4 | 0 | 1 | 1 | 0 |
| Montanez, cf | 2 | 0 | 0 | 0 | 0 | | Williams, lf | 5 | 1 | 3 | 0 | 0 |
| Johnson, 1b | 4 | 0 | 0 | 0 | 0 | | Pepitone, 1b | 5 | 1 | 2 | 0 | 0 |
| Luzinski, lf | 3 | 0 | 0 | 0 | 0 | | Santo, 3b | 5 | 1 | 3 | 0 | 0 |
| Money, 3b | 1 | 0 | 0 | 0 | 0 | | Monday, cf | 2 | 0 | 0 | 0 | 0 |
| Anderson, rf | 2 | 0 | 0 | 0 | 0 | | Kessinger, ss | 3 | 0 | 0 | 0 | 0 |
| Doyle, 2b | 3 | 0 | 0 | 0 | 0 | | Hundley, c | 2 | 0 | 1 | 2 | 0 |
| Brandon, p | 0 | 0 | 0 | 0 | 0 | | Hooton, p | 4 | 0 | 0 | 0 | 0 |
| Reynolds, p | 0 | 0 | 0 | 0 | 0 | | | | | | | |
| Selma, p | 1 | 0 | 0 | 0 | 0 | | | | | | | |
| Stone, ph | 0 | 0 | 0 | 0 | 0 | | | | | | | |
| Short, p | 0 | 0 | 0 | 0 | 0 | | | | | | | |
| Harmon, 2b | 1 | 0 | 0 | 0 | 0 | | | | | | | |
| Totals | 24 | 0 | 0 | 0 | 1 | | Totals | 35 | 4 | 12 | 3 | 0 |

| | | | | | | | | | | | |
|---|---|---|---|---|---|---|---|---|---|---|---|
| Philadelphia | 0 | 0 | 0 | 0 | 0 | 0 | 0 | 0 | 0 — 0 | | |
| Chicago | 0 | 0 | 0 | 1 | 0 | 0 | 2 | 1 | x — 4 | | |

| Philadelphia | ip | h | r | er | bb | so |
|---|---|---|---|---|---|---|
| Selma (L. 0-1) | 5 | 6 | 1 | 0 | 4 | 0 |
| Short | 1 2/3 | 4 | 2 | 2 | 1 | 2 |
| Brandon | 1/3* | 2 | 1 | 1 | 0 | 0 |
| Reynolds | 1 | 0 | 0 | 0 | 0 | 0 |

| Chicago | ip | h | r | er | bb | so |
|---|---|---|---|---|---|---|
| Hooton (W. 1-0) | 9 | 0 | 0 | 0 | 7 | 7 |

*Pitched to two batters in eighth.

266

## Burt Hooton, April 16, 1972 (continued)

Double plays: Philadelphia 1, Chicago 1. Left on bases: Philadelphia 5, Chicago 13. Two-base hit: Santo. Three-base hit: Cardenal. Sacrifice hits: Kessinger, Bowa. Umpires: Pryor, Wendelstedt, Froemming and Vargo. Time, 2:33. Attendance, 9,583.

---

## Bob Forsch, April 16, 1978 Philadelphia at St. Louis
### Cardinals 5, PHILLIES 0

| Phillies | Ab | R | H | BI | O | A | E |
|---|---|---|---|---|---|---|---|
| McBride, rf | 4 | 0 | 0 | 0 | 1 | 0 | 0 |
| Bowa, ss | 4 | 0 | 0 | 0 | 4 | 1 | 1 |
| Schmidt, 3b | 3 | 0 | 0 | 0 | 1 | 2 | 0 |
| Luzinski, lf | 2 | 0 | 0 | 0 | 1 | 0 | 0 |
| Hebner, 1b | 2 | 0 | 0 | 0 | 6 | 0 | 0 |
| Maddox, cf | 3 | 0 | 0 | 0 | 4 | 0 | 0 |
| Boone, c | 3 | 0 | 0 | 0 | 5 | 0 | 0 |
| Sizemore, 2b | 3 | 0 | 0 | 0 | 2 | 1 | 0 |
| Lerch, p | 2 | 0 | 0 | 0 | 0 | 2 | 1 |
| Garber, p | 0 | 0 | 0 | 0 | 0 | 0 | 0 |
| d-Johnstone | 1 | 0 | 0 | 0 | 0 | 0 | 0 |
| Totals | 27 | 0 | 0 | 0 | 24 | 6 | 2 |

| ST. LOUIS | Ab | R | H | BI | O | A | E |
|---|---|---|---|---|---|---|---|
| Brock, lf | 3 | 0 | 0 | 0 | 1 | 0 | 0 |
| Templeton, ss | 4 | 1 | 1 | 0 | 1 | 4 | 0 |
| Morales, lf | 3 | 1 | 1 | 0 | 1 | 0 | 0 |
| Simmons, c | 4 | 1 | 2 | 0 | 3 | 1 | 0 |
| Hernandez, 1b | 3 | 1 | 0 | 0 | 13 | 1 | 0 |
| Reitz, 3b | 3 | 1 | 1 | 1 | 0 | 3 | 1 |
| Scott, cf | 2 | 0 | 0 | 0 | 6 | 0 | 0 |
| a-Freed | 1 | 0 | 1 | 3 | 0 | 0 | 0 |
| b-Mumphrey | 1 | 0 | 0 | 0 | 0 | 0 | 0 |
| Tyson, 2b | 3 | 0 | 0 | 0 | 1 | 2 | 0 |
| c-Irog | 0 | 0 | 0 | 1 | 0 | 0 | 0 |
| Phillips, 2b | 0 | 0 | 0 | 0 | 0 | 1 | 0 |
| Forsch, p | 4 | 0 | 0 | 0 | 1 | 0 | 0 |
| Totals | 31 | 5 | 6 | 5 | 27 | 12 | 1 |

a-doubled for Scott in sixth.
b-ran for Freed in sixth.
c-walked for Tyson in eighth
d-grounded out for Garber in ninth

| | | | | | | | | | |
|---|---|---|---|---|---|---|---|---|---|
| PHILLIES | 0 | 0 | 0 | 0 | 0 | 0 | 0 | 0 | 0 − 0 |
| St. Louis | 0 | 0 | 0 | 1 | 0 | 3 | 0 | 1 | x − 5 |

Left on base: Phillies 2, St. Louis 7. Two-base hits: Simmons, Templeton, Freed. Stolen base: Hebner.

| | IP | H | R | Er | Bb | So |
|---|---|---|---|---|---|---|
| x-Lerch (L, 1-1) | 7 | 6 | 5 | 2 | 2 | 4 |
| Garber | 1 | 0 | 0 | 0 | 2 | 1 |
| Forsch (W, 3-0) | 9 | 0 | 0 | 0 | 2 | 3 |

x-faced two batters in eighth

Hit by Pitcher: by Lerch (Reitz). Umpires: Weyer, Wendelstedt, Rennert, Montague. Time, 1:56. Attendance, 11,495.

## ALL-STAR GAMES IN PHILADELPHIA
### July 13, 1943 — Shibe Park

| NATIONALS | AB. | R. | H. | PO. | A. | E. |
|---|---|---|---|---|---|---|
| Hack (Cubs), 3b | 5 | 1 | 3 | 0 | 2 | 1 |
| Herman (Dodgers), 2b | 5 | 0 | 2 | 3 | 3 | 2 |
| Musial (Cardinals), lf-rf | 4 | 0 | 1 | 0 | 0 | 0 |
| Nicholson (Cubs), rf | 2 | 0 | 0 | 0 | 0 | 0 |
| c-Galan (Dodgers), lf | 1 | 0 | 0 | 1 | 0 | 0 |
| Fletcher (Pirates), 1b | 2 | 0 | 0 | 3 | 0 | 0 |
| d-Dahlgren (Phillies), 1b | 2 | 0 | 0 | 3 | 0 | 0 |
| W. Cooper (Cardinals), c | 2 | 0 | 1 | 7 | 1 | 0 |
| e. Lombardi (Giants), c | 2 | 0 | 0 | 3 | 0 | 0 |
| H. Walker (Cards), cf | 1 | 0 | 0 | 1 | 0 | 0 |
| b-DiMaggio (Pirates), cf | 3 | 2 | 3 | 1 | 0 | 0 |
| Marion (Cardinals), ss | 2 | 0 | 0 | 2 | 2 | 0 |
| g-Ott (Giants) | 1 | 0 | 0 | 0 | 0 | 0 |
| Miller (Reds), ss | 1 | 0 | 0 | 0 | 1 | 0 |
| M. Cooper (Cardinals), p | 1 | 0 | 0 | 0 | 1 | 0 |
| Vander Meere (Reds), p | 1 | 0 | 0 | 0 | 1 | 0 |
| Sewell (Pirates), p | 0 | 0 | 0 | 0 | 1 | 0 |
| h-F. Walker (Dodgers) | 1 | 0 | 0 | 0 | 0 | 0 |
| Javery (Braves), p | 0 | 0 | 0 | 0 | 0 | 0 |
| i-Frey (Reds) | 1 | 0 | 0 | 0 | 0 | 0 |
| Totals | 37 | 3 | 10 | 24 | 12 | 3 |

| AMERICANS | AB. | R. | H. | PO. | A. | E. |
|---|---|---|---|---|---|---|
| Case (Senators), rf | 2 | 1 | 0 | 0 | 0 | 0 |
| Keltner (Indians), 3b | 4 | 1 | 1 | 2 | 2 | 0 |
| Wakefield (Tigers), lf | 4 | 0 | 2 | 3 | 0 | 0 |
| R. Johnson (Senators), lf | 0 | 0 | 0 | 1 | 0 | 0 |
| Stephens (Browns), cf | 3 | 0 | 1 | 1 | 3 | 1 |
| Siebert (Athletics), 1b | 1 | 0 | 0 | 3 | 1 | 0 |
| a-York (Tigers), 1b | 3 | 0 | 1 | 4 | 0 | 0 |
| Laabs (Browns), cf | 3 | 1 | 0 | 7 | 0 | 0 |
| Early (Senators), s | 2 | 1 | 0 | 3 | 0 | 0 |
| Doerr (Red Sox), 2b | 4 | 1 | 2 | 3 | 3 | 0 |
| Leonard (Senators), p | 1 | 0 | 1 | 0 | 1 | 0 |
| Newhouser (Tigers), p | 1 | 0 | 0 | 0 | 0 | 0 |
| f-Heath (Indians) | 1 | 0 | 0 | 0 | 0 | 0 |
| Hughson (Red Sox), p | 0 | 0 | 0 | 0 | 0 | 0 |
| Totals | 29 | 5 | 8 | 27 | 10 | 1 |

| | | | | | | | | | |
|---|---|---|---|---|---|---|---|---|---|
| National League | 1 | 0 | 0 | 0 | ᵕ | 0 | 1 | 0 | 1 — 3 |
| American League | 0 | 3 | 1 | 0 | 1 | 0 | 0 | 0 | x — 5 |

| Nationals | IP. | H. | R. | ER. | BB. | SO. |
|---|---|---|---|---|---|---|
| M. Cooper (Cardinals) | 2 1/3 | 4 | 4 | 4 | 2 | 1 |
| Vander Meer (Reds) | 2 2/3 | 2 | 1 | 0 | 1 | 6 |
| Sewell (Pirates) | 1 | 0 | 0 | 0 | 0 | 0 |
| Javery (Braves) | 2 | 2 | 0 | 0 | 0 | 3 |

| Americans | IP. | H. | R. | ER. | BB. | SO. |
|---|---|---|---|---|---|---|
| Leonard (Senators) | 3 | 2 | 1 | 1 | 0 | 0 |
| Newhouser (Tigers) | 3 | 3 | 0 | 0 | 1 | 1 |
| Hughson (Red Sox) | 3 | 5 | 2 | 2 | 0 | 2 |

Winning pitcher: Leonard. Losing pitcher: M. Cooper.

aStruck out for Siebert in third. b Singled for H. Walker in fourth. cWalked for Nicholson in sixth. dHit into double play for Fletcher in sixth. eFlied out for W. Cooper in sixth. fFlied out for Newhouser in sixth. gStruck out for Marion in seventh. hFlied out for Sewell in seventh. iFlied out for Javery in ninth. Runs batted in:Musial, F. Walker, DiMaggio, Doerr 3, Wakefield. Two-base hits: Musial, Keltner, Wakefield. Three-base hit: DiMaggio. Home runs: Doerr, DiMaggio. Sacrifice hits: Stephens, Early. Double plays: Hack, Herman and Fletcher; Vander Meer, Marion and Herman; Miller, Herman and Dahlgren; Stephens, Doerr and York. Hit by pitcher: By M. Cooper (Case). Left on bases: Nationals 8, Americans 6. Umpires: Rommel and Rue (A.L.), Conlan and Dunn (N.L.). Time, 2:07. Attendance, 31,938.

## ALL-STAR GAME
### July 8, 1952 — Shibe Park

| AMERICANS | AB. | R. | H. | PO. | A. | E. |
|---|---|---|---|---|---|---|
| DiMaggio (Red Sox), cf | 2 | 0 | 1 | 1 | 0 | 0 |
| Doby (Indians), cf | 0 | 0 | 0 | 0 | 0 | 0 |
| Bauer (Yankees), rf | 3 | 0 | 1 | 2 | 0 | 0 |
| Jensen (Senators), rf | 0 | 0 | 0 | 0 | 0 | 0 |
| Mitchell (Indians), lf | 1 | 0 | 0 | 1 | 0 | 0 |
| cMinoso (White Sox), lf | 1 | 1 | 1 | 0 | 0 | 0 |
| Rosen (Indians), 3b | 1 | 1 | 0 | 3 | 1 | 0 |
| Berra (Yankees), c | 2 | 0 | 0 | 6 | 0 | 0 |
| E. Robin'n (W. Sox), 1b | 2 | 0 | 1 | 1 | 0 | 0 |
| Avila (Indians), 2b | 2 | 0 | 1 | 0 | 0 | 0 |
| Rizzuto (Yankees), ss | 2 | 0 | 0 | 1 | 0 | 0 |
| Raschi (Yankees), p | 0 | 0 | 0 | 0 | 0 | 0 |
| aMcDougald (Yankees) | 1 | 0 | 0 | 0 | 0 | 0 |
| Lemon (Indians), p | 1 | 0 | 0 | 0 | 0 | 0 |
| Shantz (Athletics), p | 0 | 0 | 0 | 0 | 0 | 0 |
| Totals | 18 | 2 | 5 | 15 | 1 | 0 |

| NATIONALS | AB. | R. | H. | PO. | A. | E. |
|---|---|---|---|---|---|---|
| Lockman (Giants), 1b | 3 | 0 | 0 | 5 | 0 | 0 |
| J. Robinson (Dodgers), 2b | 3 | 1 | 1 | 2 | 2 | 0 |
| Musial (Cardinals), cf | 2 | 1 | 0 | 1 | 0 | 0 |
| Sauer (Cubs), lf | 2 | 1 | 1 | 0 | 0 | 0 |
| Campanella (Dodgers), c | 1 | 0 | 0 | 5 | 1 | 0 |
| Slaughter (Cardinals), rf | 2 | 0 | 1 | 0 | 0 | 0 |
| Thomson (Giants), 3b | 2 | 0 | 0 | 1 | 1 | 0 |
| Hamner (Phillies), ss | 1 | 0 | 0 | 1 | 3 | 0 |
| Simmons (Phillies), p | 0 | 0 | 0 | 0 | 0 | 0 |
| bReese (Dodgers) | 1 | 0 | 0 | 0 | 0 | 0 |
| Rush (Cubs), p | 1 | 0 | 0 | 0 | 0 | 0 |
| Totals | 18 | 3 | 3 | 15 | 7 | 0 |

| | | | | | |
|---|---|---|---|---|---|
| American League | 0 | 0 | 0 | 2 | 0 — 2 |
| National League | 1 | 0 | 0 | 2 | 0 — 3 |

Stopped by rain.

| Americans | IP. | H. | R. | ER. | BB. | SO. |
|---|---|---|---|---|---|---|
| Raschi (Yankees) | 2 | 1 | 1 | 1 | 0 | 3 |
| Lemon (Indians) | 2 | 2 | 2 | 2 | 2 | 0 |
| Shantz (Athletics) | 1 | 0 | 0 | 0 | 0 | 3 |

# All-Star Game (continued)

| Nationals | IP. | H. | R. | ER. | BB. | SO. |
|---|---|---|---|---|---|---|
| Simmons (Phillies) | 3 | 1 | 0 | 0 | 1 | 3 |
| Rush (Cubs) | 2 | 4 | 2 | 2 | 1 | 1 |

Winning pitcher: Rush. Losing pitcher: Lemon.
aGrounded out for Raschi in third. bFlied out for Simmons in third. cDoubled for Mitchell in fourth Runs batted in: J. Robinson, E. Robinson, Avila, Sauer 2. Two-base hits: DiMaggio, Minoso, Slaughter. Home runs: J. Robinson, Sauer. Double play: Hamner, J. Robinson and Lockman. Left on bases: Americans 3. Nationals 3. Hit by pitcher: By Lemon (Musial). Umpires: Barlick, Boggess and Warneke (N.L.) Berry, Summers and Soar (A.L.). Time, 1:29. Attendance, 32,785.

## July 13, 1976 — Veterans Stadium

| AMERICANS | AB. | R. | H. | RBI. | PO. | A. |
|---|---|---|---|---|---|---|
| LeFlore (Tigers), lf | 2 | 0 | 1 | 0 | 2 | 0 |
| Yastrzemski (Red Sox), lf | 2 | 0 | 0 | 0 | 0 | 0 |
| Carew (Twins), 1b | 3 | 0 | 0 | 0 | 9 | 2 |
| Brett (Royals), 3b | 2 | 0 | 0 | 0 | 0 | 1 |
| Money (Brewers), 3b | 1 | 0 | 0 | 0 | 0 | 1 |
| Munson (Yankees), c | 2 | 0 | 0 | 0 | 4 | 0 |
| Fisk (Red Sox), c | 1 | 0 | 0 | 0 | 1 | 0 |
| dChambliss (Yankees) | 1 | 0 | 0 | 0 | 0 | 0 |
| Lynn (Red Sox), cf | 3 | 1 | 1 | 1 | 0 | 0 |
| eOtis (Royals) | 1 | 0 | 0 | 0 | 0 | 0 |
| Harrah (Rangers), ss | 2 | 0 | 0 | 0 | 0 | 0 |
| Belanger (Orioles), ss | 1 | 0 | 0 | 0 | 1 | 1 |
| Patek (Royals), ss | 0 | 0 | 0 | 0 | 0 | 1 |
| Staub (Tigers), rf | 2 | 0 | 2 | 0 | 1 | 0 |
| Tiant (Red Sox), p | 0 | 0 | 0 | 0 | 0 | 0 |
| cWynegar (Twins) | 0 | 0 | 0 | 0 | 0 | 0 |
| Tanana (Angels), p | 0 | 0 | 0 | 0 | 1 | 0 |
| Grich (Orioles), 2b | 2 | 0 | 0 | 0 | 1 | 1 |
| Garner (Athletics), 2b | 1 | 0 | 0 | 0 | 1 | 1 |
| Fidrych (Tigers), p | 0 | 0 | 0 | 0 | 1 | 0 |
| aMcRae (Toyals) | 1 | 0 | 0 | 0 | 0 | 0 |
| Hunter (Yankees), p | 0 | 0 | 0 | 0 | 0 | 0 |
| bRivers (Yankees), rf | 2 | 0 | 1 | 0 | 2 | 0 |
| Totals | 29 | 1 | 5 | 1 | 24 | 8 |

| NATIONALS | AB. | R. | H. | RBI. | PO. | A. |
|---|---|---|---|---|---|---|
| Rose (Reds), 3b | 3 | 1 | 3 | 0 | 0 | 1 |
| Oliver (Pirates), rf-lf | 1 | 0 | 0 | 0 | 1 | 0 |
| Garvey (Dodgers), 1b | 3 | 1 | 1 | 1 | 6 | 0 |
| Cash (Phillies), 2b | 1 | 1 | 1 | 0 | 1 | 1 |
| Morgan (Reds), 2b | 3 | 1 | 1 | 0 | 2 | 3 |
| Perez (Reds), 1b | 0 | 0 | 0 | 0 | 2 | 0 |
| Foster (Reds), cf-rf | 3 | 1 | 1 | 3 | 0 | 0 |
| Montefusco (Giants), p | 0 | 0 | 0 | 0 | 0 | 0 |
| Russell (Dodgers), ss | 1 | 0 | 0 | 0 | 1 | 2 |
| Luzinski (Phillies), lf | 3 | 0 | 0 | 0 | 0 | 0 |
| Griffey (Reds), rf | 1 | 1 | 1 | 1 | 1 | 0 |

| NATIONALS | AB. | R. | H. | RBI. | PO. | A. |
|---|---|---|---|---|---|---|
| Bench (Reds), c | 2 | 0 | 1 | 0 | 1 | 0 |
| Cedeno (Astros), cf | 2 | 1 | 1 | 2 | 1 | 0 |
| Kingman (Mets), rf | 2 | 0 | 0 | 0 | 1 | 0 |
| Boone (Phillies), c | 2 | 0 | 0 | 0 | 5 | 0 |
| Concepcion (Reds), ss | 2 | 0 | 1 | 0 | 2 | 3 |
| Bowa (Phillies), ss | 1 | 0 | 0 | 0 | 2 | 1 |
| Rhoden (Dodgers), p | 0 | 0 | 0 | 0 | 0 | 0 |
| Cey (Dodgers), 3b | 0 | 0 | 0 | 0 | 0 | 0 |
| Jones (Padres), p | 1 | 0 | 0 | 0 | 1 | 1 |
| Seaver (Mets), p | 1 | 0 | 0 | 0 | 0 | 0 |
| Schmidt (Phillies), 3b | 1 | 0 | 0 | 0 | 0 | 0 |
| Forsch (Astros), p | 0 | 0 | 0 | 0 | 0 | 0 |
| Totals | 33 | 7 | 10 | 7 | 27 | 12 |

| | | | | | | | | | |
|---|---|---|---|---|---|---|---|---|---|
| Americans | 0 | 0 | 0 | 1 | 0 | 0 | 0 | 0 | 0 − 1 |
| Nationals | 2 | 0 | 2 | 0 | 0 | 0 | 0 | 3 | x − 7 |

| Americans | IP. | H. | R. | ER. | BB. | SO. |
|---|---|---|---|---|---|---|
| Fidrych (Tigers) | 2 | 4 | 2 | 2 | 0 | 1 |
| Hunter (Yankees) | 2 | 2 | 2 | 2 | 0 | 3 |
| Tiant (Red Sox) | 2 | 1 | 0 | 0 | 0 | 1 |
| Tanana (Angels) | 2 | 3 | 3 | 3 | 1 | 0 |

| Nationals | IP. | H. | R. | ER. | BB. | SO. |
|---|---|---|---|---|---|---|
| Jones (Padres) | 3 | 2 | 0 | 0 | 1 | 1 |
| Seaver (Mets) | 2 | 2 | 1 | 1 | 0 | 1 |
| Montefusco (Giants) | 2 | 0 | 0 | 0 | 2 | 2 |
| Rhoden (Dodgers) | 1 | 1 | 0 | 0 | 0 | 0 |
| Forsch (Astros) | 1 | 0 | 0 | 0 | 0 | 1 |

Winning pitcher: Jones. Losing pitcher: Fidrych.

aGrounded out for Fidrych in third. bStruck out for Hunter in fifth. cWalked for Tiant in seventh. dGrounded out for Fisk in ninth. eStruck out for Lynn in ninth. Errors: None. Double plays: Morgan., Concepcion and Garvey; Morgan, Bowa and Garvey; Cash, Russell and Perez; Money, Garner and Carew. Left on bases: Americans 4. Nationals 3. Three-base hits: Garvey, Rose. Home runs: Foster, Lynn, Cedeno. Stolen base: Carew. Passed ball: Munson. Bases on balls: Off Jones 1 (Brett), off Montefusco 2 (Carew, Wynegar), off Tanana 1 (Perez). Strikeouts: By Jones 1 (LeFlore), by Seaver 1 (Rivers), by Montefusco 2 (Lynn, Garner), by Forsch 1 (Otis), by Fidrych 1 (Jones), by Hunter 3 (Bench, Kingman, Seaver) by Tiant 1 (Cedeno). Umpires: Wendelstedt (NL) plate, Neudecker (AL) first base, Olsen (NL) second base, Denkinger (AL) third base, Davidson (NL) left field, Evans (AL) right field. Time, 2:12. Attendance, 63,974. Official scorers: Richard Dozer, Chicago Tribune; Ray Kelly, Philadelphia Bulletin, and Bill Liston, Boston Herald-American.

# PHILLIES 23, CUBS 22

| PHILADELPHIA | ab | r | h | bi | | CHICAGO | ab | r | h | bi |
|---|---|---|---|---|---|---|---|---|---|---|
| McBride, rf | 8 | 2 | 3 | 1 | | DeJesus, ss | 6 | 4 | 3 | 1 |
| Bowa, ss | 8 | 4 | 5 | 1 | | Vail, rf | 5 | 2 | 3 | 1 |
| Rose, 1b | 7 | 4 | 3 | 4 | | Burris, p | 0 | 0 | 0 | 0 |
| Schmidt, 3b | 4 | 3 | 2 | 4 | | Thmsn, cf | 2 | 1 | 1 | 0 |
| Unser, lf | 7 | 1 | 1 | 2 | | Bucknr, 1b | 7 | 3 | 4 | 7 |
| G. Mddx, cf | 4 | 3 | 4 | 4 | | Kingmn, lf | 6 | 4 | 3 | 6 |
| Gross, cf | 2 | 1 | 1 | 1 | | Ontivrs, 3b | 7 | 1 | 1 | 1 |
| Boone, c | 4 | 2 | 3 | 5 | | Martin, cf | 6 | 2 | 3 | 3 |
| Meoli, 2b | 5 | 0 | 1 | 0 | | Sutter, p | 0 | 0 | 0 | 0 |
| Lerch, p | 1 | 1 | 1 | 1 | | Foote, c | 6 | 1 | 3 | 1 |
| Bird, p | 1 | 1 | 0 | 0 | | Sizemor, 2b | 4 | 2 | 2 | 1 |
| Luzinski, ph | 0 | 0 | 0 | 0 | | Caudill, p | 0 | 0 | 0 | 0 |
| Espinos, pr | 1 | 1 | 0 | 0 | | Murcer, rf | 2 | 0 | 1 | 0 |
| McGraw, p | 0 | 0 | 0 | 0 | | Lamp, p | 0 | 0 | 0 | 0 |
| Reed, p | 0 | 0 | 0 | 0 | | Moore, p | 1 | 0 | 1 | 1 |
| McCrvr, ph | 1 | 0 | 0 | 0 | | WHrnz, p | 1 | 0 | 0 | 0 |
| Eastwick, p | 0 | 0 | 0 | 0 | | Dillard, 2b | 1 | 2 | 1 | 0 |
| | | | | | | Biitner, ph | 1 | 0 | 0 | 0 |
| | | | | | | Kellehr, 2b | 1 | 0 | 0 | 0 |
| Totals | 53 | 23 | 24 | 23 | | Total | 56 | 22 | 26 | 22 |

| | | | | | | | | | | |
|---|---|---|---|---|---|---|---|---|---|---|
| Philadelphia | 7 | 0 | 8 | 2 | 4 | 0 | 1 | 0 | 0 | 1 — 23 |
| Chicago | 6 | 0 | 0 | 3 | 7 | 3 | 0 | 3 | 0 | 0 — 22 |

Errors: Schmidt 2, Kingman, DeJesus. Double play: Philadelphia 2. Left on Base: Philadelphia 15, Chicago 7. Two-base hits: Bowa 2, G.Maddox 2, Rose 2, Foote, Martin, DeJesus, Boone. Three-base hits: Moore, Gross. Home Run: Kingman 3 (12), Schmidt 2 (14), Boony(2), Lerch (1), G.Maddox (6). Home Run: Ontiveros (1), Buckner (4), Martin (3). Stolen bases: Bowa, Meoli. Sacrifice fly: Unser, Gross.

| Philadelphia | IP | H | R | ER | BB | SO |
|---|---|---|---|---|---|---|
| Lerch | 1/3 | 5 | 5 | 5 | 0 | 0 |
| Bird | 3 2/3 | 8 | 4 | 4 | 0 | 2 |
| McGraw | 2/3 | 4 | 7 | 4 | 3 | 1 |
| Reed | 3 1/3 | 9 | 6 | 6 | 0 | 0 |
| Eastwick W, 1-0 | 2 | 0 | 0 | 0 | 0 | 1 |

| Chicago | | | | | | |
|---|---|---|---|---|---|---|
| Lamp | 1/3 | 6 | 6 | 6 | 0 | 0 |
| Moore | 2 | 6 | 7 | 7 | 2 | 1 |
| W. Hrnz | 2 2/3 | 7 | 8 | 6 | 7 | 1 |
| Caudill | 1 1/3 | 3 | 1 | 1 | 2 | 3 |
| Burris | 1 2/3 | 1 | 0 | 0 | 0 | 1 |
| Sutter L, 1-1 | 2 | 1 | 1 | 1 | 1 | 0 |

Hit by Pitcher: By W. Hrnz (Boone). Time, 4:03. Attendance, 14,952.

...and a Chicago newspaper put it this way....

## 45 RUNS MAY 17, 1979 IN CHICAGO

Mike Schmidt hit a three-run homer to start one of the great scoring marathons in recent baseball history, and he ended it with a tie-breaking homer in the 10th inning to give the Phillies a 23-22 victory over the Chicago Cubs.

He would like to have called it his greatest thrill, but couldn't because he has a personal love affair with Wrigley Field and recalled another epic in 1976.

That was a day in April when the Phillies trailed the Cubs 13-2 before Schmidt went to work and hit four home runs, including one in the 10th inning, for an 18-16 victory.

"We were behind in that game and came back to win it," recalled Schmidt. "That's what made that game more tasteful. This time, we got out ahead and hung on."

"Hung on" was putting it mildly. The Phillies scored seven runs in the first inning, with Schmidt and Bob Boone hitting three-run homers and pitcher Randy Lerch adding a solo shot.

The Cubs came back with six in their half of the first, with Dave Kingman hitting a three-run homer, his first of three homers in the game. The Phillies came up with eight more in the third, which Garry Maddox launched with a double and closed with a three-run homer.

Kingman hit a two-run homer in the fourth, followed by another homer by Steve Ontiveros. Bill Buckner hit a grand slam and Jerry Martin added a two-run shot in the fifth, when Chicago scored seven runs, and Kingman hit another in the sixth.

The 11 homers by the two teams tied a major league record. It now has been done six times, with the Cubs being involved three times.

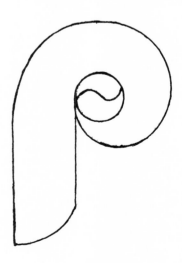

273

Jack Clements holds a major league record which will probably never be topped. In 1891, Clements caught 105 games, the most games caught by a left-handed throwing catcher.

Hall of Famer Grover Cleveland Alexander was the Phillies workhorse in the early 1900s. The big right-hander is the only Phillies pitcher to win a World Series game, beating the Boston Red Sox, October 8, 1915.

One of the Phillies top sluggers was Fred (Cy) Williams, who still holds the club record for the most home runs in one month. Cy hit fifteen in May of 1923.

The first of two Phillies to win the Most Valuable Player Award in the National League was the great slugging outfielder, Chuck Klein. The left-handed hitter won the award in 1932. Eighteen years later relief specialist Jim Konstanty became the second MVP from the Phils.

After winning the MVP in 1932, Klein had an even greater year the next season. He became one of only four National League players to win the Triple Crown: twenty-eight homers, 120 RBI, and a .368 average. (Incidentally, Jimmie Foxx of the Philadelphia Athletics also won the Triple Crown that year in the American League — forty-eight, 163, .356 — giving the city of Philadelphia a clean sweep.)

Because of his youth, Granville (Granny) Hamner (left), seventeen years old, could not sign with the Phillies until his mother had affixed her signature. General Manager Herb Pennock (right) signed the teenaged infielder in September of 1944. (Bulletin photo)

Another great left-handed hitter of the Chuck Klein era was outfielder Lefty O'Doul who set a National League and Phillies record with 254 base hits in 1929.

Granny Hamner turned out to be one of the best middle infielders in Phillies history. Originally a shortstop, Hamner was the starter for the National League in the 1952 All-Star game at that position and two years later he was a repeat starter as a second baseman.

First baseman Frank McCormick takes some batting practice in Miami Beach, Florida, during spring training of 1946. McCormick went on that season to set a National League Record, most consecutive errorless games for a first baseman, with 136.

Owner Bob Carpenter and GM Herb Pennock began to turn the Phillies around in the late 1940s. One of their biggest signings was Del Ennis, a slugging outfielder from Philadelphia's Olney High School. Ennis was the big home run and RBI man for the Phillies 1950 Championship Club.

Making his fourth start in the last nine days of the 1950 season, Robin Roberts, twenty-three, beat Brooklyn, 4-1, to give the Phillies the pennant. It was Robbie's twentieth win, the first of six straight years winning twenty or more. He wound up a brilliant career as the Phillies greatest pitcher and a member of Baseball's Hall of Fame. (Philadelphia Inquirer photo)

The 1950 Pennant winners were dubbed the Whiz Kids because of their youth. The lead-off hitter and centerfielder, twenty-three-year-old Richie (Whitey, Put-Put) Ashburn, came from Tilden, Nebraska. Ashburn wound up his Phillies career with a .311 average and the club's only two-time batting champion.

A tough clutch hitter and steady fielding third baseman on the '50 champions was Willie (Puddin' Head) Jones.

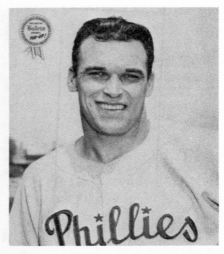

Youngest pitcher on the Whiz Kids was twenty-one-year-old southpaw Curt Simmons, winner of seventeen games. But the Army grabbed Curt in September of 1950 and he wasn't available for the World Series.

While the 1950 winners were mostly kids, it was the dramatic home run by twenty-nine-year-old leftfielder Dick Sisler who gave Philadelphia its first National League pennant in thirty-five years. (Bulletin photo)

Following the final game of the 1949 season, Manager Eddie Sawyer got his Phillies together and said, "Boys, come back here next year ready to play. We're gonna win it." Sawyer's prophecy came true and Philadelphia had a baseball champion, the first National League pennant in thirty-five years.

The Phillies of the late 1950s hit a dry spell, but things began to pick up when General Manager John Quinn brought in young Gene Mauch as manager after the first game of the 1960 season. The Phils of the 1960s became very respectable under Mauch, a shrewd strategist.

1950 National League Champions — Seated (L. to R.): Bloodworth, Donnelly, Ashburn, Caballero, Bengough, Coach; Sawyer, Manager; Perkins, Coach; Cooke, Coach; Ennis, Sisler, Jones. Middle Row (L. to R.): Wiechec, Church, Miller, Heintzelman, Silvestri, Lopata, Hollmig, Roberts, Whitman, Meyer, Hamner, Thompson, Powell, Trav. Sec. Back Row: Nicholson, Johnson, Ridzik, Waitkus, Candini, Mayo, Konstanty, Seminick, Goliat, Brittin, Stuffel, McDonnell, Simmons. Bat Boy: Kenny Bush.

Robin Roberts had pitched the final game of the season. Curt Simmons was in the service, so Eddie Sawyer made a surprise move and went with relief act Jim Konstanty (standing), the National League's Most Valuable Player, in the first game of the 1950 World Series.

Del Ennis (left) reaches a milestone, his 1,000th RBI with the Phillies, and receives congratulations from Bobby Morgan, Herm Wehmeier, and Jim Greengrass. Ennis and Ed Delahanty are the lone Phillies to surpass 1,000 RBI in their careers. (Bulletin photo)

Chris Short ranks as one of the Phillies great left-handed pitchers along with Curt Simmons and Steve Carlton. Short holds the club record for the most strikeouts in an extra inning game, eighteen in fifteen innings against the New York Mets, October 2, 1965.

John Quinn was an astute trader who built the Phillies strong club which nearly won the 1964 pennant. The star rightfielder on that club was Johnny Callison, whom Quinn had picked up from the Chicago White Sox four years earlier.

One of the most exciting products of the Phillies farm system was Dick Allen, who broke in in 1964. Allen was one of the best right-handed hitters to come along in a long time. He hit some prodigious home runs at old Connie Mack Stadium.

Rick Wise was practically the entire show June 23, 1971, in Cincinnati's Riverfront Stadium. He not only no-hit the Cincinnati Reds but homered twice, driving in three runs in the 4-0 victory. Wise also homered twice in another game that season to join a select group of pitchers to hit a pair in one game two times in one season. (William H. Gordon photo)

On Father's Day, June 21, 1964, Jim Bunning, the father of seven children, became the first pitcher in forty-two years to pitch a perfect game when he blanked the New York Mets, 6-0, at Shea Stadium. Bunning, who also had a no-hitter with the Detroit Tigers in the American League, was another big acquisition by Quinn. (AP Wirephoto)

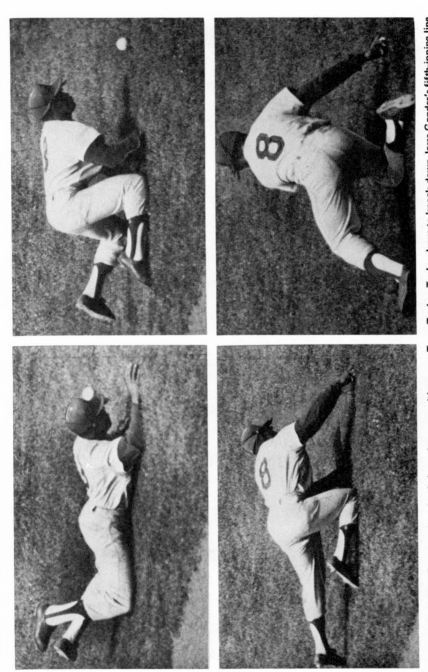

Biggest play behind Bunning that day belonged to second baseman Tony Taylor. Taylor drove to knock down Jesse Gonder's fifth-inning line drive, crawled after the ball on the outfield grass and was able to nip Gonder with a throw from one knee to first baseman John Herrnstein. (AP Wirephoto)

One of the most phenomenal pitching performances in baseball history was turned in by Steve Carlton in 1972. The big lefty won twenty-seven of the Phillies fifty-nine games, including fifteen straight; had an ERA of 1.98 and struck out 310 and easily won the Cy Young Award. Five years later, twenty-three wins produced his second Young Award. (Paul H. Roedig photo)

Paul Owens, 1972 turned out to be a key year for the Phillies. Farm Director Paul Owens replaced John Quinn as the GM on June 3. More than a month later, Owens himself replaced Frank Lucchesi as field manager. ''We had some good young players but changes were needed. I just wanted to get down in the dugout to learn as much as I could about every player so when we began making changes, I'd have a better idea who we wanted to keep,'' explained Owens.

Ken Brett made big news for the Phillies in 1973, the year the American League removed the pitcher from the batting order and inserted the designated hitter. Brett became the first star pitcher to hit home runs in four consecutive games, June 9, 13, 18, and 23. (Paul H. Roedig photo)

Owens' first major trade was a seven-player deal with the Milwaukee Brewers. The key players were pitchers Jim Lonborg (shown) and Ken Brett. (Paul H. Roedig photo)

For his manager, Paul Owens went to the Los Angeles Dodgers and selected their third base coach, Danny Ozark. A sound, fundamental baseball man, Ozark began to turn the Phillies around, finishing sixth, third, and second, followed by three consecutive firsts. (Paul H. Roedig photo)

Shortstop Larry Bowa anchors the Phillies infield defense. He set a National League record for the fewest errors in a season, nine in 1972, and holds the major league record for the highest fielding percentage, lifetime. (Paul H. Roedig Photo)

Greg (Bull) Luzinski is the club's clean-up hitter. He twice finished runner-up in National League MVP voting. In 1978, he led all National League players in All-Star voting by the fans. (Paul H. Roedig photo)

Third baseman Mike Schmidt led the major leagues in homers for three consecutive years, starting in 1974. Defensively, he received a Gold Glove in 1976 and 1977. (Paul H. Roedig photo)

The strong Phillies farm system produced three young pitching standouts in (L. to R.) Larry Christenson, Randy Lerch, and relief specialist Warren Brusstar. (Paul H. Roedig photos)

Paul Owens pulled off two major deals on the June 15 deadline which led to two division titles. In 1977, he acquired lead-off hitter and rightfielder Bake McBride (left) from St. Louis. A year later it was starter Dick Ruthven from Atlanta. McBride batted .336 for the '77 Phils, while Ruthven was 13-5 pitching for Philadelphia. (Paul H. Roedig photos)

Robin Roberts (middle) and Connie Mack, Jr., (left) became the first Phillie and Philadelphia Athletics representatives to be elected to the newly created Philadelphia Baseball Hall of Fame in voting by the fans in 1978. Warren C. Giles, President Emeritus of the National League, presided over the ceremonies. (Paul H. Roedig photo)

Bob Boone, a converted third baseman and Stanford University graduate, is one of the league's top receivers. (Paul H. Roedig photo)

Another big trade brought offense, speed, and defense to the Phillies in Garry Maddox, the fleet centerfielder described by Pete Rose as a "windshield wiper in the outfield." He won a Gold Glove in 1975, 76, 77, and 78. (Paul H. Roedig photo)

In their first venture into the new free agent market, the Phillies signed ex-Pittsburgh third baseman Richie Hebner and moved him across the diamond to first base. (Paul H. Roedig photo)

There were a few players who played with both the Athletics and Phillies and one of them was outfielder Dave Philley. The switch-hitter from Texas wound up his sixteen-year career as one of the game's best pinch hitters. (Pasquarella photo)

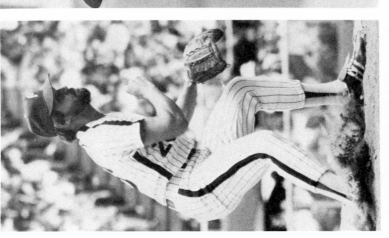

Through trades, Owens built up a strong bullpen in (L. to R.) Gene Garber, Tug McGraw, and Ron Reed. (Paul H. Roedig photos)

First baseman on the pennant-winning 1950 team was Eddie Waitkus, who nearly lost his life the season before when he was critically wounded by a deranged bobby-soxer. Ruth Ann Steinhagen, nineteen, shot Waitkus in a Chicago hotel on June 15. Waitkus couldn't play the rest of the season but was able to return for six more years in the majors.

The Phillies have had some of the best defensive shortstops in baseball and one of them was Bobby Wine, a 1963 Gold Glove winner.

The Phillies move permanently into Shibe Park on July 4, 1938, after fifty-one years in Baker Bowl. Shibe Park was renamed Connie Mack Stadium in 1953 in honor of the great manager/owner of the Philadelphia Athletics.

The final game in Connie Mack Stadium was played on October 1, 1970, the Phillies beating the Montreal Expos in ten innings on Oscar Gamble's single, 2-1. (William H. Gordon photo)

The Expos also provided the opposition as the Phillies moved into Veterans Stadium, the finest multi-purpose sports stadium in the country. Philadelphia also prevailed in that game, 4-1, April 10, 1971. (Warren Kruse, Trenton Times photo)

Veterans Stadium was the scene of the All-Star classic during 1976, when the nation celebrated the Bicentennial. With a club high five Phillies on the National League squad, the American League bowed again, 7-1. (Ed Mahan photo)

One of the most popular Phillies was a little Cuban second baseman, Cookie Rojas. In his career with the Phillies, Rojas, primarily a second baseman, wound up having played every position in a game. His one pitching appearance came in 1967.

Stan Lopata is the Phillies record holder for most home runs in a season by a catcher. "Big Stash" hit thirty-two in 1956, while driving in ninety-five runs, also a club high for a catcher.

Wally Post was an outfielder who played a little more than two years with the Phillies. He came to Philly in a big deal with Cincinnati and then returned to the Reds again.

Fred Luderus is the lone player in Phillies history to play in over 1,000 games at first base. Playing with the Phils from 1910 to 1920, Luderus appeared in 1,298 games.

One of the Phillies big bonus babies of the early 1950s was infielder Ted Kazanski was received $100,000 to sign with the Philadelphia ball club.

A three-time .300 hitter with the Phillies of the 1960s was outfielder Tony Gonzalez, who tied a club record by playing errorless ball during the 1962 season.

The 1957 Phillies featured a bunch of rookies and one of the best of that group was relief pitcher Dick Farrell, who won ten, lost two, and saved ten more with no trick pitches or pitching philosophy. The 6-foot-4 right-hander just reared back and threw fast balls.

Gene Mauch was a stickler on defense and his clubs of the 1960s had one of the best defensive catchers in the league, Clay Dalrymple (shown), whom the Phillies drafted out of the minor leagues in 1959.

Winner of twenty-three games in two seasons with the Phillies was right-hander Emory (Bubba) Church.

Catcher Timmy McCarver came to the Phillies from the St. Louis Cardinals after the 1969 season in the Dick Allen deal and returned a few years later to become Steve Carlton's catcher.

One of the characters on the 1950 Whiz Kids championship club was right-handed pitcher Russ (Mad Monk) Meyer. He averaged eleven wins in four seasons in Philadelphia, starting in 1949.

Holder of the club record for most strikeouts in a nine-inning game is righthander Art Mahaffey, who fanned seventeen Cubs in 1961.